HEINEMANN GNVQ

INTERMEDIATE

Leisure and Tourism

Peter Hayward

—HEINEMANN—
GNVQ

INTERMEDIATE

Leisure and Tourism

Peter Hayward

Edexcel
Success through qualifications

Heinemann Educational Publishers,

Halley Court, Jordan Hill, Oxford OX2 8EJ

A division of Reed Educational & Professional Publishing Ltd

Heinemann is a registered trademark of Reed Educational & Professional Publishing Limited

OXFORD MELBOURNE AUCKLAND JOHANNESBURG BLANTYRE
GABORONE IBADAN PORTSMOUTH NH (USA) CHICAGO

First published 2000

2004 2003 2002 2001 2000

10 9 8 7 6 5 4 3 2 1

A catalogue record for this book is available from the British Library on request.

ISBN 0 435 45596 6

Typeset by TechType, Abingdon, Oxon

Printed and bound in Great Britain by The Bath Press Ltd, Bath

Tel: 01865 888058 www.heinemann.co.uk

Contents

Contents

Acknowledgements

Many people and organisations have assisted in the writing of this book by providing advice or agreeing for material to be reprinted. I would like to name and thank the following: Alton Towers, Meadowhall Shopping Centre, Sheffield, British Airways, The Trafford Centre, Travel World, Nottinghamshire County Council Libraries Section, Newark and Sherwood District Council, The Jorvik Viking Centre, Eureka Museum, Museum of Modern Art, Oxford, The English Riviera Tourist Board, The Health and Safety Executive, The American Adventure, BARB, The English Tourism Council, The British Tourist Authority, The Cotswold Water Park, The Countryside Agency, The Staines Informer, The Newark Advertiser, Snowdome, Tamworth and Chessington World of Adventures. I would also like to thank Richard Shillito, Richard Brumby, Andy Hardy, Georgina Coulham and all the staff at Newark and Sherwood College, and Margaret Berriman, Gillian Burrell and Pen Gresford at Heinemann Educational for their advice and support. Finally, I would like to thank Linda for her constant support, encouragement and ideas.

The publisher would also like to thank Jennifer Johnson, picture researcher.

The author and publisher would like to thank the following individuals and organisations for permission to reproduce photographs:

ACE Photo Agency – page 99 (top right)
Bluewater – page 265
John Birdsall – page 78
Gareth Boden – page 56
Britstock-IFA – page 175 (right), 286 (bottom)
Canterbury Tourist Information – page 252
Collections/John Miller – page 200 (right)
Collections/Ray Roberts – page 170 (left)
Corbis – page 26, cover
Haddon Davies – page 46
Earls Court – Olympia – page 107
Empics/John Marsh – page 186
Eye Ubiquitous/AJG Bell – page 293
Eye Ubiquitous/David Cumming – page 296
Format/Joanne O'Brien – page 170 (right)
Format/Ulrike Preuss – page 13, 24
Sally and Richard Greenhill – page 19, 80, 132, 136, 279
Guildford Spectrum – page 180
Robert Harding – page 17, 61 (top right), 63, 241, 250, 286 (top)
Chris Honeywell – page 99 (bottom right)
Network/Peter Jordan – page 143
Network/R Drexel/Bilderberg – page 127
Network/Mike Goldwater – page 97
Photodisc – page 16, 17 (bottom left), 23, 129, 145
The Photographers Library – page 61 (top left), 84
Records Department, Liverpool City Council – page 284
Stone – page 29, 61 (bottom right), 62
Virgin – page 61 (bottom left)
John Walmsley – page 175 (left), 200 (left), 205

Every effort has been made to contact copyright holders of material published in this book. We would be glad to hear from unacknowledged sources at the first opportunity.

Introduction

How to use this book

This book has been written as a brand new text for students who are working to the 2000 national standards for Intermediate GNVQ in Leisure and Tourism. It covers the three compulsory units and four option units for the award.

These units are:

1   Investigating leisure and tourism
2   Marketing in leisure and tourism
3   Investigating customer service
4   Running an event
7   Leisure sport and recreation facilities
8   Travel and tourism organisations
13   Impacts of leisure and tourism.

Within each unit, the text is organised under exactly the same headings as the GNVQ units, to make it easy for you to find your way round the unit. By working through the units, you will find all the knowledge and ideas you need to prepare your assessment.

Assessment

Assessment in the new GNVQ is carried out on the whole unit, rather than by many smaller pieces of work. The methods of assessment are:

- one major assignment, for example carrying out an investigation into the leisure and tourism facilities in your local area
- an external test, set and marked by the awarding body, for example Edexcel.

At the end of each unit in the book, you will find a **Unit Assessment** section which provides you with practice for both these forms of assessment. The first part is a series of carefully planned tasks or ideas for assignments that can count towards your award. By working through the tasks you will have an opportunity to cover everything you need to obtain a *pass* grade. Further sections then guide you towards obtaining *merit* and *distinction* grades. The second part will help you to check your knowledge of the unit and also to prepare for the external test.

Special features of the book

Throughout the text there are a number of features which are designed to encourage discussion and group work, and to help you relate the theory to real work in leisure and tourism. These activities will also help you to build up a portfolio of **key skills** by practising **numeracy**, **communication** and **ICT**. These features are:

Think it over: Thought-provoking questions or

dilemmas about issues in leisure and tourism. They can be used for individual reflection or group discussion.

Did you know?:   Interesting facts and snippets of

information about the leisure and tourism industry.

Try it out: Writing activities that encourage

you to apply the theory in a practical situation.

Talk about it: Group exercises involving

research, discussion and/or a writing activity.

Look it up: Activities involving research.
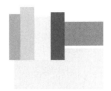

Case studies: Examples of real (or simulated) issues in leisure and tourism. Questions on the case studies will enable you to explore the key issues and deepen your understanding of the subject.

Snapshots: Examples of people working in the leisure and tourism industry and the problems and challenges they face.

Other features, included at the end of the book, are: **Fast facts** – a glossary of key terms; and **Suggestions for further reading** and useful websites. You can use these reference sections to develop your research skills.

What is leisure and tourism?

Leisure and tourism is one of the biggest and fastest growing industries in the world. Successful completion of your GNVQ Intermediate Leisure and Tourism course could lead to an exciting and interesting career within this industry.

There are many job opportunities in leisure and recreation and travel and tourism. Examples of these jobs include: travel consultants, sports centre managers, air cabin crew, holiday reps, sports coaches, tour guides, hotel managers, conference organisers, marketing executives, public relations officers and many more. These jobs can offer you a rewarding career in terms of promotion and salary, as well as variety and interest. Your studies and qualifications can help you achieve your ambitions, so work hard, enjoy your course and believe in your abilities. This way of thinking will impress any future employer.

One of the most important qualities you need to possess is the ability to get on with people and to be able to work as part of a team. This book will help you develop your customer care skills and show the importance of teamwork.

You may already have a part-time job, perhaps working in a supermarket, a restaurant or a shop.

The work may be hard, the hours long and the pay may not be that good. But also there may be variety, responsibility, friendship and fun. These parts of the job make up the 'feel good' factor – when you enjoy your work, you like the people you work with and you know you are doing a good job for the customers.

The leisure and tourism industry offers this 'feel good' factor. It can be an excellent way to make a living and develop a career. You will find that you will probably have to start your career at the lowest level, commonly known as 'the bottom of the ladder', in your first job. You must then be prepared to do anything (within reason), learn as much as you can and be enthusiastic in your work. This way you will climb the ladder and reach the top.

Another positive aspect of the work you will be doing is that you have the opportunity to make people happy. Customers you look after may thank you and recommend your organisation. This will most certainly impress your 'boss'.

Realistically, however, it will not be all fun and games. You will have to deal with complaints and calm those customers who want to let off a little steam. But you will learn to cope with this – it's all part of the job.

This book covers all the topics required for you to complete your qualification. There are plenty of interesting and motivating case studies which bring the world of work alive for you. Learning should be interesting, challenging, stimulating and fun.

Your course will include some or all of the following:

- teamwork tasks and activities
- learning new skills
- listening to guest speakers
- giving presentations
- building self confidence
- achieving things you never thought you could.

You may come across topics you have not studied before. Don't worry, this book will enable you to get through these new areas.

Finally, good luck with your studies and have an exciting journey in your chosen career. May it be full of excitement, fun and rewarding.

Investigating leisure and tourism

This unit covers the knowledge you will need in order to meet the assessment requirements for Unit 1. It will also help you understand the very important role leisure and tourism plays in today's society.

It is written in three sections. Section one looks at the leisure industry and investigates the many different activities people do in their leisure time and the facilities which have developed to meet people's leisure needs. Section one also explores the seven components which make up the leisure industry.

They are:

- *sport and physical recreation*
- *arts and entertainment*
- *countryside recreation*
- *home-based leisure*

- *children's play activities*
- *visitor attractions*
- *catering.*

Section two examines the travel and tourism industry and the six components that make up this industry:

- *travel agents*
- *tour operators*
- *tourist information and guiding services*

- *accommodation and catering*
- *attractions*
- *transportation.*

Section three describes the links between the leisure and tourism industries and explains how different organisations operate in the private, public and voluntary sectors.

This unit provides a good foundation for more detailed study of the leisure and tourism industries which you will carry out during your course.

What you need to produce

You will have the opportunity to investigate the leisure and tourism industries in an area of your choice and describe how they are linked. You will have to provide information on one or two organisations in your chosen area including brief details of their sector, activities and facilities. Finally, you will have to describe the products and services provided to local people and visitors in at least two of the major facilities in the area.

This unit is assessed through your portfolio work only. The grade awarded will be the grade for the unit.

The leisure industry
What is leisure?

Leisure is generally considered to be the time remaining after work, travel to and from work, sleep and all household tasks. Leisure time is that time when you can choose to do what you want. People are always looking for new ways to spend their leisure time. Leisure activities are many and varied, such as:

- reading
- sport – taking part or spectating
- going to the cinema or a disco
- eating out
- going to the pub
- listening to music
- visiting a tourist attraction
- watching television or playing computer games.

Key definitions
Active and passive leisure activities

Active leisure activities include gardening, playing sport, do-it-yourself (DIY), sightseeing and any other interests which require active responses from the participants.

Passive leisure activities are those which require little effort or response from the person taking part in that activity. Examples include watching the television, reading and listening to music.

Facilities

Both active and passive leisure activities take place in a wide range of facilities, such as leisure centres, clubs, cinemas, libraries, restaurants, or even involve natural features like mountains and lakes, where you can take part in outdoor pursuits such as climbing and sailing. In other words, *facilities* are the places where people can carry out their leisure activities.

Products/goods and services

Organisations offer their customers products and services. Products may include food and drink, sports clothing or gifts and souvenirs. Services may include information given by a receptionist, coaching and supervision provided by centre staff or the use of facilities like the car park or the bar.

To sum up the meaning of facilities, products and services, we can say:

A hotel **(facility)** offers weekend breaks **(products)** and provides a nightly cabaret **(service)**.

Try it out — Write a sentence similar to the one above showing the meaning of facilities, products and services using your own examples.

The development of the leisure industry

The leisure industry is currently the biggest and fastest growing industry in the world. Today, hobbies and pastimes are increasingly pursued as lack of employment, modern technology in the workplace and greater numbers of people living beyond retirement age make more leisure time available for people.

Leisure has developed as a result of advances in rapid and efficient transport systems that have opened up a worldwide opportunity for travel and the acquisition of new leisure and cultural activities. It is important that we appreciate how and why these developments have taken place, so the next section looks at some of the important milestones that have led to the present situation.

The history of leisure

The first thing to be said about leisure is that it is not new. Many of today's leisure time activities have their origins in the past when opportunities for leisure were usually associated with festivals and celebrations of a religious nature.

We would find it difficult to live in a world without cars, electricity, supermarkets or leisure centres. Many people feel they could not live without these things. These are the products of an industrialised society. In earlier times people did not have such luxuries. So how did they spend their leisure time?

Primitive society

Leisure in a primitive society probably did exist, but it was different to our understanding of leisure today. Primitive society was based on people hunting and gathering food; these were their main concerns – finding the next meal and looking for shelter.

Leisure activities that did arise were usually associated with festivals and celebrations such as the birth of children or the harvesting of food. Singing and dancing probably took place as a way of making life more tolerable and enjoyable. In reality, there would have been very little leisure time as all efforts had to be concentrated on finding food to survive.

Ancient times

In ancient times, leisure was seen as a symbol of wealth and social status. In Egypt, for example, leisure was restricted to the nobility, the military and religious leaders. Their leisure activities included wrestling, boxing, archery, art and music. Leisure activities such as hunting and falconry developed from the need for survival. Leisure gardens became ideal locations where the upper classes could relax and enjoy themselves.

The Greek civilisation

The Greeks were the first to distinguish between work and leisure. They promoted a balance between work and play as the route to a healthy lifestyle and a healthy society.

In ancient Greece, sport was an important part of the culture of everyday life. The purpose of sporting competitions was to test and improve military skills, hence the javelins were associated with spears and the discuses had spikes on them.

The modern Olympic movement is loosely based on the sporting events that the ancient Greeks adopted. Indeed, some of the words which we associate with sport today derive from Ancient Greek; for example, decathlon, gymnasium and stadium.

The Romans

In Roman times, leisure meant entertainment. The Roman calendar had 200 days of the year set aside for celebrations, 175 of which were days of games.

The great Roman engineers built public facilities for the masses to enjoy. Rome itself had over 800 public baths for use by people free of charge. The healing powers of spa waters were first recognised in Roman times. Slaves played music, competed in sports and took part in gladiatorial contests where success meant freedom, but failure meant death.

The extensive road network developed by the Romans meant that travel was faster and more convenient. These roads were built in order to conquer and trade with other nations. The Colosseum, which was a huge stadium in the heart of Rome with a capacity of 300,000, benefited from improved transport as people could travel from towns across the empire. The entertainment there was free as the emperors thought it would prevent the masses from revolting ('bread and circuses' to keep the people happy).

Many people travelling to Rome needed places to stay and somewhere to eat and drink. Stalls were set up outside the Colosseum selling souvenirs to these visitors. A leisure industry had been set up comprising hospitality, entertainment, tourism and recreation.

The Middle Ages

It has been argued that the tremendous costs associated with the lavish entertainment provided by the Romans led to the downfall of Rome; and the collapse of the Roman Empire certainly had a major impact on leisure. The very name given to the period between AD100 and AD400 – 'the Dark Ages' – suggested that these were hard times with few opportunities for the mass of the population to take part in leisure activities.

The rise of Christianity after the Dark Ages led to leisure being associated with 'holy days'. In medieval Britain religious festivals took place at key stages of the agricultural year such as:

⋄ Christmas – midwinter feast

⋄ Easter – spring festival

⋄ autumn – harvest festival

⋄ saint's and holy days – Sunday as a day of rest.

Between the tenth and fourteenth centuries (the 'Middle Ages'), leisure continued to be enjoyed by the feudal lords of the day who had time on their hands to enjoy jousting, hunting, music and dance, while the labourers were too busy tending the crops to enjoy any leisure activities.

Towards the end of the Middle Ages leisure began to take on an unpleasant blood-thirsty aspect. It came to mean drinking, gambling and blood sports, such as bear baiting and cock fighting, which became the pastimes of an increasingly corrupt nobility. However, this was soon to change.

Renaissance and Reformation

Renaissance means 'rebirth' and signals that time in the fifteenth century when the western world changed from a medieval system. There was a rebirth in the arts and learning in Europe and the Renaissance became a time when leisure was no longer available only to the privileged classes. The masses could now enjoy music, drama and dance.

However the Reformation in the sixteenth century not only changed the church but also altered attitudes towards leisure. The 'Protestant work ethic' curtailed not only the pleasure-seeking activities of the nobility, it also severely limited leisure and recreational activities for the masses. Even today certain leisure activities are restricted, especially on Sundays.

Seventeenth-century leisure

Once again attitudes towards leisure changed. From 1670 onwards the sons (and sometimes the daughters) of the nobility were sent on 'the Grand Tour of Europe' to widen their education. Places like Paris, Florence and Venice gave these young people the opportunity to experience different societies and cultures. Many of the towns and cities of Europe developed their tourism facilities as a result of these 'jaunts' by the rich, high-spending aristocrats.

In the early seventeenth century, the aristocracy began to accept the healing powers of spa water and so spa resorts like Bath, Leamington Spa and Buxton were developed as early tourist destinations.

The Industrial Revolution

The Industrial Revolution brought great changes to the society and ways of life of people in Britain, not least of which was in relation to leisure.

Towns and cities grew enormously as mechanisation and mass production resulted in people moving from the countryside to the towns to get work in the mills and factories. The cities became overcrowded and slums developed where people in badly paid jobs lived in areas of poor housing. Long working hours and low wages gave few opportunities for leisure activities for the masses. It was not uncommon, in the late nineteenth century, for men, women and children to work a 60-hour week.

On the other side of the coin, leisure was now available to those who could afford it. For those who managed the factories, the Industrial Revolution created great wealth. These 'middle classes' were able to take part in horse racing, entertaining family and friends and visiting the spa resorts, which provided an escape from the cities.

As the Industrial Revolution continued, the 'working classes' demanded greater freedom from work. Dangerous working conditions and overcrowded cities made people want to escape to the countryside and coast, if only for the fresh air and a change of scenery.

The Victorian age

By the early part of the nineteenth century seaside resorts were becoming popular. Doctors recommended fresh air and salt water as the cure for all ills. Scarborough, with the twin benefits of spa and sea water, took advantage of these resources and developed into a very popular tourist destination, especially with the middle classes. Other resorts such as Blackpool, Southend and Brighton became increasingly popular. Catering, accommodation and entertainment facilities sprang up to cater for this influx of tourists.

The period between the mid-1800s and the twentieth century was when many of today's leisure activities were developed. At the start of this period, towns and cities were unhealthy places to live with open sewers and unclean drinking water. Pressure was put on the government to improve such conditions and by the end of the nineteenth century most towns and cities had proper sewers, running water, public baths and parks and open spaces.

By the 1880s the Ministry of Health assisted local councils to develop parks, libraries and museums, swimming pools and public baths. This was the government's first direct involvement in leisure by seeking to improve the quality of life and health of its people.

From 1830 the construction of the railway network opened up the countryside and coastal regions. Rail travel became increasingly popular, especially when the public were given access to affordable travel, and the railway played a major part in developing seaside resorts. On Easter Monday in 1862 some 132,000 visitors travelled to Brighton.

One of the first people to capitalise on this new form of travel was Thomas Cook, who was destined to have a profound impact on the early development of travel. By 1885 he was running a fully commercial travel company, arranging trips and tours both at home and abroad.

In the late nineteenth century, local councils set aside land for playing fields and recreation areas. Large stadia were built on the outskirts of towns as the private sector became aware of the profitability of leisure.

Football, cricket, tennis and rugby became regulated, with rules drawn up by the governing bodies. In 1863 the Football Association was founded. In 1877 an international tennis tournament was held at Wimbledon. In 1888 the Football League was formed. This period also saw the introduction of cabaret, dance halls and the music hall shows.

At last, leisure was available to all but the most deprived in society.

Leisure in the twentieth century

The twentieth century saw people determined to take part in leisure activities which included socialising, entertainment and enjoyment. This was largely due to the influence of two World Wars (1914–18 and 1939–45), after which people were determined to make the most of life.

The inter-war years (1918–39) saw many people take up a government initiative regarding fresh air and exercise as it was accepted that many British people were generally unfit and undernourished. Also as a result, milk was provided by the government free of charge for children at school, the National Playing Fields Association was formed in 1934 and in 1937 the National Fitness Council was founded, which provided sports grants to voluntary bodies.

New forms of mass communication such as posters, guide books and radio (the 'wireless') stimulated the public to travel further afield in search of different leisure activities.

After World War II there was an economic boom which created more employment. This in turn led to people being able to spend money on new homes and labour-saving devices such as vacuum cleaners, washing machines and electric irons, as well as buying their own cars. As a result, people were able to spend more time on leisure activities both inside and away from the home.

The 1960s, 1970s and 1980s were influenced by a youth culture that was dominated by music, dancing and fashion. Television took over from the cinema and crazes like ten-pin bowling and skateboarding came and went. Indoor leisure activities, including home computers and watching videos, tended to replace the outdoor activities of the early twentieth century.

During the 1980s there was a tendency by young, wealthy people to take part in expensive and sometimes risky sports. Activities like hang-gliding, ballooning and powerboat racing became popular with this group. The terms 'yuppie' (young, urban professional) and 'dinky' (double income, no kids yet) were coined in this decade.

Also at this time sport at the highest level became dominated by big money and sponsorship and it was difficult to determine what was meant as amateur and what was meant as professional.

In the 1990s, with an increasing emphasis on health and fitness, 'going to the gym' became an important leisure activity for many people.

Most leisure activities have now become available to all, although it is still apparent, as we have seen through history, that the more wealth and status people have, the greater amount of leisure they enjoy. This pattern repeated itself in the 1990s and there is no reason to suggest it will change in the twenty-first century.

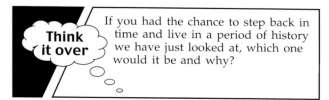

Talk about it

Working in a group, discuss what you think were the most significant developments in the history of leisure.

Think it over

If you had the chance to step back in time and live in a period of history we have just looked at, which one would it be and why?

The growth of leisure time today

There is now more leisure time available to the individual than ever before. This is due to many factors, including:

- early retirement

- a reduction in working hours

- greater paid holiday entitlement

- new technology, e.g. microwaves and dishwashers, resulting in less time being spent on household chores

- an increase in life expectancy

- an increase in disposable income – the money left over after you have paid for essentials like rent, food and clothing

- the growth in unemployment.

Not surprisingly, it is retired people who have most leisure time. The unemployed have greater flexibility over their leisure time but less choice of the activities they can afford. People in work have more money to spend on leisure activities and generally take part in these activities between 5 pm and 11 pm weekdays and at weekends.

SNAPSHOTS

Bob and Beryl

Bob and Beryl have been married for 25 years. They have three grown-up children who have all left home.

Bob is a DIY fanatic who spends hours building wall units, making garden furniture and decorating every nook and cranny in the house.

Beryl loves gardening, throwing dinner parties for friends and playing bowls.

Together they go ballroom dancing every Tuesday and Thursday evening and they spend every other weekend at their caravan on the coast.

- *Do you know other retired couples who have similar lifestyles?*

- *Where would Bob and Beryl go to find the resources they need to carry out their leisure activities?*

Jasmine

Jasmine is 17 and has just started work as a junior travel consultant after successfully completing her GNVQ Intermediate Leisure and Tourism course. Jasmine enjoys aerobics, horse-riding and going to her local nightclub with friends. She hopes to spend her future leisure time travelling abroad.

Dan

Dan is 27 and single. Dan is a biker and spends hours polishing his beloved 1200cc Honda Goldwing. He also supports Manchester United and hasn't missed a home game in two years.

Any time left over from football and his motorbike is spent with his mates down at the local pub.

Leisure activities

It is generally accepted that people now have more time than ever before to participate in leisure.

People are always looking for new ways to spend their leisure time. Leisure activities are many and varied, such as reading, sport – participating and spectating, going to the cinema, eating out, playing computer games, visiting tourist attractions.

Table 1.1 Time use: by age, Britain

Activity	Hours per week					
	16–24	25–34	35–44	45–59	60 and over	All aged 16 and over
Television or radio	14	15	13	17	26	19
Visiting friends	7	5	4	4	4	5
Reading	1	1	2	3	6	3
Talking, socialising and telephoning friends	3	3	3	4	4	3
Eating and drinking out	6	4	4	4	2	3
Hobbies, games and computing	2	2	1	3	3	2
Walks and other recreation	2	2	1	2	3	2
Doing nothing (may include illness)	1	1	1	2	2	2
Sports participation	3	1	1	1	1	1
Religious, political and other meetings	–	1	1	–	1	1
Concerts, theatre, cinema and sports spectating	1	1	–	–	–	–
Other	1	–	–	–	–	–
Total free time	40	37	33	40	52	42

Source: Office for National Statistics

Try it out

Study the facts and figures in Table 1.1 Time use by age.

How do people's leisure activities change as they get older?

Work out how much leisure time you have in one week? Show your results on a bar chart.

Work out your group's average weekly amount of leisure time. Does anyone have any unusual hobbies?

Why is there a leisure industry?

People generally work fewer hours per week than ever before. Trade union pressure and government legislation have resulted in the working week being reduced from 45 hours 30 years ago to, on average, 37 hours today. Holiday entitlement has also increased, as shown in Figure 1.1.

Leisure has developed as a direct result of improvements in technology and improved transport systems that have enabled people to travel further and faster for education and for pleasure.

? Did you know?

Some people may not be able to take part in some leisure activities because of religious and cultural traditions. For example, Muslim women following the laws of Islam are not allowed to show any part of their bodies. Obviously this restricts sporting activities. In some areas of the country, such as in Birmingham, a compromise has been reached at some leisure centres for Muslim women who want to swim. Women-only swimming sessions using female lifeguards have been introduced.

Look it up

Ask members of your family how many hours a week they work and how much holiday entitlement they have.

Now ask them the same question about their parents.

Was there a difference? Write down your findings and be prepared to share them with the rest of your group.

CASE STUDY – Bill

Bill left school when he was 14 to start work as an apprentice engineer at the local factory. His apprenticeship lasted six years. His starting pay rose from £2 and 10 shillings (£2.50) to £5 and 15 shillings (£2.75).

The factory was doing well and the engineering industry seemed to be booming. Bill had a job for life. In fact, he stayed there for 41 years. He progressed from apprentice to section supervisor and finally to factory foreman.

Last year the factory closed and at the age of 55, Bill was made redundant. He had the choice of accepting his redundancy payments and retiring early or finding another job. Early retirement could mean at least 20 years of leisure: would he know what to do with himself?

Bill initially felt he had been thrown on the scrap heap and he experienced a loss of self respect and worth. He shared his feelings with his wife who believed that Bill deserved a good rest after a lifetime of hard graft. Bill said, 'The redundancy came as a shock and I was totally unprepared for it. My life was based on hard work not free time. Well, I decided enough was enough so I retired early. It was the best thing I ever did. I now spend time doing things I want to do: spending time with my family, fishing, caravanning and doing all those jobs around the house that should have been done ages ago. In fact, I am busier now than I've ever been. The big difference is that I love every minute of it!'

Questions

- Do you know anyone in similar circumstances to Bill?

- Bill had leisure time forced upon him. What problems do people face when this has happened to them?

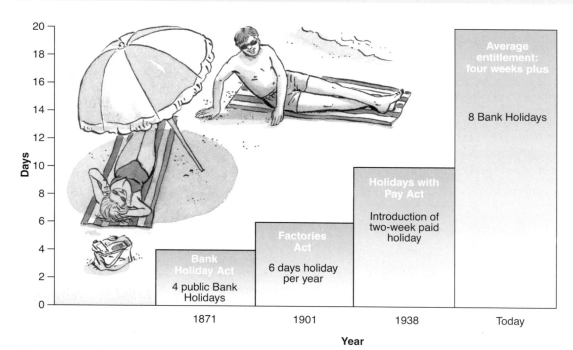

Figure 1.1   Holiday entitlement since 1871

Milestones in the development of leisure

1700s	Paid employment and regulated working hours
1750s	Beginning of the Industrial Revolution
1800s	Government involved in leisure through provision of public baths and open spaces
1815	First steam-driven sea voyage (Glasgow to Dublin)
1830	First passenger train service (Manchester to Liverpool)
1841	Thomas Cook's first 'day' excursion
1855	Thomas Cook's first Continental holiday tour
1860	Invention of bicycle – independent travel for the masses
1870	60-hour working week became the standard. Half-day holiday introduced on Saturday afternoon, later termed the weekend
1871	Bank Holiday Act establishes four public Bank Holidays
1885	Invention of the motor car
1896	Modern Olympic Games movement founded
1900s	Vast improvement in road, rail, sea and air transport
1932	First regular BBC service
1938	Holidays with Pay Act
1950s	Television becomes widely popular across the UK
1952	First jet airline passenger service
1960s	Introduction of 37-hour working week
1964	First National Sports Centre built at Crystal Palace
1964	Public Libraries and Museum Act
1968	First cross-Channel hovercraft service
1972	Sports Council established
1976	Concorde goes into service
1980s	Leisure technology in the home takes off
1990s	Eurotunnel carries first passengers
1994	First National Lottery draw
1997	Department of Culture, Media and Sport established
2000	Millennium Dome opened

Talk about it

In recent decades, automation and new technology have reduced the need for human labour. This leads to a rise in unemployment in some areas. Such enforced leisure time could possibly lead to growing crime and social disorder. This may be especially so where the people affected do not have the necessary work skills for today's society.

What does your group think about this issue?

People tend to have more time and money to spend on their leisure time, as Table 1.2 shows. In many families there are now two parents working, so families want to spend their leisure time together; hence we have:

- family tickets at theme parks, heritage centres
- pubs with family rooms
- fast-food restaurants aimed at families
- package holidays which provide activities for the whole family.

Table 1.2 Average weekly household expenditure on leisure activities and goods (£s)

	1987	1988	1989	1990	1991	1992	1993	1994/5	1995/6	1996/7	1997/8
Leisure services	18.11	18.13	19.02	21.54	22.20	27.56	25.56	31.20	32.05	33.95	38.81
Leisure goods	9.03	9.65	10.97	11.28	12.06	13.32	13.26	13.89	13.23	15.17	16.35

Source: Office for National Statistics

The statistics show that people are spending more per week on leisure services and goods.

Working in your group, can you think of any ways that leisure services could be made more accessible to people on low incomes?

How would your leisure activities be restricted if you did not have access to a car or public transport?

It's worth remembering that people like to spend their personal disposable income on doing things they like, for example going to the cinema, eating out, taking the family ten-pin bowling.

You can imagine how when someone has done a hard day's work in the office or on the factory floor they want to relax and unwind in their leisure time. For many people, especially those who don't like their jobs, their leisure time activities are more important than work.

Think it over

Many people go to work purely for the pay. There must be other reasons why people go to work, for example job satisfaction, working with colleagues, feeling wanted.

What sort of job could you do in the future that would motivate you to go to work and enjoy it?

Leisure facilities

These are places where people can go to relax and enjoy themselves. We will look at the different types of facility in turn.

Leisure centres

The first purpose-built sports and leisure centre in Britain was built at Harlow in 1960. There are now over two thousand leisure centres in the UK.

The Crystal Palace National Sports Centre was opened in 1964. The main sports catered for were athletics, swimming and diving, as well as space to stage national and international events.

The early leisure centres were built in the centre of towns so they were easily accessible for people

As a group, write down the names of some of the leisure facilities in your local area and include them on a chart like the one shown below.

FACILITY	NAME
Leisure centres	
Swimming pools	
Cinemas	
Theatres	
Museums	
Restaurants	
Travel agents	
Hotels	
Libraries	
Parks	
Community centres	
Ice-skating rinks	
Nightclubs	
Health and fitness clubs	

You may want to use the following ideas for your research:

- Yellow pages and other directories
- family and friends
- local newspapers
- local Tourist Board.

You will be able to put this information to good use for the unit assessment so make your research as detailed as possible (and don't lose it!).

to get to. This type of location, however, meant there was little or no room for expansion so they were limited in the activities they could provide.

The 1970s saw a new type of leisure centre develop as many local councils built them with surrounding track and field areas for other traditional sports such as football, netball and tennis. This development came about following the Wolfenden publication, *Sport and the Community*.

One of Europe's largest indoor leisure centres is the Dome at Doncaster. It offers more than fifty sports and leisure activities such as squash, ice-skating, aerobics, indoor bowls, swimming, martial arts and badminton. It also has facilities such as a bar, café, conference room and multi-purpose sports hall so that a variety of events can take place such as concerts, wedding receptions, antiques roadshows, exhibitions, business conferences and parties.

Some leisure centres are attached to schools to ensure maximum usage. The school pupils use it during the day and the public use it after 4 pm and at weekends.

When planning a leisure centre programme, especially one managed by a local council, with the aim of providing a service to the community, it is important to take into account the different needs of the various sections of that community. These groups include: the unemployed, people with disabilities, manual and clerical workers, senior citizens, clubs, teenagers, toddlers and pre-school age children.

As well as catering for the needs of specific groups, it is important that a leisure centre programme should cover a wide range of activities which should take into account:

- activities which are already popular
- an analysis of activities already offered
- groups which are under-provided for.

There must also be some type of balance of activities. This programming mix should cater for:

- individuals – casual bookings, open sessions
- learners – coaching courses
- clubs – training facilities, match venues
- spectators – events, casual viewing
- special groups – special sessions.

A local leisure centre should provide as wide a range of activities as possible to as large a part of the community as possible, providing them with value for money.

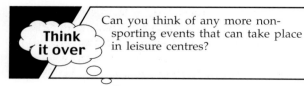

Did you know?

You can even get married in a leisure centre.

Think it over

Can you think of any more non-sporting events that can take place in leisure centres?

Look it up

What does the term 'dual use' mean?

Find out about and make notes on the meaning of Compulsory Competitive Tendering.

Facts and figures – leisure centres in the UK

There are:

- sports centres with no pool   1,483
- sports centres with pool   975
- private health and fitness clubs   2,200
- pools only   807

There are approximately 850 million visits to leisure centres each year.

SNAPSHOTS

Shona, leisure centre supervisor

Shona is 22 years old and has been a Leisure Centre Supervisor in Birmingham for two years. She left school at 16 and went to her local college where she gained a merit in her GNVQ Leisure and Tourism Course. She became a lifeguard at the town's leisure centre and took additional qualifications in Customer Care, Lifesaving and First Aid. She became a Recreation Assistant at 19 and was promoted to her present position when she was 20. She aims to become an assistant manager in two years' time. She says,

'I've always wanted to work in a sports environment. One of my strong points is getting on with people so, for me, this is the perfect job as I am in contact with the public and colleagues everyday. My advice to young people is to concentrate on work which interests you, don't just do it for the money.'

Swimming pools

In the past

Swimming was used as a form of training in ancient Greece and Rome for warriors. But swimming fell out of favour in Europe in the Middle Ages when immersion in water was associated with the recurrent epidemic diseases of the time. By the nineteenth century that prejudice was dispelled and sea bathing became popular. By the twentieth century not only had swimming become known as a means of survival or lifesaving, it was also recognised as a most beneficial form of exercise. In fact, no other form of exercise uses so many muscles so fully.

In 1843 the first swimming races took place in Britain in a public swimming pool. The Baths and Wash Houses Act in 1846 decreed that local councils should provide recreational facilities so swimming pools were built alongside the public baths. By the end of the 1880s many large towns and cities had swimming pools either indoors or outdoors. The 1936 Public Health Act again made provision for public swimming pools as the government wanted to encourage people to take up sport to improve their health and fitness. Swimming was seen as an excellent all-round type of exercise which developed strength, stamina and suppleness.

Swimming pools today

Nowadays public swimming pools come in all shapes and sizes. First there are the traditional rectangular pools, deep at one end and shallow at the other. These pools are particularly good for serious recreational swimmers (who swim to keep fit), competition swimmers, specialist clubs (sub aqua, water polo) and for teaching (swimming, lifesaving).

Many local councils and private operators have upgraded existing pools or built new leisure centres to house leisure pools. In many places the stark, chlorine-smelling atmosphere of the old pools has been replaced with leisure pools which boast slides, wave machines, warm water, music, palm trees, a tropical atmosphere, beach areas and water rapids. A leisure pool can still fulfil the needs of the serious swimmer as lanes can be incorporated into the shape of the pool. However, it is mainly for the fun swimmer.

SNAPSHOTS

Caribbean evening

Remember Shona, the leisure centre supervisor? It's her job to organise a Caribbean evening in the leisure centre pool. This is how she did it.

Stroll down to our Caribbean beach party this Saturday and sample the delights:

- A superb buffet of spicy chicken, rice, salad and barbecued spare ribs followed by fresh fruit salad with cream, iced melon and coconut surprise

- A Caribbean steel band that will serenade you to the gentle beat of Jamaican love songs

- Let our tropical wave machine lap warm water over you while you laze on our beach

- Turn up in your Bermuda shorts or bikini, depending on how the mood takes you.

MIX IT ALL TOGETHER AND YOU HAVE THE PERFECT RECIPE FOR A NIGHT OF WARMTH, SWEET MUSIC AND FUN!

Shona's customers said:

'It brings the Caribbean to the heart of Birmingham.'

'I could have stayed all night. The atmosphere was so romantic.'

Leisure centre

A modern leisure pool is mainly for the fun swimmer who wants to have a 'splashing' time

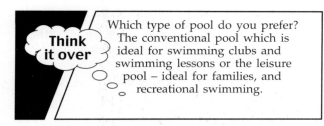

Think it over Which type of pool do you prefer? The conventional pool which is ideal for swimming clubs and swimming lessons or the leisure pool – ideal for families, and recreational swimming.

Try it out Design and draw your own leisure pool. Give it an attractive name, for example 'Ocean Waves' and include the special features like slides and flumes which would make it popular. Remember that people want fun, excitement and atmosphere.

Sports pitches

Football is our national game and you don't have to look too far to find your nearest football pitch. It may be in the local park or a club may have its own ground. There are thousands of football, hockey and rugby pitches throughout the country. Add to these, tennis courts, cricket pitches, netball courts, bowling greens, athletics tracks, dry-ski slopes and golf courses and you will get the idea of how big a part sport and recreation play in our lives.

Facts and figures – leisure centres in the UK

There are 77,946 playing pitches in England. These include 39,000 football, 11,730 cricket, 11,500 for rounders, 8,000 for hockey and 8,000 rugby.

Talk about it

What are the advantages and disadvantages of all-weather pitches?

Health clubs

Nowadays people are becoming more and more aware of the importance of leading a healthy lifestyle so facilities like health clubs have sprung up to meet this demand. They usually contain fitness suites which have all the latest 'high-tech' cardiovascular equipment such as rowing machines, exercise bikes and treadmills.

Some of the larger clubs have sauna, sunbeds and steam rooms (Turkish baths). Additional services include beauty therapy consisting of body massage, manicures and pedicures, eyelash and eyebrow treatments, aromatherapy and facial massage.

You will find now that many hotels, especially those belonging to national chains, have included health clubs within the hotel itself. This additional attraction is aimed at increasing business by offering a wider variety of activities.

Libraries

The 1850 Libraries Act permitted local councils to spend some of their money on creating and administering libraries. The 1964 Libraries and Museums Act stated that local councils should provide an efficient and free lending service to the public.

Libraries offer many sources of information. Your local library will have a great deal of secondary information which will help towards your course. As well as books, they offer videos, compact discs, cassettes and computers (so you can search the Internet for information).

There are approximately 2,600 libraries in Britain. They remain an important leisure facility and reading is still popular despite the competition from television, radio and computers.

Libraries have undergone an image change over the past 15 years. Lending systems are now generally computerised and communal areas where you can talk and read through the material you are researching have been introduced.

They are now attractive and welcoming facilities which provide the perfect setting for you to do your GNVQ coursework.

Look it up

In small groups, arrange a visit to your local library and find out what your library has to offer in addition to its book lending service.

How often do you use your public library? What do you think is the value of your local library to the community? Who do you think are its main users?

What is the purpose of the Library Service?

- to give access to information
- to support life-long learning
- to support community & social identity
- to provide cultural enrichment
- to support economic development

What can you get from your Library Service?

- books
- information
- sound recordings & videos
- newspapers & magazines
- local studies
- exhibition areas and rooms for hire
- photocopying & fax facilities
- drama/music sets
- activity programmes
- lectures and talks
- CD-Rom (in some libraries)
- Open for learning centres (in some libraries)
- Minicom service for the deaf & hard of hearing (in some libraries)

Libraries in Nottinghamshire offer a wide variety of services, ask at your local library for further information.
Comments and suggestions about the service are welcomed and any complaints are dealt with urgently.

What sorts of books, magazines and newspapers?

- novels, leisure reading and non-fiction to help with your work, school or pastime.
- paperback and hardback for children, teenagers and adults.
- BOOKS IN LARGE PRINT
- a wide range of magazines, local and national newspapers
- books and newspapers in community languages: Bengali, Urdu, Hindi, Punjabi, Gujerati, Polish, Chinese & Vietnamese.
- sets of playtexts and music scores.

What sort of recordings?

- compact discs, cassettes and records which have something for everyone including pop, jazz or light music, classical, country and western, Asian film music, African, reggae and soul.
- VHS information videos (including some with subtitles), classic films & classic foreign films.
- spoken word cassettes for children and adults.
- language courses

NB   A charge is made for most recordings - please ask staff for details of exemptions.

What is there for children?

- picture books, board books, stories, information books, spoken word, cassettes and videos.
- books in community languages.
- comics and magazines to look at in the library
- story and activity sessions, and toys to play with in the library.
- displays of art and craft work from local schools and under-fives groups.
- CD-Rom (in some libraries)

Children are always welcome in the library and can join at any age.

What sort of information is available?

The library is your local information centre. Our request service gives access to over 2.5 million items of County Library stock and, from anywhere in the U.K. (Charges are made for the request service).

- business information: directories, company information, standards, statistics.
- public information: welfare rights, benefits, education, consumer rights, government departments, tourism.
- local information: clubs, societies, education, sport, leisure, music, theatre, arts, local government, Councillors.

A library information leaflet can help you find out what services are available (1998 edition reproduced with the kind permission of Nottinghamshire County Council)

CASE STUDY – Uptown library users

Gideon

Gideon studies GCSE PE and is very interested in tennis. He needs information for a project about the past ten Wimbledon championships so he goes to his local library to find the information.

Jackie

Jackie is 38 and works part time in her local library. She likes to help people with their research. She is doing an Open University degree and uses her library as a base for her studies.

Mrs Duckham

Mrs Duckham takes her three children to the library over the half-term holidays because it is 'junior book week' for 7–11-year-olds and storytime for the under 7s. During this week Mrs Duckham's children can choose their own books, enter writing competitions and practise using a computer.

Questions

- Gideon decides to look for the relevant information himself. Which sections and resources in the library would enable him to find the information?

- Apart from the resources, why else do you think Jackie uses the library as a base when she is studying?

- How does the Duckham family benefit from their visit to the library?

The British Library

The British Library is the national library of the UK and one of the world's greatest libraries. It contains:

* the national archive of British and overseas newspapers

* western and oriental manuscripts from the beginning of writing to the present

* one of the world's finest collections of printed and manuscripted music

* one of the world's largest archives of sound recordings.

The British Library's collection consists of:

* 16 million books

* 660,000 newspaper titles

* 4 million maps

* 205,000 photographs.

It employs 2,393 staff. 4.3 million document supply requests are satisfied per year.

Video rental shops

Video recorders became popular in the early 1980s following on from the popularity of television. People could buy blank tapes and record their favourite television programmes. Video rental shops appeared soon after and enabled people to rent or buy their favourite films or video games.

In fact, you can now bring the atmosphere of the cinema into your own front room. Picture this scene . . .

> Stroll down to your local video rental shop and take out a film that everyone has been talking about. Pick up a plentiful supply of popcorn, soft drinks and sweets while you are there. Stroll back home, insert the video, put your feet up and watch the film. No queuing, no car parking problems, no comments shouted from the audience – just a totally relaxing atmosphere in which you can concentrate on your film.

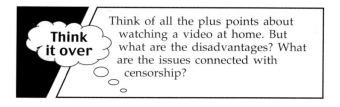

Think it over

Think of all the plus points about watching a video at home. But what are the disadvantages? What are the issues connected with censorship?

At the time of writing, video shops are extremely popular. Whether this popularity will continue with the introduction of DVD players is open to question. Another important point to note is that videos can now be hired from local corner shops. The extra competition for sales and the introduction of new technology could affect the business of video rental shops.

Talk about it

In your group, discuss whether you think videos portraying violent scenes influence the behaviour of those who watch them. Does violence on the screen lead to violence off the screen?

Cinemas

Figure 1.2 shows the trend in cinema admissions in Britain since 1952. Cinema admissions declined sharply, particularly from the mid-1950s to the mid-1960s, and since then have continued to fall more slowly.

Undoubtedly this was caused by the arrival first of television, and later video recorders.

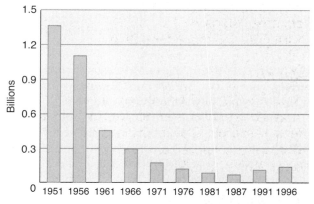

Source: *Social Trends*, National Statistics

© Crown copyright 1998

Figure 1.2 Cinema admissions in Britain, 1951–96

CASE STUDY – Mike

Mike is 30 years old and is the manager of the Majestic Multiplex, which has ten screens, a restaurant and bar next door and is located on the outskirts of the town.

Mike's job includes supervising staff to make sure everything is all right on the night.

He started working in reception when he was 16 years old and progressed quite rapidly to his present position.

He finds the most satisfying part of his job is seeing people having a good night out.

Activity

In small groups, discuss what skills and knowledge Mike might need to carry out his job as manager of such a big complex. Make a list of these and compare with the whole group.

Look it up

How do you think cinemas won back their popularity?

Find out what's on at your local cinema over a two-week period and write down the films and the range of people the films are aimed at.

Find out how often people in your group go to the cinema.

Pubs, restaurants and takeaway restaurants

Pubs

The British pub is the perfect place for adults to meet friends, socialise, tell jokes, argue, play pool, listen to music, grab a sandwich and catch up with all the local gossip. It has character all of its own.

No other country in the world can match the atmosphere of the British pub. Tourists from overseas, especially Americans, often head straight to a pub after arriving in the country, as they have no places like this 'back home'. The log fire, the gentle hum of people talking and the general character of the British pub make it unique. That's what makes it so attractive to tourists.

Nearly all pubs now serve food. This attracts more customers, which in turn brings in more income. Promotions such as 'two meals for the price of one' between certain times and 'happy hours' attract even more people.

The popularity of a pub depends on the welcome you receive, the décor, the quality of the food, the cleanliness of the toilets and the general atmosphere (as well as the quality and range of drinks it serves!).

Talk about it

In your group, what are your thoughts on the age limit of 18 years before you can go into a pub and be served achohol?

Restaurants

A wide variety means there is also competition. Some special offers help promote particular features a restaurant might like to advertise. For example:

- 'two meals for the price of one'

- an extensive menu to offer a wider choice

- vegetarian selection
- children's menus
- reduced prices between 5 pm and 7 pm
- silver saver – discount for the over 55s
- extensive wine lists
- discounts for party bookings
- a free glass of wine with your meal.

Talk about it

Working in your group, identify a range of restaurants in your local area. There are many types of restaurants nowadays as you have probably identified. These include: fast food, à la carte, wine bars, bistros, family, hotel or ethnic (Chinese, Indian, Thai, Italian and so on).

Did you know?

Eating out is one of the most popular leisure time activities. People now spend more money on eating out than ever before.

Takeaway restaurants

These are also known as 'fast-food' restaurants. In the UK, fast food includes fish and chips, hot pies and pasties, burgers, kebabs, pizzas, soups.

Drinks include milk shakes, tea, coffee and milk.

The advantage of takeaway restaurants is that a broad range of snacks and meals is instantly available to the customer. Almost every town and city in the UK has a McDonald's, KFC, Burger King or Pizza Express.

Takeaway restaurants are especially popular with teenagers and families – probably because value-for-money meals are available almost instantly, with no washing up to worry about.

Being a rapidly expanding sector of the UK food industry, takeaway restaurants have had an impact beyond what was intended. For example, an increase in takeaway food sales has meant an increase in the amount of packaging generated, which would not have existed had meals continued to be eaten in restaurants or in the home. This has negative environmental implications in terms of litter, yet positive employment implications in terms of extra jobs in manufacturing the packaging.

Facts and figures – eating out

- The average weekly expenditure on eating out is £22.
- Eating out as a percentage of food expenditure in the UK is 33 per cent.
- The total amount spent on eating out in the UK is £16 billion per year.

Talk about it

Some people have concerns over the ways in which our diet relies too much on highly processed foods that may contain high levels of refined sugars, saturated fats, salt and additives. This could lead to people eating fewer fresh, wholesome foods. The concern is that generations of people are completely replacing home-cooked meals with fast food.

In your group, discuss the advantages and disadvantages of takeaway restaurants.

Community centres

These consist of facilities built for the local community where activities such as bingo, playgroups, wedding receptions, youth club discos, tea dances, car boot sales, community theatre and even blood donor sessions are held.

They are usually located in the middle of a residential area which enables easy access for everyone in the community. These centres are usually supported by the local council and are run by a committee of volunteers.

Community centres are extremely valuable facilities for the local community in that they act as the focal point for voluntary organisations, consisting mainly of clubs, societies and associations.

It is interesting to note that in many places community centres seem to escape the vandalism which damages other parts of our communities. This is possibly because people place great value on their facility and take good care to look after it.

Profile of Wootton Community Centre

Wootton is a medium-sized village, with a very mixed population, shops and a small industrial estate. It is a very lively community, and the Community Centre is a true 'centre' for the village. The week's programme looks something like this:

Monday	9.00 – 12.00	Playgroup
	2.00 – 5.00	Whist and Bridge clubs
Tuesday	9.00 – 12.00	Playgroup
	3.30 – 5.30	After-school club
	7.30 – 10.00	Panto rehearsal
Wednesday	12.00 – 2.00	Over 60s lunch club
	6.00 – 10.00	Judo and aerobics classes
Thursday	10.00 – 12.00	Parent and toddler group
	2.00 – 4.00	Women's Institute meeting
Friday	9.00 – 12.00	Playgroup
	3.30 – 5.30	After-school club

Look it up

In geographical groups, find out if you have a community centre close to you. Find out about the range of facilities offered. How much is charged for these activities? Compare all your findings – this will also help with your assessment.

Clubs

Clubs profile

Shakers	**Hot Lights**
A club for 11–14-year-olds, open every Monday and Friday night 7–10 pm	Open every night, 18+
	Smart casual – no jeans or trainers
Chart music, soft drinks and snacks	Theme nights
	Food available, 10 pm – 2 am
Prizes and giveaways	

Look it up

Find out and list what clubs are available in your area.

Not everyone has the opportunity to go to a club or even wants to! Different cultures have different values; for example a strict Asian family would not allow their daughter to attend a club as this would not be part of their culture.

CASE STUDY — Rahul, newspaper reporter

Rahul was asked by his editor to report on the local club scene following claims by members of the public that the towns' nightspots were becoming centres for violence and drugs.

Rahul contacted the local police to ask if these claims were true. They said they had heard the rumours and so they had decided to take action. Below is Rahul's report following an interview with Chief Inspector Williams, which appeared in the local paper.

Question

Parents and guardians are obviously concerned about your welfare when it comes to alcohol, drugs and violence. How do you feel about these issues?

DOGS ON DRUG PATROL

Sniffer dogs are to be used in a nightclub to scent out drugs. The dogs will be used twice a month at weekends at 'Hot Lights'. The club's owners will not give any warning of the dogs' use, to increase the chances of catching the culprits. Staff will also be checked by the dogs, which sit beside people on whom they smell drugs. Anyone found with drugs will be detained until the police arrive. Although there have been violent incidents at the club in the past, there have been no reported problems since last year.

The club manager, Mr Terry Downes, said, 'The area in front of the club was generally accepted to be a centre for trouble and we don't disagree that patrons were involved but we are confident in the steps we have taken.'

Sports venues

Sports venues may range from the playing fields where your local team plays to Wembley Stadium.

Try it out

Match the sport with the venue:

* Lords
* Old Trafford
* Twickenham
* Silverstone
* The Crucible
* Aintree
* St Andrew's
* Wimbledon
* Crystal Palace
* Holme Pierrepoint

* Horse racing
* Golf
* Rowing
* Tennis
* Football
* Motor racing
* Snooker
* Rugby
* Cricket
* Athletics

Football match attendances

The increase in Premiership attendances in the 1992/3 season halted the decline since 1990/91 and was the highest recorded since the 1980/81 season (old League Division 1). However it is still much lower than the attendances recorded back in the 1970s, since when capacities at most major grounds have been reduced as the traditional terraces have given way to seating accommodation. Figure 1.3 shows average match attendances for the Premiership and Division 1 in the 1992/3 and 1993/4 seasons.

CASE STUDY — Sports venues in two cities

Sheffield

In 1995 Sheffield was the first city to be designated National City of Sport by the Sports Council of Great Britain.

The opening of three major sports venues in the early 1990s – Don Valley International Stadium, Ponds Forge International Sports Centre and Sheffield Arena – established the city as an important national centre for sports.

Sheffield Ski Village is the largest artificial ski-slope resort in Europe. Bramhall Lane and Hillsborough are home to Sheffield United and Sheffield Wednesday football teams.

Cardiff

Sports venues include the Cardiff Athletic Stadium, the National Ice Rink and the Millennium Stadium (costing over £100 million), which hosted the opening ceremony of the 1999 Rugby Union World Cup. Football and cricket are respectively played by Cardiff City at Ninian Park and Glamorgan Cricket Club at Sophia Gardens.

Questions

- What is the nearest city to you? What major sports facilities does it have? If you live near Cardiff or Sheffield, please choose another city.
- What sort of impacts do these facilities have on the city e.g. more jobs, traffic congestion?

20,000	10,000	23,000	12,000
Premier	Div. 1	Premier	Div. 1
1992/3		1993/4	

Source: Office for National Statistics

Figure 1.3 Average football match attendances

? Did you know?

Sunderland Football Club showed the greatest increase in supporters between the 1996/97 season and the 1997/98 season, when attendances increased from 21,000 to 35,000, i.e. an increase of two thirds. This was in part due to the new stadium called the Stadium of Light, which can accommodate more people than the old one.

Football hooliganism

Football hooliganism is not new. In 1885 Preston North End players were trapped on the field by two thousand 'howling roughs' after beating Aston Villa 5–1. They were attacked with sticks, stones and umbrellas. One player was knocked unconscious by a missile.

An 1899 semi-final replay between Sheffield United and Liverpool was abandoned at half-time. Repeated pitch invasions meant the first half took 90 minutes to complete.

The 1909 Scottish Cup Final between Rangers and Celtic was drawn, as was the replay. Spectators were incensed when extra time was not played in the replay. They invaded the pitch, destroyed goal posts and goal nets, set pay boxes on fire and fought with the police. About 130 spectators received medical treatment on the ground.

From the late 1960s, hooliganism grew to epidemic proportions throughout Europe. In Italy, supporters of Napoli went on the rampage in historic Verona after their team's shock 3–0 defeat, and there were 38 arrests, and after Sampdoria's win at Ascoli that virtually condemned the home side to relegation, it was an hour before the

CASE STUDY – Improving football's image

Sports venues of all types have been modernised over the past 20 years so that spectators can now watch their sport in comfort and safety.

During the 1970s and 1980s hooliganism, drunkenness and violence among football supporters began to bring the game into disrepute and to put people off going. Riots – before, during and after matches – and running battles in the streets between rival fans became commonplace.

It was essential for the football authorities to clean up the game on and off the field and to make life safer for spectators. This was especially true after the fire at Valley Parade, Bradford in 1985 and Hillsborough, Sheffield in 1989 when over 90 Liverpool fans were killed by overcrowding in an area of the stadium. As a result of the Taylor report, additional health and safety measures were introduced to football league grounds. More general improvements included all-seater stadia, big video screens for pre-match entertainment, facilities such as family stands to encourage women and children to attend and to promote family participation, crèches and better catering arrangements. Other features include improved surveillance by closed-circuit television cameras, stewards and police, and hospitality/executive boxes have also been installed to bring in more money. These measures have gone a long way to improve the image of the game and to encourage spectators to return to the grounds.

Questions

*   Rugby League football places great emphasis on promoting matches as family days out. How do you think football clubs could encourage more families to attend matches?
*   Some football clubs have corporate hospitality suites. What are they and who uses them?
*   What sort of pre-match entertainment could football clubs put on for

visitors could leave their dressing room. In battles outside the stadium, several police were injured, and a bus carrying Sampdoria fans was damaged by stones.

All sorts of remedies have been tried to stop hooliganism: fences, segregation of fans, all-seater stadia, closed-circuit television cameras and more careful monitoring of player behaviour.

The real causes of hooliganism are very complex. Some people believe that drinking too much alcohol leads to drunkenness, which leads to violence. One experiment which is now being carried out is to sell no alcohol or low alcohol drinks to supporters before and after the game. Let's hope this works because we don't want to see more incidents where supporters have been murdered.

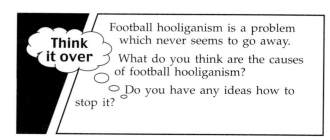

Football hooliganism is a problem which never seems to go away.

Think it over

What do you think are the causes of football hooliganism?

Do you have any ideas how to stop it?

National sports facilities

National sports centres are centres for sporting excellence, providing athletes with high quality sporting and residential facilities, for both training and competition. Each centre provides a unique range of sports facilities, equipment and expertise. The centres also offer conference facilities. In England and Wales there are five national sports centres:

- Crystal Palace, London – athletics, swimming basketball
- Lilleshall, Shropshire – cricket, football, gymnastics
- Holme Pierrepont, Nottingham – rowing, sailing, canoeing
- Bisham Abbey, Buckinghamshire – squash, football, tennis
- Plas y Brenin, National Mountain Centre Snowdonia – mountaineering, rock climbing, canoeing, orienteering.

Working in leisure facilities

Talk about it

Think about leisure in your area. As a group, discuss the following points and make a note of your answers:

- What additional leisure facilities would you like to see in your area?
- How could these be provided? By whom?
- What would prevent these facilities being built in your area?

The key components of the leisure industry

As we have seen, the leisure industry covers an enormous amount of activities ranging from trainspotting to bungee jumping. It also provides a vast range of facilities, from your local swimming pool to the biggest sports stadium, or even the Millennium Dome in London.

It is therefore useful to divide the industry into different sections or **components:**

- sport and physical recreation
- arts and entertainment
- countryside recreation
- home-based leisure
- children's play activities
- visitor attractions
- catering.

? Did you know?

In Britain 25 million people take part in sport and physical recreation at least once a month.

CASE STUDY – Working in the leisure industry

Steve

Steve has been managing Springtown Community Centre for ten years. He enjoys organising events for all age groups, working with voluntary groups and seeing local people take part in local activities.

Harindar

Harindar works part time at a takeaway restaurant. She enjoys meeting the public and working as part of a team. She classes customer care as her top priority.

Ravi

Ravi left university with a degree in Sports Studies. He is now public relations officer at a Premiership Football Club. His job includes looking after opposing teams from the moment they arrive to the moment they leave.

Question

What do Steve's, Harindar's and Ravi's jobs all have in common?

Sport and physical recreation

Some people enjoy going to aerobics classes two or three times a week where they know they will meet up with their friends and enjoy being part of a group.

Sport can also be something for the individual, for example a runner may want to achieve a personal best time or a snooker player may want to achieve a century or even a maximum break.

Whatever the reason, the popularity of sport and physical recreation is growing all the time. Thirty years ago someone running alone on a dark winter's night might have been considered slightly eccentric. Not any more; today, joggers can be seen pounding the pavements everywhere whatever the weather.

Look it up

You can find information on sport and recreation by visiting the Sport England website on www.english.sports.gov.uk.

Remember: physical recreation does not necessarily have to be sport. Activities such as gardening, DIY and walking for pleasure all:

- contain some element of physical activity
- take place in your leisure time
- are done for enjoyment.

Sport England

Sport England, previously known as the English Sports Council, is a government department which is accountable to Parliament through the Secretary of State for Culture, Media and Sports (see Figure 1.4). Its objective is to lead the development of sport in England by influencing and serving the public, private and voluntary sectors.

Sport England's aims are:

- to get more people involved in sport
- to develop more places to play sport

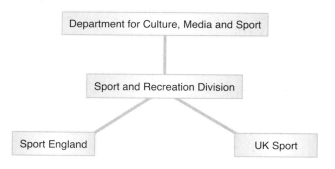

Figure 1.4   Government organisation of sport

- to win more medals through higher standards of performance in sport.

Sport England's definition of sport is:

> *'Sport means all forms of physical activity, either casual or organised, aims at improving physical fitness and well being, forming social relationships, or obtaining results in competition at all levels.'*

There are estimated to be 150,000 voluntary sports clubs in the UK.

Sport and fitness

Nowadays people are more aware of the benefits of leading a healthy lifestyle and are linking fitness and exercise to good health, hence the popularity of walking, jogging, keep fit and aerobics and the growth of leisure facilities.

Sport is important at many levels

We want to get fit, stay fit and feel younger (and look younger). Figure 1.5 shows the S factors of fitness.

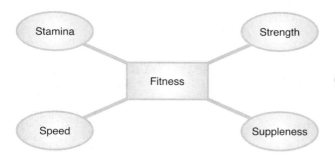

Figure 1.5 The S factors of fitness

Keep-fit classes promote the fact that exercise:

◦ is good for you

◦ helps you lose weight

◦ makes you feel good

◦ can help you make new friends.

All these claims are true providing you exercise on a regular basis, perhaps three times a week. There is a need to encourage more healthy and active lifestyles. The challenge, according to researchers, is to change attitudes among the young and develop an enthusiasm for an active lifestyle that will carry through to adult life.

Keep-fit classes have a number of benefits

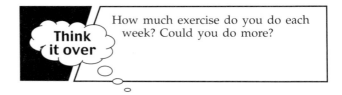

Think it over How much exercise do you do each week? Could you do more?

Talk about it

Many people give up sport when they leave school. Why do you think this is?

Sport and the economy

Sport and physical recreation is big business and plays a significant part in the national economy. It is a major factor for both local and national business in:

◦ merchandising – souvenirs, flags, pendants

◦ clothing – football strips, training shoes

◦ venues – racecourses, football grounds

◦ media

◦ transportation

◦ catering.

? Did you know?

In 1995 consumer expenditure on sport and physical recreation was £10.4 billion in the UK. This included £3.1 million on sportswear and £2 million on sports participation.

Business organisations were quick to recognise the value of sport. In 1998, £347 million was spent on sports sponsorship. Car, insurance, computer, sports clothing and alcoholic drinks companies are all examples of sports sponsors from the business sector.

Talk about it

Sponsorship attracts big money for top sports personalities. A Premiership footballer may be sponsored by a sportswear company for £1 million per year. Add his wages of £800,000 per year and you can see that take-home pay is quite good!

Do you think anyone is worth that much? How do you feel when you read about sports personalities earning £50,000 per week?

Sports spectating

Major sports events attract big crowds. Events like Wimbledon, the FA Cup Final, the Grand National and Test Match cricket attract television audiences of millions worldwide. The huge interest in either playing or watching sport creates lots of business for hotels, bus companies, restaurants and sportswear manufacturers. For example, a group of football supporters may follow their team all over the country and even into Europe. These supporters stay in hotels, eat in restaurants and obviously travel. They have become part of the leisure and tourism industry by default in that they are not holidaymakers yet they use the same facilities and pay for the same services.

Look it up

Look at a television guide and work out how many hours are devoted to sport in one week on BBC 1, BBC 2, ITV and Channel 4.

Great sporting events

Sport has great traditions. National and international events like the ones shown below boost its popularity.

- The FA Cup Final – the world's most famous football match
- The Olympic Games – held every four years at different locations throughout the world
- The World Cup – football's premier competition

Did you know?

Facilities like football and cricket grounds offer spectators much more than an opportunity to watch a game. They now have restaurants, souvenir and sportswear shops, conference suites, guided tours and even museums related to the club's history.

These additional facilities are aimed at providing spectators with a full day's entertainment, not to mention the fact that they encourage them to spend more money. The main aim is to ensure that spectators come back and bring along their families and friends. This is known as 'repeat business' and 'word-of-mouth advertising', topics we shall be studying in Unit 2.

You cannot beat the atmosphere when a crowd of people get together and start cheering on their favourite team. Imagine being at Wembley seeing your team win the cup. But you don't have to go to famous venues to experience the special atmosphere that watching sport can create. You can go down to the local park and still savour the excitement of 'the big match'.

Look it up

Some sports are classed as 'minority' sports because they do not have the same level of participation as sports like football. Examples include cycling, rowing, orienteering, table tennis and trampolining.

Investigate a minority sport which you know little or nothing about.

Try to find out where it is played, its popularity and some of its rules.

- The Tour de France – known as the toughest cycle race in the world
- The Grand National – the world's greatest steeplechase held at Aintree racecourse, Liverpool
- Wimbledon – the world's top tennis tournament
- Test Match cricket – Australia playing England at Lord's for the Ashes
- Rugby Union – The Six Nations' Cup

CASE STUDY — The London Marathon

The first London marathon took place in 1981. The race now attracts 330,000 runners of all abilities.

This is how Richard Brumby, aged 43 and a good club runner, described his first marathon:

'There was great anticipation and excitement at the start. The atmosphere was incredible as more than 30,000 runners squeezed together and waited for the start gun.

'For the first ten miles I felt great as I was carried along by the cheering crowds. After this initial feeling I had to start concentrating on my running as I had another 16 miles to

The London Marathon is world famous and attracts much publicity

go.

'Whenever I felt tired I looked round at all the sights and sounds of London in all its glory. I knew I was half way round when I crossed Tower Bridge.

'The second half of the race was a bit of a nightmare. I had to dig really deep into my energy reserves. Thank God I had spent four months training for this. My legs felt like lead but I didn't care; I could see the finishing line. I felt so proud and relieved when I knew I'd done it.

'The words "never again" sprung to mind yet the following week I started making plans for next year's race. What a glutton for punishment!'

Questions

- Why do you think people like Richard Brumby take part in The London Marathon?

- What attractions does the London Marathon have for both runners and spectators?

The Olympic Games

The Olympic Games have a very ancient history. From 776BC to AD393, Games were held every four years at Olympia in western Greece. The contests usually lasted five days and attracted male competitors from all over the Greek-speaking world. The events consisted of races for runners, chariots and horses, javelin, discus and bloody combat events. The prizes were olive wreaths – and immortal fame.

The first true modern Olympics were organised by a Frenchman, Baron de Coubertin (1863–1937). He believed that sport could be the 'religion' of the modern world, a force to inspire the best in people and bring nations closer together. His hope and vision drove the Olympic movement forward.

? Did you know?

Many events at the 1900 Olympics were disorganised. Some sprints were run downhill. The discus and hammer were held in a city park where competitors kept hitting the trees. Swimming took place in a river with a strong current.

The Olympic Games have now developed into a worldwide event incorporating summer and winter Games.

The Olympic motto is 'Citius, Altius, Fortius' which is Latin for 'Swifter, Higher, Stronger'. There is a second, longer, unofficial motto which describes what could be called the true Olympic spirit, 'The most important thing in the Olympic Games is not to win but to take part'.

This might seem hard to believe nowadays in a world when winning often seems to mean everything and coming second is often portrayed in the media as failure.

Talk about it

What does your group think about the unofficial Olympic motto? Do you agree with it?

In pairs, investigate and discuss the major controversies and incidents which took place at: the 1936 Olympics in Germany, Mexico 1968, Munich 1972, Montreal 1976, Moscow 1980, Los Angeles 1984 and Seoul 1988.

Think it over

What do you think about racism and sport?

A 'Kick Racism out of Football' initiative was recently launched in a bid to stop racist comments being hurled at black footballers at matches. The campaign has the backing of the football authorities and any spectators found guilty of this type of racism will face legal action and be banned from grounds.

? Did you know?

Until recently, Yorkshire Cricket Club only allowed players born in Yorkshire to play for Yorkshire. This appeared to restrict playing opportunities for people from other countries and other cultures. Yorkshire Cricket Club has now changed with the times and abolished this policy. Today, the doors at Yorkshire Cricket Club have been opened to West Indian, Asian and other cultures in a bid to offer more opportunities for people to play for it.

Working in sport and recreation

If you are interested in a career in sport and recreation there are a number of ways to begin your search for paid employment or voluntary positions. Many vacancies are advertised in local and national newspapers. The following magazines, which may be found in your local library, also advertise vacancies in this industry:

⋄ *Health and Fitness*

⋄ *Leisure Week*

⋄ *Leisure Opportunities*

⋄ *Leisure Management.*

Magazines covering specific sports, particularly those published by the governing bodies of sport, generally list jobs in coaching and administration.

? Did you know?

Sport and physical recreation provides over 400,000 paid jobs.

If you are interested in sport and people you may well be suited to a job in sport and physical recreation.

Arts and entertainment

This component of the leisure industry covers a large range of leisure activities, both inside and outside the home (see Figure 1.6).

We have already studied pubs, nightclubs and cinemas, so we shall concentrate here on other leisure activities and facilities. Home-based leisure activities, shown in Figure 1.7, will be covered on pages 42–5.

Figure 1.6 There is a wide range of leisure activities

? Did you know?

136 million people visited the cinema in 1997.

There are 2,000 museums and galleries in the UK.

The Arts Council received £243,000 in 1998 from Lottery funding.

Local authorities support the arts at a cost of £190 million per year.

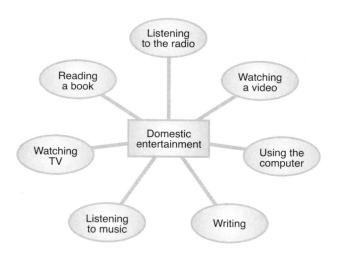

Figure 1.7 Some types of entertainment are available inside the home

The statistics show that one in four adults in Britain attended plays whereas fewer than one in ten went to the ballet or opera. Table 1.3 shows attendance at cultural events.

Table 1.3 Attendance at cultural events in Britain

	Percentages		
	1986/87	1991/92	1996/97
Cinema	31	44	54
Plays	23	23	24
Art galleries/exhibitions	21	21	22
Classical music	12	12	12
Ballet	6	6	7
Opera	5	6	7
Contemporary dance	4	3	4

Source: *Social Trends 1998,* National Statistics © Crown copyright

Think it over

Do you know people who go to the opera/ballet/theatre? What do you think attracts people to these activities and facilities? What about going to the cinema?

Theatres

You can go to the theatre to see a famous play by Shakespeare or a clown being hit in the face by a custard pie. It can make you laugh or cry, or frighten you. It can be acted, sung, or danced, or all three. If you turn on the television tonight you will probably see a drama.

However, there is nothing to beat the excitement of a live audience watching live performances on stage. Think about watching these performers on television and then imagine them on a stage in front of you, only a few feet away. Theatre is alive and exciting for everyone – from the audience, to the actors on the stage, to the many people behind the scenes.

It should be noted that theatre does not mean just drama. Increasingly, theatres are used for a wide range of performing arts, such as concerts, cabaret and light entertainment. Many provincial theatres run clubs and workshops, as well as family membership schemes, designed to increase the interest of young people.

Theatres have traditionally provided an opportunity to socialise, with drink intervals available midway through the evening and bar facilities available before and after performances.

Many theatres offer some form of food and drink provision by the way of a coffee shop, bistro and theatre bar. A very popular event in theatres now is to offer a combined dinner and theatre ticket; this happens more in city theatres and is listed with a specific hotel or restaurant near the theatre. The package includes your first and main courses served, then a break to attend the theatre performance, and then back to the hotel to conclude your evening with dessert and coffee.

This package benefits both the theatre and the hotel or restaurant as each will promote the other by providing adverts in the theatre about the hotel and in the restaurant about the theatre and its attractions.

Talk about it

There's more to theatre than Shakespeare. In your group, write down all the other activities which are held at your local theatre throughout the year.

The UK is one of the world's major centres for theatres and is associated with a lot of tradition. There is an enormous range of shows and plays with the larger productions being located in the major cities. Single, 'one-off' performances can be staged in leisure centres, village halls, schools, colleges and community centres. Many theatre companies, including the RSC (Royal Shakespeare Company), also go on tour around the country, setting up in sports halls or leisure centres.

Local authorities often subsidise theatres and other venues while the Arts Council supports many regional and local theatre companies. Funding is also generated through sponsorship and donations. The voluntary sector has many amateur drama groups which put on performances either in the local theatre or church or village halls.

The theatre is not a highly profitable market for the private sector. One reason for this is the fees commanded by 'stars', who could actually make more money in film and television work. Secondly, the high levels of subsidy received by the national companies make it very difficult for the commercial sector to compete. London theatres are becoming increasingly dependent on audiences of overseas visitors. Financial problems also mean rising ticket prices, emphasising the view that drama is primarily for the well-off middle classes.

Therefore many of the more popular shows in London's West End are musicals. Although they are extremely expensive to put on, they are very popular and can be supported by the additional sales of tapes, CDs and other merchandise. Musicals require a large stage set and have high costs, which makes it difficult to stage them in the smaller theatres.

West End theatres

These are the venues for professional drama in London. The 'West End' is the phrase to describe about 40 commercially owned theatres in Central London. The equivalent in New York is Broadway.

Four of the theatres have permanently resident companies. The Coliseum is the home of the English National Opera, while the Royal Opera House, Covent Garden houses the Royal Opera and Royal Ballet companies. On the South Bank, the Royal National Theatre mounts its own productions in three auditoriums (the Olivier, the Lyttleton and the Cottesloe).

Outside the West End other London theatres include the Lyric at Hammersmith, the Mermaid and Sadler's Wells, as well as many fringe, pub, community and club theatres.

West End theatres

These include the following:

Adelphi	London Palladium
Apollo	Piccadilly
Dominion	Prince Edward
Drury Lane	Victoria
Duke of York's	Victoria Palace
Gielgud Savoy	Whitehall

Some frequently asked questions about London theatres are:

Q. Do I have to wear formal or informal clothes when I go to the theatre?

A. It does not matter what you wear nowadays. You will not look out of place whether you wear a suit and tie, or jeans and a T-shirt.

Q. Where can I get cheap tickets?

A. The half-price ticket booth in Leicester Square sells top-price tickets for most shows at half price plus a small service fee. Nearly all theatres offer concessions to students, senior

A theatre can offer many kinds of entertainment from concerts and musicals to children's plays and 'serious' drama

citizens and the unemployed, normally one hour before the performance.

Q. How far in advance can I buy tickets?

A. Usually two weeks in advance, except for very popular shows where several months may be needed. There is a possibility, if you are lucky, to buy tickets on the day.

Look it up

Find a copy of a national Sunday newspaper which gives a 'What's on' guide of the London theatres. In pairs, write down the name of six London theatres and make a note of what is being performed at them. Can you find out the ticket prices? What seems to be the most popular type of show?

Facts and figures

There are 500 professional theatres in the UK, of which 96 are located in or around Greater London.

London has two national theatre companies: the Royal Shakespeare Company (RSC) at the Barbican and the Royal National Theatre on the South Bank.

Job opportunities in the theatre

Employment opportunities in the theatre include the following:

- cashiers – box office manager
- lighting and sound technicians
- manager
- make-up artist
- scenery assistants
- sales and marketing
- acting roles
- directing.

Look it up

Does your school/college have a media or performing arts section? What sort of productions do they put on? Talk to these students and find out what type of career they aim to follow. Discuss your findings with the rest of the group.

Did you know?

Making people laugh is a serious business. There are two basic types of gag or joke: those which are verbal, such as funny lines; and those which are physical, like falling flat on your face. There is often comedy in serious plays. This is because, as in real life, laughter keeps breaking in at serious moments.

Theatrical terms which are useful to know include:

- understudy – actor prepared to take over another actor's role in an emergency
- auditorium – the part of a theatre building where the audience sits
- props – any articles or objects used in a play, except for the scenery and costumes
- audition – a trial performance to judge an actor's skills and suitability for a role.

Museums

A museum is an institution housing collections of objects of artistic, historic or scientific interest, which are conserved and displayed for the education and enjoyment of the public.

It was during the Renaissance that the term 'museum' was applied to a collection of objects of beauty and work. Museums as they are known today were first established in Europe in the eighteenth century. Since then, special museums have developed such as university museums, history museums, science museums and specialist museums dedicated to a single subject, for example the National Railway Museum in York, the Theatre Museum, London and the National Museum of Photography, Film and Television, Bradford.

Museums appeal to people with a desire to understand the past and to consider how the past can inform the future. Research has shown the most common reason for visiting museums was the chance to 'learn and find out about things'. The second most popular reason was to take advantage of 'facilities under cover protected from the weather'. Millions of people visit museums each year, seeking knowledge, enjoyment and understanding of times gone by and the world around us. Altogether there are about 110 million visits to museums each year.

There are approximately 900 museums in the UK. Over half of this total are housed in listed buildings, themselves a source of public interest. There is a wide variety of museums in the UK, as shown in Table 1.4.

Museums have always been popular places to visit for educational purposes and many museums are developing their appeal to the younger market.

Another trend in museum development is the appearance of more open-air museums. These attempt to recreate the past by reassembling old buildings on a single site. They provide an appropriate setting for demonstrations of old crafts and skills central to an agricultural or industrial way of life associated with the region's past. An example of this type of museum is St Fagans, Cardiff.

Table 1.4 Different types of museum

Type of museum	Example
National	British Museum, London
Local history	Colchester City Museum
Science and technology	Museum of Science and Technology, Manchester
	Catalyst Museum, Widnes, Cheshire
Fine arts	Victoria and Albert Museum, London
	Barber Institute, Birmingham
Film and photography	Museum of the Moving Image, London
	National Museum of Photography, Film and Television, Bradford
Industrial heritage	Wigan Pier
	Ironbridge Gorge Museum
Historical	Howarth Parsonage, West Yorkshire
	Beamish Open Air Museum, County Durham
Archaeology	Corinium Museum, Cirencester
Natural history	Natural History Museum, London
Maritime	Portsmouth Maritime Museum
	National Maritime Museum, Greenwich
	Merseyside Maritime Museum
Transport	National Railway Museum, York
	Great Western Railway Museum, Swindon
	National Motor Museum, Beaulieu

Facts and figures – numbers of visitors to the top ten museums and galleries, 1999

1	British Museum, London	5,460,537
2	National Gallery, London	4,964,879
3	Tate Gallery, London	1,822,428
4	Natural History Museum, London	1,739,591
5	Science Museum, London	1,480,000
6	Royal Academy, London	1,390,000
7	Kelvingrove Art Gallery and Museum, Glasgow	1,051,020
8	National Portrait Gallery, London	999,842
9	Victoria and Albert Museum, London	945,677
10	Royal Museum of Scotland, Edinburgh	759,579

Source: English Tourism Council

? Did you know?

(Photo courtesy of Eureka, The Museum for Children)

Museums can bring education to life

Children's museums are becoming ever more popular, particularly with regard to science and technology. Craftspeople have been brought into the museums and galleries to enable the public to watch processes they would not normally see. 'Hands-on' experiences, with lots of buttons to push and things to touch and see, are used to bring education to life. The Jorvik Viking Centre at York, the new Royal Armouries Museum in Leeds, Tales of Robin Hood, Nottingham and the Eureka Children's Museum in Halifax are examples of a new kind of museum in action. Ironbridge Gorge Museum, Beamish Museum, Wigan Pier and the National Maritime Museum in Liverpool are examples of museum sites which recreate historical times so that visitors can witness the sights, sounds and often even smells of times gone by.

Many town centres now have museums which depend largely for their financial survival on being commercially successful. Examples include 'The Oxford Story' and 'The White Cliffs Experience' in Dover which are run on a commercial basis, relying on admission charges and what customers spend in the shop for their continued success.

Such museums can use a wide range of promotional activities such as radio, television, posters, letters to schools, attendance at exhibitions and public relations.

London's museums

London's museums and art galleries contain some of the most comprehensive collections of objects of artistic, archaeological, scientific, historical and general interest. The British Museum in Bloomsbury is one of the biggest and most famous museums in the world. Its collections range from Egyptian exhibits and Classical antiques through Saxon treasures to more recent artefacts.

The Victoria and Albert Museum in South Kensington is an assembly of fine and decorative art collections from all over the world. There are magnificent examples of porcelain, glass, sculpture, fabrics and costume, furniture and musical instruments, all set in a building of Victorian grandeur. Nearby are the Museum of Natural History and the Science Museum, also housed in splendid buildings. On the other side of London, in the City itself, is the Museum of London, which has exhibits dealing with the development of the capital from its origins to the present day.

Other important collections in the capital include the Imperial War Museum, the National Army Museum, the Royal Air Force Museum, the National Maritime Museum, the Wallace Collection (of paintings, furniture, arms and

CASE STUDY — The Jorvik Viking Centre, York

The Jorvik Viking Centre has become one of Britain's most popular museums. It is a new kind of museum, built on the site of the Viking City of York. A specially designed 'time-car' takes visitors on a journey through Jorvik, the name by which the Vikings knew York. The Centre is a reconstruction of life in the Viking city.

A cassette commentary is provided as the time-car carries its passengers back through time, past life-sized models of people from the thousand years which separate Jorvik from today.

Technology allows the noises and smells – both pleasant and unpleasant – of Viking York to be experienced. The Centre allows visitors to experience at first hand, life as it once was, without the need for barriers or 'keep-off' signs. After the time-car journey, visitors can walk through a display of the actual artefacts and then visit a shop selling souvenirs, craftwork and books.

(Photo courtesy of the Jorvic Viking Centre)

The Jorvik Viking Centre reconstructs life in Viking times

Questions

- Why do you think the Jorvik Viking Centre is especially popular with foreign tourists?

- The Jorvik Viking Centre brings displays to life. How would you bring a music museum to life?

armour, and objets d'art). Sir John Soane's Museum (founded by the architect of the Bank of England in the City) and the London Transport Museum in Covent Garden. The Queen's Gallery in Buckingham Palace has exhibitions of pictures from the extensive royal collection. The Theatre Museum displays the history of the performing arts, while the Museum of the Moving Image traces the history of film and television.

Working in museums

Job opportunities in museums include museum attendant and also positions in catering, sales and marketing, security and guided tours.

A museum attendant could be required to move and arrange exhibits. The age range could be 17 plus and the person will require an interest in the arts, be fit and able to work without supervision.

Curators, conservators and managers act as mediators between the needs and interests of the museum, their departments and the public. Tasks include collection building, research, working on and the monitoring of temporary special exhibitions. A degree or equivalent is usually expected for this position.

Art galleries

An art gallery is a building or room for the public exhibition of works of art. In art galleries run by local authorities, works of art are usually exhibited for public enjoyment or education; in privately run commercial art galleries, works are usually exhibited for sale.

Most major national art galleries were established in the nineteenth century. In those days collecting was seen to be more of a national entitlement

(Photo courtesy of the Museum of Modern Art)

Museum of Modern Art, Oxford

rather than the preserve of the elite. There was a desire to preserve the nation's art collections and natural artistic traditions. Private collections were opened to the public.

In recent times, the commercial art gallery has played an important role both for collections and as the means by which living artists can sell their work and receive public recognition. Research has shown that attendance at art galleries is very much class-based, with a lower proportion of people from unskilled, manual occupations attending than those from the professional classes.

London art galleries
The National Gallery in Trafalgar Square contains one of the finest mixed collections of paintings in the world. Next door is the National Portrait Gallery, whose collection includes more than 9,000 portraits. The Tate Gallery, situated on the Embankment between Chelsea and Westminster, houses the largest collection of British paintings from the sixteenth century to the present day. In 1987 an extension opened to house the paintings bequeathed to the nation by J. M. W. Turner. There is also now a new Tate Gallery of Modern Art constructed at the disused Bankside power station in Southwark, near the reconstructed Shakespearean theatre, the Globe.

Bingo halls

Bingo was at its most popular during the 1960s and 1970s but slumped in the 1980s due to the video 'revolution' and increased home entertainment.

Bingo is still popular in seaside towns. Try walking along the promenade in Blackpool or Margate without being enticed in by a bingo 'caller'. Bingo still attracts three million people, employing 24,000 people in 900 clubs providing £96 million in revenue.

Many bingo halls were converted into nightclubs during the 1980s but some new bingo halls have since opened and there has been a campaign which aims to bring bingo back to its previous popularity.

Theme and leisure parks

Theme and leisure parks have become very popular since Disney resurrected the amusement park industry in 1955 in the United States.

The bigger British theme parks have been modelled on North American examples, principally the immensely popular Disneyworld, Florida and Disneyland in California.

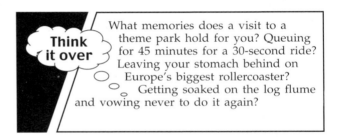

Think it over
What memories does a visit to a theme park hold for you? Queuing for 45 minutes for a 30-second ride? Leaving your stomach behind on Europe's biggest rollercoaster? Getting soaked on the log flume and vowing never to do it again?

Britain's first theme park was Thorpe Water Park at Chertsey, its theme being maritime history. Britain's best-known theme park now is Alton Towers, Staffordshire. It offers a combination of magnificent surroundings, historic heritage and fun. Alton Towers has been transformed from a stately home and gardens into one of the finest leisure parks in the world.

Theme parks as attractions have developed from the idea of amusement parks with thrilling rides, such as rollercoasters, or old or interesting exhibits to look at. Theme parks stretch over vast areas of land and for this reason most are situated in the countryside. The individual attractions in a theme park are more numerous, more terrifying and involve more high technology than in traditional fairgrounds or amusement parks.

The biggest theme parks attract millions of visitors each year which can result in long queues for individual rides at peak times. However, there are usually plenty of souvenir shops, fast-food outlets, amusement arcades, adventure playgrounds and laser games to keep visitors occupied between rides.

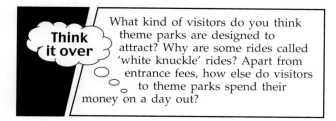

Think it over

What kind of visitors do you think theme parks are designed to attract? Why are some rides called 'white knuckle' rides? Apart from entrance fees, how else do visitors to theme parks spend their money on a day out?

Some theme parks charge a fixed-rate admission for the whole day, with the rides coming free.

Others do not charge an admission fee, for example Blackpool Pleasure Beach, which attracts around 9 million visitors a year. Others include the Palace Pier, Brighton, Pleasureland, Southport and Laserbowl, London.

As theme and leisure parks attract many people, there has been a massive financial investment in the rides offered. The Pepsi Max 'big one' cost £12 million, Nemesis at Alton Towers cost £10 million and the whole of Legoland cost £85 million to build.

The one major disadvantage faced by British leisure parks is the climate. Although these facilities have indoor attractions and some undercover rides, there is usually no escape from the rain and people do not want to queue up for a ride in the pouring rain. Virtual reality simulation enables visitors to experience a wide range of exciting activities indoors, so a new type of attraction may be developed in some theme parks.

CASE STUDY – Disneyworld

The first theme park, Disneyland, opened in California in 1955. Disneyland was so successful that the operators decided to open a second park in Florida, called Disneyworld.

Today Disneyworld is one of the world's most famous theme parks; 20 million people visit Disneyworld each year.

As well as the attractions on offer, other factors help its success:

- Location – central Florida is a popular holiday destination for both Americans and foreign visitors. Many cheap package tours operate from Europe.

- Climate – Florida's hot summers and warm winters attract visitors all year round. Europeans like the hot summer, Americans like the warm winter, especially if they come from northern USA and Canada where winters can be severe.

- Accessibility – central Florida can be reached easily from other parts of the USA and from Europe. There are many other attractions within easy reach of Disneyworld, including: Sea World – the largest sea-aquarium in the world, the Wet 'n' Wild Water Sports Park, the Everglades and the resorts of the Gulf Coast and Miami.

Activity

- Find out what attractions Disneyland has to offer, for example The Epcot Centre, MGM studios.

Jobs in theme parks

Employment opportunities in theme parks can include jobs in:

- catering
- customer liaison
- entertainment
- health and safety
- ground maintenance
- publicity and marketing
- security.

CASE STUDY – Alton Towers

'The park grounds are open from 9.30 am each morning until one hour after the rides and attractions close. Closing times are shown daily, usually this reflects the time it gets dark!

The magic gets stronger

At Alton Towers, Britain's No 1 theme park, there are more mega thrill rides than anywhere in Europe; there's also 80 hectares/200 acres of stunning parkland and loads to do for tiny tots or dotty aunties – so whether it's white knuckles or green acres you're after, there's something for everyone. And in 2000 there's more than ever before!

More than a theme park

There's much more to Alton Towers than the themed attractions you'll find there. With acres of green landscape and woodland walks, punctuated with delightful unexpected

Alton Towers publicity

(Reproduced with kind permission from Alton Towers)

surprises from the Chinese Temple to bubbling fountains, there's tranquility alongside the thrills. And, of course, there are the Towers themselves. Still majestic, with origins dating back 1000 years, they cast an invisible aura around the Park. In their shadow stands the Gothic style chapel, designed by Augustus Welby Pugin; yet another touch of the unexpected in a land of magic.

Visitors will find no shortage of great value restaurants and snack bars at the Park. Whether you want a full three-course meal, fish and chips, a sandwich or just a soft drink, there's something to suit everybody's taste and pocket.'

Some facts about Alton Towers

- Alton Towers is the UK's largest theme park with around 3 million visitors a year.

- Alton Towers opened its themed hotel on 16 March 1996.
- It was the first hotel operated by a theme park to open in the UK.
- Alton Towers has won Tommy's Campaign Parent Friendly Oscar as Britain's top theme park for families with children.

Questions

- After reading the case study, write down why you think Alton Towers is so successful.
- Alton Towers is open between March and October. What events do you think it could stage during the winter months?
- What do people want from a day out at a theme park?

Countryside recreation

Introduction

In Britain there is a wide variety of countryside locations, from the Lake District mountains to the open spaces of Dartmoor. Some city dwellers escape to the countryside to get away from the noise, rush and hustle of the city. They find that the peace and quiet of the open spaces, the mountains, rivers and lakes, helps them relax. Similarly, some people who live in the countryside enjoy the noise of the city as a contrast to the peace and quiet of the countryside.

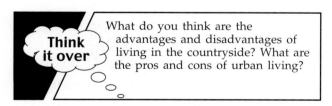

Think it over What do you think are the advantages and disadvantages of living in the countryside? What are the pros and cons of urban living?

The creation of urban lifestyles in the Industrial Revolution inspired a longing by city dwellers and townspeople to take part in recreational activities traditionally associated with the countryside, such as going for a walk and enjoying the colours of the countryside. This led to the creation of parks and 'green' spaces by local councils in many cities. Legislation has been introduced to protect the area of countryside around cities, the 'green belt', so that building development cannot encroach on the countryside.

Look it up

Does your area have green spaces? What are the benefits of parks and gardens in cities?

Many people are attracted to the dramatic scenery offered by the countryside and places like north Wales and the Scottish Highlands attract millions of visitors. The attractive natural features of the countryside, such as rugged landscape, coastlines and picturesque dales, act as a magnet for visitors from home and abroad.

Many people simply like to sit and enjoy the scenery whereas the more active take part in camping, sailing, pot-holing, hang gliding or even fell running.

National government, local councils and voluntary sector organisations are all involved in the provision of countryside recreational facilities, such as picnic sites, allotments, open spaces, parks and gardens.

? Did you know?

In 1998 two-thirds of the population visited the countryside during the course of the year, and each visitor spent on average £7 per visit.

The Countryside Agency

The government has recognised the importance of the countryside and set up the Countryside Agency, which was a merging of the Countryside Commission and the Rural Development Commission.

Its aims are:

- to ensure and enhance the countryside

- to help everyone, wherever they live, to enjoy this national asset

- to reduce the impact of traffic growth on the rural environment and quality of life while overcoming the rural isolation some people suffer

- to enable people to enjoy the countryside on foot, or horse or cycle.

Details of the Countryside Agency can be obtained on their website: www.countryside.gov.uk.

Areas of Outstanding Natural Beauty

The Countryside Agency is responsible for designating Areas of Outstanding Natural Beauty and advising the government on how they should be protected. (see Figure 1.8).

National Parks

The first ten National Parks in England and Wales were created between 1951 and 1957. Since then only two more have been designated. Figure 1.9 shows the location of each of the Parks. The National Parks were defined as:

'an extensive area of beautiful and relatively wild country in which, for the

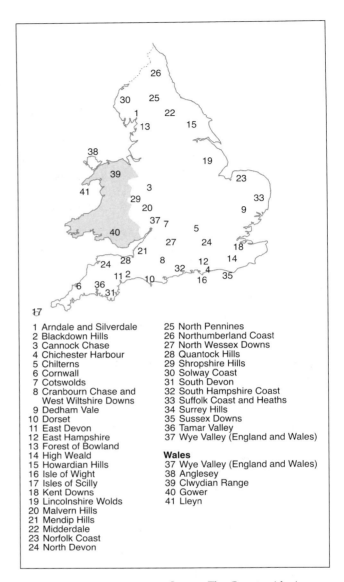

1 Arndale and Silverdale
2 Blackdown Hills
3 Cannock Chase
4 Chichester Harbour
5 Chilterns
6 Cornwall
7 Cotswolds
8 Cranbourn Chase and West Wiltshire Downs
9 Dedham Vale
10 Dorset
11 East Devon
12 East Hampshire
13 Forest of Bowland
14 High Weald
15 Howardian Hills
16 Isle of Wight
17 Isles of Scilly
18 Kent Downs
19 Lincolnshire Wolds
20 Malvern Hills
21 Mendip Hills
22 Midderdale
23 Norfolk Coast
24 North Devon

25 North Pennines
26 Northumberland Coast
27 North Wessex Downs
28 Quantock Hills
29 Shropshire Hills
30 Solway Coast
31 South Devon
32 South Hampshire Coast
33 Suffolk Coast and Heaths
34 Surrey Hills
35 Sussex Downs
36 Tamar Valley
37 Wye Valley (England and Wales)

Wales
37 Wye Valley (England and Wales)
38 Anglesey
39 Clwydian Range
40 Gower
41 Lleyn

Source: The Countryside Agency

Figure 1.8 Areas of Outstanding Natural Beauty in England and Wales

nation's benefit, and by appropriate national decision and action,

a) the characteristic landscape is strictly preserved

b) access and facilities for public open-air enjoyment are amply provided

c) wildlife and buildings and places of architectural and historic interest are suitably protected.'

Source: The Countryside Agency

Figure 1.9 The National Parks in England and Wales

Table 1.5 Visitors to National Parks, 1997

Park	Area (sq. km)	Visitor days (millions)
Peak District	1,404	20.0
Pembrokeshire	583	12.5
Lake District	2,280	12.0
North Yorkshire Moors	438	11.0
Yorkshire Dales	1,761	8.5
Dartmoor	945	7.8
Snowdonia	2,170	7.5
Brecon Beacons	1,350	7.0
Exmoor	685	2.5
Northumberland	1,031	1.0

Source: The Countryside Agency

Services provided in National Parks include:

- information and interpretation services – information centres, leaflets, books

- a ranger or warden service

- facilities for improving access for visitors – footpaths, stiles, waymarking

- provision of car parks and picnic sites

- assistance to voluntary conservation and wildlife groups.

The number of visitors to National Parks is shown in Table 1.5.

Threats to National Parks

The legal protection afforded to our National Parks does not make them sacred. There are changes within the Parks and some of these are threatening to the concept of a National Park. The natural beauty can be adversely affected and the scope provided for open-air recreation restricted.

The main threats are:

- changes in agricultural practice

- military use – live firing and road building

- quarrying and mineral extraction

- urban encroachment – housing developments

- afforestation with non-indigenous species

- new roads.

Heritage Coasts

Around 32 per cent of scenic English coastline is conserved as Heritage Coast. These special coastlines are managed so that their natural beauty is conserved and, where appropriate, the accessibility for visitors is improved.

The first Heritage Coast to be defined was the famous white chalk cliffs of Beachy Head in Sussex. Now much of our coastline, like the sheer cliffs of Flamborough Head with its huge sea bird colony, is protected as part of our coastal heritage.

The National Cycle Network

This is an ambitious scheme, funded by National Lottery contributions, to create 10,000 miles of cycle paths across Britain. It is promoted by a charity called Sustrans, which stands for Sustainable Transport. Sustrans is dedicated to designing and building routes for cyclists and walkers. As well as the National Cycle Network, it also promotes the Safe Routes to Schools Project.

In June 2000 the first 5,000 miles of network were opened. The next 5,000 miles is to be developed by 2005.

Look it up

Sustrans has a website: www.sustrans.org.uk

In small groups, access the website and using a map of Britain, see if you can trace the 5,000 miles now opened. You might even find part of the network is near you, and could organise a cycling event with your group!

National Trails

Many stretches of coast – as well as the wider countryside – are made easily accessible by a network of public footpaths and bridleways, some of the most challenging of which are designated as National Trails.

Long distance footpaths

The Countryside Agency has designated a number of long distance routes, and pays for most of their upkeep and waymarking (see Figure 1.10). Where possible the routes have used existing rights of way and the remaining sections have been established largely through negotiation.

Country parks

Country parks give people the opportunity to enjoy the countryside. They usually have refreshment facilities, toilets, picnic areas and information centres. Most are administered by local councils, and sometimes they receive grants from the Countryside Agency.

Regional parks

The first regional park was the Lee Valley Regional Park to the north-east of London. It was so successful that a number of other regional parks have been established, including the Colne Valley Park on the western side of London.

Voluntary and private sectors

The voluntary sector serves as both a leisure

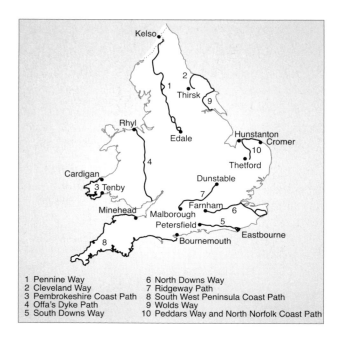

1 Pennine Way	6 North Downs Way
2 Cleveland Way	7 Ridgeway Path
3 Pembrokeshire Coast Path	8 South West Peninsula Coast Path
4 Offa's Dyke Path	9 Wolds Way
5 South Downs Way	10 Peddars Way and North Norfolk Coast Path

Figure 1.10 Long distance footpaths in England and Wales

provider and countryside protector. In Britain, the National Trust, a charity founded in 1895, owns more than 1,047 square miles of countryside and 530 miles of coastline.

Many voluntary organisations were founded during the later part of the nineteenth century as a reaction to the Industrial Revolution, encouraging people in the towns and cities to return to the rural values of the past.

The private sector has become increasingly involved in promoting countryside leisure through the creation of theme parks and the expansion of farm tourism. Tables 1.6 and 1.7 show the number of visitors to gardens and country parks in 1998-99. The private sector tends to promote the countryside as an important part of a healthy lifestyle in marketing campaigns.

The impact of tourism on the countryside

There is a problem maintaining a happy balance between providing public access to the countryside and conserving the countryside environment. Private car ownership has opened up the countryside to town and city dwellers, but as the

Table 1.6 Visits to gardens, 1999

Attraction	Entry	Number of visitors
Hampton Court	Free	1,200,000
Kew Gardens	Pay	864,269
Botanic Gardens, Belfast	Free	630,000
Wisley Gardens, Surrey	Pay	614,487
Royal Botanic Garden	Free	609,488
Botanic Gardens, Glasgow	Free	400,000
Pavilion Gardens, Buxton	Free	352,000
Westonbirt Arborehem, Tetbury	Pay	300,240

Source: *Visits to Tourist Attractions 1998*
published by the English Tourism Council

Table 1.7 Visits to country parks, 1998

Attractions	Estimated number of visitors
Strathclyde Country Park	4,220,000
Bradgate Park, Leicester	1,300,000
Sandwell Valley Park	1,100,000
Clent Hills, Romsley	1,000,000
Clumber Park, Worksop	1,000,000
Crawfordsburn, Belfast	1,000,000

Source: *Visits to Tourist Attractions 1998*
published by the English Tourism Council

number of visitors has risen enormously it becomes increasingly difficult to protect the countryside.

The problems include:

◦ overcrowding – traffic congestion

◦ pollution – litter, noise, air

◦ inappropriate development – buildings out of character with locality

◦ loss of natural habitat – erosion, excessive use.

Camping in the countryside

The attractions of camping include:

◦ freedom

◦ economy

◦ flexibility

◦ the open air experience.

Local bye laws prohibit camping on many commons and areas where the public have access rights. However, in practice the activities of the backpack camper are considered to be within the range of activities which are compatible with the philosophy of a National Park, provided that the back packer is sensitive to the issues.

The camping code

Back packers should:

1 obtain permission (where possible) before setting up camp

2 be as unobtrusive as possible

3 stay in small groups

4 avoid pitch marks left by other tents

5 remove all litter

6 dispose of excrement and waste water sensitively,

and should not:

a camp in enclosed moorland without permission

b stay on one site for more than two nights

c make unnecessary noise

d camp within 100 metres of a road

e camp within sight of a house or road

f camp in a reservoir catchment area

g camp on small common areas

h camp on areas heavily used for informal recreation.

Facts and figures – parks, open spaces and the countryside

- Going for a walk is the most popular recreational activity.

- 14 per cent of urban areas are Open Green Space and 73 per cent of people live in urban areas.

- Approximately £1.5 billion is spent each year on the management of and maintenance of parks and open spaces.

- Total employment supported by visitor attractions to the countryside is estimated to amount to 354,000 jobs

- Spending by all visitors to the countryside was estimated at £11 billion in 1998, 77 per cent from day visits, 22 per cent from UK tourists and 6 per cent from overseas tourists.

Working in the countryside

Countryside Ranger's Assistant

Duties
Work locally or away from home

Constant maintenance and tending of natural resources such as ponds, walks and coastal pathways

Outdoor work which sometimes involves clerical/administration and office duties

Candidates
18+, driving licence, GNVQ Intermediate Leisure and Tourism, good communication skills, initiative, prepared to work unsociable hours

SNAPSHOTS

Serge, rock climber

Hi, I'm Serge and every weekend I go to Matlock, Derbyshire to take part in my favourite activity – rock climbing. I started three years ago at school and I've been a regular climber with the local club since then. I am now able to lead climbs. This is a massive responsibility as not only have I got my own safety to think about, but also my colleagues below me.

The things I like about rock climbing are the challenges of the climb, the sense of achievement (and relief) when reaching the top and the friendship that goes with the sport.

My ambition is to progress to mountaineering, and

Think it over

Are you the adventurous type? What skills and qualities do you think you need to take up abseiling, rock climbing or orienteering?

Look it up

Research some information about Plas y Brenin National Sports Centre and list the activities available there.

Talk about it

People like to visit the countryside to enjoy the scenery, have picnics and take part in activities such as rambling or fell walking.

As a group, discuss what precautions can be taken in order to protect the countryside but which will still encourage people to visit it.

SNAPSHOTS

Home-based leisure

We have seen above how entertainment takes place in cinemas and theatres. However, the majority of our entertainment today is of our own making and takes place in the home.

Home-based leisure activities include those shown in Figure 1.11.

You can even keep fit in your own front room thanks to the introduction of exercise bikes and rowing machines. The trend in keep-fit videos showing famous personalities 'working out' means we can now do aerobics in the comfort and privacy of our homes.

Look it up

Working together as a group, try to find three different keep-fit videos and bring them into your class. Evaluate each video in terms of value for money, motivation and entertainment.

Figure 1.11 There are many home-based leisure activities

'Do it yourself' (DIY) continues to keep people occupied at home. There are many large DIY retail outlets which are busy every weekend. DIY advertising on television recommends that you build your own patio, assemble your own furniture and put up your own bookshelves. In addition there now seems to be television programmes on gardening, cooking and DIY every day.

Try it out

What are the advantages and disadvantages of keeping fit at home?

List five famous people who have become part of the 'keep-fit' craze.

Video rental shops have enabled us to watch our favourite films at home, which works out cheaper than going to the cinema and means that parents with young children do not have to pay for babysitters. Of course, watching videos at home does not offer the same atmosphere as a cinema and can lead to social isolation; although against this is that you can invite friends round for an evening to watch a favourite film.

? Did you know?

The annual expenditure on home-based leisure is £40 billion. The number of UK households with access to the Internet in June 1997 was almost 1 million. As of November 1999 there were 7 million adults registered with access to the Internet.

Television

Figures show that watching TV is the most popular home-based leisure activity, followed by listening to the radio.

Look it up

Look in a TV guide and count the number of hours per week devoted to cookery, DIY and gardening programmes. This will give you an idea of their popularity. Only soaps and sport have more viewing time.

Talk about it

Do you and your friends and family match the profile shown in Table 1.8.

How much television do you watch per week?

Look at Table 1.9. What can you work out from these figures?

Table 1.8 Participation in selected home-based leisure activities

Activity	Hours per week
Watching TV	17.1
Listening to the radio	10.3
Listening to CDs, tapes or records	4.0
Reading books	3.8
Reading newspapers	3.3
Caring for pets	3.1
Gardening	2.1
Cooking for pleasure	1.9
Watching videos	1.7
DIY or house repair	1.6
Sewing and knitting	1.3
Reading specialised magazines	1.0
Reading other magazines	0.7
Exercising at home	0.5
Using games computer console	0.5
Car maintenance	0.5

Table 1.9 Television viewing in the UK: by age

Age groups	Hours and minutes per week		
	1986	1991	1993
4–15	21:06	18:20	19:12
16–34	21:38	22:20	22:42
35–64	27:56	27:38	26:24
65 and over	37:47	37:27	35:47
All persons	26:32	26:04	25:41

Source: BARB

Did you know?

Eighty per cent of households in Britain have a video recorder. In addition to taping programmes, the Cinema Advertising Association's survey showed that in an average month, 45 per cent of the population watch a hired video.

The home has developed as a leisure centre. Over the past 20 years home entertainment has expanded with television, video recorders and computers becoming commonplace. The introduction of cable, satellite and digital television has increased the popularity of television viewing (see Figure 1.12).

Four out of the top five weekly magazines in Britain are connected with television, reflecting television viewing as the most popular home leisure activity. Of these magazines, the most popular is the *Radio Times*. Among all magazines, however, the most popular title is the *Reader's Digest* (see Table 1.10).

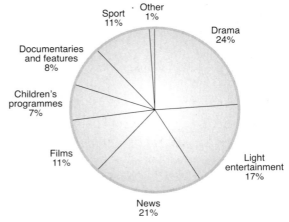

Source: *Social Trends*, National Statistics © Crown copyright 1998

Figure 1.12 Television viewing in the UK: by type of programme

Table 1.10 Magazine readership

	Percentage of adults reading each magazine in 1996			Percentage of each age group reading each magazine in 1996				Readership (millions)		Readers per copy (nos.)
	Males	Females	All Adults	15—24	25—44	45—64	65 and over	1971	1996	1996
General magazines										
Radio Times	18	19	19	20	20	18	17	9.5	8.5	2.9
TV Times	18	19	19	21	19	18	15	9.9	8.4	3.0
Reader's Digest	14	13	13	8	13	17	14	9.2	6.1	3.9
What Car	7	1	4	6	5	3	1	n.a.	1.8	12.2
National Geographic	5	3	4	4	4	4	2	1.1	1.7	n.a.
Exchange & Mart	5	2	3	5	4	3	1	n.a.	1.5	8.2
Women's magazines										
Woman's Own	3	16	10	10	11	9	8	7.2	4.3	4.2
Bella	3	15	10	12	11	8	6	n.a.	4.3	n.a.
Woman's Weekly	2	11	7	4	5	9	10	4.7	3.1	2.6
Woman	2	11	7	6	8	6	5	8.0	3.0	3.2
Best	2	11	6	9	8	5	3	n.a.	2.9	3.1
Prima	2	10	6	7	8	5	2	n.a.	2.6	3.0

n.a. – not available

Look it up

How many soaps are there on television nowadays? Why are they so popular?

What is meant by having 'square eyes'?

Do you think we watch too much television?

Types of activity

People's choice of home-based leisure is affected by factors such as availability of a garden, housing conditions and standard of living. The use of leisure time will vary according to the home itself, family interests and material possessions, such as radio, television, computer or video. It also depends on the number of timesaving appliances, like microwaves, dishwashers and washing machines, which release members of the household from household chores, thus creating more leisure time.

Another often-understated factor regarding leisure at home is the keeping of pets, including the many millions of domestic cats and dogs.

Children's play activities

Young children love to play; in fact, it could be said that play is children's 'work' as well as being their main leisure-time activity. It helps to develop their social and physical skills and is part of the growing up process. Play also gives children the opportunity to use their imagination and to develop their creativity skills. It has been said that without play, there would be no sports, no arts and no games.

Play is an essential part of learning

Play areas

Through play, children experiment and use every opportunity to touch, look, feel and listen, so play areas should offer opportunities for these sensory experiences.

Any provision of play areas by local authorities, the private sector or individuals should take the following into account:

- safety

- supervision

- equipment which would be interesting and challenging to children in terms of size, shape and colour

- equipment which children would enjoy using.

Play areas should be well maintained and within sight of housing developments so they can be overlooked and supervised.

Look it up

Visit two play areas and compare them in terms of safety, location and equipment.

Talk to parents and children there and ask what they think of the play areas, how often they use them and how far they have travelled to use them.

Holiday playschemes are usually run by local authorities and aim to provide worthwhile activities such as sports, day trips, nature walks and camping. Other types of play provision include adventure playgrounds, activity centres, after-school clubs and youth clubs.

Try it out

Design and draw a play area for children, taking the following factors into account:

- location
- type of equipment (including safety)
- fencing
- toilet provision
- main roads
- far enough away from adult playing areas, e.g. cricket pitches
- seating for adults.

You should say what age of children your play area is intended for.

SNAPSHOTS

A day in the life of Shazia, a summer playscheme assistant

Before the children arrive, I talk to the other assistants to plan the day's activities. We then get the equipment out and wait for the children.

This is how the day goes:

9.00 am Take names, addresses and telephone numbers just in case we need to contact their home.

9.10 Our first activity is rounders. I enjoy taking them for sports and organising them into teams.

10.00–10.15 Break time: soft drinks to organise.

10.15–11.30. Nature trail.

11.30–12.00 Pop quiz.

12.00–1.00 Lunch and playtimes.

1.00–3.00 Trip to swimming pool.

3.00–3.30 Say goodbye to the children and clear up.

3.30 pm Exhausted!

Believe me, there's never a dull moment!

Visitor attractions

Some of the facilities we looked at under the heading of Arts and Entertainments overlap with this component. In this section we shall look at facilities which attract tourists to an area and give them something to do during their stay.

There are several definitions of visitor attractions. These include:

⬦ 'All those things that draw visitors to a particular place.'

⬦ 'A designated permanent resource which is controlled and managed for the enjoyment, amusement, entertainment and education of the visiting public.'

⬦ 'A permanently established excursion destination, the primary purpose of which is to allow public access for entertainment, interest or education, rather than being principally a retail outlet or a venue for sporting, theatrical or film performances.'

The English Tourism Council categorises visitor attractions as:

'Historic buildings, museums and galleries, wildlife attractions, gardens, country parks, steam railways, leisure parks and other attractions'.

Visitor attractions give tourists something to do; they are the reason why tourists visit a destination. When people go on holiday or short breaks, first they find their accommodation and then they look for entertainment. Visitor attractions should provide them with fun, interest and entertainment.

Many visitors from overseas are attracted to the UK because of the culture and history, whereas others like to explore the countryside. As a result, both artificial and natural attractions have been developed. Natural attractions include beaches, lakes, mountains, rivers, National Parks, Areas of Outstanding Natural Beauty, forests and hills.

Man-made attractions can include:

⬦ *artistic and cultural heritage* – stately homes and castles, historical, buildings and monuments, cathedrals and churches, arts and music festivals, museums and galleries, battlefields, historic ships

⬦ *sports facilities* – leisure pools, ice rinks, golf courses, leisure centres, ten-pin bowling centres

⬦ *leisure shopping* – hypermarkets, shopping centres, gift and antiques shops

⬦ *entertainment* – pubs, clubs, discos, fairgrounds, cinemas, zoos, theme parks

⬦ *transport and rides* – coaches, steam railways, ballooning.

Look it up

Write down three visitor attractions from each of the six categories mentioned above. What is the group's most popular visitor attraction?

Visitors to English visitor attractions

Figure 1.13 shows the percentage breakdown of visitors to English visitor attractions. This covers 200 million visits, including those made by foreign visitors. It can be seen that Britain's history and culture are vitally important to the tourist industry, as museums, galleries and historic buildings account for about half of the visitors.

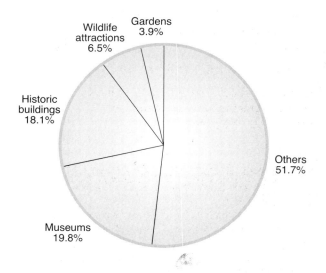

Source: *Sightseeing in the UK,* published by the English Tourism Council

Figure 1.13 Percentage breakdown of visitors to English visitor attractions, 1998

? Did you know?

The British Tourist Authority estimates that there are 400 million visits to attractions in the UK each year.

Look it up

Sixty per cent of all incoming tourists visit London for the shopping and attractions connected with heritage. Carry out some research and list some of the visitor attractions in London which act as a magnet to visitors.

Talk about it

What is the most popular visitor attraction according to the figures in Table 1.11?

Which is the next most visited attraction?

In what order of popularity would your group place these attractions?

SNAPSHOTS

George and Donna come from New York. They visit Britain every three years to visit relatives and see the sights. 'We just love looking at your castles and stately homes. We haven't got anything like that back home, and we sure do like these Beefeaters at The Tower of London. They are so cute. We're moving on to Stratford to see Shakespeare's house and hopefully take in a play.

'We usually spend a few days in Oxford to look round all the university buildings and then it's on to Scotland to sample the delights of Edinburgh and the Highlands.

'We can't get used to driving on the wrong side of the road and your cars are so small. Next year we hope to do Europe for three months, spending six weeks in Great Britain. We just can't keep away.'

Compare George and Donna's thoughts to those of Bill Bryson, author of Notes from a Small Island.

'I wandered through the city examining hotels from the street, but they all seemed a bit grand for me and I eventually ended up at the central tourist office, feeling lost and far from home. I looked through the racks full of leaflets advertising shire-horse centres, zoos, falconry centres, miniature pony centres, model railways, butterfly farms, and something called Twiggy Winkle's Farm and Hedgehog Hospital.

'Nearly all of them padded out their lists of featured attractions with things like 'Free Car Park', 'Gift Shop' and 'Tea-room' and the inevitable 'Adventure Playground'.

'Who goes to these places? I couldn't say, I'm sure.'

Table 1.11 Top UK attractions – free and paid admissions, 1999

Free admission		Paid admission	
Attraction	**Number of visitors**	**Attraction**	**Number of visitors**
1 Blackpool Pleasure Beach	7,200,000	1 Alton Towers	2,650,000
2 British Museum	5,460,537	2 Madam Tussauds	2,640,000
3 National Gallery	4,964,879	3 Tower of London	2,422,181
4 Palace Pier, Brighton	3,750,000	4 Natural History Museum	1,739,591
5 Seaworld, The Trocadero, London	3,454,690	5 Legoland, Windsor	1,620,000

Source: *Visits To Tourist Attractions 1999*, published by the English Tourism Council

CASE STUDY – Meadowhall Leisure Shopping

Location

- Meadowhall is situated 3 miles (4.8 km) north east of Sheffield in the county of South Yorkshire (population 1.3 million), at the eastern end of the Lower Don Valley.
- The Lower Don Valley is an area approximately 2,000 acres stretching 3 miles (4.6 km) between Sheffield city centre to the west, and the M1 motorway.
- Around 7.2 million people – or 1 in 8 of the UK population – live within an hour's drivetime of the site.
- Major towns and cities within this drivetime include Leeds, Nottingham, Manchester, Hull, Leicester, Barnsley, Doncaster, Wakefield and Rotherham.
- The Centre occupies a level site extending 78.3 acres (31.6 hectares) immediately to the west of the M1 motorway. The site is bordered by an orbital ring road.
- The River Don flows in a clockwise direction around the northern site boundary and the riverside setting has been comprehensively landscaped to incorporate trees, walkways, cycling paths, seating and play areas.

Statistics

Since Meadowhall opened in 1990, the statistics have been impressive:

- Over 80% of the multiple retailers at Meadowhall are in the 'Top Ten' of their company outlets, including 24% which are the best performing outlet in the country.
- 54% of customers travel under 10 miles or fifteen minutes drivetime to Meadowhall, with 77% travelling under 20 miles, or 30 minutes drivetime.
- An average of 150,000 cars use Meadowhall each week.
- 20% of customers use public transport.
- The 'average party' consists of 2.4 shoppers during peak periods.
- The length of the average shopping trip is 2.4 hours 7 minutes.

Infrastructure

- *Motorway*: The M1 motorway immediately adjoins the site, providing access from both northbound and southbound carriageways at Junction 34.

(Photo courtesy of Meadowhall Centre)

Meadowhall Centre, Sheffield

- *Roads*: A sophisticated computer-controlled traffic management system employing extensive CCTV coverage enhances road capacity and optimises traffic flow.
- *Car parking*: 12,600 free car-parking spaces are provided; 350 of these parking spaces are specifically allocated for the disabled and people with children.
- *Supertram*: The Passenger Transport Interchange serves as a terminus for Sheffield's Supertram, completed at an overall cost of £270 million. A total of 88 trams run per day, every 10 minutes at peak times, linking Meadowhall with major city suburbs and the city centre.
- *Coaches*: The Meadowhall coach park provides parking for up to 200 coaches and is linked directly to the Meadowhall Centre by a footbridge.
- *Trains*: Two stations accommodate regional railway trains, serving 240 routes nationwide every day. Intercity trains are also routed through the station.

Source: Meadowhall Key Fact Pack

Activity

Meadhowhall is said to offer an exceptional combination of all the attributes most commonly required of the local shopping environment. Working in groups, make a list of what you think these are.

Talk about it

What do you think are the advantages and disadvantages of out-of-town shopping complexes like Meadowhall?

Look it up

Look again at the visitor attractions we have studied. As a group, write to some of them for information and make a display, putting them into their appropriate categories, for example artistic and cultural heritage, transport and rides, etc.

Try it out

Have a go at making a leaflet which describes or 'sells' your area as a tourist attraction. Include pictures and other illustrations to make it lively and interesting.

Visits to top tourist attractions by category, 1999

Historic houses/monuments
1 Tower of London	2,422,181
2 Windsor Castle	1,280,000

Cathedrals
1 York Minster	1,800,000
2 Canterbury Cathedral	1,350,000

Gardens
1 Hampton Court	1,200,000
2 Kew Gardens	864,269

Museums and galleries
1 British Museum	5,460,537
2 National Gallery	4,964,879

Wildlife attractions
1 London Zoo	1,067,917
2 Chester Zoo	965,721

Steam railways
1 North York Moors	277,870
2 Severn Valley	227,922

Leisure parks and piers
1 Blackpool Pleasure Beach	7,200,000
2 Palace Pier, Brighton	3,750,000

Vistitor centres
1 Cadbury World	496,446
2 Lulworth Cove Heritage Centre	452,766

Source: *Visits to Tourist Attractions 1999*, published by the English Tourism Council

Catering

Catering is connected with eating out, now classed as one of the most popular leisure activities in the UK. As a result, the catering industry has grown to meet this demand.

Catering is so much a part of modern life that it is estimated that up to a quarter of all food is now consumed away from home or taken into the home in a form in which it is ready to eat.

Fast-food outlets, bars and cafés, restaurants and pubs offer customers a wide choice of eating from quick snacks to à la carte meals. You can have your meal brought to you by a waiter or waitress or help yourself to a choice of dishes in a buffet. Takeaway services, in particular for Chinese and Indian meals, have become increasingly popular. You can even have your meal delivered to your front door.

Probably the biggest growth in catering is in pub food. Many pubs now provide cooked meals, sandwiches and snacks. As families want to eat out together pubs have introduced family rooms, play areas and children's menus to further attract this target market. Another reason for the popularity of pub food is it is sometimes cheaper than restaurant food and yet can still be of a high quality.

Families are also attracted to fast-food outlets such as McDonald's, Wimpy, KFC and Burger King. Relatively inexpensive food like pizzas, burgers and chips in particular have a great appeal to children. Shopping centres like Meadowhall in Sheffield and The Trafford Centre, Manchester, have enormous eating areas where you can choose just about any food you like from any part of the world.

Talk about it

Fast food is quick and convenient but is it good for us?

What about the impact of fast-food outlets on the economy and the environment? Does one cancel out the other?

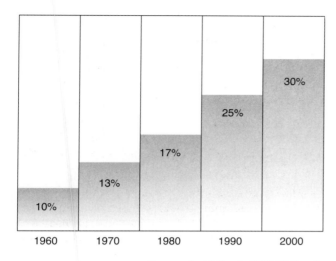

Source: *Social Trends 1998*, National
Statistics © Crown Copyright 1998

Figure 1.14 Eating out as a percentage of food expenditure in the UK, 1960–2000

As Figure 1.14 shows, eating out has become a popular leisure activity as well as a necessity.

Food facts

Here is an example of how much food was consumed at Alton Towers in 1999:

- 260 tonnes of chips – equivalent of eating the American Statue of Liberty
- 4 million litres of fizzy drinks – enough liquid to have a bath a day for 101 years
- 85,000 pizzas – stacked up that's 3.5 times the height of the Empire State Building in New York
- 147,000 packets of crisps – enough crunch for nearly 2 years at 8 hours munching a day
- 89,000 Snickers and Mars Bars – a day's calories for nearly 21,000 people
- 594,000 cups of teas and 598,692 cups of coffee – an average kettle would have to be boiled 298,173 times.
- 1 million doughnuts – the weight of four dinosaurs
- 300,000 hot dogs – if laid end-to-end would easily stretch across the Channel and back
- 9,000 kilos of popcorn – a 93-year supply for one popcorn addict
- 9,298 lb of peanuts – that would produce enough calories to last one person 34 years
- 774,701 sticks of rock – which if joined together end-to-end would be 733 times higher than the Eiffel Tower in Paris.

CASE STUDY – Elizabeth

Elizabeth is in the sixth form. She has just started work as a waitress in a small market town hotel. She works every Saturday 7.00 am to 2.30 pm and 7.00 am to 10.00 pm.

This is how her day goes.

'Breakfast is served between 7.30 am and 8.30 am. My first job is to make sure all the tables are set up and that everything is ready for the guests. Full English is very popular around here and I can only dream of bacon sandwiches, as there's no time for me to grab a snack. After the rush of breakfast it's time to prepare for the senior citizens' coffee morning which starts at 10.00 am, although they usually start to arrive anytime from 9.30 am onwards. I enjoy the friendly banter with them but I have great difficulty getting rid of them (in the politest possible way of course). It's all very well to tell me about their vegetable patches and grandchildren, but I've got tables to set for lunch.

'My shift finishes at 2.30 pm and restarts at 7.00 am. This is known as a split shift. Time flies by. As soon as one job is done, another needs doing. At the end of the day I am absolutely shattered. My feet are killing me and my mind is set on only one thing – a long, hot bath.

Questions

'I like the work really as it pays for my social life and I work with some great characters.'

- What are the disadvantages of shift work?

- Are there any advantages?

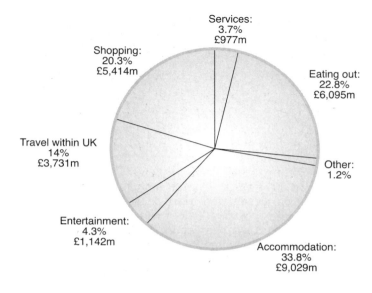

Services:
3.7%
£977m

Shopping:
20.3%
£5,414m

Eating out:
22.8%
£6,095m

Travel within UK
14%
£3,731m

Other:
1.2%

Entertainment:
4.3%
£1,142m

Accommodation:
33.8%
£9,029m

Source: British Tourist Authority

Figure 1.15 Breakdown of tourism spending, 1998

You can see from Figure 1.15 that only accommodation exceeds eating out when it comes to tourism spending.

Leisure facilities providing catering include the following:

- cinemas – confectionery in foyer
- leisure centres – vending machines and café
- theatres – bars and restaurant for interval drinks and meal after performance
- theme parks – fast-food outlets, restaurants, cafés, bars.

Where do people in your group like to eat out? Make a list and then classify the venues into four groups: pub food, fast food, ethnic and other restaurants. Which is the most popular?

Employment in catering

There are many job opportunities in catering and it is still a major growth area (see Table 1.11).

Table 1.11 Main areas of employment growth, 1990s

| 327,000 more jobs in pubs and bars |
| 295,000 more jobs in restaurants |
| 281,000 more jobs in hotels |
| 138,000 more jobs in clubs |
| 115,700 more jobs in contract catering |
| 40,000 more jobs in air transport |
| 20,000 more jobs in theatre and television |

What type of meal would you expect to be served in:

- a transport café
- McDonald's
- a high class restaurant?

Why is there a need for different catering facilities?

Talk about it

Nearly everyone has had a bad experience of eating out; either the service has been terrible or the food has been equally bad. Share your worst experience of eating out with the rest of the group. What could have been done to improve the situation?

The interrelationship between the different components of the leisure industry

We have looked at the different components of the leisure industry separately but they are often interrelated. For example, mountaineering can be classed as both a sport and a countryside activity. In the same way, going to the theatre and then having a meal is a mixture of arts and entertainment and catering. A theme park may have a children's playground which means there is a mixture of visitor attractions and children's play activities.

So, although the leisure industry is made up of different components, it is not very often that they are treated in isolation; they are all more or

CASE STUDY — Laura

Laura is 24 and leads a very full and active life. She loves going to aerobics classes at the sports centre with her friends because they have a good laugh and end up having a drink together afterwards.

Laura's weekends are hectic. She will often drive up to the Lake District on Saturdays to escape from the mad rush of the city, spend a few hours hiking and will have a pub meal. She will then drive home, put her feet up, watch a bit of television and fall asleep on the sofa.

Laura spends Sundays with her two cousins aged 6 and 8. She takes them to the play area, treats them to a happy meal at McDonald's and then takes them to the cinema to watch the latest children's film.

She looks forward to getting back to work on a Monday morning for a rest!

Question

Can you identify the different components of the leisure industry and their interrelationship from this case study?

---

less interrelated. Looking at them separately is the best way to show what exactly goes to make up the whole of the leisure industry.

Products and services

Products are things that we can see or touch – they are real, such as a newspaper, a meal in a restaurant or a pair of training shoes. We buy them, own them and use them.

Services are intangible products. They often support the sale of a product, such as waiter or waitress service in a restaurant, coaching swimming lessons at the leisure centre or serving behind a bar. We have them, use them but do not take ownership of them.

Facilities in the leisure and tourism industry offer their customers products and services. For example, a cinema may show the film as the product, and provide telephone booking, a choice of films and a range of confectionary and soft drinks as the service.

The main products and services offered by the leisure industry include those shown in Figure 1.16.

- *Sports participation* People take part in a wide variety of sports ranging from fishing to football, basketball to badminton, cricket to croquet. In order to play these sports people must buy the products that go with them, for example a cricket bat.

Figure 1.16 Products and services offered by the leisure industry

Sports and leisure centres sell different goods and services, such as a month's membership for the gym or a six-week lifesaving course, in addition to selling goods and equipment from their own shop.

- *Catering* The products provided by all catering services are food and drink. You can either order a takeaway product, such as a pizza, or sit in the restaurant to eat the meal.
- *Outdoor activities* Products and services offered in National Parks and Areas of Outstanding National Beauty include guided

walks, orienteering instruction, information at the visitor centre, cycle hire and basic catering.

◦ *Play schemes*   The main aim of play schemes is to keep children happy and occupied with worthwhile activities when their parents are at work. Activities like sports, painting and games can all be classed as products. The main service is looking after the children.

◦ *Sports spectating*   The product in this case is what you are going to watch – either live or on television, for example tennis at Wimbledon or football at the local park.

The services you find at these events include catering, action replays on the big screen, music at half-time and cheer-leading before, during and after the event.

◦ *Accommodation*   The products on offer here include a 'murder mystery' weekend in a hotel, a 'swinging 60s night' at a holiday camp or an activity weekend at a university during the summer break.

◦ A hotel's services might include room service; a guest house might provide newspapers; and a self-catering apartment might be cleaned and tidied every two days.

◦ *Arts and entertainment*   Museums put on exhibitions and displays, cinemas show films; theatres put on plays; galleries put on exhibitions. The services they provide include catering, information and entertainment – anything to ensure that people enjoy themselves during their visit.

◦ *Heritage sites*   An example of a heritage site is a castle and it is the main thing visitors want to see – therefore it is a product. Some of the services included in a heritage site might include guided walks, information from staff and gift and souvenir shops as well as a café or a tearoom.

Try it out

Imagine an ice rink is about to open in your town. What products and services could it offer?

A two-storey derelict building is about to be converted into a massive fast-food restaurant. What products and services could it provide to cater for families?

Try it out

Can you identify the products and services offered by:
• a restaurant
• a theme park
• a hotel?

The travel and tourism industry

Talk about it

In no more than 15 words describe what you believe the meaning of travel to be.

Then in no more than ten words describe what you think tourism is.

The development of the industry

The word 'travel' comes from the French word *travail*, which means work. The word 'tourism' also comes from a French word *autour*, which means around. In the nineteenth century before the building of good roads and railways, travel really was hard work. For example, a trip from London to Edinburgh by coach today would take around 12 hours. The coach of 200 years ago would have been a horse-drawn carriage over bumpy, rutted tracks, not motorways. The journey time would have been 12 days not 12 hours.

Few people attempted to travel long distances. In some countries, people were not allowed to travel away from their home area. Two hundred years ago travelling was so difficult and uncomfortable that it is hardly surprising that few people travelled for pleasure. There was no real tourist industry because tourism needs the following:

◦ *Leisure time*   Two hundred years ago the only holidays or 'holy days' for many people were at Christmas and Easter. There were no paid holidays and most people could not take time off work.

◦ *Fast and comfortable travel*   Two hundred years ago there were no cars, railways, aircraft, steamships or even bicycles. Poor roads made travelling uncomfortable and dangerous. There were no computers, credit cards, telephones or travel agents so making arrangements for travel was time-consuming and complicated.

- *Money* Transport was expensive and most people could not afford the cost of travelling (or to stop work for the time it would take).

The first tourists were wealthy people of the seventeenth century who visited spa towns like Bath, Harrogate and Baden Baden in Germany because they believed that drinking and bathing in water containing special minerals was good for their health. In the late eighteenth century sea water was recommended as a health cure and royalty and the wealthy travelled to Scarborough and Brighton to bathe in the sea.

Thomas Cook

The travel and tourism industry did not really take off until after the arrival of the railways. In 1841 Thomas Cook organised an excursion by rail to a temperance meeting from Leicester to Loughborough (look up the meaning of temperance). The was such a success that Cook arranged several similar trips over the next three years.

In 1851 Cook was asked to organise the travel arrangements of workers from Yorkshire and the Midlands to the Great Exhibition which took place in Hyde Park, London. About 150,000 people were transported by Cook. He soon became a household name.

Cook began to stage more complicated excursions involving train, boat and accommodation in hotels for his customers. This took a lot of worry out of the travel for his passengers and his fame quickly spread.

Foreign travel was still beyond the means of many people until in 1855 Thomas Cook led a long-distance tourist excursion through Europe for a group of very wealthy tourists. This was to become known as Cook's 'Grand Tour'. This trip was similar to today's package tours. Cook offered people transport, accommodation, meals and sightseeing tours at a single, all-inclusive price.

By 1872 Thos Cook And Son, as Cook's company had recently become known, was an agent for the sale of domestic and overseas travel tickets. It was the first travel agency, and it is still one of Britain's largest travel agents. As more and more people began to want to travel abroad, more travel agencies were set up to cater for them.

Cook's name was so good with hoteliers that he was able to develop two important travel systems – the 'hotel coupon' which travellers could use to pay for hotel accommodation and meals instead of using money, and the 'circular note', a forerunner of the traveller's cheque, which enabled tourists to obtain local currency in exchange for a paper note issued by Thomas Cook.

Mass tourism

In the early twentieth century ordinary working people were given paid holidays. This meant that they could afford to go away for a day or two, or perhaps even a week, often to popular seaside resorts like Blackpool and Southend. This was really the beginning of tourism for all or 'mass tourism'. Foreign travel was still too expensive for working class people at this time.

The period between the two World Wars saw an increase in both domestic and European holidays. Domestic holidays flourished, with the traditional resort towns of Brighton, Scarborough and Blackpool seeing new competition from places like Llandudno, Skegness, Clacton and Colwyn Bay.

During World War II (1939–45) thousands of British servicemen and women travelled abroad as members of the Allied Forces and many acquired a taste for foreign travel which they continued after the war.

The 1950s and 1960s saw an increase in prosperity for many. People enjoyed a higher standard of living than ever before and had longer, paid holidays. Advances in technology meant that travel became faster and more comfortable. The holiday industry boomed. Travel companies competed with each other to offer cheap package deals to Mediterranean resorts.

In 1950, 25 million foreign holidays were taken worldwide and by 1990 the number had increased to 330 million.

Package holidays became increasingly popular in the 1950s and 1960s

In the mid-1970s young people wanted holidays which included parties, fun, sea and friendship. This led to the introduction of Club Med and 18–30 holidays.

The travel and tourism industry is now one of the world's biggest industries and there is no reason to suggest that tourism will decline as an international activity in the future.

Talk about it

Have you ever been a tourist?

What do you like about going away? What attracts you to a tourist destination?

Look it up

Find out all you can about Billy Butlin and the holiday camps he set up.

The ever-increasing economic importance of tourism has now gained the attention of most

countries of the world. Tourism was given little political relevance as recently as ten years ago. Now most countries, developed and developing, have some sort of tourism policy. Many countries devote considerable amounts of money to tourism promotion. In the words of the World Tourism Organisation:

> 'Tourism is one of the most important economic, social, cultural and political phenomena of the twenty-first century'.

Figure 1.17 highlights the economic value of tourism.

? Did you know?

In 1997 total tourism spending in the UK was estimated to be £53 billion, comprising £22 billion spent on domestic tourism day visits, £15 billion spent on domestic holidays of one night or more, and £13 billion spent by overseas visitors while in the UK.

Tourism defined

Perhaps the most widely accepted definition of tourism is:

> 'the temporary, short term movement of people to destinations outside the places where they normally live and work and the activities they take part in during their stay at these destinations' (*Tourism Society 1976*).

- *Incoming tourism* Those visitors who come from overseas to visit this country and spend their holidays here. The USA still generates the greatest number of overseas tourists to the UK.

- *Domestic tourism* Those visitors from this country who spend their holidays or go on day trips within this country.

- *Outgoing tourism* Those people who spend their holidays (and their money) overseas. This means that economies in America, Spain, France and Italy all benefit from UK outgoing tourism.

An essential part of tourism is the traveller's intention to return home afterwards. The purpose of a visit could be:

- a holiday – two weeks in Majorca soaking up the sun

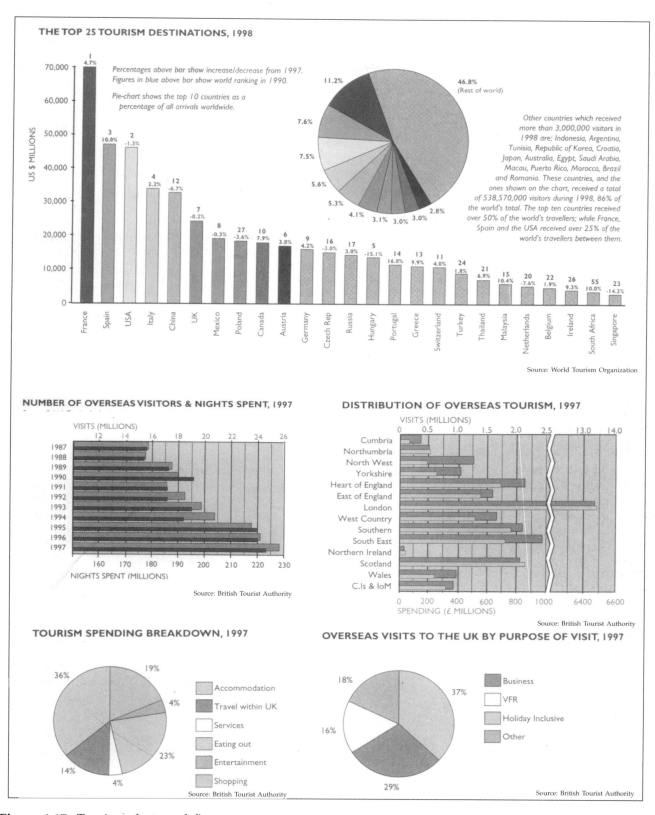

Figure 1.17 Tourism: facts and figures

- one week in Skegness enjoying the delights of the seaside

- three weeks' trekking in the Himalayas.

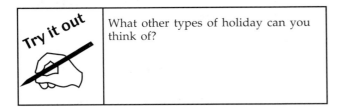

Try it out | What other types of holiday can you think of?

Sightseeing – literally seeing the sights of a location and taking in the atmosphere, for example a weekend break to London or a day trip to the Lake District.

Visiting an attraction – there are thousands of places a tourist might visit at any given time. In Britain these range from seaside funfairs to art galleries and museums, historic country houses to theme parks and shopping malls. Just about the only thing they have in common is that people want to visit them.

Visiting friends or relatives – in terms of tourism this type of visit is usually associated with travelling away from home. This type of tourism accounted for around 25 per cent of all holidays taken by UK residents in Britain in 1998. This type of tourist usually enjoys free accommodation thanks to the hospitality of friends or relatives. The money saved on accommodation will be spent on eating out, visiting leisure facilities and travelling around the area.

Going to a sports event – imagine going to the Olympic Games, one of the world's biggest sporting events. As a tourist you would stay in a hotel, use restaurants, buy souvenirs and go sightseeing, as well as watching the Games themselves.

Other major events, like the Tour de France and Wimbledon, all attract tourists who not only spend their money at the event site but also in the surrounding area. This boosts the local economy by bringing in money and creating jobs.

There are two main types of tourism: leisure tourism and business tourism (see Figures 1.18 and 1.19).

Leisure tourism

Figure 1.18 Reasons for leisure tourism

Leisure tourism includes:

- *Holidays*
  - two weeks in Gran Canaria
  - a week-end break in Cambridge
  - a four-week cruise in the Caribbean

- *Visiting friends and relatives*
  - a family reunion in Blackpool, 140 miles away
  - staying at a penfriend's house in France
  - an American father visiting his son at Cambridge University

- *Health and fitness*
  - a cycling tour of Holland
  - a walking holiday in Ireland
  - a three-day break at a health farm

- *Sport*
  - the British team's visit to the Olympic Games in Sydney
  - going to Trent Bridge in Nottingham to watch England play the West Indies in a one-day cricket international
  - a day out at Holme Pierrepont National Water Sports Centre

- *Education*
  - an Open University summer school at Leicester University
  - a weekend diving course in Portsmouth

– a Spanish student on a four-week crash course in English in London

* *Culture and religion*
  – a Muslim's pilgrimage to Mecca
  – a weekend in Lincolnshire studying historic churches
  – a Catholic visiting Rome to take part in Mass given by the Pope
  – going to Lourdes.

 **Try it out**

Write down your own examples for each of the categories of leisure tourism given above.

Business tourism

Business tourism includes:

* *Business meetings*
  – a British sportswear manufacturer flies to India to meet suppliers and negotiate prices
  – a local politician travels by train from London to Leeds and back again the same day to meet constituents
  – a marketing director flies to Saudi Arabia to meet potential clients and set up new products

* *Exhibitions and trade fairs*
  – a tourist development officer from Lincoln visits the UK travel trade fair in Manchester
  – an architect travels to attend the Ideal Homes Exhibition at the NEC, Birmingham

Figure 1.19 Reasons for business tourism

* *Conferences and conventions*
  – the Conservative Party holds its annual conference in Brighton
  – the Institute of Leisure and Amenity Management's annual conference, Leisure 2000, in Bournemouth

* *Incentive travel*
  – a two-week Mediterranean cruise for life assurance salespeople for exceeding their sales targets
  – a one-week family holiday in Florida for a manager who has just clinched an important deal.

Tourists

Tourists are people who are:

* away from home

* on visits which are short term and temporary

* travelling for leisure or for business.

Facts and figures – tourism

* Tourism provides 1.7 million jobs (7 per cent of the UK workforce).

* Tourism creates one in five of all new jobs.

* Over 200,000 businesses, mainly small independent ones, hotels and guest houses, restaurants, holiday homes, caravans and camping parks are responsible for the bulk of tourism services.

* It is estimated that every £30,000 spent by visitors supports one full-time job.

* Britain welcomed 26.2 million overseas visitors in 1997.

* The domestic market accounts for 65 per cent of tourist trips.

* 83 per cent of short breaks are taken in England, 7 per cent in Scotland, 8 per cent in Wales and 1 per cent in Northern Ireland.

Look it up

In pairs, contact the English Tourism Council and the British Tourist Authority and gather the following information:

How much money does tourism generate each year from incoming and domestic tourism?

You can telephone or e-mail to contact each organisation.

Facts and figures – activities on holiday

A recent survey showed that around three-quarters of British people enjoyed sightseeing while on holiday, around half had enjoyed sunbathing, while a third enjoyed reading. Only an eighth stated that they had enjoyed the more energetic and adventurous activities such as skiing, parascending and water skiing.

Talk about it

List the top five activities you enjoy while on holiday. What about others in your group?

Developing tourism

The way tourism works can be seen in Figure 1.20.

As transport systems improve and leisure time increases it follows that the tourism industry is set for a bright future. There is also an increase in the number of retired people, many of whom have both the time and money to spend on travel and tourism, as well as a growing trend for young people to travel overseas.

Talk about it

What are features in your area which could be called 'tourist attractions'?

How would you promote tourism in your area?

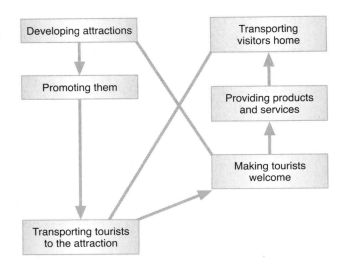

Figure 1.20 How tourism works

SNAPSHOTS

Students invade Ibiza

George, Ben and Ziad had just completed their 'A' levels; now they were ready for the fun. The plane landed at 2 pm so it was down to the beach to seek out the sun. The lads had worked hard for their exams and had managed to save up for this holiday through their part-time jobs in McDonald's and the local cake factory.

For two glorious weeks they were going to enjoy themselves, and enjoy themselves they did. Social activities and nightlife started at 11.30 pm and finished at 6.30 am, just in time for breakfast.

The clubs held upwards of 3,000 young people, all out to have a good time. Day time was spent sun bathing, sleeping and playing cards. Food consisted of beans on toast, pizza and sandwiches.

After two weeks of constant fun, romance and enjoyment, the lads arrived back in England – needing another holiday to recover from the last one!

Look in the travel section of one of the weekend newspapers and find a tourist destination which would appeal to you. Explain your reasons for choosing it.

Travel

We have seen that tourism is a vast industry that ranges in its scope from visiting friends or relatives to going to a sports event. The key fact to the development of tourism is travel. Without it, theme parks and tourist destinations in London would find the business connected with tourism extremely difficult to run. Therefore, when looking at the structure of the tourist industry, travel is regarded as the main feature.

Travel is concerned with how people get to their chosen destination and how they travel around the area they are visiting. This section will look at the seven main methods of travel (see Figure 1.21).

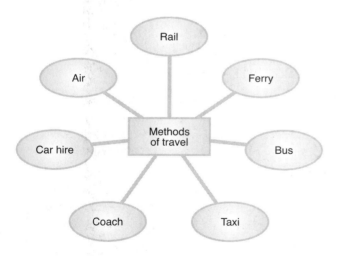

Figure 1.21 How people get to their chosen destination

Transport

Transport is a capital-intensive industry. Airlines, railways and shipping companies need to invest large amounts of money in buildings, planes,

Modern methods of travel emphasise comfort and speed

trains or ships and equipment in order to provide modern, efficient services to their customers. Governments also need to provide money to build roads and motorways for car owners and coach operators. Tourism has developed as an industry as a result of the improvements made in transport technology.

Without transport there would be no travel or tourism. The importance of transport can be summed up in three ways:

- a means of travel to a destination, i.e. from a tourist's place of origin
- a means of getting around a destination, for example the use of a taxi to visit the Tower of London
- a major feature of the tourist trip such as a journey on the Orient Express or on a cruise liner.

We will now look at each of the different methods of travel in turn.

Air travel

By far the largest number of overseas trips, both outward and inward to the UK, are by air. International passenger statistics suggest that around 85 per cent of all holidaymakers prefer to fly to their overseas destinations.

Air travel has the advantage of being able to take a direct route and coming up against no natural barriers. The only things which prevent aeroplanes taking the shortest route between two points are adverse weather conditions, air traffic congestion and countries which restrict flights across their air space for political reasons.

There are three broad headings under which air transportation can be categorised:

* *Scheduled air services* – scheduled flights which regularly operate specific domestic or international routes according to published timetables or schedules which are fixed in advance.

* *Charter flights* – services organised to meet travel needs at specific times, which are not fixed to a specific timetable and so can be altered or cancelled if passenger numbers fall off. Most charter flights are usually organised by tour operators for the purpose of transporting holidaymakers, and for this reason the majority of the flights are organised in the summer to holiday destinations such as the Mediterranean. If a tour operator cannot sell enough seats on a particular flight it can seek to combine those passengers on another flight to the same destination. This is known as consolidation.

* *Air taxi services* – these are generally offered by small private charter companies, who carry upwards of 18 passengers to specific destinations. Being small, these aircraft can often utilise the runways of small as well as large airports. As such, they are of particular interest to business executives in that, for example, they allow the passengers to fly out to a meeting in a specific location and fly back the same day.

Travelling by air has the great advantage of speed but also has some disadvantages:

* limited departure/arrival point

* transfer time needed into city/destination

* luggage restricted.

Working in the air travel industry

When considering job opportunities in air travel, most people immediately think of the air steward or stewardess or cabin crew, as they are known. The vast majority of people see these staff as airbound waiters, which is not the case. Air stewards need to be able to handle any kind of emergency and initiate the appropriate safety procedures straight away. First aid skills, social skills and initiative are all qualities required by cabin staff.

Other aspects of air travel will include jobs such as:

* airline manager

* airline sales representative

* airport manager.

SNAPSHOTS

Melanie, flight attendant
I'm Melanie Eason. I have been a cabin crew member for three years.

Let me first of all say that it is not the glamorous job that everyone seems to think it is.

Long before I meet the passengers I have to check that everything is ready. Are there enough meals? Is the emergency equipment intact? Are there enough stocks of drinks and duty-free goods?

When the passengers board I have to show them to their seats, demonstrate the emergency procedures and make sure they are all settled in and ready for take off. Once we are up in the air I have to work really hard: serving food and drinks, dealing with passenger enquiries, selling perfume.

I gained my Intermediate GNVQ Leisure and Tourism at college and worked for a few years in a travel agency. I managed to get through the six-week airline training course and started off on domestic flights: Birmingham to Edinburgh, East Midlands to Belfast.

I was then promoted to work on long-haul flights and I can safely say I've fulfilled my ambition of seeing the world – in fact I've done it four or five times over!

The work is very hard, harder than you could imagine. However, I've seen some wonderful places and I work with some brilliant people.

Rail travel

Trains play an important part in moving people between and within countries. Trains are particularly used for domestic tourism – leisure and business. They are a quick and convenient way of travelling between cities and in Britain, for example, 17 per cent of all business travel involves trains. The majority of people who travel first class on trains are people who are travelling around the country for business purposes.

Most trains offer passengers a choice of facilities and services: sleeping accommodation, restaurant cars, snacks and meals, bar, and telephones. Most train services offer different classes of travel, varying according to the price paid for the ticket.

A major growth area in train travel has been the re-emergence of private steam railways. In Britain there are now some 45 such lines in operation. Locomotives, both full size and narrow gauge, have been lovingly restored by volunteers and attract visitors to take nostalgic rail journeys in locations like Ffestiniog in Wales, the Severn Valley and Minehead in Somerset.

The *advantages* of rail travel include:

- speed, particularly over long distances
- normally 'walk on' so no need to book (although at some peak times you have to)
- choice of joining points
- catering on many trains (although this is not cheap)
- least impact on the environment.

The *disadvantages* include:

- restriction to rail-routes, so some cross country journeys take a long time
- restriction to timetable service – you cannot go wherever and whenever you want
- luggage limited to what you can carry
- cost – despite special offers, still more expensive than road journeys
- standing room only on busy trains, sometimes for long journeys.

The construction of the **Channel Tunnel** has meant that Britain is no longer an island as the Tunnel now links us to mainland Europe. This simple geographical fact has important outcomes for the travel industry:

- It takes 40 per cent of cross-Channel passengers.
- 5,000 people have been employed to staff the tunnel
- Thousands of other jobs have been created in engineering, transport and, not least, tourism.

Look it up

Try to find out some statistics about the Channel Tunnel, for example length, journey time, how long it took to build, etc. Secondly, try to find out some information about Eurostar and the Shuttle.

Working in rail travel

Jobs in rail travel include:

- buffet car waiter
- dining car chef
- guard
- ticket inspector/conductor
- Pullman class stewards/stewardesses
- train driver.

Ferry travel

Britain is linked by regular ferry services to all mainland European countries with North Sea coasts and to Ireland. These ferry services are usually used by passengers in combination with some form of local transport, for example coach, train or car, which carries them to the ferry ports from their places of origin, and on to their final destination after the sea crossing. Despite the opening of the Channel Tunnel, ferries remain a popular means of holiday travel to continental Europe.

The success of ferry companies depends on being able to get cars and passengers on and off ferries rapidly. This again reinforces the need for good transport links, in this case between the port and the road system leading out of it. Demand varies according to the season, peaking in the holiday months of July and August. Day trips to France, often involving shopping in French hypermarkets, have been a recent growth area, boosting low season demand.

However, all ferries, including services operated by hovercraft and hydrofoils, can be seriously affected by adverse weather conditions. Delays and cancellations are always a risk in winter. Ferry services form a vital link with Ireland, and with smaller islands like the Isle of Wight, the Isle of Man, the Hebrides and the Shetlands.

Look it up

Make a list of as many different ferry companies you can find. Collect some information about hovercrafts.

Why might some people prefer to cross the Channel by ferry rather than going through the Channel Tunnel?

The *advantages* of ferry travel are that:

- sometimes ferries are the only transport form available (e.g. Isle of Wight)
- you can put a car on board vehicle ferries.

The *disadvantages* of ferries are that:

- the timetable can be restricting
- some services are passenger ferries and cannot take vehicles.

Bus/coaches

Bus and coach operators offer a wide choice of tourist services by way of:

- private hire service
- express trunk routes for domestic and international travel
- tours and excursions
- transfers, for example from airports to tourist destinations.

Although not much used by business travellers, this form of travel is popular with the young and the elderly since it offers one of the cheapest means of travel as well as one of the most convenient (i.e. local pick-up and direct delivery right to the resort). New express coaches seek to

attract other users by way of providing a much wider range of services, including such extras as on-board toilets, reclinable seats, telephone, video, as well as snack bar refreshments, and even stewards.

Local bus services, too, are often used by visitors in large towns and cities. London Transport has estimated that over 20 per cent of all passengers on its famous red London buses are tourists.

The *advantages* of travelling by bus or coach include the following:

- you get straight into a town/city
- there is a choice of 'joining' points
- the overall cost is relatively low
- you can only travel if you have a seat, so there is no standing
- many services have catering and on-board toilets.

The *disadvantages* are that:

- you are restricted to service routes
- you are restricted to timetable service
- luggage is limited to what you can carry
- you have to book to guarantee a seat
- the service is slower than rail/air.

Taxi/car hire

Taxis provide an important service to leisure and business tourists. Many of the customers of taxi companies in cities are visitors who use taxis as a fast and convenient way of moving around unfamiliar streets.

In the UK alone, car rental generates £600 million a year. Within the UK the majority of car hire rentals are for business people or for overseas tourists. Travel agents regard car hire as an important add-on to a sale. For example, when they book a rail, air or coach inclusive holiday for a customer they can also offer to make a car rental booking for them. The customer may not have considered hiring a car at his or her destination.

Some of the major car rental companies are Avis, Budget, Dollar, Rent a Car and Hertz.

Travel by car

The increase in private ownership of the motor car was a factor in the decline of the railway system in many countries. Today, the car is the most popular means of transport by far for tourists. In the USA, journeys by car account for 85 per cent of all holiday travel.

The car offers people greater freedom than most other forms of transport in terms of where they go, the route they follow and where they stop on the way.

Alongside the growth in car ownership has been a growth in the purchase of camping gear and caravans. Services like roadside catering, car hire and motels have also flourished.

The *advantages* of travelling by car include the following:

- highly flexible, you decide where and when you travel
- you can carry large amounts of luggage easily (useful for families)
- door-to-door service (useful for people who cannot walk far)
- cost per mile is low
- you can hire a car if you do not own one.

The *disadvantages* of car travel include:

- high initial cost in buying, maintaining, licensing and insuring, even though the cost per mile is low
- parking can sometimes be a problem
- traffic congestion can cause delays
- the negative environmental impact of so many cars.

The key components of the travel and tourism industry

The travel and tourism industry industry is so vast that we shall divide it into seven key components (as we did for the leisure industry). These can be seen in Figure 1.22.

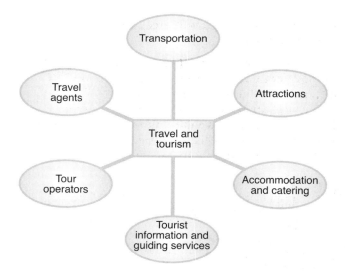

Figure 1.22 The seven key components of the travel and tourism industry

Travel agents

Every high street nowadays will include a large number of travel agents and obviously they are all in competition with each other.

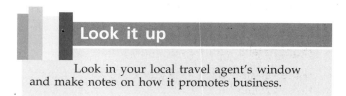

Look it up

Look in your local travel agent's window and make notes on how it promotes business.

The main aims of travel agents are:

- to sell holidays and associated products like insurance, car hire and currency exchange
- to provide information
- to advise clients.

Travel agents provide the following services:

- plan travel itineraries
- work out costings
- issue tickets
- keep accounts
- book airport car parking spaces.

Much of the information provided by travel agents to clients is delivered through the medium of brochures. Specific data on travel and accommodation arrangements are checked through computer reservations systems. Travel consultants who have been on educational visits to some destinations can also draw on personal experience. Some travel agents will also lend videos which feature popular resorts to their clients.

Travel agents sell their products and services in much the same way as high street shops in that they advertise what they sell and supply customers with what they want. However, there is one big difference which is that travel agents do not charge their customers for their service. They are paid commission by the companies whose products they sell. In other words, they act as agents for the industry's suppliers or 'principals' as they are known. These consist of tour operators, airlines, rail companies, hotels, ferry companies and car hire companies.

Retail travel agents tend to sell a wide range of popular summer sun and winter holidays; for example, two weeks in Gran Canaria or a week's skiing in Andorra.

They also deal with long haul flights, i.e. those that go beyond Europe to places like Australia, America and the Far East.

There is another type of travel agent. The **business travel agent** specialises in arranging transport and accommodation for business people who want to see existing suppliers, attend conferences, see new suppliers and develop new business. The business travel agent arranges flights, transfers and accommodation in much the same way as retail travel agents do for holidaymakers.

Some big companies like Boots of Nottingham, whose business travel requirements are high, have a travel agent on site. This is known as an 'in plant' travel agency.

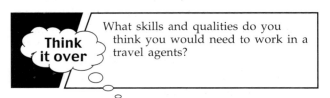

Think it over

What skills and qualities do you think you would need to work in a travel agents?

The retail travel industry in the UK is dominated by 'national multiples' who have agencies throughout the country, for example Lunn Poly

and Thomas Cook. There are also many **independent travel agents** who do not form part of a national chain. They usually consist of one retail unit although they can still be classed as independents if they have up to six branches.

Independent travel agents are not usually found on the high street but are tucked away in an office above another retail outlet. They tend to provide a local service in the suburbs or villages. Independents are vulnerable to take-overs by national multiples.

Another type of travel agent is the regional multiple which enjoys close connections with business and leisure travellers in their region. They sometimes start out as one shop in a family business and develop over time.

Look it up

Try to find one business and one independent travel agent in your area.

Currency exchange

As mentioned earlier, one of the services provided by travel agents is currency exchange. This is provided because at some stage where overseas travel is involved, sterling will have to be exchanged for another currency. The main means of exchanging currency include:

- changing sterling for foreign currency or traveller's cheques

- traveller's cheques, which business travel agents, in particular, tend to deal in, while some of the larger ones, such as Thomas Cook and American Express, issue their own cheques

- Eurocheques, which allow the holder to pay for items or draw cash in European currencies.

Despite some fears within the travel industry about travel agents going out of business because holidays can now be booked on the Internet as well as over the phone, travel agents are still very much in evidence on the high street. Many people still like to book their holiday through travel agents because of the personal service they offer. What's more any questions about the holiday can be made face to face and if necessary complaints about the holiday afterwards can be dealt with personally.

Tour operators

A tour operator puts together holiday packages which consist of:

- travel – road, sea, air, rail
- accommodation – hotels, guesthouses, self-catering
- travel services – transfers, car hire, excursions.

Tour operators organise package holidays to a range of different domestic and international destinations. Most tour operators are *wholesalers* in that they produce a package holiday and then negotiate the product with the travel agent (the 'retailer') who then sells on the product to their clients.

There are two types of tour operator:

- **wholesale operators,** who put together and operate tours only through retail travel agents
- **direct sell** operators, who do not make their products available through travel agents but sell the package direct to the public.

Some tour operators specialise in domestic tourism, that is organising tours within the UK for UK residents. Incoming tour operators on the other hand specialise in tours for overseas visitors in the UK. In both cases, money is spent in Britain which therefore helps the economy.

Examples of well-known tour operators include Thomas Cook and American Express, both of whom operate worldwide.

A tour operator needs to take the following into account when doing the budget for a holiday package:

- marketing of brochures
- employment and training of staff, e.g. holiday reps
- market research – which principals and clients to sell to
- reservations – maintaining booking systems.

Of course, there are some people who like to arrange all their own travel and accommodation so it is not part of any package. These people are known as independent travellers and they like the freedom and control of organising their own itineraries.

Talk about it

What do you think are the advantages of travelling independently?

Tourist information and guiding services

Information for tourists is provided by national and regional tourist boards and local tourist information centres (TICs). Their job is to market and monitor the quality and development of the particular tourist area they serve.

There are four national tourist boards, one for each of the individual countries that make up the United Kingdom. They are responsible for ensuring that visitors to England, Wales, Scotland and Northern Ireland get the facilities, services, information and welcome they expect.

To help the national tourist boards in promoting each country, there are a number of regional and area tourist boards which concentrate their efforts on smaller, specific regions or areas within each individual country.

Local TICs inform visitors about accommodation, car hire, visitor attractions, restaurants and transport. They also provide maps of the town and region they serve. Tourist information centres are mainly funded by local councils, which sometimes own and manage tourist attractions themselves – for example theatres and museums. Councils usually have their own tourist sections in their leisure services departments.

On a wider scale, tourist information is provided by the English, Welsh and Scottish tourist boards, whose main job is to encourage tourists to visit their respective countries and to improve tourist facilities. They are funded by central government. The British Tourist Authority aims to encourage overseas visitors to Britain.

Guiding services

You yourself may have been on a guided tour, perhaps of a castle or stately home, the aim of

67

which is to make the tour as informative and interesting as possible. Some of the best guided tours can be made on open top buses around cities like London, York and Bath. The tour guide gives a running commentary which usually includes interesting stories about people and places on the route.

Some tour guides are volunteers who have a special interest in the history of a place. Others are retired people who possess a wealth of knowledge about an area and who have time on their hands to spread their knowledge and enthusiasm to tourists.

Talk about it

What skills and qualities would you need to be a tour guide?

Look it up

Using your research skills, gather information about The Blue Badge Guide scheme.

Accommodation and catering

The hotel and catering industry today is essentially concerned with providing accommodation, food and drink for those who are away from home. The accommodation can be in hotels, motels, guesthouses, inns, farmhouses, holiday cottages and chalets, caravan parks and camp sites.

This component of the industry employs 20 per cent of the UK tourism workforce and brings in money to both the national and local economy. Overseas visitors spend about one-third of their 'holiday' money on accommodation and catering.

Facilities in this component of the travel and tourism industry include:

- hotels, motels and guesthouses
- caravans and camping sites
- bed and breakfast
- holiday centres
- timeshares
- youth hostels
- restaurants, cafés, fast-food outlets, bistros, motorway service areas.

Accommodation

Accommodation can be divided into two basic categories:

1 **serviced accommodation**, where meals are provided, for example hotels, guesthouses

2 **self-catering**, such as cottages, chalets and some hotels.

Tourists decide for themselves the type of accommodation they want. When it comes to eating arrangements, they can choose the following options:

1 **full board**, known as the '**American Plan**' – three meals provided

2 **half board**, known as the '**modified American plan**' – breakfast plus midday or evening meal

3 **bed and breakfast,** known as the '**Continental plan**'.

Location affects the type of accommodation available. For example, in a city there are likely to be a wide range of hotels including five-star hotels. These may be part of an international chain, such as Holiday Inn. In a small town or rural area there are more likely to be guesthouses and farmhouses offering bed and breakfast. In a seaside resort you are likely to see rows upon rows of guesthouses along the promenade, usually offering family accommodation.

Hotels can be placed under several headings according to their location:

- city centre hotels
- beach hotels
- resort hotels
- country house hotels.

Each serves a different type of client.

Grading schemes
These help tourists distinguish different types of accommodation. The English Tourism Council, the AA and the RAC run a joint scheme in England.

Accommodation is awarded stars, from one to five, which symbolise overall quality, level of service, food standard and the range of facilities available. These schemes classify accommodation into groups according to their facilities and quality. Accommodation facilities operating these schemes are checked to see if they meet the required standards.

Catering

Tourists 'eating out' want a wide choice of catering outlets to choose from. A family of four may want to go to McDonald's. a young couple may want a romantic candlelit dinner in a bistro, whereas a group of lads may want a few pints in the local pub, followed by a curry.

The standard of catering in hotels can sometimes make or break a holiday. This can be a reason why some people like to play safe and choose self-catering.

Talk about it

Who do you think might stay in the following types of accommodation:
- a country house hotel
- a Blackpool guesthouse
- a city centre hotel?

Attractions

We looked at visitor attractions on page 47 and saw how these can be divided into two types:

- natural attractions, such as the Lake District, the National Parks, the Giant's Causeway and so on

- man-made attractions, such as Alton Towers, The Albert Dock, Liverpool, Disneyland Paris, the Leaning Tower of Pisa, Hadrian's Wall or Stonehenge.

The reason why many people make trips is to see attractions. For example, tourists go to Blackpool to see the Tower, to stroll along the 'prom', to go on the Pleasure Beach and to see the 'lights' (the illuminations) which are promoted as 'the greatest free show on earth'.

Theatres, museums, country parks and historic buildings are all classed as attractions. They all provide some type of entertainment for visitors. It stands to reason that the more attractions an area has, the more tourists will visit that area. This will benefit the local economy.

A big sporting event could also be classed as an attraction. The London Marathon attracts 25,000 runners and thousands of spectators, many of whom want overnight accommodation. Other sporting events which attract thousands of visitors include the Olympic Games, the Tour de France and the FA Cup Final.

A National Code of Practice ensures that visitor attractions have agreed to provide a high standard of customer service, cleanliness, courtesy and maintenance. They must also deal promptly with enquiries and provide proper access for people with disabilities.

Look it up

Find and draw symbols for the following attractions. You may find a map useful.

Abbey or cathedral	Historic house
Aquarium	Information centre
Camp site	Nature reserve
Caravan site	Picnic site
Castle	Wildlife park
Country park	Zoo
Golf course	

Transportation

Rapid and efficient transport systems by road, rail, air and sea have given tourists the chance to travel far and wide and gain a greater knowledge of the world. Choice of transport depends on:

- price

- destination

- time – how much is available

- reason – visiting family or friends, business or leisure

- departure points – how easy it is to get there.

The increase in travel, particularly by car, has raised a number of issues about congestion and pollution, especially in cities, on motorway routes and the countryside. The busiest weekend of the year in England is the one when schools break up for summer. Traffic jams form on the M55 into Blackpool, the A17 to Skegness and the M5 into Cornwall. People often set off at 3.00 am to try to avoid the chaos.

The government has invested heavily in road and motorway systems to try to ease traffic congestion and is now constantly urging people to use public transport and not their own cars.

New developments such as the Channel Tunnel have made travel easier and faster. Heathrow is one of the busiest airports in the world and long-haul flights are now available from Manchester and Birmingham. In order to satisfy the demands of their customers and stay one step ahead of the competition, airlines, shipping and railway companies have to keep investing in buildings, staff and equipment.

Look it up

Trace a map of Britain and mark on it the main air and sea ports.

The travel and tourism industry: a summary

Tourism involves travelling away from home. It has developed because it is now easy to travel to our chosen destinations. Such destinations usually have facilities which both the local population and tourists can use.

Tourism is promoted by central and local government to encourage domestic and incoming tourism.

The travel and tourism industry, as seen through the components we have studied, is growing all the time. This means there are lots of job opportunities for people like you who are studying to gain relevant qualifications.

Links between leisure and tourism

Although we have looked at the leisure industry and the travel and tourism industry separately, they are linked in many ways. Each depends on the other for its customers. For example:

- a visit to a theme park is both a leisure activity which involves travel (getting to the park) and tourism (a day out)
- a trip to London to watch the FA Cup Final involves leisure (sports spectating) and tourism (travelling away from home)
- visiting friends and relatives (tourism) and going to the cinema with them (leisure)
- going to Spain for a two-week holiday (travel and tourism) and windsurfing (leisure) while you are there.

The public, private and voluntary sectors

The leisure and tourism industry is made up of the following three sectors:

1 The **private sector**: this is made up of commercial organisations whose aim is to make a profit for their owners and shareholders.

2 The **public sector**: organisations funded by central and local government whose main aim is to provide a service but at the same time generate enough income to survive.

3 The **voluntary sector**: non-profit making organisations run and managed by volunteers.

The private sector

Activities and facilities connected with the private sector include:

- eating and drinking – e.g. restaurants, pubs, clubs, wine bars
- home-based leisure – e.g. DIY
- travel and tourism – e.g. holidays, accommodation

- sport and recreation – e.g. aerobics, squash, ice skating
- entertainment – e.g. cinemas, theatres, clubs
- visits – e.g. to theme parks, attractions, zoos

The income generated from these activities is from paying customers.

Commercial organisations are owned by individuals or companies whose main aim is to make a profit. Businesses in the private sector can be sole traders (one person), for example fitness consultants, owners of guesthouses, sports coaches, couriers, or at the other end of the scale there are huge companies like Adidas, American Express, McDonald's, Thomas Cook.

All private sector organisations have to make sure that the income they generate exceeds running costs such as wages and stock, otherwise they go out of business.

The public sector

Public sector organisations are funded by central and local government and include:

- parks and open spaces
- leisure centres
- playing fields
- swimming pools
- public halls
- tourist information centres, libraries, museums.

Public sector organisations aim to provide a community service, not necessarily making a profit. However, they must still be seen to be giving value for money.

Commercial competitive tendering (CCT) now operates in public sector facilities such as sports centres. This means that private companies can bid to operate public sector services such as the catering, cleaning and even the management of a sports centre. As a result, public sector organisations have had to adopt a more commercial outlook to protect their status.

Central government does not get directly involved with leisure provision. It has departments like Sport England, The Arts Council and the British Tourist Authority to award grants.

The voluntary sector

Non-profit making organisations are run by volunteers and include:

- youth clubs
- Scouts and Guides
- amateur dramatic societies
- St John Ambulance
- the Youth Hostel Association.

People with similar interests often form clubs or societies where they can meet and share ideas. Committees are sometimes then elected and a more formal structure is developed. A voluntary organisation usually has a chairperson, secretary and treasurer. These people are elected by the club members to co-ordinate the smooth running of their organisation.

Voluntary organisations vary greatly in size and aims. One group of keen runners may form a local running club. In contrast, voluntary organisations such as the Youth Hostel Association and the YMCA employ paid staff and have budgets of millions of pounds. Examples of voluntary clubs in your area will probably include local football clubs, model railway societies and bridge clubs.

Try it out

Write down which sector these organisations belong to:

- a fast-food outlet
- a hotel
- a local council swimming pool
- a tourist information centre
- the Countryside Agency
- the Boys' Brigade
- a youth club
- the National Trust.

Talk about it

What differences might there be between a local council sports centre and a privately operated gym?

The public, private and voluntary sectors: a summary

The leisure, travel and tourism industries provide a service to the public irrespective of which sector they belong.

The public sector aims to give value for money and offer a service to the community. The private sector aims to make a profit and build up the business. The voluntary sector is run by volunteers and is non-profit making.

Leisure services in towns and rural areas is usually provided by the public and voluntary sectors, whereas in cities the contribution to leisure activities is greater from the private sector.

Links between the public, private and voluntary sectors

All three sectors sometimes work together on projects.

Dual use

Many sports and leisure centres are deliberately built on school sites. The idea behind this is that the school uses the centre in the day and the public use it after 4 pm and at week-ends. This is an example of a local education authority working with the local council to provide a facility which can be used by the whole community, some of whom would be from the voluntary sector. This shows co-operation between the two sectors.

A form of co-operation within the same sector is known as *joint provision* which can be defined as,

'The joining together of two or more groups to design and construct a facility for mutual benefit'.

The concept has proved in the past and continues to prove very popular with some local authorities. It often involves a local authority working closely with another local authority or private organisation in providing certain facilities; for example, two neighbouring local authorities may each wish to build a leisure centre in their local area, but cannot afford to build and run the centre. However, by choosing to build one, possibly larger, leisure centre located so as to be able to serve both communities, both authorities may be able to benefit from sharing the costs.

Grants

Public, private and voluntary organisations can apply to central government for grants to support new developments, for example a new sports pavilion for a football team. The government is now able to offer grants to sports organisations through lottery funding.

Sponsorship

The public and voluntary sectors sometimes receive sponsorship in the form of financial support from private sector organisations. In return, the organisation usually seeks publicity. Sponsorship can also give the organisation a good image, especially if it is seen to be offering some benefits for the local community.

Unit I Assessment

Tracksuits and sunglasses Scenario

Congratulations on your new job. You have just been appointed assistant to the Leisure and Tourism Development Officer for your area. This is a newly created position so you have to prove to people, especially your boss, that you are up to the challenge.

Your boss is well known for throwing new staff 'in at the deep end'. He's just told you that a group of American councillors is visiting your area next week to set up a town twinning link. This is what you have to do.

Obtaining a pass grade

Task 1

Prepare a presentation for your American guests to include:

- a brief description of your area in terms of population, features, recent developments
- your own definition of leisure and tourism, relating it to your area
- a clear description of the leisure and tourism industries in your area
- an accurate description of at least three links between leisure and tourism in your area.

Task 2

Produce an information pack showing two examples of organisations in your area which make up the following components of the leisure and tourism industries:

- sports and physical recreation
- arts and entertainment/countryside recreation

- home-based leisure
- children's play activities
- visitor attractions
- travel agents and tour operators
- accommodation and catering
- transportation
- tourist information and guiding services.

In your information pack give brief details of the sectors to which your organisations belong and then describe the facilities and activities which go on in these organisations. Photographs would certainly add something extra to your pack.

Task 3

Finally, for a presentation again:

- describe at least two of the major leisure and tourism facilities in your town. In your description outline the products and services available to local people and visitors in these facilities.

Obtaining a merit or distinction grade

To obtain a merit or distinction grade your work must show an ability to seek, use and interpret a wide range of relevant information in your investigation, including a variety of examples for the components of Leisure and Tourism.

You must give an accurate description of at least three links between the leisure and tourism industries in your area, at least one of which should explain in detail a link between the different sectors.

Finally, you must give a comparison and contrast of the products and services offered by the two major facilities.

UNIT I ASSESSMENT

73

Obtaining a distinction grade

To achieve a distinction, you should provide a detailed explanation of how leisure and tourism facilities in your area could work together to improve the products and services they provide. You must identify any gaps in provision and explain how these could be addressed by the facilities.

To achieve a merit or distinction you need to improve the quality of your work, not necessarily produce more work.

Key skills available

Communication: C2.1a, C2.1b, C2.2
IT: IT2.1, IT2.2, IT2.3

Useful tips

Your work can be presented in a number of ways, for example as a presentation, an information pack or a video. You could produce a report or even a guide book.

Try to investigate your own area if possible so you can draw on your own experience and therefore have fairly easy access to organisations. There may be areas that do not feature all the components of the leisure and tourism industries. If this is the case, it may be possible to study an area where you have been on a day trip or a residential course.

Resources

1   Leisure and tourism organisations, especially tourist attractions, produce information packs about their facilities. This resource would help you with your presentations and the contents for your information packs.

2   Tourist boards or local tourist information centres provide much useful information.

3   Activities within the text will give you an opportunity to go out and investigate facilities.

4   The Internet has many websites on locations and specific facilities. It also has information on local events, accommodation and leisure and tourism facilities in an area. The FEDA GNVQ Support Programme has a free materials list for Leisure and Tourism GNVQs (e-mail: publications@feda.ac.uk or phone 01207 840 5302/4).

Unit I Test

1   Into which component of the leisure industry would you put Stonehenge?

2   Crystal Palace offers participation in which component of the leisure industry?

3   You and your family are going to France for a week. What sort of tourism do we call this?

4   What is the main aim of an organisation in the private sector?

5   Which sector of the travel and tourism industry would run a tourist information centre?

6   What type of activities does a summer playscheme provide?

7   Why would an outdoor activities centre be best located in the countryside?

8   What is the best location for a theme park?

9   Give four sources of information which would help you find a job in the leisure and tourism industry.

10 What sort of sports activities would you do in Snowdonia?

11 Why might people in a village object to the development of a tourist attraction nearby?

12 Which job do you think would be most suitable for you after you have successfully completed your course?

13 What skills and qualities would a hotel receptionist require?

14 What products and services do travel agents provide, apart from selling holidays?

15 How can leisure facilities be designed to cater for everyone, including people with disabilities?

Marketing in leisure and tourism

Marketing is about people. It involves finding out about people's wants and needs and developing effective ways of meeting them in order to make a profit.

The leisure and tourism industry is highly competitive, and customers are becoming more discerning and demanding, which means that organisations which fail to market their products and services effectively will fail.

This unit will help you to understand the importance of marketing. It introduces three aspects of marketing that are used in leisure and tourism organisations:

- *marketing research*
- *target marketing*
- *the marketing mix.*

The next section looks at the different promotional materials used in marketing and the final section examines promotional campaigns.

This unit builds on the introductory work you completed in Unit 1: Investigating leisure and tourism and links well with Unit 3: Investigating customer service.

What you need to produce

You will be expected to show your understanding of the marketing activities of a leisure and tourism organisation. This includes describing the products or services it offers; the products and the services which are available.

In addition you need to describe promotional techniques and the market segments the organisation has chosen to target. Finally, you have to produce some promotional material for the organisation.

This unit will be assessed only though an external assessment. The grade you achieve in this assessment will be your grade for the unit.

Introduction
What is marketing?

If you asked people in the street the question, 'what is marketing?' you might get an assortment of replies. Many of them would be inaccurate!

Marketing is about finding out what customers need and want and developing effective ways of meeting them.

Marketing puts the consumer or customer at the centre of the organisation's decision-making. It is all about attracting customers and keeping them. After all, if there are no customers, there will be no organisation. So – marketing is concerned with getting the right product to the right customer at the right price, in the right place at the right time. That is the theory.

Try it out

Product: A two-week summer holiday in Playa del Ingles, Gran Canaria.

- Who would be the right customer?
- What would be the right price?
- Where would it be promoted?
- When would be the right time?

Compare your answers with those on page 78.

Marketing is just as important in the public and voluntary sectors as it is in the private sector because they all have customers. Since customers are at the centre of all marketing activities, it is vital that everyone in an organisation should know that marketing is everyone's responsibility.

One of the main aims of marketing is to generate income and make a profit. These aims are related to the customer, the product and the way the product is sold. Leisure and tourism organisations market themselves in the same way, as can be seen in Figure 2.1.

One of the main aims of marketing is to attract customers and keep them. Customers spend money on products and services like food and drink, theatre tickets, swimming lessons. Finding out what customers want, charging them the right price and promoting the product (such as swimming lessons) creates an awareness which means that people will be attracted to a facility,

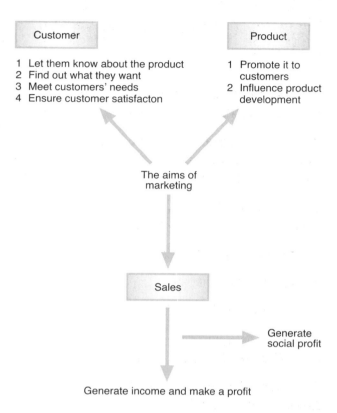

Customer

1. Let them know about the product
2. Find out what they want
3. Meet customers' needs
4. Ensure customer satisfacton

Product

1. Promote it to customers
2. Influence product development

The aims of marketing

Sales

Generate social profit

Generate income and make a profit

Figure 2.1 Generating income and making a profit

and will spend their money. Hopefully, they will return and tell their friends about it.

CASE STUDY – Paul

Paul opened his gym three years ago. After working as a deputy manager of a local authority leisure centre for five years he had decided to 'take the plunge' and start his own business.

At first Paul had a 12-station multi-gym and five sets of 'free weights'. As membership increased, he was able to invest in two treadmills, five rowing machines and five exercise bikes. Next year he plans to add a health suite incorporating a sauna, steamroom and sunbeds.

The profit Paul makes looks like this:

PROFIT = Income generated from subscriptions and fees MINUS overheads such as rent, wages, fuel bills and equipment.

Question

Paul receives £32,550 from annual subscriptions, £51,795 from fees and £28,275 from catering. He has to pay £5,650 rent per year for the premises, £30,000 on staff wages, £8,765 on heating and electricity and £15,000 on equipment. How much profit does he make per year?

One of the main aims of marketing is to attract customers and keep them. Customers spend money on products and services like theatre tickets or swimming lessons. Finding out what customers want, charging them the right price and promoting the product creates an awareness which means that people will be attracted to a facility, and will spend their money. Hopefully, they will return and tell their friends about it.

Making a profit

When organisations have met the expense of all the running costs, any money left over is classed as profit. This profit enables the future investment and survival of the organisation. Effective marketing leads to customers spending their money and thus creating profit. Marketing campaigns are therefore aimed at attracting customers and which is why many organisations have a marketing budget or a marketing department to ensure this happens.

Generating social profit

Not all organisations aim to make financial profit from their operation. This is particularly true in

CASE STUDY – Jenny

I manage a Community Centre, a non-profit making facility operated by the local council. The centre is right in the middle of a housing estate  which means we can provide activities for local people.

Our users include senior citizens, parents and toddlers and people who want to get out of the house and mix with others. I go into the community and talk to people and ask them what they want out of the Centre. To me, this is what marketing is all about. I then try to provide what they want.

The best form of advertising round here is word of mouth because it is a fairly tight knit community. I also put posters up at the Health Centre, the library, the local playgroups and dentists' surgeries.

Although we struggle to break even financially every year, we make up for it in terms of social profit – by providing the type of activities the Community wants.

Questions

- What skills and qualities would Jenny need in her job as manager of the Community Centre?

- What role does a Community Centre play within the local community?

the public and voluntary sectors where the main aim may be to provide a community service. However, these organisations still market their products and services, as shown in the case study on page 78.

Informing customers

Organisations need to let people know exactly what they are offering in terms of location, activities, prices and facilities. This information could be included in brochures, leaflets and newspaper advertisements. In addition to this, probably one of the most understated ways of spreading information to customers is through staff explaining the work of the facility and using their knowledge and expertise to answer customer enquiries.

Customer satisfaction

Satisfied customers tell their friends and return for more. How do organisations satisfy customers? Marketing helps to keep customers happy by:

- finding out what they like
- giving them what they want
- asking them for their ideas
- being interested in them.

Meeting customers' needs

Meeting the needs of customers is another way of keeping customers happy, for example:

- providing facilities for disabled people, i.e. ramps, wider car parking spaces
- senior citizens on a coach trip want an interesting and knowledgeable courier and plenty of toilet stops!
- young children want interesting, colourful and challenging play equipment in play parks, while their carers want seating, toilets and a location which is safe for their children.

Marketing research, which we shall look at in the next section, helps determine what people need and want.

Promoting products

Promotion of products plays a substantial part in marketing. We are overwhelmed nowadays with posters, brochures, newspaper advertisements and television 'ads' for everything from special holiday offers to 'what's on' at the local theatre.

This type of promotion aims to attract customers to facilities and encourage them to spend their money on the products and services on offer.

Products and services in the leisure and tourism industry need to be marketed effectively if organisations are to survive. The types of products and services which are marketed, include:

- holidays *marketed by* travel agents
- sports activities *marketed by* sports centres
- concerts and shows *marketed by* theatres
- films *marketed by* cinemas
- meals and menus *marketed by* restaurants
- day trips to the coast *marketed by* coach operators.

Influencing product development

Market research shows what customers want. The result of market research should be analysed and changes should be made to the product/service if it is found that existing products do not match their customers' needs and wants.

If organisations do not keep up with present trends and do not change, it is likely that they will go out of business. The leisure and tourism industry is constantly changing and new products have to be developed to meet this change. Table 2.1 shows some of these changes over the past 40 years.

New products and services have to be marketed so that customers can choose what they want.

Influencing customer choice

This can be done by marketing campaigns which show activities that will benefit customers, for example 'Keep fit and healthy lifestyle classes help you lose weight, get you fit and make you feel good'. With promises like that, you would be only too happy to join.

Table 2.1 Some changes in the leisure and tourism industry

1960s	2000+
Foreign holidays for the minority of people	Overseas package holidays popular with the mass market
One-car family	Two- or even three-car families
Cricket and football (traditional sports)	Hang gliding, jet ski-ing, windsurfing and parachuting
Home entertainment: black and white TV, radio	Computers, videos, CDs, DIY, exercise at home
Day trips to the countryside or walk to see a friend	Trips to theme parks, multi-screen cinemas, indoor shopping and leisure pools
Eating out a rare treat	Fast-food outlets, pubs with family rooms, family restaurants with play areas.

Marketing research

Marketing research gathers together the likes and dislikes of consumers so that an organisation can act on the information and (hopefully) improve the product. Marketing research is a method that helps organisations find out their customers' needs.

Anyone involved in making decisions will appreciate the value of accurate and up-to-date information such as that collected by Renate in the case study below. The better the information, the more likely organisations are to achieve their aims.

Marketing research enables organisations to answer the following questions:

- Who will be our typical customers?
- What will they want?
- Why will they buy from us and not our competitors?
- How much will we sell as a result of our marketing research?

Other information gained by marketing research includes answers to such questions as:

- How can we improve the existing product?
- How much are customers prepared to pay?
- How often will they buy it?
- What sort of image will sell the product?
- What new products shall we develop?

CASE STUDY – Renate

You may have seen someone like Renate in your town centre. She is the one with the clipboard, usually seen asking people questions and then writing down their responses. Renate is carrying out marketing research. She is employed by an agency on a part-time basis. Her main task is to find out what washing powder people use.

The questions might go something like this:

What powder or liquid do you use? Have you always used it? Why do you use it? How often do you see it advertised? Is it good value for money? Do you use other wash powders?

Questions

- Why is Renate asking all these questions?
- What would the organisation do with Renate's research?

Marketing research involves forecasting. Good forecasting can reduce the risk of making bad decisions, so we can see that marketing research helps with product or service development.

Doing marketing research successfully

There are many sources of information for marketing research but you have to work out which are the most useful. Imagine that you run a health and fitness centre. Figure 2.2 shows some of the groups of people who might be useful sources in your research.

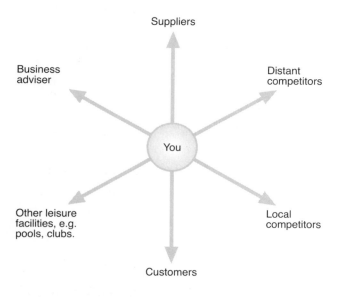

Figure 2.2 Sources of marketing research

Look it up

Imagine you are the manager of a health club. Visit a similar facility in the area and ask about joining. This will give you information about membership, fees, equipment and training programmes. Ask as much as you like because if they think they have a potential customer, it is guaranteed that they will do 'the big sell'.

Remember that so-called 'mystery shopping' is an accepted practice. It goes on all the time. The aim is to gain information and ideas and then use them.

The marketing research process

The process of marketing research is outlined in Figure 2.3.

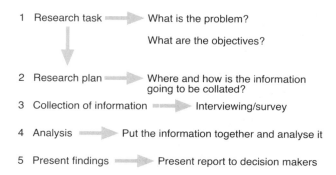

Figure 2.3 The process of marketing research

Marketing research methods

Marketing research is about collecting information. There are four widely used methods for collecting primary marketing research data:

- postal surveys
- telephone questionnaires
- personal surveys
- observation.

Postal surveys

Postal surveys are a very common method of research used in leisure and tourism. It involves the posting back of a completed questionnaire so it is important to include a stamped addressed envelope. It is unlikely that people will reply if they have to pay for the response themselves.

Postal surveys can reach a lot of people in a very short time. There is no interviewer training required and it is usually cheaper than doing face-to-face interviews. Respondents also have time to consider their answers, which can be an advantage or a disadvantage – depending on the question.

CASE STUDY – Penny

Penny is the manager of a local authority swimming pool. Attendances have fallen over the past three months, mainly due – it is thought – to the opening of a privately owned leisure pool. Penny has been asked by the council's leisure services committee to reverse this trend.

Penny went to visit the new leisure pool, as a paying customer, to find out what attractions it held and why people were going there and not to the pool she managed. She was able to listen to comments made by other users and observed them enjoying themselves.

Penny then put together a questionnaire and carried out over 200 personal interviews in the town centre during the following two weeks. Her main aim was to find out how her swimming pool could regain its popularity.

After completing the interviews she put all the information together and found that people who wanted fun and excitement went to the new pool, whereas 'serious' swimmers preferred the local authority pool. Penny then presented her report to the councillors and made the following recommendations:

- introduce early morning swims for those people who want to swim lengths, either for recreation or training purposes

- introduce fun sessions on Saturday mornings and afternoons for 7-to-11-year olds, using inflatables in the shape of animals, monsters and aliens

- increase the provision of swimming lessons for both adults and children

- carry out a promotional campaign to raise awareness of these new activities.

Question

Can you recognise the five stages in Penny's marketing research process?

One way of encouraging people to complete surveys is to offer incentives such as: 'Complete and return this very simple questionnaire in the pre-paid envelope and you could win a holiday for two in the Caribbean'.

Some travel agents send out questionnaires to find out if customers were satisfied with their holiday and all the arrangements that go with it including transfers, excursions and the service provided by the holiday representative. See Figure 2.4 as an example.

The advantages and disadvantages of postal surveys are shown in Table 2.2.

Postal questionnaires can be distributed in a number of ways:

- posted to clients as soon as they have returned home

- the questionnaires may be on 'site' in reception or in the rooms – they can be

```
Cheap 'n' Cheerful Travel
1 The High Street
ANYTOWN
Yorkshire
AN1 2CC
```

On a scale of 1–5 where 1 is excellent and 5 is poor, how would you rate the following?

	1	2	3	4	5
1. Service provided by the travel agent	☐	☐	☐	☐	☐
2. In-flight service	☐	☐	☐	☐	☐
3. Hotel facilities	☐	☐	☐	☐	☐
4. Holiday representative	☐	☐	☐	☐	☐
5. Entertainment	☐	☐	☐	☐	☐
6. Accommodation	☐	☐	☐	☐	☐
7. Overall enjoyment	☐	☐	☐	☐	☐

Figure 2.4 An example of a postal survey

Table 2.2 Advantages and disadvantages of postal surveys

Advantages	Disadvantages
Data can be cheaply collected from a large number of respondents	Postal questionnaires often suffer from a poor response rate
No problem with the behaviour and appearance of the interviewer influencing results	Responses may be largely from people who have strong opinions on the subject (and are therefore not representative)
Respondents have time to consider answers and consult others if necessary	No check on whether respondents have really understood the questions
Postal methods may be the only way to contact some respondents	No control over who actually completes the questionnaire
	No opportunity to observe respondents' reactions to the questions
	Cannot expect to collect respondents' spontaneous answers
	No control over order in which questions are answered
	Respondents are limited to the question and answer options presented and their authentic views may not be revealed

posted back when they have been completed

◦ given out at the end of a coach trip or on the flight home from a holiday and posted back.

Postal questionnaires can be expensive for the organisation in terms of postal costs. One way to get round these is to ask clients to complete questionnaires there and then, and place them in a sealed box before they leave.

Telephone surveys are becoming more popular than ever

Telephone questionnaires

Telephone surveys are growing rapidly as a means of obtaining a quick response to an event or activity. For example, organisers at the National Exhibition Centre might phone exhibitors after the event to find out if everything had been satisfactory for them. A hotel may phone guests to see if they had enjoyed their stay

Talk about it

Have you ever been telephoned about a product or service? In a group, discuss what do you think are the advantages and disadvantages of a telephone questionnaire.

You might have thought of the following *advantages*:

◦ a larger number of interviews can be carried out covering a wide geographical area

- there are no transport costs for the interviewers – they do not have to move around

- costs per interview are low.

Disadvantages can include:

- only a short questionnaire can be used because of the time factor

- there is a general distrust by customers of speaking to people they cannot see and have never met

- telephone surveys can be expensive.

It is difficult when conducting telephone surveys to convince people you are not trying to sell them anything. This is because there are so many calls

CASE STUDY – Caterina

Caterina works for a marketing research company. Her job is to phone customers about the service they receive from their telephone company.

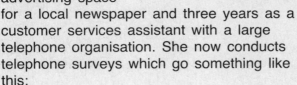

Caterina spent two years selling advertising space for a local newspaper and three years as a customer services assistant with a large telephone organisation. She now conducts telephone surveys which go something like this:

Caterina: Good afternoon, Mrs Stewart, my name is Caterina and I work for ABC telephone company. We are carrying out a customer care survey and I would just like to ask you a few questions.

Mrs Stewart: You're not trying to sell me anything, are you?

Caterina: No, we are just carrying out a survey. Do you have any additional services, such as call back?

Mrs Stewart: We had 'family and friends' and 'call back' added at Christmas.

Caterina: Is there anything else you might be interested in?

Mrs Stewart: Well, I've heard we can get e-mail and the Internet. Is that right?

Caterina: It certainly is. For a minimum charge of £5.99 per month you will be able to surf the net and e-mail friends 24 hours a day.

Mrs Stewart: Would I need an additional line?

Caterina: We would have to install an extra telephone point but this is included in the £5.99 monthly line rental. Our engineers could sort this out for you and it would only take one hour.

Mrs Stewart: It sounds good to me. But I would like to talk it over with my husband first. I'll call you when we've made a decision.

Caterina: Thanks very much Mrs Stewart. We look forward to hearing from you.

Mrs Stewart: Goodbye and thank you.

Question

What sort of telephone techniques does Caterina need if she is to do her job well?

from double glazing companies, motoring organisations and so on, all trying to sell us things over the phone.

Working in a group, write your own script for the first few minutes of a telephone survey. After you are all satisfied with the script, see if you can try it out on another group. How successful was it?

A good way to start a telephone survey call might be:

'Good morning. I am a student from Anytown College and I'm doing a survey about how much exercise people take each week. I'm not trying to sell you anything. I only want to ask you a few simple questions about our courses. It won't take up too much of your time. Would you mind?'

The request is harmless and it's not going to cost anything so the chances are that people will take part in the survey. However, you must always remember that the person being interviewed may just tell you what they think you want to hear in order to get you off the phone so they can go back to watching their favourite television programme.

Personal surveys

Personal surveys involve face-to-face interviews with either an individual or a group of people. The interview may be structured around a questionnaire upon which answers are recorded and analysed. On the other hand, an interview can be in the form of a discussion, with the interviewer having a list of topics of interest to discuss. The interviewer can also create questions and seek responses as the interview progresses.

Personal surveys in the form of **questionnaires** can:

* provide information about the customers of an organisation

* give customers the opportunity to air their views and opinions

* reveal the habits and preferences of customers.

It is important to design the questionnaire and ask the right questions in such a way that the required information will be received. Questionnaire design is a skilled job and can take a lot of time.

Here are some basic rules for designing questionnaires:

1 Keep questions simple.

2 Leave questions about age, occupation and marital status to the end of the questionnaire, after some type of relationship has been built up with the person being interviewed.

3 Don't ask irrelevant questions, i.e. those that have nothing to do with your aim of finding out what customers want.

4 Ask no more than eight questions.

5 Ask open questions by using the words 'what' 'why' and 'how'. For example, 'What do you look for in a holiday?'.

6 Interview a large enough sample to give you valid results.

7 Do not include questions which test the respondent's memory, such as 'How much did you spend on food each day during your first week here?'.

It is common practice to test or 'pilot' a questionnaire to check if the right questions are being asked and to see if they are easily understood.

There are two **types of question** – closed and open. *Closed questions* usually require an answer to be selected from a range of options, including simply 'Yes' or 'No'. Closed questions are used in quantitative surveys. They can be answered quickly and can easily be analysed later.

For example:

* Do you come swimming on your own? Yes/No

* Have you stayed in this hotel before? Yes/No

* Do you watch television every evening? Yes/No

Open questions allow the respondent to express an opinion and show their feelings. Although these give useful information the results are more

CASE STUDY — two questionnaires

Two questionnaires are given below. In pairs, read through them and decide which is effective and which is not. Give reasons for your answers and compose your answers with the rest of the group.

LEISURE AND TOURISM QUESTIONNAIRE

I'm doing a survey. Can I ask you some questions?

Q1   How old are you?

Q2   Where do you live?

Q3   If you won the lottery where would you go?

Q4   How much would you pay to go on holiday?

Q5   Are you a non-smoker?

Q6   How many children have you got?

Q7   How much do you spend on food per day for the first week of your holiday?

Q8   Don't you agree that rail travel is expensive?

Q9   How much does the main breadwinner in your home earn?

Q10 Who decides where you go on holiday?

Questionnaire A

LEISURE AND TOURISM QUESTIONNAIRE

Good morning/afternoon.
I am carrying out a survey on holidays and tourism for a national travel company. Would you mind if I asked you a few questions? It won't take long.

Q1   Did you go on holiday last year?
Yes ☐
No ☐

Q2   How often do you go on holiday each year?
Once ☐
Twice ☐
More ☐

Q3   Where did you go?
UK ☐
Europe ☐
USA ☐
Elsewhere _____
(*Include destination and country.*)

Q4   Who goes on holiday with you?
Family ☐
Friends ☐
(*Please give details.*) _____

Q5   When booking your holiday do you:
make your own arrangements ☐
use a travel agent ☐
go direct to a tour operator? ☐

Q6   If a new travel agency was to open in this area, where do you think would be the best location?
On the high street ☐
In a shopping centre ☐
In a side street ☐
Elsewhere ☐

Q7   What opening times would attract you to visit the travel agency?

Monday–Friday	Saturday	Sunday
9–12 pm ☐	9–12 pm ☐	10–1 pm ☐
1–5 pm ☐	1–5 pm ☐	1–4 pm ☐
5 pm onwards ☐		

Q8   What sort of holiday would you like to see on offer? _____

Q9   What type of travel arrangements would you like to see on offer? _____

Q10 Where do you live? _____

Q11 Which age group do you belong to: 16–24 ☐
25–39 ☐
40–59 ☐
60+ ☐

Observation:
Male ☐   Female ☐

Thank you very much for taking part in this survey. The answers you have given will be treated in strict confidence.

Questionnaire B

difficult to analyse because people have so many different opinions.

For example:

- What do you think about this swimming pool?
- What do you look for in a holiday?
- What improvements would you like to see in the fitness suite?

Look at the two questionnaires in the case study. It is not hard to see that questionnaire B is effective and questionnaire A is not!

Questionnaire A is ineffective and would be considered bad for many reasons, including:

- the introduction is not clear as to the purpose of the survey and is unwelcoming
- questions 1 and 2 should be asked at the end of the interview; question 1 is too personal
- question 5 is irrelevant
- question 6 assumes the person has got children, which could be offensive or upsetting to some people
- question 7 is too long
- question 8 is a leading question
- question 9 is far too personal
- there seems to be no thanks or mention of confidentiality at the end.

Questionnaire B is effective for several reasons:

- it has a good introduction
- all the questions are in a good running order and stay focused on the subject of holidays
- the information is easy to collate and analyse
- questions relating to address and age are left to the end to ensure that a feeling of trust has been built up
- the people being interviewed are thanked for taking part in the survey.

Try it out

In groups of four, you are to carry out the following tasks:

Your group has come up with the brilliant idea of setting up a health and fitness club in your area. Design a questionnaire which would give you sufficient marketing research evidence to see if your idea would work.

Divide your group into pairs. Each pair should interview ten people, using the questionnaire you have designed.

As a group, compare your questionnaire with those of other groups, analyse your results and present your findings to your tutor.

The advantages and disadvantages of personal surveys are shown in Table 2.3.

Table 2.3 Advantages and disadvantages of personal surveys

Advantages	Disadvantages
Very good response rates are possible	Time-consuming interviews can mean that only a small unrepresentative sample is chosen
Interviewer is available to clarify questions and prevent misunderstandings	Interaction between respondent and interviewer can lead to distorted answers being given
Probes allow extra lines of enquiry to be followed up	Respondents are limited to the question-and-answer options presented, and their authentic views may not be revealed
Pace of questioning can induce spontaneous responses	
No uncertainty over who actually answers the questions	
Interviewers can observe and collect useful background data	
Uniformity of interview technique and content makes quantitative analysis of the data possible	

Face-to-face interviews

A much-used type of primary marketing research includes face-to-face interviews. Personal interviews are time consuming and expensive but they do achieve a higher response rate than telephone and postal surveys.

A marketing research interview uses two types of questions. Closed questions can only be answered by 'yes' or 'no' (such as 'Do you use the gym?') while open questions allow interviewees to express their opinions (such as 'Why do you go there?').

The researcher carrying out the interviews must be careful not to influence the respondent, for example by agreeing or disagreeing with an answer that is given. Therefore the interviewer should be fully trained in research techniques in order to elicit the right information.

During an in-depth interview the interviewer usually has a list of topics to discuss rather than a set of questions to ask. As the interview progresses the interviewer can ask more searching questions and, if necessary, use probes to clarify the responses. This can help if questions are of a confidential or embarrassing nature, such as 'How many cigarettes a day do you smoke?' or 'How much weight have you lost since you started going to this keep-fit class?'.

Face-to-face interviews can take place in the street, at a tourist attraction, at home or at work. In a face-to-face interview you can find out what customers:

- want in terms of a product or service
- think of your competitors
- think of your organisation
- think about your product
- think about the name of your organisation – is it easy to remember, can they pronounce it?
- feel are the best words to describe what you offer, e.g. 'value for money', 'cheap', 'good quality'.
- think of your advertising and promotional material.

Interviewing is costly in terms of time but it is an investment well worth making. By asking the right questions you should get the answers which will tell you about your product and organisation.

Discussions

This method of marketing research is used to generate new ideas when finding answers to questions like, 'What new activities would you like to see in the leisure centre?' or 'What type of performances would you go to watch at the theatre?'.

Discussions can also be used to find out what consumers think about a new promotion or idea before it is widely available, for example a different colour or type of packaging for a product or even a name change. Sometimes group discussions are recorded or video taped to assist in preparing a summary of the group's responses.

Try it out

You have been asked to develop a new type of chocolate bar. Using some carefully designed questions, carry out some marketing research and, after analysing what people want, aim to come up with the best selling chocolate bar of all time.

Your marketing research could be done in your school/college.

Observation

Observation is a popular and useful research technique. Observation means studying by looking and data is collected by observing people.

The advantages of observation as a technique is that it means you can see what people actually do rather than what they tell researchers they do.

There are two types of observation: direct observation and participant observation.

Direct observation

Subjects are watched as they go about their normal business and observations are recorded by the researcher. Naturally, observations can usually only take place where permission has been granted – otherwise the observation could be seen as unethical.

Examples of direct observation include:

- watching and listening to a hotel receptionist dealing with guests' enquiries observing a trampoline instructor coaching a student – the observer could be an examiner watching to see if the coach passes the requirements of the qualification.

Direct observation does not always have to be carried out by a member of staff. For example, it can be done by closed-circuit television (CCTV) which monitors the movements and actions of people, such as in a town centre or at a football match. With this form of direct observation, however, participants do not always give their permission!

Organisations such as libraries use an electronic counter to record the numbers of people using the facility, and turnstiles are used at sports stadia to keep a check on the numbers of spectators coming into the ground.

Participant observation

This means that the researcher becomes part of the group being studied. There is probably no better way of really getting to understand the way groups work than to join them.

Examples of participant observation include:

- joining a group of recreation assistants throughout their shifts for a week

- working alongside the kitchen staff in a restaurant.

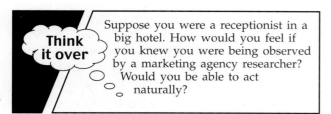

Think it over Suppose you were a receptionist in a big hotel. How would you feel if you knew you were being observed by a marketing agency researcher? Would you be able to act naturally?

Cameras capture crime

Street cameras are already beginning to pay dividends in the fight against crime.

Police reports show that the 18 town-centre cameras are pinpointing crime and aiding detection just two weeks after being switched on.

A 24-year-old man has been released on police bail after being filmed allegedly stealing a bag of clothes from outside a charity shop on Millgate at 9.30 pm on Monday.

Three juveniles were arrested at 5 pm on Sunday on suspicion of taking clothes from outside the same charity shop. An 11-year-old girl and a 10-year-old boy have accepted cautions, and another 11-year-old girl has been released on bail.

Inspector Ward said: 'The camera system has really only just gone on line but already it is proving its worth. This system will greatly benefit the town centre, its businesses, its residents and its visitors.'

Think it over Many town centres now have CCTV. Do you think this takes away a person's liberty and is too intrusive? In other words, is 'big brother' watching you?

Would you feel your every move was being watched if there were CCTV cameras in a sports centre?

How do you think facilities can benefit from the use of CCTV observation?

CASE STUDY – marketing research

Bridgetown Leisure Centre is to open in three months' time. The local council wants to make sure that the activities available at the Leisure Centre are the ones the customers want.

Marketing research will help find out customer needs. This is what you have to do:

Divide into four groups so that each is responsible for one method of marketing research: postal surveys, telephone questionnaires, personal surveys, observation.

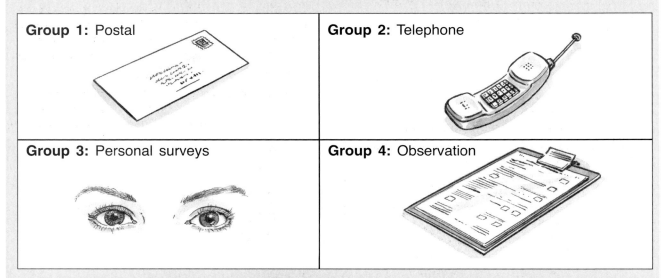

Group 1: Postal

Group 2: Telephone

Group 3: Personal surveys

Group 4: Observation

Helpful hints

1 Group 1 – design a questionnaire which will give you information about customer needs and wants at the Leisure Centre. Send out 20 letters and act on their responses.

2 Group 2 – phone 30 people and find out what they would want to do at the Leisure Centre, making sure you have a lot of questions to ask them.

3 Group 3 – design a questionnaire and interview 30 people.

4 Group 4 – observe the customers at your local leisure centre. What are the most popular activities? How long do people stay there? It is essential that you ask the Leisure Centre Manager for permission to conduct this observation.

Activity

When all your information has been gathered list the activities you would put on at the Bridgetown Leisure Centre and say why.

Target marketing

Target marketing is concerned with matching the right products with the right people. The market for a product or service is the total number of existing customers who currently use or buy the product. It can also consist of potential customers who could buy or use the product or service.

A target market consists of:

1 existing customers – those who have bought in the past and will continue to do so

2 potential customers – those who may buy in the future and could become regular customers.

Target marketing is aimed at both groups.

Try it out

Match the product to the target market.

Product	Target market
Club Med holidays	Senior citizens with money to spend
Long winter breaks in Spain	12–16 age group
Swimming lessons	18–30-year-olds
Youth club	Senior citizens
Old Tyme dancing	Children, non-swimmers

? Did you know?

We are constantly being targeted by banks, mail order firms and credit card companies who want our business.

Try it out

Who would be the target market for:

• a week at Butlin's Funcoast world, Skegness

• a day at Alton Towers

• a game of bowls?

It is important to get the right product to the right people – but how do we know who the right people are? The answer is to divide the market into smaller sections or segments. This enables organisations to serve these segments specifically so the customers are given what they want. This way both the organisation and the customer benefit.

Different market segments have different needs. For example, if we say that all people who take part in sport are a target market, we can then divide this market into segments according to their needs.

Different age groups will have different sports needs. For example, men aged between 16 and 35 years may want to play football whereas senior citizens may want to play bowls. Organisations need to know who their customers are and what they want. Advertising and promotion can be targeted more effectively if market segments are recognised.

There are five basic ways of segmenting the market, which enable organisations to build up profiles of their customers. These five segments are:

◦ age

◦ gender

◦ social group

◦ lifestyle

◦ ethnicity.

Age

Different age groups tend to have different leisure interests and needs. Senior citizens often prefer to go out in groups, for example, on day trips, or they may want to 'winter' in Spain. One organisation which specialises in holidays for the over-50s age group is Saga Holidays, which was established in 1952. The owner of a hotel wanted to attract guests during the low season and found that the target market was retired people. Saga is now an international travel company offering all types of holidays for older people with varying levels of disposable income.

In contrast, young people aged between 18 and 30 years of age may prefer fun-packed holidays where they can dance and party all night and every night. Club 18–30 targets this market. Young people may also be attracted to adventure type holidays, such as climbing in Snowdonia, or trekking in the Himalayas.

Table 2.4 Life cycle classification by age

Bachelors, spinsters	Young single people with reasonable level of personal disposable income. Enjoy nightlife, music and package holidays in Spain/Greece
Newly weds/groups living together	Higher disposable income. Eat out a lot. Holidays in Florida/India/Far East
Full nest 1	Young couple/married/living together, youngest child less than 6. Family trips to zoo, parks. Self-catering holidays
Full nest 2	Young couples with children, youngest over 6. Falling disposable income. Less money to spend on leisure activities
Full nest 3	Older couple with older children who are still dependent, probably studying. Lower disposable income – home is base for entertainment: TV, video, radio, computer
Empty nest 1	Older couples. No children or children left at home and dependent. Disposable income not restricted. Weekend breaks, eating out, theatre and annual holidays abroad
Empty nest 2	Older couples, chief breadwinner retired. Income once again restricted. Home entertainment, DIY, gardening, TV
Solitary survivor 1	Single/widowed person. Restricted income. Gardening/home-based leisure
Solitary survivor 2	Single person retired. Little spare cash. Little to spend on leisure

Talk about it

How might a leisure centre target a family of two adults and two children under ten?

Targeting a market segment by age or life cycle classification as shown in Table 2.4 can give leisure and tourism organisations a focus. The life cycle classification puts a person into one of nine categories which are based on where that person is on his or her life cycle.

Talk about it

In your group, can you identify people you know who fall into the life cycle concept? Do you agree with the different categories?

Look it up

Saga Holidays and Club Med cater for specific age groups. Using brochures from travel agents, describe the types of holidays on offer for them.

Gender

Leisure and tourism organisations have recognised the different needs and interests of men and women. This is because:

- most women prefer aerobics to playing rugby. In other words, men and women enjoy different leisure activities

- men and women have different tastes, a gym for women may be decorated in pastel shades and have no loose weights whereas men do not even notice the décor. They want to concentrate on weightlifting and weight training

- women may prefer all-female classes for their workouts.

It is important that organisations recognise the need to cater for each gender as this could increase business and improve the image of the organisation. For example, hotels can make the effort to cater for business women as well as business men, particularly for women travelling alone who might want room service rather than eating alone in a restaurant.

In these days of equal opportunity, women have been able to do things which were previously the domain of men; for example, in athletics, women now take part in the pole vault and triple jump. Women jockeys race alongside men. However, there are still some sports which women cannot take part in with men, for example football and rugby. What do you think about this?

Talk about it

What sort of leisure activities could be aimed specifically at each sex? For example, a 'knit and natter' club for women over 60 or a mother and toddler swimming group. (But what about the dads...?)

Think of some activities specifically for men and women.

Does this encourage sex discrimination? What about boxing for women?

? Did you know?

It's not too long ago that some pubs had a male-only bar – no women allowed! Thankfully, times have changed and pubs now encourage women and families by providing a warm welcome and facilities like family rooms.

? Did you know?

As an equal opportunity measure men can now take paternity leave and get paid for it.

Social group

This is sometimes referred to as socio-economic grouping. It is a way of categorising people under the headings of marital status, education, jobs and income. In general, people who have similar incomes and similar jobs, have similar leisure interests.

The most widely used method of grouping people for marketing purposes based on income and occupation is shown in Table 2.5.

It is assumed that the people in each category have similar amounts of disposable income and similar buying habits. It is also assumed that people in social grade A have the highest level of disposable income.

However, there are some problems with this type of classification system. For example, some C1 and C2 people may have a higher disposable income than those in A and B grades who might have to pay out for private education for their children and private health care for the family.

Table 2.5 Social status and occupation (based on the Registrar-General's social classification)

Grade	Social status	Occupation	Products and services used
A	Upper middle class (1)	Lawyers, chief executives, managing directors	Expensive holidays Exclusive golf club
B	Middle class (2)	Doctors, teachers, middle managers	All-inclusive holidays
C1	Lower middle class (3A – non manual)	Supervisors, junior managers	Fly/drive holidays
C2	Skilled working class (3B – manual)	Plumbers, electricians	Package holidays
D	Working class (4)	Semi and unskilled – labourers, cleaners	Cheaper package holidays
E	Unskilled people (5)	State pensioners, widows, casual workers	Coach holidays Day trips

If a hotel targeted people in the 'A' category the price of rooms, the decor, style and exclusiveness of the place would reflect this; whereas a seaside hotel might consist of basic, friendly accommodation and service to those in the C1 and C2 categories. The system is used purely for marketing purposes: for selecting market segments to match the products and services available.

Talk about it

Do you think this method of categorising people is accurate? What newspapers would you expect people in A and B grades to read? What newspapers would you expect C1s and C2s to read?

Lifestyle

Efforts have been made to look at groups of people according to their lifestyles, that is, the way they live, their interests and opinions and their activities. Advertisers in particular look at lifestyles and target their advertisements to hit the right target market. Examples of this include services such as banking (including credit cards) and insurance, both of which have been heavily marketed.

One method of marketing research is ACORN, which stands for 'A Classification of Residential Neighborhoods'. This method classifies people under the following categories:

- **mainstreamers** – average people doing ordinary things, buying branded products like Heinz beans and Adidas sportswear

- **aspirers** – tend to go for exclusive and expensive products like fast cars and luxury holidays

- **succeeders** – those who have been there and done it; a powerful group who can afford a lifestyle to which they have become accustomed

- **Reformers** – those concerned about the quality of life, for example preserving the environment.

Leisure and tourism organisations can target these groups, for example:

- an exclusive health club – aspirers

- a local leisure centre – mainstreamers

- a high-class five-star hotel – succeeders

- an organic whole-food shop – reformers.

Try it out

In your group design and make a collage for each of the lifestyle categories and include a family that would go with it.

Ethnicity

Different cultures and ethnic groups have different interests and needs, and leisure and tourism organisations have to take this into consideration. Religious customs, food and language have to be taken into account when promoting products and services for different ethnic groups. For example:

- A London hotel may have to change its menu to suit overseas visitors. A group of American tourists may expect to be served burgers and fries not cottage pie and gravy.

- Special Saturday morning films at the cinema may be shown to attract the Asian community, as this is part of their culture.

- Sports and leisure centres may provide women-only swimming sessions for Muslim woman. Female lifeguards only will be on duty, a provision which respects their culture.

- A Caribbean centre which acts as a meeting place for people of West Indian origin, where they can take part in activities such as singing, dancing and organising fund-raising events for local charities.

CASE STUDY — John

John is the manager of a large hotel in central London. It is very popular with tourists from all over the world. Part of John's responsibilities is to ensure that each guest is really well looked after and that they all get what they ask for.

John says, 'There is no other job quite like it for variety and challenge. A German guest may want rye bread, sauerkraut and saveloy for breakfast every day so I have to arrange this with our chef. American tourists like cinnamon rolls and bagels for their breakfast, so once again, I check this out in the kitchen.

'It's quite fun really; our French guests want to read French newspapers, our Australian guests insist on drinking Australian beer and our Chinese guests prefer to eat with chopsticks rather than knives and forks.'

Question

Can you think of any other ways John's hotel could cater for the needs of guests from particular ethnic groups?

The marketing mix

The 'marketing mix' describes the four key factors which an organisation has to take into account when meeting the needs of its customers, i.e. product, place, price and promotion. These four factors are often referred to as the 4Ps of the marketing mix; which is one of the most important concepts in leisure and tourism marketing (see Figure 2.5). An example of a marketing mix for a leisure centre is shown in Figure 2.6.

Figure 2.5 The marketing mix

Talk about it

Fantasy Travel has introduced a holiday package with a difference: 'Around the world in 80 days'.

This holiday does exactly what it says, taking in 40 countries in an incredible 80 days. It costs a mere £25,000. It will be advertised in the *Sunday Times Magazine* for just two successive issues.

Tour organiser, Michaela Dalby, says, 'It's the absolute trip of a lifetime for anyone with time on their hands and money to spend. It's the ultimate in fantasy travel.'

What do you think about this package?

Which of the 4Ps of the marketing mix can you see at work here?

Marketing decisions which are made by using this method can help increase business and boost sales if the organisation gets the right product in the right place at the right price using the right type of promotion.

Some leisure and tourism organisations may adjust the emphasis of the 4Ps, depending on their objectives. For example:

- A local authority leisure centre may have opened a private health and fitness centre. As a result, the manager of the fitness centre may reduce prices to compete with the new rival.

- A pub may find that more and more families are coming in for meals so the landlord may

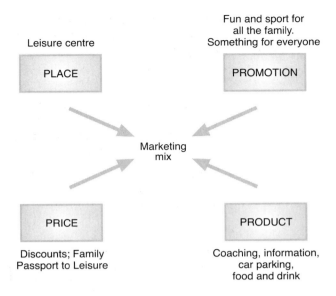

Figure 2.6 An example of the marketing mix for a leisure centre

adjust his product accordingly, for example creating a special children's menu or building a play area.

- A new restaurant has opened in town and the owner carries out a lot of promotions to raise awareness of the new facility.

- A sports goods shop has decided to expand to bigger premises so it looks for a place in the centre of town which is easy to locate for a large number of people.

Draw a diagram similar to Figure 2.6, but instead of using a leisure centre, one group show a hotel, one group should show a cinema and another group use a restaurant.

Compare your completed work.

Product

The product is the term used to describe the products or services offered for sale by organisations. It is only through these that customers' needs are satisfied. But leisure and tourism is primarily a 'service' industry. Although there are products such as books, training shoes,

squash racquets and so on, much of the leisure and tourism industry is connected with the customers' experience and how those experiences are delivered to the customer.

Figure 2.7 shows some examples of leisure and tourism products.

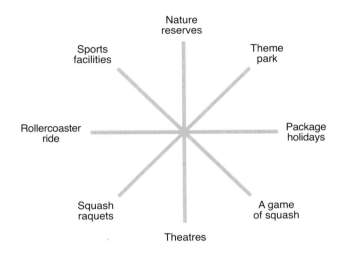

Figure 2.7 Some different examples of leisure and tourism products

Some products are tangible, i.e. you can touch a tennis racquet and can see a theatre and its facilities. Many leisure and tourism products are intangible, for example you cannot touch or see a package holiday or a session in the gym – but you can experience it.

Customer satisfaction

The leisure product is made up of a set of **satisfactions** which organisations deliver to their customers. These satisfactions include:

- quality of customer service – if a theatre receptionist treated a customer badly, that customer would either make a complaint, not return or both; so customer care training for staff is essential

- standard of facilities – nowadays people expect value for money, not shoddy goods or out-of-date equipment or dirty changing rooms

atmosphere – facilities should be bright, warm and friendly, creating a welcoming image.

The moral of Jack's story in the case study below is that leisure and tourism products are made up of different elements, like Jack's night out, but all these elements should combine to form a satisfying leisure experience. If something goes wrong, it can badly affect the overall experience.

Product development

Products have to be continuously improved and developed as customers are always seeking something that is new and improved. For example:

- Blackpool Pleasure Beach and Alton Towers open new and exciting rides such as The Playstation and Oblivion each year

- new adventure sports like paragliding, jet skiing and windsurfing have grown in popularity with those who like adventure and are prepared to take risks

- leisure centres provide crèches for the children of the women taking part in keep-fit sessions or doing sports; this makes it possible for the mothers to take part in such activities

- health and fitness clubs now provide much more than 'keep fit'. The complete package can include personalised fitness programmes, dietary advice, massages and manicures.

This constant product development is aimed at satisfying customer needs, pleasing new customers and maintaining quality.

Try it out

In pairs, can you think of some other products which have been improved to make them more attractive to customers?

CASE STUDY – Jack

Jack works in a shoe factory and decided to go to a rock concert with his mates. The tickets weren't cheap but it was a once-in-a-lifetime opportunity for him. Jack thought the band was brilliant, everything he expected. Unfortunately, the whole night overall was a bit of a let-down. The coach to the venue arrived 20 minutes late which meant they almost missed the show. What's more, there were no apologies from the driver. Although Jack could hear the band, his view was partially blocked by one of the hall's supporting columns. What's more he had to pay a fortune for a programme and queue for ages at the bar for a drink. The band were great. Pity the rest of Jack's leisure experience didn't match them.

Questions

- Have you ever had a similar experience to Jack?

- What elements were missing from your overall experience?

The brand name

The brand name given by an organisation to one of its products or services aims to make recognition of the product easier and to differentiate the products or collection of products from those of their competitors. In other words, it establishes a product in the mind of the customer. Brand names include Heinz, Kellogg's, Hoover, Nescafe. Brand names in the leisure and tourism industry include Reebok, Adidas, McDonald's, Thomson, Holiday Inn, and Little Chef.

In the eyes of a customer, these brands tend to suggest quality, trust and reliability, so people are prepared to pay a higher price for them because they feel they are superior to other similar products. Organisations therefore encourage this brand loyalty to be built up in order to take advantage of this feeling.

The brand name gives a product identity and organisations promote it to encourage the potential customer to buy. The characteristics of a good brand name are:

- it is easy to remember and pronounce, e.g. Puma, Reebok, KFC

- the name is short and catchy, e.g. Pepsi, Levis, Donnay

- the brand name is adaptable in that it covers a number of different products, e.g. Adidas produces clothes, footwear and aftershave.

Some organisations link a brand name to particular segments of a market. For example, an airline may have 'standard' class, 'executive' or 'gold' class seating for specific travellers who fall into those categories.

Talk about it

Can you think of any brand names – both in the leisure and tourism industry and outside it?

Think of a product, for example a chocolate bar. Make up a brand name for it which is catchy and easy to remember.

After-sales service

Good after-sales service should provide additional business for organisations. For example, a leisure centre may design a course for people in the fitness suite to help them lose weight. It could be advertised as a 'Gym and trim' course. It would be successful if people lost weight.

But what about marketing weight loss? Why not put on another course which would help customers maintain their fitness, keep to their reduced weight and keep them motivated? A follow-on course could be: 'Look good, feel good' – an aerobics class, or 'Gym, swim and trim' – a combination of activities.

Other services should be reviewed to establish a link to improve customer satisfaction and produce increased income for the organisation. One example could be in a college where students studying for the primary ABTAC (Travel Agent's Certificate) could then progress to the Advanced ABTAC course.

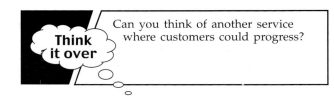

Think it over

Can you think of another service where customers could progress?

The other point of after-sales service is ensuring continual customer satisfaction with the product and the service received. For example, selling a holiday and issuing the tickets to the client is not necessarily the end of the sale for either party. The travel agent could phone the client after the holiday to find out if the person enjoyed it.

This would demonstrate three things:

1   Genuine concern that the product was right.

2   Finding out if the customer's needs were met.

3   Good public relations, that is, creating a good image for the organisation.

Talk about it

In your group, think of some other examples of after-sales service.

After-sales service also includes dealing with complaints. The quicker problems are dealt with and sorted out, the more likely it is that the customer will return and use the organisation again.

Place

Place refers to two things: the actual *location* of the facility and how the product is *distributed* to the customer. This is concerned with getting the right product to the right people at the right time.

> **Talk about it**
>
> Where are restaurants, cinemas, sports centres and schools located in your area?
>
> Why do you think location is so important?

Location

Facilities in leisure and tourism need to be located near to a well-populated area where customers and potential customers live. Restaurants, theatres, cinemas and concert halls usually have a town or city centre location.

In addition, there should be good signposting and sufficient car parking spaces. Accessibility is very important. Are there transport links to the facility? Is it easy to get access to the facility for people with disabilities, i.e. are car parking spaces one metre wide, is there a ramp into the main entrance?

> **Think it over**
>
> What is the ideal location for a community centre, a leisure centre and a youth club?

Hotels

Should **hotels** be located in city centres, on the outskirts of towns, at the seaside or near a motorway?

Many seaside hotels were built in Victorian times when resorts became increasingly popular

Since hotels serve the needs of many different customers, they can be found in all these locations because:

- business people use city centre hotels, such as railway hotels or those near airports
- holidaymakers stay at seaside hotels
- travelling salespeople use hotels near good motorway links.

An example of an ideal location is Blackpool Pleasure Beach. This is located in a town which has other attractions such as:

- Blackpool Tower
- the Illuminations

Hotels near good transport links are essential for modern travellers

◇   seven miles of golden sand

◇   the Promenade.

Blackpool is well served by the motorway system and has plenty of accommodation. You could even use it as a stopping-off place before moving on to the Lake District.

Distribution channels

This covers how the product reaches the customer. Leisure and tourism products and services should be made available to customers when they want them. Some of these products and services can be 'delivered' and paid for at the point of production, for example a game of badminton in a leisure centre, a round of golf at the golf club or a concert at the theatre.

Some products and services are made away from the place where the customers want them, so channels of distribution are created, such as **communication channels**. These will give advice on ticket availability, information on flight times and directions to destinations. For example, it is easy to book a holiday in Bournemouth as most travel agents could do this and most tourist information centres could supply information about accommodation. This distribution of information allows people to book holidays with the minimum of fuss in the knowledge that the destination is easy to reach.

Other examples of communication channels for a hotel might be:

◇   ringing up and making a reservation

◇   using the same hotel chain and asking the receptionist to book a room

◇   through a tourist information centre

◇   via the Internet.

Other distribution channels can include:

◇   stockholding – making sure there are enough products in stock, ready for the customer to buy, such as enough hotel rooms, training shoes, airline seats or squash racquets

◇   transportation – making sure the product is delivered to the right place at the right time

◇   packaging and display – the product should be displayed in such a way that it looks attractive to customers and at the same time is practical for the shop itself, not taking up too much space.

Many products are sold through third parties because it is not always possible to sell direct. These intermediaries are usually retailers and wholesalers who deliver the product to the customer. For example, the distribution channel for a holiday can be seen in Figure 2.8. There are advantages and disadvantages to this system, as can be seen in Table 2.6.

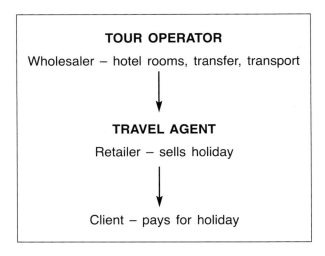

Figure 2.8 A distribution channel for a holiday

Table 2.6 Advantages and disadvantages of the 'third party' system

Method	Advantages	Disadvantages
Travel agent	Good location, loyal customers Image could be well presented within premises	High overheads for renting high street location
Tour operator	Reputable and well-known organisation	No face-to-face contact with customers

Price

Customers will usually buy products if they feel they are getting value for money. This means the organisation's objectives must be met so that:

1   the private sector can make a profit

2   the public sector can provide a service at break-even point.

Organisations can only stay in business if customers are prepared to pay the price of their products. So, prices must be fixed to provide an income which covers costs, makes profits and enables organisations to stay in business.

Price is the only part of the marketing mix that generates income. Place, promotion and product all create costs, which can be covered if the right price is charged.

Setting a price

When pricing products the following factors must be taken into account:

- the cost of producing the product
- the price customers are prepared to pay
- the prices competitors charge
- the profit margin.

Put very simply, profit is the difference between sales and costs.

Sales less costs = profit

What importance do you place on price when buying clothes?

What about other products?

Figure 2.9 shows some of the factors which influence pricing.

Arriving at the right price is not easy. Organisations have to be aware of the value customers put on a product or service and

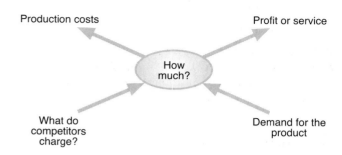

Figure 2.9 Factors which influence pricing

somehow the organisation has to find out what the customer is willing to pay. Marketing research can help with this. If potential customers are asked what they are willing to pay, the organisation would have a good idea of what price to charge.

Another way of setting a price would be to find out what competitors charge. If people shopped around for a similar product, for example a two-week holiday in Crete, and found the same holiday was £200 more at one travel agent than the other, it is likely that they will go to the lower priced one. It is known as **market-led pricing** when organisations offer similar products and services at a similar price.

Sometimes an organisation has to work out a special price for a customer because there is no standard price for the product. For example, a businesswoman might want to fly to Thailand for a week, move on to Singapore for three days and finally spend two days in Bombay completing her business before flying back to the UK. This is quite a trip and it cannot be worked out like a package holiday. This is called **one-off pricing**, as the product is very different to normal travel requests.

Another method of arriving at a price is called **cost-plus pricing**. For example, the owner of a fitness centre would work out the costs of operating the place. He then adds on a flat rate or percentage to his products or services in order to arrive at a selling price which covers his cost and creates a profit.

An example of cost-plus pricing

Three Peaks Leisure Centre Crèche

- Running costs = wages of part-time assistants: £100

- Operating costs (e.g. heating, lighting): £50

Total costs per week: £150

If 25 children were charged £6, income = £150

To make a profit, 25 children could be charged £10 = £250

So profit would be £100.

Peak and off-peak pricing

Organisations in the leisure and tourism industry have to adjust their prices for the same product at different times of the year, week or even day. For example, a ferry operator might halve the price for its trips between January and March compared to its summer prices, and rail fares can vary for travelling the same distance. For example, a single ticket to London from Newark costs £35 before 9 am but is £24 after 9 am and at weekends.

Peak and off-peak levels

Peak times	Off-peak times
5–10 pm weekdays	9–5 pm weekdays
9–6 pm weekends	6–10 pm weekends

Holidays in the UK

Low season (cheaper rates)	*High season* (higher rates)
Jan, Feb, March	June, July, August

Holidays overseas

Prices rise during the school holidays, especially summer and Christmas.

Low season
Winter (except for skiing) – reduced prices

Leisure centres often reduce the price of activities during off-peak or less busy times, i.e. from 9.00 to 5.00 when many people are at work. The aim of off-peak pricing is to encourage people to use facilities at quiet times.

Look it up

Find out the peak and off-peak rates at your local leisure centre for badminton, squash, swimming and hire of the hall. Are there any other special deals? Is there a gym with different rates according to the time of day?

Look it up

Using holiday brochures compare the prices of a two-week holiday in Menorca for two adults and two children in March and in August.

Group and special discounts

The idea of offering discounts is to:

- offer as many people as possible the opportunity to take part in leisure activities

- increase usage of facilities

- increase income.

For example, a leisure centre may offer discounts for the unemployed such as:

- low cost or free activities

- free equipment hire.

A pub may offer discounts on meals to senior citizens at certain times, for example 'silver' three-course meals for the over 60s at £3.50 every Tuesday between 12 and 2 pm.

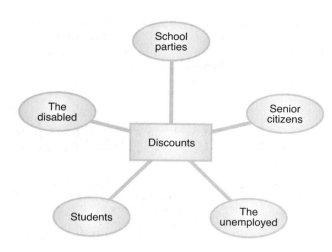

Figure 2.10 Discounts may be offered to a variety of groups

Figure 2.10 shows the kind of groups who might benefit from discount.

Talk about it

Can you think of some examples of discounts offered by leisure and tourism organisations?

Special offers

SNAPSHOTS

Special offer
A new pub has just opened in town and has a special offer of beer at just 99p per pint for the first six weeks of opening. This is likely to attract customers in the hope that they become 'regulars'.

SNAPSHOTS

80s night
Every Thursday evening is 80s night at the local club. Special offers include 80p admission and 80p for drinks for the first 80 minutes.

Quite a novel idea: the club is full every Thursday.

SNAPSHOTS

Discounts
Special discounts on late bookings:

1   *Flight-only £99 to Ibiza departing this Saturday (three days to book!).*

2   *Two weeks in Gran Canaria, self-catering, £199 per person, departing next Thursday.*

Such discounts are aimed at filling the plane. You may find someone sitting next to you on the plane who has paid twice as much but has been unable to take full advantage of the special offers.

Credit terms

Credit terms are arranged when goods and services are supplied but payment is not requested at the time of purchase. Credit may be given at no charge, for example 'Buy now, pay later' with no interest charged.

Credit cards entitle the holder to a free period of credit. They can be used to make payments for accommodation, meals and holiday bookings. Theatre and concert tickets can also be booked by credit card and over the phone.

Promotion

The promotional activities of a hotel will be geared towards filling its rooms. Similarly with an airline the aim will be to sell all the seats.

Promotion is the most easily recognised aspect of marketing. It is all about communication with existing and potential customers so that they react by buying the product. People cannot buy a product if they have never heard of it. Promotional activities can be put into action once the product, place and price of the products have been determined.

SNAPSHOTS

The Coral Beach Hotel

Set in ten acres of grounds amidst beautiful landscaped gardens, this impressive complex offers impeccable standards of comfort and service. Its serene and hospitable ambience makes it the perfect environment in which to thoroughly pamper yourself with revitalising massage and beauty treatments at the on site health and beauty spa. You can even pre-book a health and beauty package and look forward to an invigorating course of treatment! Customers seeking more in the way of action will not be disappointed either, as down on the beach, a huge array of watersports ranges from sailing and paragliding to speed-boating and canoeing. The accommodation at the Coral Beach is exceptional in every way and all rooms are immaculately furnished and extremely well equipped.

FACILITIES INCLUDE: Two swimming pools (one outdoor, one indoor) • Beach • Gardens • Jacuzzi • Five restaurants • Three bars. Lounge • Snack bar • Squash court • Mini golf • Gym • Health & beauty spa • Windsurfing • Waterskiing • Paragliding • Pedaloes • Catamarans • Canoes • Bananas • Disco • Children's club

Elegantly decorated rooms feature one double or two twin beds, air-conditioning, satellite TV, radio, telephone, mini bar, bathrobes, hairdryer, bathroom and balcony.

SNAPSHOTS

Classic Airlines

Travel in style. Classic Airlines offers luxurious seats, lots of leg room and first-class service. Your flight includes a champagne breakfast, free drinks, the latest film releases and complimentary souvenirs.

'A flight with us is a flight to remember.'

Promotion aims to:

◦ make customers aware of the product

◦ promote understanding of the product

◦ persuade customers to buy the product (which increases sales)

◦ encourage customers to return – repeat business (see Figures 2.11 and 2.12).

Organisations need to know:

◦ Who are my customers?

◦ Where are they?

◦ How can I tell them about my product?

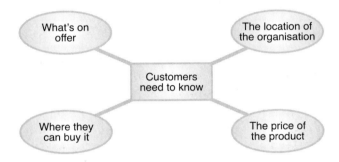

Figure 2.11 Promotional activities must offer information

Figure 2.12 There are many different promotional activities

Advertising

The aim of advertising is to communicate with potential customers so that they will buy the product, thus increasing sales. As many customers as possible within the target market should be reached. Advertising can be expensive and costs vary according to space, frequency and how long the advertisements run. Figure 2.13 shows the sorts of places where adverts can be found.

Try it out	In a group, think of as many adverts as possible which immediately spring to mind. Why are they memorable? Does everyone think of the same ones?

One method is to use the 'shotgun approach' – spraying as many potential customers as possible in the hope that some of them will be persuaded to buy the product.

Local advertising attracts local people and using local newspapers and radio is one example of shotgun advertising. This could be used by a leisure centre wanting to promote its new swimming courses. This type of advertisement would be within the centre's budget, far more so than advertising on television, and local people would most likely be the ones who would use local facilities.

Figure 2.13   Advertisments can be found in many places

Money can be wasted if an advertisement does not reach its target audience. But also the message must be put across effectively. Probably the most expensive form of advertising is on television. A 30-second commercial during the break in *Coronation Street* would cost thousands of pounds. This timeslot is classed as peak-viewing time when there is an audience of around 15 million people. The advertising costs would reflect this. Production costs in making a television advertisement should also be taken into account.

Advertising on television is usually restricted to large commercial organisations who are able to afford it. Examples include Adidas, Lunn Poly, Thomas Cook, Coca Cola and Nike.

Newspaper advertising can also be expensive. A full-page advertisement in a national newspaper would cost thousands of pounds whereas one in a local paper may cost only £100.

Look it up

Contact your local newspaper to find out the costs of a half and full page advertisement.

Does the cost vary according to its location in the newspaper? Are there any discounts offered if the advertisement is placed over a period of time every week?

Direct marketing

This is sometimes known as direct mail advertising where leaflets are posted through doors to try to get a response from potential customers. These leaflets may be delivered with magazines and newspapers.

You have probably been on the receiving end of direct mail (sometimes known as 'junk mail') on quite a few occasions. Personalised letters addressed specifically to you are sent direct by post from organisations with which you may have had no contact. Examples can include American Express, finance companies, the Reader's Digest and double glazing companies.

These organisations have obtained your name and address from a database and have written to you explaining the benefits you would receive if you took up their special offers and used their products. They have been able to obtain the names and addresses of people in a certain age group on certain incomes. This allows them to target their market segment accurately and directly.

The most common direct marketing techniques used in the leisure and tourism industry are:

- direct mail
- telemarketing – by phone
- door-to-door distribution – by post
- direct response advertising – where the customer responds either by phoning (to collect a gift) or completing a coupon which will be entered in a prize draw.

Talk about it

What sort of direct mail do you receive? Did you receive incentives like a free gift for you to respond? Have you ever responded to direct mail?

Public relations

The main aim of public relations (PR) is to boost the image of an organisation. It also aims to:

- put the organisation in a good light
- promote a good image for its products and services
- publicise what it offers.

PR involves organisations contacting the media to inform them of forthcoming events and interesting stories.

PR is all about making organisations look good in the eyes of the public. The holiday destinations featured in the various 'holiday' programmes on TV create a favourable image for those particular destinations, encouraging people to go there. In the same way travel journalists are often given free holidays by travel companies and overseas tourist boards in the hope that their published articles will give a favourable impression of the area.

Public relations officers help to create a good image for their organisation. If, however, an unfortunate incident took place, for example a chemical leakage at a swimming pool, or food poisoning at a hotel, it would be up to the PR officer to limit any bad publicity and give out accurate information rather than let journalists speculate.

Look it up

Can you find a story in your local newspaper which creates a good image for an organisation?

CASE STUDY – PR at work

In 1982, as a manager of a leisure centre, I contacted the local press to say I had an exclusive story which would benefit the local community.

Ours was the first centre to provide a mother and baby changing and feeding room. This allowed complete privacy for mothers to feed and change their babies in a purpose-built room. We even managed to get Boots to provide the nappies free of charge. This story showed the community that we were:

- a 'caring' centre
- providing facilities for all ages – even babies!

I saved the newspaper time by writing the story for them. This meant all the information was detailed and accurate.

This story gave the leisure centre a lot of publicity and, what's more, it was free.

Questions

- How would the leisure centre have benefited from this press release?
- Why do you think it is important to build up good working relationships with the local media?

Personal selling

Personal selling involves face-to-face communication, with the seller trying to persuade the customer to buy the product. It also includes giving out information about a facility. This is the job of receptionists in leisure centres and tourist information offices.

Obviously the most important aspect of selling is actually to *make a sale* – selling a holiday, selling club membership or sports equipment. It is the selling of products which keeps organisations in business as income is generated, costs are covered and profits are made.

It is quite likely that your first job in the leisure and tourism industry will include selling. How you inform customers about your products and services and how they match your customers' needs will determine your success as a salesperson.

One of the first tasks of the salesperson is to find the target market to sell the goods to and to match the product to the target market. For example:

- a businesswoman may need to fly to New York and return as soon as possible; answer – a flight on Concorde

- a family wants to be able to access information for their children's homework and keep in constant contact with friends; answer – a personal computer with Internet and e-mail facilities.

The salesperson's main aim is to sell the product, whether this is a holiday or a pair of training shoes, and also to search for new clients and offer after-sales back-up.

The advantage of personal selling to the organisation is that the salesperson can adopt the sales presentation to suit the individual. The salesperson can show an in-depth knowledge of the product and can therefore answer any queries immediately. The one disadvantage of personal selling is the high cost attached to selecting, training and operating a sales force.

Displays

If ever you go to a trade fair or exhibition you will see displays set up by organisations aimed at promoting their products and services. A member of staff will be on hand at the display to answer any queries that potential customers may have and to give out promotional materials, such as pens, keyrings, T-shirts and carrier bags.

The displays which attract most interest from passing customers are the ones which have incentives to attract people to stop and look. Free food and drink may be on offer or even the chance to win a prize in a competition.

'Hands-on' displays which entice people to 'have a go', for example test a computer or ride an exercise bike, are often the most successful.

If you ever have to help with a display at an exhibition you will find that customers come in three types: customers, potential customers and time wasters. The crucial issue is to identify prospective customers and lead them towards a sale, rather than spending time with those who are 'time wasters'. Customers mainly come for something new: new ideas, new products, new services. They like to collect information. Customers walk past a display in about three to six seconds and stay at a major exhibition on average for four hours.

Customers are attracted by noise, music, crowds and demonstrations.

It is worth noting the following points when working at a trade fair or exhibition. Staff:

- must be open, warm and welcoming

Trade fairs are used to promote many different products and services

- should not cluster in a group talking to each other

- should not pounce on customers – or ignore them

- should have a product working or at least something to attract passers-by.

When in the conversation with customers, remember to:

- smile. Approach customers and open the conversation. Ask open questions

- show interest and listen. Make customers feel important

- find out what they want and provide it if possible

- record details so you can follow up later

- follow up fast.

A display should be colourful, attractive and different from all the hundreds of other displays. Staff need to be friendly, knowledgeable and informative. A recent travel trade exhibition in Manchester had over five hundred displays. Some examples included the following:

Display	Incentive
The Scottish Highlands	A free glass of whisky
Melton Mowbray	Free pork pie
The Bahamas	Chance to win two-week holiday
Blackpool Pleasure Beach	Free tickets to ride on 'The Big One'
'Sunny Scarborough'	Free stick of rock

Try it out

In your group, think of a holiday destination and design a display which would be so eye catching that people would be attracted to it straightaway.

Sponsorship

Sponsorship is a way of getting the organisation's name known to the public.

Organisations will sponsor teams or events by providing them with financial assistance. In return, sponsors expect to receive lots of good publicity and increased sales. For example:

- Vodafone sponsors Manchester United
- Going Places sponsors *Blind Date*
- Carling sponsors the Premiership.

Most football teams, both local and national, have sponsors. A walk to the local park on a Sunday morning will reveal teams with sponsors' names on their shirts. Many are even sponsored by the local pub, which makes a lot of sense to the landlord who will reap the benefit of 'his' team either drowning their sorrows or toasting their victory in his pub.

Probably the best known sponsorship on television is by Cadbury's confectionary which sponsors *Coronation Street*. The company aims to make its chocolate 'The nation's favourite' just as *Coronation Street* is the nation's favourite 'soap'.

The advantages of sponsorship are that it:

- leads to increased recognition of the sponsor through advertising, for example on football shirts

- promotes a favourable image, especially if an organisation is sponsoring a good cause, for example raising funds for the local hospital

- gains prestige for sponsoring a well-known event, for example the Embassy World Snooker Championship or the AXA FA Cup

Some sports have found it difficult to gain sponsorship if they are not popular enough, especially for television, for example canoeing, or if they have a poor image, for example boxing.

Talk about it

Think of two examples of local and national sponsorship.

Demonstrations

These enable customers to see:

- what a product can do
- how it can benefit them.

Watching a demonstration can also tempt customers to buy the product.

SNAPSHOTS

Computerised till demonstration

Imagine you are the manager of a leisure centre and you want to buy a 'state of the art' computerised till for your centre. A demonstration would show you:

1 *how all receipts issued should reconcile with takings*

2 *bookings for each activity on a daily, weekly and monthly basis*

3 *trends in usage.*

Staff who use the till could also be involved in watching a demonstration, as their questions could be answered and they would feel part of the decision-making process. This is good for employee relations.

SNAPSHOTS

Carpet cleaner demonstration

Imagine you are the manager of the local theatre and you have £1000 to spend on a top-of-the-range industrial carpet cleaner which is what your theatre needs.

A demonstration of the vacuum cleaner by the salesperson would show its speed, effectiveness and power on your carpets. The results could be seen instantly. (Would you be persuaded to buy it straightaway?)

Every demonstration should be clear, simple and informative. The benefits of the product to the customer should be stressed throughout the demonstration.

Talk about it

Imagine you are a salesperson and you have to demonstrate a product to a group of customers. In pairs, decide what product you could demonstrate and be prepared to give your demonstration to the rest of the group.

Sales promotions

The leisure and tourism industry is extremely competitive. Every organisation does its utmost to get business. Sales promotions make an offer of a feature in a specific time limit. They are always aimed at their target market; for example, the target market for a sales promotion of 'two meals for the price of one' would be families. A daytime 'gym and swim' offer would be aimed at those who are at home during the daytime.

Examples of sales promotions might include:

- one child goes free if the holiday is booked before the end of September

- buy one meal, get one free – this week

- stay three nights for the price of two this weekend only

- no charge for cars with four paying passengers on all ferry crossings this month.

Talk about it

As you can see, sales promotions last only for a limited time. Why do you think this is?

Here are some more examples of sales promotions or incentives which can be offered to customers:

- taster sessions – try out our health suite for free

- coupons – money-off vouchers in newspapers for entry to theme parks, or coupons for discounted meals

- competitions – enter our prize draw and win a holiday

- special offers – beer 99p a pint this week

- free gifts – free T-shirt when you spend over £30

- loyalty incentive – Air Miles when buying a product, loyalty points when shopping at the supermarket.

The *advantages* and uses of sales promotions include the following:

- to exploit special opportunities, for example supporting an advertising campaign

- to motivate staff – this has to be short term or it loses its effectiveness

- where brand loyalty is low

- there is a direct response which can be evaluated.

In pairs, find some examples of sales promotions. They do not all necessarily have to be connected with the leisure and tourism industry.

Promotional techniques and target markets

Promotional techniques such as advertising and direct mail have to be targeted at specific market segments if they are to be successful and therefore effective.

For example, the following factors need to be taken into account when promoting holidays:

1   Who is the target market?

2   What appeals to them?

3   What do they read?

4   What do they think about price?

5   Where do they go?

An 18–30s holiday could be advertised in magazines such as *Hello* or *OK* which are often read by this age group. Posters could be located in travel agents and the London Underground.

The aim is to reach the target audience with a message which they all like and a product they cannot resist. A local leisure centre would advertise in local newspapers and place posters in the centre to promote a keep fit campaign, as financial resources would not stretch to television or radio advertising (and this would not be cost effective).

Talk about it

How could a local football club promote a summer soccer tournament?

How could a travel agent promote a four-week Caribbean cruise?

The effectiveness of promotional materials

Advertisements

Effective advertising arouses the interest of customers and can reach a large number of people. It is vital therefore that advertisements motivate customers to buy the product.

Advertisements attempt to persuade potential customers that there is something special about the products being advertised. They claim that the products cannot be matched by those of any other organisation. But an advertisement cannot stimulate sales unless it is read; therefore it must be seen and must grab your attention.

It is, of course, the attention and interest of the target market and not the world in general that the advertisement seeks to attract.

CASE STUDY – Andy

Andy is manager of a town centre hotel and one of his responsibilities is to advertise the hotel's facilities. He uses a set format when creating his advertisements by asking himself the following questions:

• What do I want the advertisement to say to people and who am I aiming it at?

• Where's the best place to advertise?

• How much will it cost?

• How should I design it – catchy headline, benefits, action to be taken – AIDA (see below)?

• What illustrations should I use?

Activity

Based on the format used by Andy, design an advertisement for the hotel's restaurant.

Advertising agencies usually prepare advertisements for larger organisations. A team of creative writers put the advertisement together, which the organisation then approves. Smaller organisations prepare their own advertisements (in order to save costs). They are more likely to advertise in local newspapers whereas larger organisations would advertise on television and radio.

Any good advertisement should use the AIDA formula:

◇ Create **Attention.**

◇ Promote an **Interest.**

◇ Motivate the customer to **Desire** the product.

◇ Enable the customer to take **Action**.

(Reproduced with kind permission from The American Adventure)

Would you consider this to be a good ad? Why?

A good advertisement will attract attention, arouse interest, create desire and make it easy to take any necessary action to buy the product.

 Try it out Find two advertisements in your local newspaper and show how they use the AIDA formula.

Creating your own publicity

1 White space
Look at a page of advertisements in a newspaper. Notice how a large advertisement with a lot of white space stands out from the rest.

It is a brave decision to produce an advertisement with a lot of white space because you are paying for the space and not giving into the temptation to fill it with information. But when used properly, this type of advertisement is eye-catching.

2 Border
A border can make an advertisement stand out and seem important. Like a frame round a picture, it can make what is inside look really good.

3 Colour
Spot colour in a newspaper draws attention to an advertisement, especially if it is the only one with spot colour on that page. Evidence suggests that full colour advertisements in magazines attract twice the readership of black and white.

4 Illustration
This is an effective way of getting the reader's attention and interest. Illustrations say things quicker than words and more vividly too. Don't forget – seeing leads to believing.

The best illustration of all is the one which shows that the product or service is being happily used. Happy customers and smiling faces are a powerful way to get the message across. This is especially true if you can use a 'before' and 'after' illustration, demonstrating the benefits of the product.

5 Headline
You must try to grab the reader's attention and arouse interest. The most important headline words are YOU, FREE and NEW. For example:

◇ Instant hot drinks from new 'Supervend' will save you time and money
◇ A quiet word to the hard of hearing
◇ How little need you pay for a restful night?

These advertisements mention the target customer, promise benefits and arouse curiosity.

Try it out

In pairs, design an advertisement for a product which will grab the readers' attention and act as an incentive for them to buy it.

Try it out

Go into a travel agent for a holiday brochure. Make some notes about what you think of it as a piece of promotional material. How did you choose that particular brochure?

There are two types of advertisements that can be placed in newspapers. These are display ads and classified ads.

Display ads are usually placed among news stories so they stand out and get noticed. They are generally bigger and more expensive than classified advertisements. They use headlines and logos to catch the reader's attention.

Classified ads consist normally of only a few lines of copy listed under category headings. They are an essential form of advertising for newspapers as they generate a lot of income. Publications like *Exchange and Mart* are full of classified ads and do not carry any news stories.

Try it out

Find an example of each of the above types of advertisement. List the advantages and disadvantages of each.

Brochures and leaflets

A good brochure should convert an enquiry into a sale. It must therefore be informative, interesting and persuasive.

Brochures come in different shapes and sizes although most are in colour. A tour operator's summer brochure shows the product – the holiday destination – in a tangible form in that it shows golden sands, deep blue sea, magnificent scenery and happy holidaymakers. Brochures are displayed on the shelves at travel agents and tourist information centres and because there are so many only the most eye-catching ones will stand out from the rest of the crowd.

Using direct mail, brochures can be sent directly to customers, so making it easier for them to take their time and choose what they want.

Leaflets are not as expensive as brochures to produce. They are less bulky than brochures and are usually in single A4 or A5 format. They advertise things like keep fit sessions at the local fitness centre or give details of forthcoming events, for example a riverside water festival.

Large organisations tend to produce leaflets which have been designed by a graphic designer. They are usually printed in colour on good quality paper with pictures or illustrations to make them stand out. However, smaller organisations do not have large advertising budgets. Their leaflets are usually word-processed and printed in one or perhaps two colours at the local printers. But their content (the copy) can still make them effective.

Posters

Posters are seen on billboards, at stadia, on buses and at bus stops. If they catch your attention and you have time to read them they can carry a very effective message which can stay in your mind. This is especially true if there is an image or photograph on the poster – *every picture tells a story.*

A shop window is an ideal location for posters and you have only to look at a travel agent's window to see some examples. Black lettering on a yellow background is an effective format for a poster. Look at a travel agent's window next time you are in town and see the type of posters they use.

One poster campaign which proved to be a great success was the English Riviera posters of the 1986 and 1987 seasons which relied on artistic quality and which were widely displayed in London underground stations.

Posters are used as point-of-sale advertising (see below) within travel agents. However, good quality, full colour printing on large sheets can be expensive. It is also difficult to evaluate their effectiveness.

Source: English Riviera Tourist Board

These posters proved to be very successful

Point-of-sale material (POS)

This is an example of a sales promotion which takes place at the point of sale. It is an eye-catching display of the product, or information about the service, and is seen at the point at which the product is sold to customers. The point of sale is the actual place where products are sold, for example the counter in a shop or the reception in a leisure centre.

When customers arrive at the point of sale they are usually in a position to buy. If they do have doubts about products then there are special offers, promotions and discounts to tip the balance and make them part with their money.

Point-of-sale materials on display in shop windows entice the customer in to look further. Examples of point-of-sale materials include pens, key rings, flags, banners and stickers. This is when the assistant should take over and convert the interest into a sale.

Merchandising materials

Merchandising materials include T-shirts, mugs, calendars, bracelets, books and photographs. A Disney shop is a classic example where merchandising material is on full display; in this case associated with the Disney theme.

Football clubs sell merchandising materials which include diaries, photographs, shirts, pens, books and scarves. Manchester United Football Club generates more money on merchandising material than it does from its gate receipts.

Many tourist destinations and theme parks merchandise their own material because they know people want something to remember their visit by.

Talk about it

What do you think about the price of some of the merchandising materials some organisations charge? Give your reasons.

Videos

This type of promotional technique is relatively new and can be highly effective.

Travel agents can sometimes give clients a video about a destination they are interested in. This is an excellent selling tool as a video can give a powerful and lasting impression of a place. Disneyland uses videos to promote its facilities and holidays. Potential customers simply have to call a free telephone number to get their own free copy.

From the customer's point of view, it is worth remembering that videos only portray favourable images; they never show the bad side of things.

Press releases

Press releases include details of events or activities which can be forwarded to the media in advance of them happening. The main advantage of a press release is that, if published, it creates free publicity. A good press release will provide sufficient detail for a journalist to include in a newspaper without actually even having to attend the event.

If organisations can build up a good relationship with the media they may find that they are able to have their press releases published on a regular basis.

The other big advantage of a press release is that people are more likely to read it rather than an advertisement, which may have the same content but is written in a different format.

STARS TO DAZZLE IN AID OF CHARITY

A DRUMMER who supported many well-known bands in the sixties and seventies is among the many chart-topping acts who will be appearing at the forthcoming Fiesta in the Park, which will be held in Green Park, Westbridge.

Roger Sparkey and a number of other musicians, who have donated their time, will be joining masses of children from local schools throughout the county in an attempt to become the largest choir on record. A recording of the performance will be made with a percentage of the proceeds going to local charities. The organisers have agreed to donate £1 from every ticket to the causes.

Throughout his long career, Sparkey who was a member of the popular band, The Allstars, got to play with a wide range of world-famous stars.

The event, which features a large number of chart-topping acts, will take place on Sunday 10 September and is expected to attract huge crowds.

Mr James Smith, event coordinator, said: 'We are extremely delighted that Roger Sparkey has agreed to help us with this attempt in aid of such a worthwhile cause and we hope that this year's event will be even more successful than before.'

An example of a press release

How to write a press release

- Answer the questions like *who, what, where, when* and *why* in the opening paragraph.
- Don't make it longer than it needs to be.
- Submit it well before deadline dates.
- Put in a quotation from the contact person at the end.
- Give details of the contact person.
- Use double spacing – this allows for editing.
- Include a picture if it will help tell the story.

 Try it out Using the guidelines given, write a press release about a forthcoming event at your school/college.

Planning a promotional campaign

The many products and services available in the leisure and tourism industry need to be promoted in such a way that customers will be encouraged to buy them. For example:

- the local leisure centre wants to encourage more people to join a 'healthy lifestyle campaign' so it uses the local media to advertise it
- a national sportswear company wants to promote a new range in sweatshirts and so places advertisements on television and in national newspapers.

Objectives of a promotional campaign

Objectives are things you want to achieve. Any organisation, no matter how big or small, should have objectives. Objectives enable organisations to focus on what they want to achieve. The success of a promotional campaign can be judged on whether the objectives have been met (see Figure 2.14).

Objectives should be SMART:

- **Specific** – aimed at one area of operation
- **Measurable** – the effectiveness of the campaign can be assessed

Figure 2.14 The objectives of a promotional campaign

- **Achievable** – realistic enough to ensure objectives can be met
- **Realistic** – fit in with the aims of the organisation
- **Timed** – deadlines can be met.

Some examples of promotional campaign objectives could include the following:

- visitor attraction – attract 15,000 visitors per month over the next six months
- travel agent – sell ten summer holidays by the end of next week
- leisure centre – double the number of senior citizens using the indoor bowls centre next season
- theatre – reduce overtime by 10 per cent during July and August

CASE STUDY – The Palace Theatre: a promotional campaign

This 100-year-old variety theatre is owned by the local council and sponsored by a building society and a local newspaper. In 1974, the Palace Theatre was refitted, refurbished and re-opened after having fallen into a state of disrepair. Since then the theatre has flourished, offering a variety of entertainments to as wide an audience as possible.

June 2000 marked the one hundreth anniversary of the theatre opening and the manager planned a week-long celebration to mark the event.

The product

The week-long celebration was to include a play by local schoolchildren, guided tours, a theatre workshop, a pantomime, a concert by the local brass band and a special showing of the film *The Full Monty*, 'Voulez-Vous', a tribute to Abba and on the last night a music hall variety concert, with Jim Davidson as compère. This would be a grand finale, as the very first performance back in 1900 was a music hall variety show.

Planning for this campaign started a year before the anniversary.

Objectives

- To celebrate 100 years of the Palace Theatre
- To raise the awareness of the theatre both in the town and the surrounding area
- To get as much media coverage as posssible and therefore create a high profile
- To get the community involved

Marketing research

The manager went out into the community to ask for ideas about the centenary celebration. He did this through face-to-face interviews. He also rang up an old friend who managed a theatre 200 miles away, who had just put on a similar campaign. This could be seen as secondary marketing research.

Target markets

- Senior citizens who would enjoy a good night out
- Schoolchildren who would watch a pantomime
- Regular theatre-goers who would enjoy a backstage tour
- Film fans who would like to see *The Full Monty.*

Promotional methods

- Advertising – paid advertising placed in the local newspapers
- Publicity – a press release written by the manager and interviews on local radio
- Sponsorship – local companies would be invited to sponsor individual performances
- Direct mail – to existing customers, details of whom could have been obtained from the customer database
- Posters and leaflets around the town

Type of media

- Local radio and television
- Point of sale in the theatre foyer
- Direct mail – leaflets
- Local newspapers – advertising publicity

Question

Can you think of any other areas that the manager might have covered?

- health and fitness centre – increase club membership by one-third between now and the end of the year.

It is worth taking a more detailed look at the objectives of a promotional campaign.

Raising awareness

Customers will not buy an organisation's products or services if they are not aware of them. Attracting the attention of customers is an essential first step in communicating with them.

Informing customers

Promotional campaigns involve sending messages to potential customers about the product or service the organisation provides.

Holiday destinations, accommodation, discount prices and new facilities like a restaurant can all be promoted. Leaflets and brochures could be used for this type of promotion where a lot of information is being given out.

The type of media used to inform customers will depend upon the size of the market and the target market the organisation is informing.

Making people buy the product and improving sales

Promotional campaigns are aimed at motivating customers to take action and buy the product,

which will lead to increased sales and greater use of the facility.

Selling, sales promotions and displays are aimed at getting customers to take some form of action, for example visiting a theme park or buying a holiday.

Promotional campaigns use advertising to increase sales. Good advertisements, as we have already seen, should grab the reader's attention (AIDA) and motivate people to buy the product.

Sales can be increased through the use of promotions like buying two for one, offering free gifts and reduced prices. Direct mail and personal selling do the same job.

Improving the image

Leisure and tourism organisations try to promote a good image to their users and the public in general, in the hope that people will continue to buy their products and use their facilities. This can be achieved by:

- improving the products and services
- creating an up-to-date impression
- reaching out to a new target market.

Facilities sometimes suffer from bad publicity. A promotional campaign could attempt to put that right (see case study below).

CASE STUDY — Chemical leak

A swimming pool had a chemical leakage and had to be evacuated. Fortunately no one was injured and there was no negligence on the part of the pool. But in the eyes of the public, the pool was classed as being unsafe so the damage had been done.

The manager invited the press to watch him take his two young daughters to be the first people to take the plunge in the pool once the leak had been repaired. This was done in the hope that it would show the public the pool was perfectly safe to swim in. He also organised a public meeting where people could voice their concerns over the incident. At the meeting the manager was totally open and honest with the public and gave a full and frank explanation of what had happened. He slowly rebuilt the confidence and trust of his customers. Rebuilding the image of the pool was a long and difficult task which had to be done carefully and honestly.

Questions

- What would have happened if action hadn't been taken after the chemical leak incident?

- Why do you think it is always better to be honest and give the full facts, like the manager did?

Attracting new customers

Examples of this could include the following:

- A new leisure centre is about to open next week. New customers will be attracted to the facility by advertising in newspapers, direct mailing of leaflets and writing press releases.

- Imagine a pub has just opened a bistro. Why not offer two meals for the price of one between 12 noon and 2.00 pm for the first month? Better still, invite the press for a free meal which they can then write about in the local paper.

- A theatre has recently undergone a major refurbishment programme which has brought it into the twenty-first century. New plays, new concerts and up-to-date films will create a new image to attract new customers.

Maintaining existing customers

Customers who enjoy using a facility are likely to return on a regular basis and stay loyal to it. They also usually tell their friends about how good it is. Customer loyalty should be rewarded. Why not introduce a system whereby regular customers receive discounts? A loyal customer base is essential. Don't let them go to your competitors.

Identifying target markets

Marketing research helps to define what group of people (the target market) the promotional campaign should be aimed at. It will also help organisations decide what type of promotion is best for the product or service by using research techniques such as:

- observation – who is using the facility?

- questioning – why do you use this facility?

This helps organisations to decide the right mix of promotional techniques to use. As we found out earlier, this is known as primary or field research. Secondary or desk research, for example in libraries, can tell us how people spend their leisure time, and how much disposable income different groups have to spend on their leisure activities. There is even information available on the best types of media to use to target different market segments.

The objectives of a marketing campaign should therefore state what market the organisation wants to target. This can save money and ensure an effective response and a successful outcome.

Techniques to use in promotional campaigns

The big question organisations have to ask themselves when they are about to embark on a promotional campaign is: how do we get the message across to our target market?

Advertising is an excellent way of creating awareness and interest in a product. However, it does not always get people to act or buy the product, so it is advisable that promotional campaigns use two or more techniques to get the message across.

Table 2.7 shows some of the advantages and disadvantages of different promotional techniques.

Promotional materials used in marketing campaigns

No matter how much money is invested in promotional materials, it will be wasted if it is not used effectively. Selecting the right media for the campaign is essential for success. The choice of media is wide, ranging from television and radio advertising to magazines, posters and point-of-sale material.

The type of media used depends on the objectives of the campaign, the target market the organisation is trying to reach and what it can afford. For example, a tour operator may decide to promote a new holiday destination, so one

objective of its promotional campaign would be to attract as many people as possible across the country. The most suitable media for such a campaign would be television and national newspapers and magazines. A local theatre may want to increase attendances for its Tuesday and Wednesday film evenings as its main objective. In this case, advertisements in the local press and the use of direct mail or leaflets would be suitable.

There are different ways a message can be put across to customers. Where movement and sound are considered to be necessary in adding impact to the message, television, radio and video (for example Disneyland) would be the most appropriate media. Messages delivered using printed materials such as leaflets, brochures and advertisements in newspapers, can also be very effective.

If these messages are sent via direct mail they can provide a lot of information over longer periods of time, for example theatres sending their 'What's on' brochures to their regular customers to attract advance bookings.

Monitoring and evaluating the success of a promotional campaign

Two of the most common reasons for monitoring and evaluating promotional campaigns are to show that money has been well spent and that the promotional campaign has contributed to sales.

Table 2.7 Advantages and disadvantages of different promotional techniques

	Advantages	Disadvantages
Advertising	Reaches a large audience	Can be expensive
	Stimulates interest	May not be seen/heard
	Targets the market	Also hits people not interested in the message
Publicity e.g. press release	Increases awareness	May not hit target audience
	Presents good image	May not be read/heard
Sales promotion	Rapid increase in sales	Short term
	Moves slow items or times (e.g. off-peak usage)	Provides little information
Personal selling	Increases sales	Expensive
	Good for targeting customers	Limited target audience
	Interactive and responsive	Takes a long time to cover a large audience

Promotional campaigns aim to increase sales. This is done by motivating people to buy products or services, attracting new customers and retaining existing customers. Monitoring can take place by checking the till rolls (to see how much income has been generated), counting visitors on an electronic counter or seeing how many rooms have been booked in a hotel.

Evaluation is the final stage of a promotional campaign. Evaluation enables an organisation to assess the success, or otherwise, of the marketing campaign. Questions to ask as part of an evaluation include:

- Did we meet our objectives?
- Will the campaign increase business?
- Was it all worth it? Did we make a profit?
- Did we improve our image?

Evaluation should not be just gut feeling and guesswork. There are several methods which can be used for evaluating a campaign:

- Face-to-face interviews by market researchers could ask for people's views on the products recently advertised.
- Existing customers could also be asked face to face or they could be sent questionnaires to complete as their names and addresses would be on the database.
- Sales of the products or services could be analysed before and after the campaigns. This could be done quite early by checking the till roll and comparing the income before and after the campaign.
- A sports centre would be able to count the new members joining up after the campaign.
- Staff could ask people in a friendly and informal way how they thought the campaign had gone. Comments and suggestions could be invited.

A promotional campaign is usually a team effort. Individuals within the team could evaluate their own performance and the overall team performance could then be evaluated.

Self-evaluation questions might be:

- Did I do what I was supposed to do?
- Could I have improved my performance?
- How might I do it differently next time?

A **team evaluation** will also be useful. It can be a good idea to hold a team meeting based on the premise that all comments will be constructive, no one will be criticised or blamed for anything and everyone will come out of the meeting having learned from the experience and be ready to improve and build upon a future promotional campaign.

Marketing: a summary

- Marketing involves finding out what people want and then providing it for them.
- Marketing research helps to find out what the customer wants and answers the question, 'Who will be the typical customer for this product?'
- Target marketing matches the right product to the right customer.
- A market segment consists of people with similar characteristics and likes.
- The marketing mix, or the 4 Ps, enables the right product to reach the right customer at the right price.
- There are many ways of advertising and promoting products and services. The trick is to choose the one which is the most cost effective.
- A good promotional campaign should raise interest in a product and increase sales.

UNIT 2 ASSESSMENT

Unit 2 Assessment

Although this unit is externally assessed, the following assessment and the 'check it out' questions will help to provide you with the necessary knowledge.

To market, to market

Scenario

Your organisation has just been presented with a cheque for £1000 for winning a prestigious marketing award. As Marketing Officer you have every right to be proud of this achievement because you did all the work for it. What's more, your boss is equally delighted. Never wanting to miss out on an opportunity for gaining publicity, she has asked you to write an article for a national marketing journal stating exactly how you went about marketing your organisation.

What you have to do
Obtaining a pass grade
Task 1

Choose a leisure and tourism organisation in your area, preferably one with which you are familiar. You have to produce a report that:

- includes a description of the products and services it offers

- gives details of the pricing of the products and services, mentioning discounts, special offers, sales promotions, etc.

- describes the methods of distribution and the outlets used to get the products and services to the customer

- describes the following promotional techniques: advertising, direct marketing, public relations, personal selling, displays, sponsorship, demonstrations, sales promotions

- describes the following methods of research: postal surveys, telephone questionnaires, personal surveys, observation

- describes the market segments the organisation targets.

Task 2

Produce a leaflet which promotes the facilities, products and services of the organisation. Be original; produce your own leaflet, not a copy of an existing one.

Your work must show a basic understanding of marketing by using some technical language correctly. Your promotional leaflet must provide information in a way that is suitable for the target market.

Obtaining a merit or distinction grade

To obtain a merit or distinction grade your work must show how you can analyse relevant information to give an accurate account of the marketing activities of the leisure and tourism organisation you have chosen. Try to make your leaflet imaginative, accurately presented and appropriate for the target audience.

Obtaining a distinction grade

In order to obtain a distinction your work must show that you can analyse relevant information to produce a detailed and accurate account of the marketing activities of your chosen organisation.

Your work must also show how you would evaluate the success of the organisation's promotional techniques and materials.

Finally, you must say how successful you think the organisation's promotional techniques and materials have been.

Key skills available

Communication: C2,1A, C2,1B
IT 2.2, 2.3

Improving own learning and performance:
LP2.1

Resources

Examples of promotional materials can be obtained by writing to a variety of leisure and tourism organisations or visiting local ones.

Visits to the British Travel Trade Show or the Recreation Management Exhibition will provide opportunities to collect a variety of promotional leaflets from different sections of the industry.

Unit 2 Test

1   A theatre produces a brochure showing forthcoming events. What is the main marketing reason for doing this?

2   The use of television advertising is an example of what part of the marketing mix?

3   A restaurant is offering 'two meals for the price of one' between 5 pm and 7 pm, Monday to Friday. What type of marketing activity is this?

4   A city hotel uses its customer database to send out a mailshot giving information about weekend breaks. What type of promotional activity is this?

5   A restaurant in York is promoting a range of midweek lunches. What market segments are being targeted?

6   A coach operator is planning to offer tours to the Women's Institute. This is market segmentation by what?

7   Which market segment is most likely to be targeted by a travel agent offering holidays that include parties, barbecues and fun?

8   How might a café encourage local college students to use it?

9   A sports centre offers reduced prices for day-time use of its facilities. Which group is most likely to benefit from this scheme?

10   Following the staging of a riverside festival, the organising committee meet to discuss how successful the event has been. What part of the promotional campaign is this?

11   A leisure centre runs an open day which includes free swims for children. How will the centre benefit from this promotion?

12   A theatre has run a promotional campaign in the local newspaper with discount vouchers. How could this promotion be evaluated?

13   How could a local museum promote a forthcoming exhibition?

14   A major theme park has run an advertising campaign on television. How could the success of this campaign be evaluated?

15   What part of a promotional campaign involves a group of people meeting to discuss ideas?

UNIT 2 ASSESSMENT

Investigating customer service

This unit explains why customer service is so important in leisure and tourism. The unit is written in five sections. You will learn about:

- *different types of customers and their varying needs*
- *the customer service provided to both external and internal customers and the benefits of excellent customer service*
- *the importance of personal presentation*
- *dealing with customers and handling complaints*
- *keeping accurate customer records.*

What you need to produce

You need to produce evidence which shows your understanding of customer service in leisure and tourism. This includes a review of the customer service provided by a leisure and tourism organisation and a record of your involvement in a variety of real or simulated customer service situations.

This unit is assessed through your portfolio work only. The grade awarded will be the grade for the unit.

What is customer service?

Before working through the different sections of this unit, we will look at the overall concept of customers and customer service.

Customer service is all about looking after customers so well that they want to return: *customers come first.*

Leisure and tourism organisations cannot survive without customers. Giving excellent customer service plays an important part in helping organisations to keep their customers and attract new ones. Once you have got customers, you have to look after them. Why? *Because unhappy customers don't come back.*

If customers are upset by poor service, for example from a grumpy receptionist, or poor facilities, like dirty toilets, they will take their custom elsewhere. And where will they go? *To your nearest competitor.*

Try it out

Think of a time when you have experienced poor customer service. It may have been on holiday, in a restaurant, in a shop or in a club. Use the following headings to help you make notes on your experience.

- What was the organisation?
- How were you greeted?
- How do you think you were regarded by the person dealing with you?
- How do you feel you were treated?
- What do you think of the organisation?

Talk about it

Working in your group, work out what you think gives an organisation a bad name.

Leisure and tourism is a **service** industry. Whether you become a flight attendant or a sports centre supervisor, a waitress or a holiday 'rep' you will have to deal with customers.

Some may ask you questions, 'How far is it to the beach?'.

Some may not feel well, 'I think I've had too much to drink'.

Some may not be very nice, 'I'm sick and tired of this hotel, I want my money back'.

Some may even say, 'Thanks very much; you've been very helpful'.

In other words, dealing with customers can be very hard work. So when you've been on your feet all day, you are hungry and you want to go home, you must still treat every customer as if they were your first. Whatever happens, *don't* use the following phrases:

- 'Oh yes, everybody complains about that'
- 'Ah well, you can't believe everything the sales department tells you'
- 'Sorry, it's nothing to do with me'
- 'I can't help you with that. Besides, I'm on my coffee break'.

Instead you need to say:

- 'I'll take care of that for you right away'
- 'Is there anything else I can help you with?'

Think it over — Can you think of any other words and phrases to use which show good customer service?

Good customer service

Examples of good customer service might include:

- at a supermarket checkout, the cashier helps you to pack your bags
- in a fish and chip shop, not only do they provide a plastic bag, but they also put the fish and chips into it for all the customers.

SNAPSHOTS

Zoe

Zoe went into town with a friend and her friend's mum to have her belly button pierced. She had the money, she had plucked up the courage and she had even chosen the bar.

Before the girl doing the piercing got started, she asked if anyone had any last questions. Zoe's friend's mum, Linda, said,

'Zoe is going to Majorca in two weeks' time. Does that matter?'

The assistant then advised Zoe not to have it done until she returned from holiday, as there was a chance of infection either from swimming pool water or sand.

This was sound, honest advice and an example of good customer service. It would have been easy for the assistant to go ahead and do the piercing and collect the fee. Instead she was caring for the customer.

Did you know?

Your customer care skills will keep your customers happy. Happy customers not only bring their custom back, they also bring their friends.

Ten rules of customer service

1. The customer is always right.
2. Never underestimate the importance of good customer service.
3. Always be positive and enthusiastic.
4. Communication must be open and honest.
5. A customer is satisfied when his or her needs have been met in a friendly and professional manner.
6. Customers who receive consistently good and friendly service stay loyal.
7. Each customer should be treated as an individual.
8. Every member of staff is responsible for effective customer service.
9. As a customer you should expect and demand good service.
10. All customers are different and all customers are special.

Caring for customers

Is it caring **for** customers or caring **about** them? It is both and all staff play an important part in providing good customer service, even if they don't all come into contact with customers. For example, the person washing the dishes in a restaurant might never meet the customers face to face. The cleaner in a travel agency never meets the clients. The housekeeper doesn't usually see the hotel guests. But all these staff play a vital part in making sure the customer is satisfied with both the product and the service. In all these cases the customers would not be happy if the dishes weren't sparkling clean, if the toilets were dirty and if the beds weren't made properly. When staff don't meet customers it is called *indirect contact*.

Try it out

Can you think of other examples of indirect contact?

Now give some examples of where staff come into *direct contact* with customers, e.g. a hotel receptionist greeting guests. List your examples and discuss them with the rest of the group.

When you work in leisure and tourism you should try to put yourself in your customers' shoes. Think about how you like to be treated, how annoying it is to be ignored, how good it feels to be made to feel important.

Different types of customer

Leisure and tourism facilities are used by people of all ages, types and nationalities, including those with specific needs, such as disabled visitors and people with young children. To provide excellent customer service, you will need to identify and meet the needs of a variety of customers, for example:

- individuals
- groups
- people of different ages
- people from different cultures

- non-English speakers
- people with specific needs, such as people needing wheelchair access or those with young children
- business men and women.

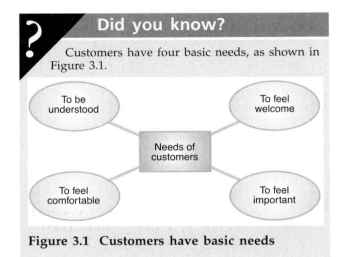

Did you know?

Customers have four basic needs, as shown in Figure 3.1.

Figure 3.1 Customers have basic needs

Establishing the different needs of different customers can be quite a complex task as it is not possible to ask each and every customer what his or her needs are. So organisations often use some of the following methods to try to establish customer needs:

- direct discussion with customers
- feedback from staff
- analysis of customer complaints and comments
- market research (as discussed in unit 2)
- questionaires – written, phoned or personal interviews
- user group discussions.

We shall now look at some different types of customer.

Individuals

Dealing with people on a one-to-one basis means you can give them your full attention, thus enabling you to find out their needs. For example:

- in a hotel, you may find out that a businessperson wants the *Financial Times* newspaper left outside the bedroom door every morning

- working as a flight attendant you may find out that one of the passengers is a vegetarian

- a first-time user of the gym may need advice about how to use the equipment and what training programme to follow.

Talk about it

In pairs, think of other examples of individuals using leisure and tourism facilities and identify their needs. Discuss your answers with the rest of the group.

Customer service in practice

This is what some people working in the leisure and tourism industry have to say about customer service:

'Making it our responsibility to give individual paying customers a quality leisure service – it's not just a top management job, we all need to do it' *Theme park supervisor*

'Providing each customer with customer satisfaction – giving them a level of service that satisfies their leisure needs in every way' *Sports Centre manager*

'Making customer satisfaction our most important sale. Yes, we are actually selling enjoyment not just holidays' *Travel consultant*

'Viewing every guest as a valued customer and treating them all in a very special way' *Hotel manager*.

Groups

Think about a holiday representative talking to a group of holidaymakers on their first morning at their resort. The group might be made up of families, young couples, senior citizens and people holidaying alone. Although the holiday representative may look on these guests as a group, he or she must also remember that the group is made up of people who should be treated as individuals.

It can be daunting to stand up and talk to a group, although some people make it look easy: a tour guide speaking to visitors from overseas, a

CASE STUDY – Sally

Sally is a leisure centre receptionist. She gets a great deal of job satisfaction by helping the centre users.

Sometimes Sally is approached by people who have just moved into the area asking about the activities that go on in the centre. Today, Kay has come into the leisure centre to look around. The conversation goes something like this:

Sally: Good evening, how can we help you?

Kay: I'm new to the area so I'd like to look around.

Sally: That's fine. What sorts of activities do you like doing?

Kay: Squash, badminton and a bit of keep-fit.

Sally: How often do you take part in these activities?

Kay: About three times a week, but I am just a beginner.

Sally: We have lots of sports courses and keep-fit sessions. Why don't you have a look around the centre then I can tell you about our family membership scheme?

Kay: Thank you. I'll be back soon.

Question

What customer service qualities has Sally shown which may encourage Kay to become a member?

Different groups have different needs:

- **holidaymakers**

Information about attractions, entertainments, restaurants, shops, foreign exchange, excursions

- **families on holiday**

Activities for children, baby-sitting service, crèche, restaurants and pubs which will accept families

- **conference delegates**

Four-star hotel, access to fax machines, computers, photocopiers and meeting rooms.

Try it out

Match the group with the needs below.

Group	Needs
Senior citizens' day trip to Blackpool	Stopping off points for refreshments, early arrival at ground, location of pubs, safe journey back
Club 18–30 holidaymakers	A tour guide who can speak their language, lots of tourist attractions, opportunities to take photos and buy souvenirs
Foreign visitors on a tour of London	Lots of parties, great nightlife, sea, sun and fun
Children's birthday party	Interesting lessons, day trips, guest speakers, friendly tutors, relevant assignments, new friends
A coachload of football supporters	An entertainer (magician), bouncy castle, crisps, sandwiches, balloons, games, prizes, fun
Leisure and tourism students	Lots of toilet stops, friendly driver who tells jokes, Jim Reeves on tape, fish and chips, and a good old sing song.

sports coach talking to a class of children or a businessman talking to conference delegates. You need to prepare your talk well beforehand, make your voice sound interesting and look around the group to make sure they are all listening. It takes practice, and then more practice. But once you have acquired the skill, you never lose it.

CASE STUDY – Maria

Maria is a holiday representative for Pastime holidays, a tour operator which specialises in all-inclusive package holidays for retired people.

She says, 'We offer a wider range of holidays to cater for different people with different needs. Some of our clients want a totally relaxing time spent in the warmth of a country like Portugal. They like to take things very easy and may go out only occasionally on one of our sightseeing excursions.

'Other groups may want a more active time so we organise bowls competitions, lessons in a foreign language and sightseeing trips, which include stopping off at souvenir shops and places of interest. These activities suit the

more energetic over-50s. In fact I sometimes have trouble keeping up with them!

'We have to make sure that the hotels have lifts, few outside steps and a nearby beach. This ensures that less mobile guests can still enjoy their holiday. It's a demanding job because you are constantly bombarded with questions like, "Is there any ballroom dancing in this area?" or "Where can I buy a stamp?". I find our over-50s groups great fun, they're always ready for a laugh.'

Question

What other sort of activities could be provided for these groups when they are on holiday?

CASE STUDY — Brendan

Brendan is a courier with a tour operator which specialises in safaris to Kenya. The holidays are in the luxury price bracket and Brendan's company offers camping expeditions with a courier or a stay in one of the luxury game lodges established by the government in Kenya's National Parks.

Brendan says, 'My guests are usually young couples with no children or older couples whose children have grown up and are no longer living at home. In other words, these are people with sufficient disposable income for them to afford an adventure holiday with a touch of luxury added.

'I take groups of people into the natural parks where they want to get close-up camera shots of the wildlife, particularly the big game animals. After a hard day in the bush, my guests dress for their four-course dinner in the hotel's five-star restaurant. The believe they deserve a spot of luxury on holiday.'

Question

What sort of occupations do you think these people might have?

People of different ages

Customers have different needs and groups of customers are often made up of different age groups; for example, grandparents, mum and dad and three children. This complicates matters slightly as they all have different needs: granddad and grandma want to relax by the pool, mum and dad want to go down to the beach, while Ravi, Sanjit and Hira want to join the other children in the organised games.

Figure 3.2 shows how customers can be classified by different ages.

Talk about it

Into what sort of age groups might you classify customers?

How is this helpful?

Try it out

You are the assistant manager of a leisure centre and you are responsible for programming activities. What sort of activities would you put on for:

- senior citizens
- under-fives with their parents
- teenagers aged between 17 and 19 years?

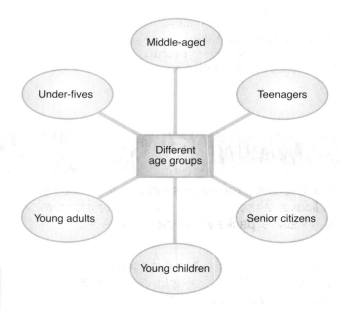

Figure 3.2 Customers can be grouped together by age

People from different cultures

Culture can be a difficult word to define. It relates to the character, history and traditions of people.

People from different cultural backgrounds have different needs. When you start your career in the leisure and tourism industry you will learn to respect the beliefs and traditions of people from different cultural backgrounds. It is useful to know the cultural background of customers so you can provide for their varied needs.

You may have experienced different cultures if you have been abroad on holiday. You may have found cultural differences which include diet, language, dress. For example, in Spain shops close at lunchtime because of the heat, so a siesta is taken during the afternoon. The nightlife may start at 11 pm and finish at 6 am. In Scandinavia, breakfast might be pickled herring and dark rye bread, while in France, breakfast often consists of a bowl of coffee and a croissant. In Australia, Christmas dinner could be a barbecue on the beach.

Talk about it

Can you think of some other examples which show cultural differences?

Share these as a group together.

Non-English-speaking customers

When working in the leisure and tourism industry, you may become involved in helping the many foreign visitors who come to Britain who do not speak English. This language barrier can be overcome in a number of ways:

- leaflets in different languages

- headphones and tapes in different languages may be provided, e.g. on a guided tour of a castle

- guides and translators who can speak the language of different visitors from overseas.

In order to communicate with non-English-speaking customers, remember:

- smile

- do not shout – they are not deaf

- speak slowly and clearly

- use maps to help with directions

Sometimes symbols can be used in place of written words

- use gestures

- be patient

- keep checking to see if they have understood

- if there is a real problem, see if you can find a translator.

Patience is the key word. Remember that you are providing a very valuable service to these customers. It is reassuring to them that they are dealing with someone who can help them.

Look it up

Many people in Britain expect everyone to speak English when they go abroad. But what about when foreign tourists come to Britain? Not everyone can speak English and why should they? You may come across these people during your career. To break down the language barrier a little bit, look up the following words and phrases, in French, Japanese and Spanish.

- 'Welcome, hello, goodbye, thank you.'
- 'Where is the railway station?'
- 'Could you direct me to the Post Office?'
- 'How much is this?'

Customers with specific needs

All customers have their own special needs and wants. Some customers have more specific needs and require extra understanding and sensitive treatment. These customers include people with disabilities, who usually like to be as independent as possible and to be treated in the same way as other people.

Remember that if customers with disabilities are accompanied by someone, you should not ignore the disabled person by directing all your attention to the helper.

An understanding of customers with disabilities is essential for all employees who come into direct contact with customers. Knowledge of the facilities which are available for people with disabilities would also be very useful. It is worth remembering that we should see customers as people with difficulties not difficult people. All customers should be greeted initially with a friendly welcome, regardless of their specific needs.

We will now consider some customers with particular needs.

Customers with restricted mobility

These range from people in wheelchairs to those suffering with stiff joints. Many buildings are equipped to deal with this by providing:

- lifts

- ramps

- wider car parking spaces

- car parking spaces near the entrance to the building.

Visually-impaired customers

When helping people who are visually impaired, consider the following tips:

- When guiding a blind person, ask how they would like you to guide them. Most prefer you to walk slightly ahead while they take your arm.

- Explain exactly what obstacles are ahead, e.g. a set of stairs going up.

- Try to avoid intrusive background noise, such as loud piped music – blind people rely far more on their hearing than sighted people.

SNAPSHOTS

Ahmed
'I once took a blind student up the Eiffel Tower. He asked me to describe the view overlooking Paris. This was quite a challenge since the student had been blind from birth. I found myself trying to describe colours, shapes and sizes. It was amazing – putting myself in his position. We had a wonderful time. He said he felt like he was on top of the world.'

Hearing-impaired customers

Consider these points when dealing with customers who have hearing difficulties:

- Face the customer on the same level, with your face to the light.

- Speak the words clearly.

- Do not shout, as it distorts the visual effect of words.

- Allow more time for customers to work out what you are saying.

Think it over

What sort of special facilities are provided in places like leisure centres, theatres and cinemas for people with disabilities?

Talk about it

Try this exercise which your tutor will organise. One person will be blindfolded and another has to lead that person round college and give all the necessary warnings of obstacles and explanations. This will give some idea of what it is like to be visually-impaired and is good practice for when you have to deal with this situation.

Other special needs

There are other customers as well who have special needs. These can include mothers with young children who may face a number of difficulties, such as always being on call for their children, financial constraints or a lack of confidence. These difficulties can be overcome by providing breastfeeding and crèche facilities, baby changing rooms and programming sports activities for families.

Another group with special needs is people who are unemployed. They may not be able to take

take advantage of our award winning Shopmobility scheme

Simply visit our dedicated Shopmobility desk on Market Street and complete an application form. You will receive one of our Membership cards, which will enable you to take advantage of the following:-

❖ Free wheelchair hire - available from the Market Street Customer Service Desk.*

❖ Free self drive scooter hire* - we have a number of electric scooters for hire free of charge. Demand is high and we cannot guarantee scooters.
   We do however operate a booking system just call 0845 600 6800.
      ❖ Nine toilets for the disabled.
         ❖ Over 350 parking spaces designated for the disabled.
            ❖ Accompanied shopping available on request (please call the Careline for full details).

❖ A special area set aside in the Coca-Cola Oasis with extra room for your ease and comfort.**

❖ A complimentary magnifier to use with all our Customer Services literature.

❖ Walking sticks and wheelchair cushions are also available on request (subject to availability).

❖ Members of the Customer Services team trained in sign language.

All areas of the Centre are fully accessible by wheelchair with four lifts to transport wheelchair users between floors.

* Two forms of identification are required (one with current address).
**Area only available before 11.30am and must be pre-booked by calling the Careline.

Care for the disabled

The Meadowhall Crèche has facilities for special needs children - places are limited and can be booked in advance by calling **0114 256 9313**.

For more information on Shopmobility, call the Careline on **0845 600 6800** - alternatively join the Shopmobility scheme by visiting the Customer Services Desk on Market Street (two forms of identification are required).

Toilets

Toilets and parent and baby changing facilities can be found at the following locations:

❖ Lower Oasis in the Lanes

❖ Lower Arcade

❖ Upper Park Lane entrance

❖ Market Street next to Massarellas

❖ Upper Oasis next to Rock Island Diner.

Disabled Facilities

Disabled facilities are also available at the following stores and restaurants:

❖ Boots

❖ Debenhams

❖ House of Fraser

❖ Burger King

❖ Pollards Tea and Coffee

❖ Bradwell's English Restaurant

❖ Mamma Amalfi

❖ Marks & Spencer

For further information call the Careline on 0845 600 6800

12.   13.

(Reproduced with kind permission from Meadowhall Centre, Sheffield)

Help for customers with special needs at the Meadowhall Centre, Sheffield

part in sports activities due to the lack of money, lack of adequate sports equipment and lack of confidence. The ways these customers may be encouraged to take part in sport and recreation activities include off-peak pricing, free use of equipment, and the provision of special sports sessions.

Business people

People on business, especially if they are staying away from home, use many of the facilities which we normally associate with holidaymakers.

SNAPSHOTS

Dwayne

Dwayne is the chief executive of an engineering firm. His business frequently takes him all over the country and sometimes abroad.

Dwayne says, 'A typical business trip would mean flying down to London, staying overnight and meeting clients. I usually stay in a hotel which has facilities to allow me to work, i.e. e-mail, fax, photocopier. I make sure there's a desk and chair in my room along with the other usual facilities. One thing I do need is a trouser press because looking smart is important when meeting clients.

'After I've completed my work in my room, I enjoy a nice meal in the hotel restaurant and a quiet drink in the bar. This sets me up for another busy day tomorrow.'

The increasing number of businesswomen need the same office-type facilities as men in hotels. Business travellers still appreciate the extra details and services that can be made available, such as a range of toiletries and magazines, flowers, fruit and water.

Good customer service is about detail. It's about getting lots of little things right. In other words: *detail makes the difference.*

Try it out

A businesswoman is staying in a big city hotel for a week. Write down the sort of service from the staff, and the kind of attention to detail she might expect over the five days.

Customer needs

Remember that the four basic needs of customers are to be understood, to feel welcome, to feel important and to feel comfortable.

More specifically, customers need:

- help
- advice
- information
- security
- safety
- the right product at the right time in the right place.

These need to be examined in a little more detail.

Help

For example:
- directing a family to the nearest McDonald's
- carrying a guest's luggage from the car to the hotel
- showing a person in a wheelchair to the lift.

Advice

You might be asked questions like:
- 'Which is the best wine to accompany my meal?'
- 'Which hotel is suitable for families?'
- 'Which show do you think I should see first?'

Information

Requests for information might include:
- 'What are the opening hours of the Leisure Club?'

- 'What type of visa will I need for visiting South Africa?'
- 'How often do the buses run to the beach?'

Security

Customers need to know that:

- personal belongings will be safe
- night-clubs will not tolerate violent behaviour
- airports check all luggage.

Safety

In everybody's interests it is essential that safety rules are enforced, for example:

- sports equipment, such as trampolines are checked regularly
- fairground rides are well maintained
- fire exits are kept clear at all times.

The 1974 Health and Safety at Work Act obliges the employer to safeguard the health and safety of two groups of people: his or her employees and clients and visitors to the premises. The case study below looks at a day in the life of Aisha, an office supervisor in a large travel organisation.

Look it up

In pairs find out about the regulation of the working conditions regarding heat, lighting and noise in two working environments. It could be in the place you work part time or somewhere you are familiar with or a place where one of your family works.

The right product at the right time in the right place

This means, matching the product to the customer. For example:

- honeymooners wanting a trip to 'Paradise'
- families wanting value-for-money accommodation
- young people wanting designer wear clothes.

Talk about it

In pairs, add extra examples to each of the categories mentioned above, i.e. help, advice, information, security, safety, the right product. Discuss these in your whole group after you have completed the exercise.

CASE STUDY – Aisha

Aisha's office is overcrowded. Ten people work in a space suitable for only six. Her first job when she arrives is to open the windows, which means climbing on the top of the desk and pulling the windows open. It's a bit of a risky operation but because there's no other ventilation and no air conditioning, it would be unbearable without some fresh air.

Aisha works on the computer from 9 am to 1 pm, without a break. She often finds herself squinting at the screen because of the reflection of the sunlight bouncing back at her off the screen.

Aisha went to the doctor's last week to complain about her bad back which the doctor diagnosed was a result of sitting in a chair with insufficient back support.

At around 3.30 pm Aisha can feel herself dozing off. The poor lighting and lack of ventilation has created a very stuffy atmosphere. She can't wait until 5 o'clock!

Question

What do you think could be done to improve Aisha's working conditions?

External and internal customers

External customers are the visitors or consumers who use the facilities of an organisation and pay for the products and services. They play a vital role in the leisure and tourism industry because without them there would be no business! They must be given the very best customer service so they will return and use the facilities again. External customers will also recommend an organisation to their friends if they feel they have been treated well.

Internal customers are the people you work with and we will look at them on page 137.

The benefits of excellence

Excellent customer service brings a number of benefits for leisure and tourism organisations, as can be seen in Figure 3.3. We will look at these in more detail.

Figure 3.3 The benefits of excellent customer service

Increased sales

Good news travels fast. An organisation which has a good reputation and is recommended by existing customers to other people will usually find an increase in the number of their customers. This means more people will spend their money there as the scenario outlined in Figure 3.4 shows.

SNAPSHOTS

Good news from Kelly

'I always like going to our local sports centre because the staff are so helpful and friendly. Nothing seems to be too much trouble for them. We play badminton there every Sunday morning. It's now become a social event as we meet our friends there and have a drink and a meal in the sports bar after our game.'

Bad news from Shilpa

'I just knew I wasn't going to enjoy my meal as soon as I walked in. The tables were full of empty plates and the ashtrays were full to overflowing. We had to wait 20 minutes before someone took our order. When the food did arrive, it was cold and I'm sure I didn't ask for a child's portion. Sorry, but we won't be going back there again.'

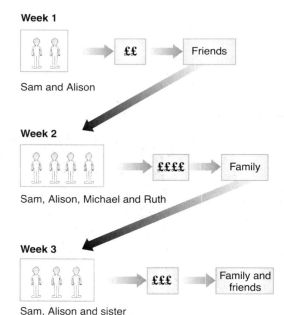

Figure 3.4 How recommendations lead to increased business

Private sector organisations like restaurants and travel agents aim to make a profit. Increased numbers of customers brought in by excellent customer service leads to increased sales and the necessary profit.

CASE STUDY – Geoff

Geoff manages a ten-pin bowling alley. His staff are all trained in customer service and everyone has gained their Welcome Host-

Customer Care qualification. Geoff has financial targets to meet each month and he monitors the usage figures. He also monitors the effectiveness of the centre's customer service – the number of complaints, the repeat business, and what is revealed by customer surveys, and from chats with customers.

Geoff says, 'Customers not only come for the product – bowling – but also for the service. We treat them like royalty, make them feel important and encourage them to stay for a meal or a drink. To them, it's a total leisure experience. In other words, customers know that when they use our centre, they will be treated in a special way. We spoil them.

'By the way, when it comes to customer service, we have two rules for our staff:

Rule 1 The customer is always right

Rule 2 If the customer is ever wrong, re-read rule 1!'

Questions

- Have you ever been to a place where you have been 'spoiled' by the level of customer service given to you? Let the rest of your group know.

- What would Geoff do if his receptionist was not giving excellent customer service?

Public sector organisations, such as local authority leisure centres and libraries, should also adopt a customer service policy which increases usage.

The English Tourism Council has the following customer service policy:

- exceeding customers' expectations
- putting the customer first all the time
- finding out what the customer wants and making sure that it is delivered
- making sure that every customer recommends us
- getting the details right first time and every time.

Good customer service encourages customer loyalty and spreads the word to potential customers. So why do organisations lose customers? The Wales Tourist Board gives a number of reasons, as set out in Figure 3.5.

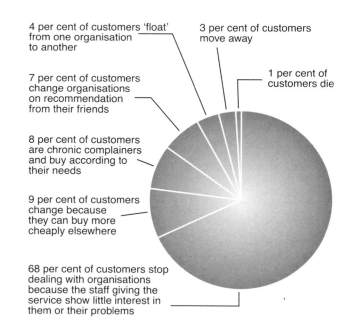

4 per cent of customers 'float' from one organisation to another

3 per cent of customers move away

7 per cent of customers change organisations on recommendation from their friends

1 per cent of customers die

8 per cent of customers are chronic complainers and buy according to their needs

9 per cent of customers change because they can buy more cheaply elsewhere

68 per cent of customers stop dealing with organisations because the staff giving the service show little interest in them or their problems

Source: Wales Tourist Board

Figure 3.5 How organisations lose customers

Satisfied customers

Customers who are happy with the product or service they have paid for and the way they have been treated by staff are satisfied customers.

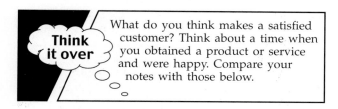

Think it over

What do you think makes a satisfied customer? Think about a time when you obtained a product or service and were happy. Compare your notes with those below.

Satisfied customers are happy because they have:

* had value for money

* been very well looked after

* been given accurate information about the product

* had their wishes fulfilled.

Satisfied customers can also motivate staff. Customers who have been treated well will sometimes show their appreciation to staff by thanking them and smiling. This means that staff are then motivated to deliver the same type of service to the next customer, i.e. *satisfaction spreads*. If customers thank you for a job well done it makes you feel good about your work. You will be enthusiastic and motivated – you will want to work! Everyone will feel good about working in an atmosphere of good teamwork and enthusiasm.

The postcards opposite show one satisfied customer and one not so happy one.

Statistics show that it is five times cheaper to retain a customer than it is to obtain a new one, and that if you upset a customer, they tell at least 12 other people about it. That's why in today's fiercely competitive environment, customer service will be the key to survival in the twenty-first century.

'dissatisfied customers tell an average of 12 other people about it'

TEN COMMANDMENTS OF CUSTOMER CARE

1 **Our customers**
are the most important people in our business

2 **Our customers**
are not dependent on us – we depend on them

3 **Our customers**
like to be welcomed and recognised, listened to, smiled at, cared for, thanked and invited back

4 **Our customers**
are not an interruption to our work but the reason for it

5 **Our customers**
are not people to argue with or match wits with

6 **Our customers**
are not cold statistics but human beings with feelings and emotions just like our own

7 **Our customers**
want value for money and enjoyment, quality products served correctly and promptly in relaxed and welcoming surroundings

8 **Our customers**
give us an opportunity to serve them

9 **Our customers**
are deserving of our most courteous and attentive treatment

10 **Our customers**
are the lifeblood of our business and have paid for our service

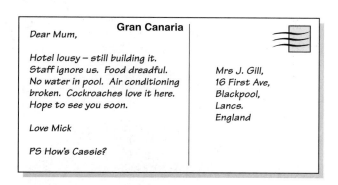

Gran Canaria

Dear Mum,

Hotel lousy – still building it. Staff ignore us. Food dreadful. No water in pool. Air conditioning broken. Cockroaches love it here. Hope to see you soon.

Love Mick

PS How's Cassie?

Mrs J. Gill,
16 First Ave,
Blackpool,
Lancs.
England

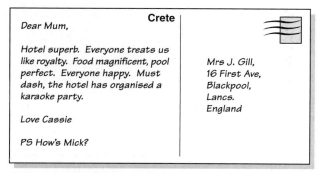

Crete

Dear Mum,

Hotel superb. Everyone treats us like royalty. Food magnificent, pool perfect. Everyone happy. Must dash, the hotel has organised a karaoke party.

Love Cassie

PS How's Mick?

Mrs J. Gill,
16 First Ave,
Blackpool,
Lancs.
England

Where would you rather be?

(Reproduced with kind permission from Alton Towers)

TEN MAGICAL RULES OF CUSTOMER SATISFACTION

1 **Warm welcome** – the key to a successful attraction

2 **First impressions** – are lasting and our visitors will remember the impression you give

3 **Stars of the show** – you are part of the show, your presence can bring the attractions 'alive'

4 **Appearances count** – you are on show, look the part to meet our visitors

5 **Excuse me** – know the park/hotel and be ready to answer questions

6 **Fun, fun, fun** – you are in the entertainment business, show you enjoy your work

7 **Be prepared** – for unexpected emergencies and know how to handle any situation

8 **Positive thinking** – take the initiative, make suggestions to make your attraction even better.

9 **Litter** – is everyone's problem. so take pride in your site

10 **Winning team** – work together and use your talents to the best

(Reproduced with kind permission from Alton Towers)

The customer service guide for staff at Alton Towers

Repeat business and recommendations

Good customer service can lead to repeat business, that is, existing customers coming back for more. In fact, if they continue to return, they will tend to build up loyalty to an organisation. This is also the best and most cost effective way of advertising – recommendation by word of mouth. There is no better phrase than 'I recommend':

- 'I recommend you go for a meal there' will lead you to one particular restaurant

- 'I recommend these boots to anyone' means you may well buy some

- 'I recommend Ritzy's Nightclub' means you will go there rather than anywhere else.

On the other hand, an unhappy customer will probably tell between ten and 15 other people of their unhappy experience.

Try it out

Look at the ten commandments of customer care and the ten magical rules of customer service of Alton Towers. In pairs, make up your own customer care charter for a leisure and tourism organisation of your choice.

Think it over

Is there a facility which you keep going back to? Why would you recommend it?

Good public image

All leisure and tourism organisations like to promote a good public image. This is a way of showing customers that the product is value for money and that the service they receive is second to none. The good image will not exist without excellent customer service.

Leisure and tourism organisations often promote a better public image by using endorsements from satisfied customers to promote their products. They also use pictures of people having fun as a result of using the organisation's products and services. The aim of this is to encourage new custom and to build up loyalty.

Restaurant of the Year

'The setting was perfect. The staff knew just what we wanted'

'The food was superb, the service was excellent'

'The staff are so helpful, they couldn't do enough for us'

A good public image depends on excellent customer service

List the things which give organisations good and bad reputations.

Try it out

Who would be the Trafford Centre's competition?

List the type of customers who benefit from the centre's customer care policy.

The Trafford Centre Customer Services

Committed To Excellence

Help & Assistance If you need help of any kind whilst you are in The Trafford Centre, ask one of our team. Their red uniforms make them easy to pick out and you will find plenty of them on duty in the malls, around the Orient and out in the car parks.

Services for Children There is a children's entertainment programme in the Wonder World. Situated above the Festival Village there are regular performances from The Trafford Centre Bears, real-life magicians, jugglers and a host of other entertainment. More fun is available in Kidz Klub – a soft toy play area and crèche and specially decorated party rooms which are available to hire for special celebrations. We can even arrange the catering and entertainment. Our on-site crèche caters for 65.

Services include:

Crèche for two up to eight year olds.
Children's buggies available from Customer Services Desk and security wrist bands.
Unisex parent and child toilets.
Baby changing facilities and breast-feeding rooms.
Babies bottles can be warmed up in a special unit in the food court within the Orient.

Customer Comfort If you find it hard to manage in the food court - or you are in a wheelchair or juggling with children, shopping and lunch - then ask the catering staff to page one of our Orient team members who will be on hand to carry your tray and see you comfortably seated.

Most of our team are fully trained First Aiders, so whether you suffer a simple cut or serious emergency, all you have to do is alert one of our staff. The meeting point for lost persons is at the Dome Customer Services Desk.

The Operations Room links our customers, stores and staff on the ground with each other and the outside world. It monitors the traffic on the surrounding roads so that when you finally have to tear yourself away, we can help you find the easiest route home.

Hourly visits to our Viewing Gallery will be conducted by a member of The Trafford Centre team, highlighting safety and security procedures for your comfort.

Shopmobility There are car park facilities for visitors with disabilities around the Centre and 65 spaces next to the Centre's Festival Village entrance. Inside, you can pick up a battery-operated scooter or manual wheelchair from the Shopmobility unit. All the public areas, toilet blocks and elevators are designed for wheelchair use.

Two forms of identification are required for equipment hire, one must show the customers current address. Orange badges, drivers licence or similar are acceptable.

Lenses for the visually impaired are available free of charge at the Customer Services Desk and the Shopmobility unit.

Parking The Trafford Centre provides 10,000 free spaces for customers' cars, plus 300 coach spaces.

The Operations Room is in constant touch with our car park staff and with the Traffic Police. So when you arrive at The Trafford Centre, electronic signs on the motorway slip roads will start directing you to a section of car park where space is available.

For more information on buses and taxis please contact our Customer Services Desk.

(Reproduced with kind permission from The Trafford Centre)

A customer services leaflet from a major shopping centre

Competitive edge

By providing excellent customer service – better than that of competitors – you will give your organisation more chance of maintaining existing customers and also attracting new ones. A travel agent may, for example, sell the same package holiday at the same price as a competitor, but it is the one which gives the very best in customer service, that will attract the business.

Internal customers

Internal customers are the people you work with, for example other employees of your organisation working in another department. It might seem strange to think of your colleagues as customers, but you have the same responsibility to each other as you do to your external customers. So you should treat your internal customers the same way you treat your external customers.

It is very important to remember that all members of staff should give a high level of service to each other. Imagine you work in a travel agency. We know that your external customers are the people who want to book a holiday or arrange travel insurance etc. To reach that stage in the transaction head office would have provided you with the posters to advertise the holidays, the computer systems to enable you to make the reservation and the skills you need to operate the computers.

In this case, *you* are the internal customer because *you* need the product, that is, the advertising material, the equipment and the necessary skills to do the job properly. All these things are provided by your organisation – see Figure 3.6.

Imagine you work as a waiter/waitress in a popular restaurant. It's very busy and customers just keep coming in as your restaurant is renowned for its value-for-money meals and excellent customer service. Your job is purely to take the food and drinks to the tables. But you need the following people to enable you to carry

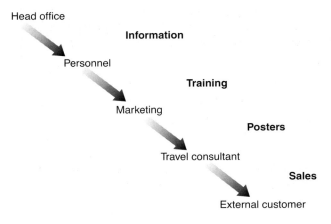

Figure 3.6 The internal customer chain in a travel agency enables holidays to be sold to the external customer

out your work:

- The table clearers make sure the tables are clean and clear.

- The dishwashers make sure the plates are clean.

- The kitchen staff make sure the meals are prepared.

- The cashier makes sure the customers pay.

- The manager makes sure everything runs smoothly.

In other words, there is a great deal of teamwork, where everyone relies on everyone else. Imagine if one link in the chain was weak, the whole operation would suffer.

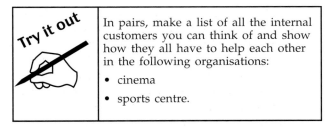

Try it out   In pairs, make a list of all the internal customers you can think of and show how they all have to help each other in the following organisations:

- cinema
- sports centre.

It can take a while to get used to the idea of your colleagues at work as internal customers. However, it must be remembered that staff who come into direct contact with customers cannot provide them with good customer service unless they receive the same type of service and support from their colleagues.

'We believe in teamwork. Every member of staff is important and we all treat each other with importance. Our external customer service is reflected in our internal customer service.' *Hotel manager*

There are several benefits of providing excellent customer service to internal customers. Some are obvious, and some are not so obvious; for example, good internal customer service provides a pleasanter place to work for everyone.

Imagine what it would be like if you had a job which you didn't enjoy – perhaps it was boring, perhaps because the pay wasn't that good. Now imagine if you were working with people who didn't help you, talk to you or listen to you. That would be a even worse and, what is more, it is likely that your feelings would be apparent to external customers, which would be bad for the organisation. On the other hand, if colleagues are friendly, polite, supportive and helpful, the result would be a happier you and a happier workplace, providing better service for external customers (see Figure 3.7).

So remember that it is important to:

- co-operate with colleagues at all times

- work well together

- be friendly and polite

- help and support each other.

Figure 3.7 The benefits of providing excellent customer service to internal customers

CASE STUDY – The right answer

Look at this situation in a travel company, when one employee telephones another.

'Hi, Melanie, it's Ashra from the Truro branch. We need some more posters for the Spanish promotion before Saturday. Could you send me some please?'

Answer A: 'Ashra, you've got to be joking. Do you think I'm superwoman? It's Thursday today and you expect me to produce miracles with the workload I've got. You are joking. No chance.'

Answer B: 'No problem, Ashra. I'll get them from the storeroom right now and put them in this afternoon's post so you'll have them tomorrow. Hope your Spanish promotion is going well. What else have you got lined up at your branch?'

Obviously, no one would like to have been on the receiving end of Answer A. That would not have been good for staff morale and certainly wouldn't solve the poster problem. Answer B is helpful, friendly and interested in what is going on, which is exactly how external customers are treated *and* how internal customers should be treated.

Questions

- You may have a part-time job. Do you know anyone with an Answer A attitude?

- What do you think builds up a good atmosphere when working with colleagues?

People who work well together usually enjoy their work more. A happy workforce leads to good teamwork and greater efficiency. This is good news for the external customer, who will end up on the receiving end of some truly excellent customer service.

One of the best examples of people working together outside the leisure and tourism industry is on the road. Next time you see a group of sub-contractors digging up the road, laying pipes and resurfacing have a good look at the way they work together. They all rely on each other (usually), they all have set tasks, they all get on with it and, as a result, the job (usually) gets done on time.

If other employees are treated in the same way as external customers, there will be improved job satisfaction – employees will enjoy their work and take pride in it. An organisation should provide an expected level of service to internal customers which should include:

- being valued
- being kept informed as to how the organisation is performing
- being treated with respect
- receiving appropriate training.

Job satisfaction leads to a sense of pride in the organisation, an increase in self-confidence and competence, and the motivation to continue to do well.

If you take an interest in your job, attend training courses and work well with others in your organisation, the chances are that your enthusiasm and positive attitude will be noticed by the management. People who can work well with others have a habit of motivating them. This is especially useful in supervisory and management positions. Providing excellent internal customer service can result in co-operation from colleagues, recognition from management and improved chances of promotion.

CASE STUDY — All right on the night

Jake is organising a New Year's Eve dinner dance for 300 people as part of his job as Entertainments Officer with a Borough Council. This task means working with colleagues to make sure everything all goes well on the night. This is how the internal customer chain looks:

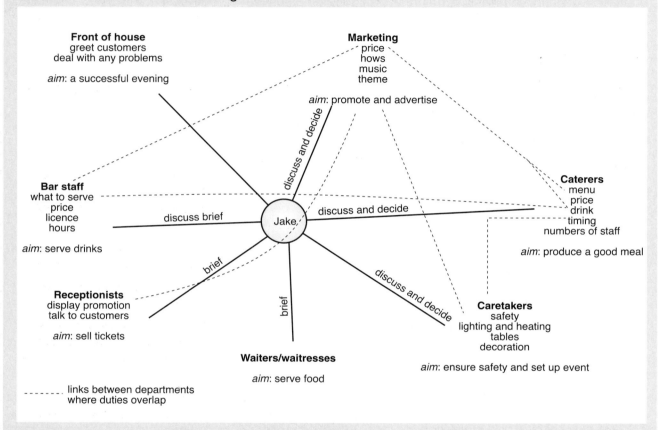

Front of house
greet customers
deal with any problems

aim: a successful evening

Marketing
price
hows
music
theme

aim: promote and advertise

Bar staff
what to serve
price
licence
hours

aim: serve drinks

discuss and decide

discuss brief

Jake

discuss and decide

Caterers
menu
price
drink
timing
numbers of staff

aim: produce a good meal

Receptionists
display promotion
talk to customers

aim: sell tickets

brief

brief

discuss and decide

Caretakers
safety
lighting and heating
tables
decoration

aim: ensure safety and set up event

Waiters/waitresses

aim: serve food

------- links between departments where duties overlap

Everyone to clean up

Everyone had to work together and treat each other with the same respect as they would treat external customers. All this led to:

- teamwork
- high staff morale
- sense of achievement.

At 3.30 am everyone finished, exhausted but happy, knowing they had done a good job.

Questions

- What would be the consequences at such a function if staff didn't work together?

- Some people just don't get on; it might be a personality clash, it might be jealousy. How would you, as a supervisor, overcome any conflict among your staff?

Personal presentation

Whether you like the idea or not, your customers will judge you and your organisation by the way you look – your appearance – and the way you treat people – your attitude. First impressions count in any business but particularly in the leisure and tourism industry where dealing with people is a very important part of the job.

You may think that how you look and how you behave is your own business, and so it is away from work, but at work you represent your organisation, and this is important. If you present a 'good' image then customers will be impressed with both you and the organisation you represent.

? Did you know?

You never get a second chance to make a good first impression!

CUSTOMER CARE

1. Customer service at Alton Towers must be top quality.
2. The quality is right when customers, staff & shareholders are happy.
3. Failure to meet customer expectations will mean they will not return & may put others off coming.
4. If staff are unhappy employees' standards of service often fall. All staff are encouraged to look for ways that will improve customer service.
5. If shareholders are unhappy with the financial returns from their investment they may be unwilling to re-invest in Alton Towers.
6. Alton Towers therefore must know:
   who its customers are
   where they come from
   what their expectations are of the product
   what they expect of the Alton Towers experience.
7. The word '**magic**' has become central to the theme park and sets an expectation in the minds of customers. The service quality programme must reflect this and has to deliver the magic.
8. Delivering the magic: The Alton Towers magic means delivering good memories to all customers that visit. Alton Towers must provide quality:
   Tangible aspects of the product – rides, shops, restaurants, grounds, gardens.
   Intangible aspects – the service that delivers the tangibles.
   The intangible aspects rely on the service quality training programme.
   This programme has to deliver the magic.
   The staff at Alton Towers are trained to deliver this magic.

(Reproduced with kind permission from Alton Towers)

The magic of customer care at Alton Towers

Talk about it

In pairs think of an example of good and bad first impressions you have experienced as a customer. It may have been a greeting from a sales assistant in a shop, a receptionist in a doctor's surgery or an attendant in a leisure centre.

SNAPSHOTS

Shaheen

Shaheen works in a big sports and leisure store at the customer services desk. It's always busy, but especially on Saturdays and in the summer. Shaheen says, 'The golden rules are:

- *customers come first – whatever other tasks you may have, your first duty is to look after your customers*
- *personality – aim to be friendly, polite, calm and approachable at all times*
- *be organised – keep your working area tidy and as clean as possible. Make sure you are familiar with the layout of the building and where other members of staff work*
- *accuracy – be accurate when taking messages, remembering to record the date and time the message was taken.*

'Appearance is important but what is acceptable in one situation may not be in another. For example, if you work in a club then a stud in your tongue and gothic make-up may be acceptable. But I have to wear a jacket and skirt or trousers and not too much make up!

'Above all, courteous service is the important thing. I love my job and try to communicate that.'

When you walk into a reception area you should find:

- a clean and tidy entrance
- doors clearly marked 'Reception' and 'Welcome'

- the reception area tidy, with fresh flowers

- brochures and leaflets on display

- a receptionist smartly and appropriately dressed in uniform

- a receptionist who deals with customer's enquiries promptly and courteously.

Try it out — Make a chart with the heading 'Tips to make a good impression'. Try to include all the things covered so far, and then add your own.

The way you present yourself to customers has a direct influence on their enjoyment, your job satisfaction and the future success of the organisation that employs you. In particular, you will need to appreciate the importance of:

- dress

- personal hygiene

- personality

- attitude

- behaviour.

Depending on whether you deal with customers face-to-face, over the telephone or in writing, some or all of these points may be important.

Of course, it is not just a member of staff who gives a good first impression, it is also the actual place itself. For example, imagine walking into a cinema foyer where the carpets are dirty and the litterbins are overflowing with empty cans and popcorn cartons. In addition to this, the toilets are smelly and dirty. What sort of impression does this give you?

Try it out — Think of a place you go to regularly, for example a fast-food restaurant. Picture the place itself and write down your impression of the building; the décor, how clean it is, how welcoming it feels.

Dress

Many organisations provide staff with uniforms. There can be many advantages in this, because:

CASE STUDY — First impressions

When it comes to making a good first impression there's no one more important than the receptionist. That crucial first impression makes all the difference as to how customers see your organisation.

A receptionist should be:

- able to put customers at ease

- able to listen and understand the needs of customers

- tactful, reliable and self-motivated.

Questions

- What impression do you get from the receptionist shown here?

- List all the things you can see that are examples of poor reception.

Wearing a uniform can show that you are part of a team

- a professional company image is presented
- staff can be easily recognised as being part of the company
- staff can be easily found by customers
- staff feel a sense of belonging to a team.

If you are not provided with a uniform make sure your clothes are clean and ironed. Polish your

Make a list of all the staff you can think of in the leisure and tourism industry who wear uniforms. What impression does this give?

shoes and get them reheeled when they need it – this means they will last much longer as well as looking smarter, so it does make sense!

Some leisure and tourism organisations have made up expressions which show the importance of creating a good first impression.

- 'First impressions are lasting impressions'
- 'Customers can always see your attitude'
- 'Take pride in yourself and your appearance'
- 'You are always on show – play the part'

Write down two or three expressions of your own which show the importance of first impressions in customer service.

A good way of remembering the importance of first impressions is to think about when you go for a job interview. At an interview you need to impress the interviewer, who is going to be looking for someone who will please the customers both internal and external and conform to the standards of the organisation. In other words, someone who will make a good first impression. You might think that the way you dress is a statement about yourself. It is. But you want to impress your potential employer and think about putting the customer first. You may

CASE STUDY – The Rutland Hotel

Standards for staff

- Uniform – to be worn at all times when on duty. To be cleaned and well maintained
- Shoes – black, well polished
- Jewellery – no earrings for men
- Hair – tidy and smart; men – no pony tails
- Personal hygiene – clean, fresh, no body odour. No excessive perfume/aftershave
- Nails – clean and tidy

- Tattoos – none to be visible
- Shaving – men to be clean shaven
- Make up – conventional and not excessive.

Questions

- What do you think about these standards?
- Would you be able to work in this hotel? Discuss this in your group.

not do so if you wear jeans, a casual top, training shoes, a ring through your nose and a stud in your tongue.

Personal hygiene

Customers notice details: they notice dirty nails, untidy hair and clothes that may not have seen the washing machine for the best part of a week resulting in an unpleasant smell in the atmosphere. It is important to attend to personal hygiene.

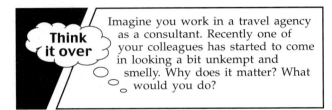

Think it over

Imagine you work in a travel agency as a consultant. Recently one of your colleagues has started to come in looking a bit unkempt and smelly. Why does it matter? What would you do?

Try it out

Staff who work in catering have to ensure that personal hygiene is a top priority, especially if they are handling food. What additional hygiene precautions do they have to take?

Personality, attitude and behaviour

It is important to be polite and friendly but there is more to making a good first impression than that. It means doing something extra – '**going the extra mile.'**

The following list outlines the type of attitude, behaviour and personality that customers look for:

- A friendly smile goes a long way – customers like staff who are friendly and welcoming.

- Customers don't want to hear your problems. Your facial expression will reveal your problems – so smile to hide them.

- Act positive, think positive; act enthusiastic, be enthusiastic – these attitudes tend to spread.

- Having a bad day? The customer doesn't care if the world is against you so don't let it show.

- A good positive attitude will enable you to build up a speedy relationship with the customer.

- The way you look and behave will affect the way the customer regards you and your organisation.

- Customers want to enjoy themselves in leisure and tourism organisations and your attitude should promote that feeling.

- Patience – you have been asked the same question a *dozen* times already today. You may even have answered it all week. But, everytime is the first time you have been asked it.

Your behaviour will influence the customer.

It follows then that the impression people have of you is based on the behaviour they see as well as the words they hear.

Your behaviour is like a beacon, sending out signals to all the people with whom you have dealings. The signals you send are vital because they are a major influence on the reactions of the other person. They can help or hinder every transaction you make with people.

Telephone techniques to make a good impression

The telephone can play an important part in any good customer service strategy when it is used properly.

Talk about it

Look at these expressions and discuss what you think they mean.
- Smile when you dial
- Don't phone a groan

The sayings mean that if you are actually smiling when you are making or receiving a call your voice will automatically reflect that smile – it will

CASE STUDY – Jade

Jade is a flight attendant with an international airline. She takes great pride in her appearance. In fact she has to: before each flight the senior flight attendant inspects each cabin crew member. Jade has the following advice for anyone who wants to become a flight attendant:

'It's not the glamorous job it's sometimes made out to be. The hours are long, you are always on your feet and you have to work shifts. And, to be quite honest, some of the passengers can be a bit of a pain.

'Fortunately, I have a very positive attitude which allows me to overcome the downsides of the job. If ever I feel tired, all I have to do is picture the many fantastic places I've seen around the world, think of the great people I work with and remind myself of the many opportunities for promotion.'

Question

What sort of personality would you need to be a:

- flight attendant
- sports centre supervisor
- travel agent?

make your voice sound more assertive and friendly. Try it sometime and then keep practising it. You will find it works and is far more welcoming than a voice which is full of misery, which sums up expression number two.

The way that a receptionist uses the telephone is particularly important. A receptionist should:

- make sure he or she knows how the telephone system works
- learn as soon as possible the names and jobs of the staff in the organisation
- always answer incoming calls in a friendly and professional manner
- take messages quickly and accurately
- be able to answer questions about the organisation's products or services.

Checklist for dealing with customers by phone

- Give all your attention to the customer.
- Get the customer's name, write it down and use it.
- Get other details, such as address, and write them down. Use a specially prepared form.
- Ask plenty of questions.
- Listen hard and show them you are listening.
- Keep your voice interesting by varying the speed and emphasis.
- Pause, to show you are thinking about what they have said.
- At the end of the conversation, summarise what you have agreed.

Callers can experience some very frustrating results when they telephone an organisation. For instance:

- not getting an answer quickly enough when you know someone *must* be there

- being put through to the wrong extension and/or cut off

- being left hanging on without an explanation of what is happening and/or being left 'on hold' listening to piped music

- being greeted by an answerphone

- being put through before you've finished what you are saying.

Communicating with answering machines

Telephone answering machines have a tendency to make some callers go dumb. They just can't bring themselves to talk to a machine; perhaps that's how you feel. But why waste your time by having to call again? Better to leave a message. Here are six tips for making the most of a recorded message:

1   Ignore the fact that you are talking to a tape. Imagine a human being at the other end. Say hello and don't apologise for calling. The person you're calling obviously wants to hear from you, otherwise the machine wouldn't be left on!

Confidence is important when using the telephone

2   Date and time your call. That way it won't get overlooked.

3   Speak more slowly and more clearly than usual.

4   Repeat names, addresses and phone numbers. They may be hard to catch first time round.

5   Keep the message brief.

6   Be sure to wait for the 'beep' before starting to talk. Otherwise part of your message might be lost.

Good impressions in writing

The way you present a piece of information in writing can affect the customer's impression of the overall service given by your organisation. It is certain that poor grammar, spelling mistakes and a badly set out format will give a bad impression.

Try it out

Look at this letter.

What would Mr Johnston's impression of Twilight Travel be? Find all the errors in the letter.

3 Main Street
High Wycombe
Bucks

29/4/2000

Dear Mr Johnson

I am writing to confirm your booking for a two week holidayin Gran Canaria between [*2]June 29thX 30th June and July, 13th, 20000.

Your tickets will be sent when I have recieved the full payment of acommodation for which you have asked for and I hope you have a good time.
Yours faithfully

J Painstakinly

Mannager
Twilight Travel Services

Written communication should:

- be easy to understand
- be properly set out
- use language and grammar correctly
- contain correct spelling.

First impressions: a summary

- Be enthusiastic – enthusiasm spreads.
- Be confident – the customers will put their trust in you.
- Be welcoming – everyone likes to be liked and approved of.
- Be polite – manners are important.
- Show you care – treat customers as individuals and make them feel important.

Dealing with customers

Everybody working in the leisure and tourism industry will, at some time, come into contact with customers. Receptionists, waitresses and sports centre assistants deal with customers face-to-face on a daily basis. There are occasions when the contact might be unexpected; for example, cleaners or lighting technicians in a theatre may not expect to deal with the public. All staff need to know how to communicate with customers and use different skills in different situations. This will come in time. You will become more confident in communicating with customers as you get to know more about the job and the organisation you work for. When communicating with customers, you will need to use appropriate:

- language
- pitch and tone of voice
- pauses and silence
- body language.

Language

The way in which we say things is as important as what we say. Our verbal communication, either face-to-face or on the phone, will affect what our customers think of us. Examples of face-to-face communication include:

- sharing ideas and opinions – group discussion
- working with other people – teamwork
- offering information and advice – e.g. restaurant opening times
- giving instructions and awaiting feedback – supervisory roles.

In a customer service situation the language you use to talk to your customer should be simple and easy to understand. After all, communication is not only about sending a message, it is about the other person receiving it and understanding it.

Try it out

We have seen that there are many different types of customers so our communication, and therefore our language must be geared towards that customer. With a partner, write down what sort of language you would use and how you would talk to the following customers:

- a young child
- a foreign tourist.

When speaking to people, try to avoid the following:

- *jargon* – language specific to your industry. For example 'Your ETA is 20.00 hours'. Customers might not understand that ETA means estimated time of arrival or even that 20.00 hours is 8 pm
- *slang* – words and phrases that are not standard English. For example, *innit* (isn't it), *quid* (£1), *wanna* (want to), *ain't* (isn't) and *cos* (because)
- *colloquialism* – words or phrases used in a specific locality. For example, *mardy* (bad tempered), *moidered* (worried about), *appen so* (that may be the case).

Tips to remember:

- Don't complicate what you say with difficult language.

- Speak clearly and concentrate on what you are saying.

- Ask the other person questions to check he or she has understood what you have said.

- Try to vary your voice so you don't send the caller to sleep.

Talking to groups

Imagine that you are a holiday representative: one of your first tasks is to introduce yourself to the group and tell them all about the hotel, the nightlife, the do's and don'ts. Here are some points to remember if you are ever in this situation:

- Face all the guests – don't turn your back on any of them.

- Plan what you are going to say and say it with confidence.

- Be prepared to answer the questions that they may fire at you.

- Don't just look at one person in the group, speak to them all.

Imagine you are that travel rep. Prepare a welcoming speech to your guests – use your imagination as to the location and type of accommodation – and prepare to give your 'welcome' to the group of holidaymakers.

Imagine you have to give directions to a group of foreign tourist who can speak little English. They want to find a hotel which is half a mile (2 kms) away. Can you give them the right directions?

Pitch and tone of voice

What happens if someone speaks to you in a dull and very monotonous tone? The chances are that you will stop listening. Think about the expression: put some life into your voice. Customers will not want to listen to someone whose voice is boring and monotonous. But

making your voice sound interesting takes practice.

Talk about it

Read the following news story to your group, adjusting the pitch and tone of your voice.

'Last night England won the World Cup by defeating Germany 3-0 at Wembley. Street parties broke out everywhere and the Prime Minister declared that everyone could have the day off work.

Fans filled the streets in a mood of great joy and happiness never before seen in the country. Flags were flying, glasses chinked, car horns blasted out and the national anthem rang out in every village, town and city.

No one, but no one, could ever remember such scenes of joy and happiness. Every football fan in the land cried tears of joy.'

Did your voice go up and down? Did it range from loud to soft? If it did, you were altering the pitch and tone of your voice. Did your group find you easy or dull to listen to?

The pitch and tone of your voice – whether it is high or deep – is often affected by fear and nervousness. The muscles in your throat and your vocal chords tighten so the sound becomes a squeak or high pitched.

Talk about it

Take a deep breath and, as you breathe slowly out, say a few short words like 'I love to talk'. You should find your voice sounds better since it is physically impossible to breathe out and keep your muscles tight at the same time.

It's not just what you say that is important, it is also the way you say it. You can, if you want, sound angry, full of life, enthusiastic, bored or downright miserable. Customers can tell by your voice what mood you are in and how you feel. The way you talk about something will affect their judgement of it.

For example, if you talk enthusiastically and positively about a local hotel, the customer will feel it will be worth staying there. At the same time, if you talk in a boring and unenthusiastic manner about a show at the local theatre, you are unlikely to encourage people to go and see it!

Talk about it

Try this in your group and have some fun. You can make the same word mean several things. Try saying the word 'holidaymaker' and sound:

- bored
- surprised
- pleased
- overjoyed
- angry
- tired.

Adjusting the pitch and tone of your voice to situations takes practice and time. It is worth it because people will listen to you and your message will be received and understood.

Pauses and silences

People can only absorb so much information in one go and they tend to 'switch off' when they can't take any more. This is worth remembering when dealing with customers because you want to keep their attention and interest when you are talking to them. That is why it is important to pause now and again, and also to maintain silence at the appropriate time. If you use these techniques it will give:

- the customer time to absorb the information you have given them

Talk about it

Using pauses and silences is a skill that requires practice. Try this exercise, working in pairs. One of you should be the customer, the other the sales assistant. Sell the following items using the 'pause and silence' technique:

- a holiday
- a mobile phone.

CASE STUDY — Selling and silence

In a selling situation the 'sound of silence' can win or lose a sale. The following example illustrates this.

Assistant: How can I help you?

Customer: I'd like to look at some training shoes.

Assistant: What size do you take, please?

Customer: Size 10.

Assistant: What colour would you like?

Customer: Blue with white strips.

Assistant: These are the latest design in your size. Would you like to sit down and try them on? They look great. How do they feel?

Customer: Very comfortable.

Assistant: Good. There's 10 per cent discount on these at the moment. Would you like me to take them over to the counter and I can put them in a box while you pay for them?

Questions

- At which crucial moment must the assistant pause and keep quiet while the customer is making up his mind?
- When should the assistant let the power of silence take over?
- What might the consequences be if the assistant rushed the customer?

- the customer the opportunity to comment or ask questions
- you the opportunity to think what you are going to say next.

Body language

Not all face-to-face communication involves using words. We can also convey our feelings and attitudes without speaking. This is known as *body language* or *non-verbal communication*.

In fact 80 per cent of all communication is non-verbal. Being able to read someone's body language will be a big help when you are dealing with customers as you will be able to work out how they are feeling. It will also be useful for you to monitor your own body language so that you know you are sending out the right signals.

You can usually tell by looking at a person's face if they are feeling happy or angry – a smile will show happiness, a scowl will show anger. In fact the face is probably the most expressive area of our body as it can show many emotions (see Figure 3.8).

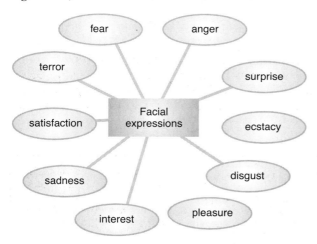

Figure 3.8 Faces can express many emotions

 In groups of four, take it in turns to try to depict all the facial expressions shown in Figure 3.8. Remember not to use any words!

You will be able to tell if a customer is angry merely by looking at him or her. This will give you time to plan your reaction. Likewise, if you see someone is distressed you can be ready to be understanding and sympathetic.

Some body language gestures are open and positive, for example leaning forward with open palms facing upwards shows acceptance and a welcoming attitude. Some others are closed and defensive, such as leaning backwards, head down and arms folded. This may show someone is not interested or can express rejection.

If you use plenty of gestures other people will probably interpret you as being warm, enthusiastic and emotional. This would be appropriate if you want to generate enthusiasm for a new idea. Using gestures only now and again would make you seem cold, reserved and logical. This might be useful if you had to convey cold facts or bad news.

Using eye contact is a way of acknowledging customers, making them feel welcome and showing that you are really listening.

You can gain a general impression of customers from a combination of their facial expressions, head movements and gestures. Being able to judge what the other person is thinking through their body language is a very powerful tool which you can use when dealing with customers.

Talk about it

How would you describe the examples of body language shown in Figure 3.9?

Now try to act out the examples.

One 'volunteer' should stand in front of the class and perform an example of body language which the rest of the class has got to guess within 20 seconds.

Did you find this easy or hard?

Working accurately

Dealing with customers can be hard work. Your job is to try and handle every situation which may occur, such as giving someone directions, sorting out a complaint, finding accommodation for tourists or selling souvenirs.

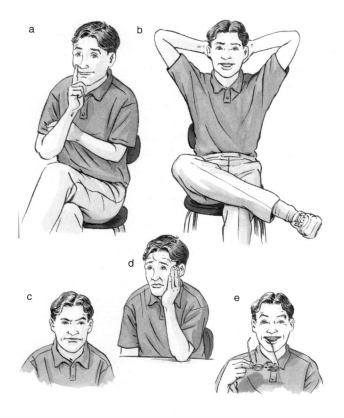

Figure 3.9 What types of body language can you see here?

In order to provide good customer service you will need to be able to *work accurately*. For example, if you are making a reservation for someone wanting to stay at the hotel where you work, it is important that you give them accurate information about:

- room charges
- meal times
- methods of payment
- room service
- types of accommodation
- local entertainment.

Customers expect you to be accurate because they are paying for the service and they are relying on you to help them. If ever you don't know the answer to a question asked by a customer you will have to say, 'Sorry, I don't know, but I will find out straightaway'.

Listen and respond to customers

One of the most important yet under-used skills in customer service is that of *listening*. You have to concentrate when someone is speaking to you. You must also resist the temptation to interrupt – this annoying habit puts people off what they were going to say.

Most people love to talk about their favourite subject – themselves! Many of your customers will tell you their life story, given half a chance. The important point to remember is that by listening to customers carefully, you will find out what they want.

Ask appropriate questions

Open questions These allow customers to give an answer other than 'no'. For example:

- Where would you like to go?
- How long would you like to go for?
- What type of accommodation would you like?
- How many people are going?
- When would you like to go?

These open questions are particularly useful in a selling situation. An expression used by salespeople is '*Selling isn't telling, it's asking*'. So a sales assistant will ask, 'How can I help you?' to which the customer may reply, 'I'd like to look at some training shoes, please'.

 Try it out | In pairs, think about the reasons why open questions are used. Make notes of your answers and then compare them with the list that follows (don't cheat by looking at the list first!)

Figure 3.10 shows some words used to begin open questions. But why do we ask open questions? Some of the reasons are:

- to give customers the opportunity to talk
- to show interest
- to find out how customers feel
- to keep control of the conversation

Figure 3.10 These questions 'open' up a conversation

- to make customers feel important
- to understand any complaints
- to understand exactly what the customer wants.

Closed questions, These, on the other hand, begin with 'is' 'can' 'does' 'have' and 'are'.

A closed question would be, 'Can I help you?' to which the answer could be simply 'Yes please' or 'No thank you'. 'No' is a real conversation killer, especially when you are trying to sell something, which is why open questions are always best in a selling situation.

Use open questions to gain as much information as possible. If you feel a customer is ready to buy a holiday and you have asked plenty of open questions, you can close the sale by using a final open question, 'How would you like to pay?'.

Obviously you will not be selling things all the time. The point to remember is that open questions give you information and make the customer feel that someone is interested in what they want.

When you are dealing directly with customers there are many different situations in which customer service is provided. These can include:

- providing information and advice
- receiving information and passing on messages
- keeping records
- providing assistance
- dealing with problems
- dealing with dissatisfied customers
- offering extra service.

We will look at each in detail.

Providing information

The more you know about your organisation, the area in which you work and the leisure and tourism industry in general, the more you will be able to help your customers.

For example, imagine you are working in a big hotel during your college holidays and a guest wants to see the manager to make a complaint. Do you know the manager's name? Do you know when he or she is on duty? Do you know the procedure for handling complaints? Do you know where the deputy manager is? Well, you should know. The customer will certainly expect you to know. The customer won't care if you have only worked there for two days. He has paid his money and expects answers. It is a good idea to find out straight away as much as possible about your organisation so that you can provide information confidently and accurately, rather than saying, 'Sorry, I don't know'.

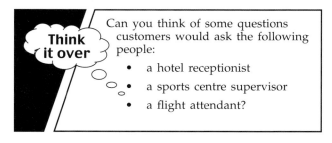

Customers expect you to know most things about your organisation and the particular facility you work in. A thorough knowledge of your workplace will create a good image of both you and your organisation.

CASE STUDY – Maxine

Maxine has just moved into the area. She likes sport so she goes to the local leisure centre to find out the type of activities they offer.

Maxine: Can you give me some information about your aerobics classes please?

Receptionist: I think they run on a Monday and Wednesday, but we've just changed them so I'm not sure.

Maxine: Have you got a membership scheme?

Receptionist: We have but it's too complicated to explain. There's family, child, young, free and single, over-sixty – the truth is there are so many types of membership that I can't remember them all.

Maxine: How much is it for an adult swim?

Receptionist: If you come on Wednesday, I think it's half price, if you come at peak times it's double that rate and if you come on Sundays, it's double time and a half.

Maxine: Where is the nearest public swimming pool please?

Questions

- Why is it important for staff to have sufficient knowledge about their organisation's products and services?

- How would you overcome a situation where staff don't know enough about the organisation they work in?

Giving advice

Some customers need advice: which wine to have with the meal, what is the fastest train to catch to London, which is the best club in town? Holidaymakers especially often seek reassurance because they are on 'unfamiliar territory' so they constantly want to know if they are going to the right places or doing the right things. As a result they need to ask lots of questions. You may have even asked similar questions yourself, such as:

- Which club plays the best music?

- Is it safe to drink the water?

- Is it best to go by taxi or bus?

Leisure and tourism staff are often bombarded with questions so they should:

- be trained when and how to give advice

- know about the area they work in

- ask someone in authority if they don't know what advice to give.

Receiving information and passing on messages

There is a big difference between hearing and listening. You may hear something but not necessarily take in the message. For example, you may hear your tutor at the front of the class but are you taking in what is being said?

If you listen, and listen carefully, you should be able to absorb what is being said.

When receiving information:

- make eye contact with the person who is speaking to you – this shows that you are interested in what they are saying

- give your full attention by facing the person, nodding and commenting to show you are listening. This also encourages people to continue talking

- check every now and again that you have heard correctly by giving a quick summary

- make a note of the main points if there are quite a few.

Talk about it

In pairs, tell each other about your family, your home, the area where you live and your interests. This is a listening exercise. When each person has finished talking, make a note of everything you've heard and then tell the rest of the group what you have discovered about your colleague.

When passing on a message it is important to:

- speak clearly. This may seem obvious but it is easy to mumble when you are concentrating only on what you are saying, not how you are saying it

- check that the other person has understood what you have said by asking them

- vary the tone and pace at which you speak so that your voice is interesting to listen to.

A simple *feedback loop* shows how messages are sent, received and understood (see Figure 3.11).

It is always a good idea to check that the customer has understood the information you have provided. This ensures that:

- you have recognised their needs

- you are providing the right product

- the customer knows what is being provided.

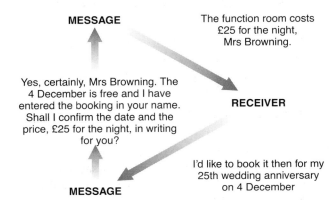

MESSAGE

The function room costs £25 for the night, Mrs Browning.

RECEIVER

Yes, certainly, Mrs Browning. The 4 December is free and I have entered the booking in your name. Shall I confirm the date and the price, £25 for the night, in writing for you?

I'd like to book it then for my 25th wedding anniversary on 4 December

MESSAGE

Figure 3.11 A simple feedback loop – how messages are sent, received and understood

Talk about it

Chinese whispers is a simple party game which shows what can go wrong when messages aren't passed on properly.

In groups of ten (or if that is not possible, the nearest to that number), stand in one long line. The person at one end of the line has to whisper the following message to the next person, who passes it on to the next person and so on. 'The 8.45 train leaving London's Kings Cross will arrive in York at 12.30 pm, stopping at Stevenage, Peterborough and Newark. There is a buffet car available.'

The message has got to be whispered so quietly that only the sender and receiver can hear it. In theory the last person to receive the message should be able to repeat exactly what the first person said. Your tutor will help organise this exercise.

Was your team successful? Did you communicate effectively or were there some very funny changes by the end?

Keeping records

This plays an important part in customer service and as such is dealt with separately in more detail in the section on page 161.

Providing assistance

As you know, when working in the leisure and tourism industry it is your job to help customers as much as possible by providing them with all the assistance they need. This may include helping to carry their luggage or directing them to the beach.

Sometimes it seems that customers do not want your assistance, especially if you ask a closed question like, 'Can I help you?' to which the automatic reply could be, 'No, I can manage'. It would be better to ask, 'How may I help you?'. It is very difficult to say 'no' to this open question.

The following phrases show how you can offer assistance:

- 'I'd be glad to help'

- 'I'll go and get it for you myself'

- 'I don't know, but I'll ask someone'

- 'I'll ask him to ring you as soon as he gets back'

- 'We'll do all we can to help'.

No matter how you are feeling you must always provide the very best assistance to your customers. This can include:

- using a master key to open a customer's locker because they have lost their key

- helping a tourist fill in an insurance form after having her handbag stolen

- helping to carry someone's luggage into the hotel foyer.

Dealing with problems

A wide variety of problems can crop up for anyone working in leisure and tourism. For example:

- table 4 has been double-booked for eight o'clock by two parties of six

- the showers in the changing rooms are freezing

- the till has 'crashed' and the assistant can't take money or issue tickets

- the safe keys are lost and the centre is due to open in ten minutes

- the roof is leaking and the main hall floor is under two inches of water

- there is a chemical spillage in the boiler room which is spreading outside.

Before trying to solve these problems, think about the process involved:

- keep calm, don't panic and think clearly – go and see the problem for yourself

- if the problem is life-threatening, act straightaway and call the emergency services

- if you can solve it, do so

- if you need assistance, send for it

- if the problem has occurred previously, think about what action was taken before

- think of the consequences of your decisions, 'If I do this, what will happen?'

- make a note of the incident and the action taken

- if the problem cannot be solved immediately, make alternative arrangements

- if the problem is going to affect staff and customers, erect hazard signs

- alert customers due to arrive if the problem is going to affect their use of the facilities.

Talk about it

In groups of three, choose one of the problems shown above and, using the guidelines given, say how you would solve it. Report your solutions to the rest of the group.

Dealing with dissatisfied customers

All the customers quoted below were dissatisfied with the service they received (or didn't receive) or the state of the facilities:

'My chips are cold, what are you going to do about it?'

'The toilets are filthy, when was the last time they were cleaned?'

'I've paid good money to watch this show and it's a load of rubbish.'

'This is the second time my squash court has been doubled booked. I want to see the Manager.'

'The hotel was a mile from the beach, the entertainment was non-existent and the pool wasn't supervised. I want my money back.'

Remember the golden rule: *the customer is always right.*

The first thing to do is to **listen** to the reason for the complaint. The customer can then say what he or she wants. This also gives you time to think of a suitable response.

Secondly, apologise and be sincere about it – really show your concern.

Thirdly, take whatever action is necessary to try to diffuse the situation. Say you will do something about the complaint as soon as you have carried out the necessary investigation into the problem. You may have to offer a full or part refund or another booking in the future depending on the problem. A written apology may be needed, probably from the head of the organisation.

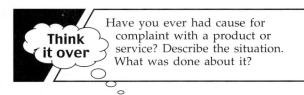

Think it over

Have you ever had cause for complaint with a product or service? Describe the situation. What was done about it?

Offering extra services

We know about the products and services which leisure and tourism organisations provide – cinemas show films, travel agents sell holidays and so on. These are standard services. But what about the extra services that leisure and tourism organisations offer?

- Cinemas also provide booking by phone using your credit card number and collecting your ticket from a machine in a wall, no queuing necessary.

- Theatres offer special seating areas for the disabled and allow you to order interval drinks from the bar.

- Travel agents will sell insurance, exchange currency, book theatre tickets.

- Restaurants provide no-smoking areas, high chairs for babies.

Try it out

Can you think of extra services provided by
- shopping centres
- leisure centres
- hotels?

Providing something extra can encourage customer loyalty and gives an organisation a good image, showing that it cares for its customers.

Handling complaints

Everyone in the leisure and tourism industry has to deal with complaints at one time or another. A customer who complains is giving you the chance to put things right. It is the unhappy customer who doesn't complain who is more worrying,

CASE STUDY – Oakleaf Travel Hotline

Oakleaf Travel is a tour operator which has a telephone hotline specifically to deal with complaints.

Client: My holiday was ruined by the staff at the hotel. They were, unfriendly and unhelpful.

Oakleaf: Well did you try and make an effort to get on with them?

Client: Why should I? It's their job.

Oakleaf: Well madam, if you take that sort of attitude with our overseas staff, I'm not surprised they didn't like you.

Client: How dare you! I'll report you to the Manager.

Oakleaf: I am the Manager actually.

Question

What was wrong with Oakleaf's handling of this complaint?

CASE STUDY — Nathan's sports emporium

Nathan: How can I help you?

Customer: I bought these training shoes three months ago and there is already a hole in one of them.

Nathan: I'm very sorry to hear that. Can I take a look at them? How often do you use them, sir?

Customer: I do 50 miles every week in them which includes road running and cross country.

Nathan: I see. Actually sir, the training shoes you bought are more designer wear than sports shoe.

Customer: To me, a training shoe should last at least a year, not three months.

Nathan: I can understand why you are upset sir. You need a really good pair of training shoes, suitable for off-road and road running. I will send your present pair back to the manufacturers and meanwhile I can show you a pair of training shoes which will be ideal for your purposes. With a £20 discount for the inconvenience caused, they will only cost you £20. How does that sound sir?

Customer: Well perhaps I should have got these in the first place, I'll take them. Thanks.

Question

How well do you think this complaint was handled?

because that customer says nothing but goes elsewhere in the future.

You will need to understand that it is important to listen to customers and to keep calm when handling complaints. You will also need to know when to refer a customer to a more senior member of staff if you are not able to deal with an enquiry.

Talk about it

Have you ever complained about a product or service? In a group, make a list of things that people complain about. Compare your results with the list below.

What makes us complain?

There can be many reasons why people feel the need to complain. For example:

- products and services that do not live up to the manufacturers' claims, for example 'You said the batteries in this phone would last for six months. They've run out after two'

- queuing up and waiting for long periods, for example, 'I've been in this restaurant for 25 minutes and still no one has taken my order'

- poor customer service – staff not listening

- mistakes – being given the wrong product.

Talk about it

What sort of complaints might you expect to hear in the following facilities:

- changing rooms in a sports centre
- a swimming pool
- a staff canteen?

CASE STUDY – Food safety

Rod was having a great time with his mates on a day trip to Brighton. They all ate fish and chips except for Rod who had home-made steak pie and chips. Two hours later Rod was being violently sick, and had to be taken to hospital. He stayed there for three days, with a bad case of food poisoning.

When he had recovered, Rod went back to the place where he bought his steak pie and complained to the owner, who didn't seem to take any notice.

So Rod contacted the local council's environmental health officer. The inspectors

who looked into Rod's case checked the kitchen and found cooked and fresh meat together in the same fridge, dirty work surfaces and food still stocked beyond its sell-by date.

Under the Food Safety Act (1990), which demands high standards of cleanliness at all times in the preparation and storage of food, the Local Authority inspectors closed the premises and prosecuted the owners.

Question

Do you think Rod was right to complain? Why?

When people complain, they tend to show a range of human emotions including anger and frustration, which can lead to aggressiveness. It is very important to learn how to handle complaints properly, both for your benefit and protection and for the benefit of the organisation. If you can stay calm and cope with a frustrated and angry customer, then this should mean that:

- staff should not suffer verbal abuse
- the customer should not lose his or her temper
- the image of the organisation will not be tarnished.

This is how to do it:

- Keep calm – this way you won't get into an argument with the customer.
- Listen and don't argue – this way you hear the full story and you give yourself time to come up with a suitable reply.
- Do not take complaints personally and become defensive; try to think of a complaint as a cry for help.

- Be sympathetic that the person has a complaint without necessarily accepting the blame.
- Do not put blame on to others, for example saying, 'It's the advertising department again, they got the dates wrong'. This is no consolation and it puts the organisation in a bad light.
- Use 'open' questions to find out about the complaint – don't guess or jump to conclusions, but let the customer tell you exactly what he or she wants.
- If you are unable to handle the complaint yourself, refer to someone higher up in the organisation.
- Try to come to an agreement which will satisfy the customer, for example suggesting alternatives. Make sure that whatever has been agreed is carried out as soon as possible. Do not suggest any alternatives you cannot deliver.
- Make the most of your opportunities – if you deal successfully with a complaint it is

possible that the customer will return and become one of your most loyal customers!

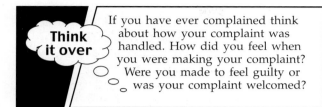

If you have ever complained think about how your complaint was handled. How did you feel when you were making your complaint? Were you made to feel guilty or was your complaint welcomed?

Handling complaints well will put your organisation in a good light. It also shows that you care for your customers.

You might have included: expensive car parking fees, people smoking in non-smoking areas, uncomfortable seating in the passenger lounge, not enough waste bins, escalators and lifts not working, not enough toilets, no television in airport lounges.

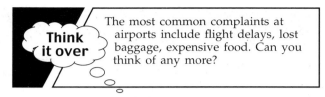

The most common complaints at airports include flight delays, lost baggage, expensive food. Can you think of any more?

Types of complainer and how to handle them

The aggressive complainer

People who lose their temper and get aggressive when they have a complaint need careful handling so that the situation does not get out of control.

The passive complainer

These people often have to be encouraged to complain. This is necessary so that the problem can be discovered and then put right.

CASE STUDY – Airport rage

It was going to be one of those days for Helen at check-in. Fog had enveloped the airport so flights could not get in or out. Delays meant crowds and crowds sometimes caused problems. Today was no exception. One passenger was expecting to fly out to Spain at 11.00 hours and it was now 14.00 hours. He decided to spend his time in the bar and after several pints of lager he was becoming quite loud.

As he approached check-in he tripped over someone's suitcase and went sprawling. He decided to take his anger and frustration out on the nearest person wearing a uniform, which just happened to be Helen.

'If you don't get me on that ... plane soon there will be big trouble. I'm sick of ... waiting. You in your fancy uniform, what are you going to do about it?'

Helen listened to him, kept calm and did not raise her voice. She looked him right in the eye as she apologised for the flight delay and said everyone was having to wait.

This did not pacify the man who continued to swear and accuse Helen of being stupid. Again, she stayed calm, asked him to sit down and said she would ask her supervisors to help him. Helen not only called her supervisor on the phone but pressed the security button under her desk. The man was escorted to security where he stayed overnight. The fog cleared but he wasn't allowed to fly in such a condition. Helen calmly carried on dealing with the other passengers.

Questions

- How do you feel Helen coped with this aggressive complainer?
- Have you ever had to deal with awkward customers?
- Share your experiences with the rest of the group.

CASE STUDY — Restaurant disappointment

Gianni enjoyed his job in his uncle's restaurant. He felt he was becoming a good waiter. One night a young couple were sitting at the window table drinking their wine. Gianni sensed there was something wrong. The woman seemed to be unhappy and annoyed. Gianni went over and asked if they had enjoyed their meal.

'Well, er, actually, er, it was OK,' said the man. The girl stared at him in amazement.

Gianni then asked if there was anything wrong with the meal. 'Well . . .' said the man.

'Please, we like to know if our customers are happy with the food and service they receive. Now if there's something that isn't quite up to standard . . .?' encouraged Gianni.

'Very well,' said the man, 'our lasagne was stone cold and the wine has got little bits of cork in it.'

Gianni apologised and told his uncle what had happened. He immediately offered the couple a free meal and a bottle of wine on an evening of their choice.

Gianni had spotted that his customers were dissatisfied, and so checked if something was wrong. He gently persuaded them to tell him the problem, despite their reluctance. He made them feel comfortable about airing their complaint.

There are two points to remember about passive complainers:

- Nice customers may not return.
- They may tell their friends their complaint was dealt with properly and promptly.

Question

It's never easy to spot the silent complainer. What sort of things should you look for if you sense your customers are not totally satisfied with either the service or product they have received?

CASE STUDY — Queue crisis

Janice travelled a lot by train because of her work. She was always frustrated when buying her ticket because of the way some queues moved faster than others.

Janice suggested to the station master that a one-queue system should be introduced. Passengers should wait in one line behind a roped area and move forward to a cashier as each one becomes free. Cashiers would press a button to indicate when they are ready to serve the next customer. This would lead to a fair and orderly queuing and serving system.

This was a very constructive suggestion by Janice. You will find this system is already

used in major Post Offices, banks and some shops.

The stationmaster should:

- thank Janice for bringing the situation to his attention
- try to resolve the problem.

Remember this type of complaint often raises issues that can also be a problem for other customers.

Question

Can you think of any situation, similar to Janice's, which can be solved constructively?

The constructive complainer

Constructive complaints help you to find solutions to problems and if handled well can bring benefits all round.

Look it up

There are two publications, *Which?* and *Holiday Which?* published by the Consumers' Association. Try to find out something about this organisation and look in either publication to see the type of situation they report on.

Keeping customer records

Many leisure and tourism organisations keep records of their customers. They record relevant information about customers that may be used for future membership and marketing purposes. Creating and using up-to-date records gives an organisation a clear picture of its business and helps it to plan for the future. For example, a health club might have records of its members' names, telephone numbers, and personal fitness plans. On some occasions, it is a legal requirement to keep records, for example for VAT purposes and the Inland Revenue.

Some examples of places that find it useful to keep customer records can include:

- a hotel, which will have a list of guests' names and addresses

- a leisure centre, which will have an activity booking sheet to show who is playing what sport and when

- a fitness centre, which will have records to show the progress of members in their fitness programmes.

Another example of keeping a record is the accident report book. This would give the following details of any accident:

- details of casualty – name, address and telephone number, age, and gender

- details of accident – date, time, place, what happened, nature of injuries

- names and addresses of witnesses

- action taken – if first aid given, casualty taken to hospital, to whom incident reported.

Keeping such records allows the management to monitor health and safety and, if there is ever a court case, all the facts can be presented as they will all have been written down. Other health and safety records include:

- dates on which fire extinguishers were checked

- times when pool water is tested

- lifeguard training and qualifications.

Try it out

Look at the sample report of an injury or dangerous occurrence and read all information. Design your own simple accident report form and complete it following this incident:

Eloise was playing volleyball when she suddenly screamed out in pain as she hit the ball. Her finger had bent right back on itself and Eloise was left in agony.

Remember that your report should give full details of the incident.

Look it up

By law your school or college will have a first aid box, accident book and a health and safety statement. Find out where these are all kept and ask if you can examine them in detail.

Creating customer records

Accurate records are an essential part of good customer service. You will need to know how to create customer records, either on a computer system or manually. You should also understand the issues involved in data protection.

(Reproduced with permission from Health and Safety Executive)

An injury report form

Data Protection Act 1998

This Act means that all records about clients which are filed will be seen as data, whether they are held electronically or on paper. The 1998 Act provides people with a range of rights, and specifies obligations which organisations must follow. Among these rights are included:

- the right to know what information is held about a person

- the right to refuse to provide information

- the right that data should be accurate and up-to-date

CASE STUDY – Cathy's holiday from hell

When you are on holiday you don't expect too many things to go wrong. You naturally think you will be looked after and nothing untoward will happen to you. Not so in Cathy's case.

Cathy booked the holiday with 'Wing and a Prayer' airlines. She was looking forward to a week in the sun in Crete. And it was hot! The hotel room was meant to have air conditioning and a balcony. But although there was a fan, it was broken, and although there was a balcony, the sliding door to it wouldn't open. The room with a view turned out to have a view of a 24-hour building site complete with all the noises made by bulldozers, cement mixers and raucous labourers.

Cathy thought she might escape to the poolside. Unfortunately the pool water was so dirty she couldn't see the bottom, there was broken glass on the poolside and there was no lifeguard to complain to.

Things did not improve. What was supposed to be a relaxing week in the sun turned out to be a holiday from hell. The tour rep. did keep promising to transfer her to another hotel but that never happened.

Cathy complained to the travel agent when she got home, as her solicitor had advised her that, as a result of a European Directive in 1990, the tour operator is responsible for every part of a holiday, including travel and accommodation. She is still awaiting the outcome of her claim.

Questions

- What would be the best way that Cathy could make her complaint?

- Have you or anyone in your group ever experienced a 'holiday from hell'? Share your experiences with the rest of your group.

- Imagine you are Cathy's tour operator. Write to her to say what you intend to do about her complaint.

- the right that information should not be kept for longer than necessary

- the right to confidentiality – that the information should not be accessible to unauthorised people.

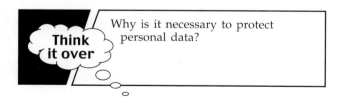

Think it over — Why is it necessary to protect personal data?

Many people and organisations hold information about us – on computer or in paper files. This growth in the recording and use of personal information has many benefits, for example better medical care and helping to fight crime. There are also some possible problems, for example if information is entered wrongly (perhaps onto a database), is out-of-date or is confused with data belonging to someone else. A person could find themselves unfairly refused benefits, credit, housing or even a job or a place at college.

Computer systems have largely taken over from manual systems for keeping records and are used in libraries when bar coding books and in pubs for stock control. Manual systems which are still in use include accident report forms, maintenance sheets and card index records. However, regardless of which system is used to keep records they must be:

- accurate

- clear

- legible

- up-to-date

- easily accessible.

Finding and changing existing records

You will need to know how to find and change customer records because customers' details change; for example, people move house, they have children, and so on. Records may be kept on computer, in filing cabinets, in diaries, daybooks, or on record cards. They must be easily accessible so it is helpful to keep them all centralised, either on a computer database or in a filing cabinet.

If finding records has to be quick then changing them has to be done accurately. If a customer changes address, and the new address is not taken down properly then all future correspondence will be lost, which could mean a loss of business for the organisation.

Accuracy and confidentiality

Customer records need to be accurate so if you enter information the details must be correct and double checked if necessary. Imagine if you made someone ten years older than they really were, or gave their partner a new name; that could lead to all sorts of complications.

Customers give information about themselves in the knowledge that this information will not be passed on to other people. It is essential therefore that records are kept secure and that only authorised personnel have access to them. You also need to be aware of the Data Protection Act which limits the amount and type of information you can place on computer about people (see page 162).

Organisations are also required to inform the authorities that they will be storing information about customers on computer systems.

Customer service: A summary

- People shop around for similar products which are priced more or less the same. Excellent customer service can make the 'browser' stay, buy and return so that they become regular customers.
- First impressions are lasting impressions. It takes only three seconds for a customer to gain an impression. Make sure it is a good one.
- Different customers have different needs. Identifying and meeting these needs will enhance the image of both you and your organisation.
- Internal customers or work colleagues are just as important as external customers. Good teamwork, co-operation and support between internal customers lead to excellent customer service for external customers.
- Dealing with customers takes skill, personality and patience. This is one of the most enjoyable parts of working in leisure and tourism.
- A complaint handled properly and professionally can in fact lead to repeat business.
- Customers demand high standards of service – treat them as you yourself would like to be treated – put yourself in their shoes.

CASE STUDY – Confidentialty

Anil works as an assistant in a leisure centre. One day when the phone rang in the office Anil answered this call as the receptionist was out of the office:

'Hello, I was wondering if you could help me with some information about one of your staff. I need his address and telephone number. Would you mind helping me out?'

Unfortunately, Anil was too eager to please and did what he was asked.

The next day, the employee who had been the subject of the phone call came in looking puzzled. He wondered how his old employer had managed to get in touch with him at his new home address.

Question

The information that Anil so gladly offered was confidential and should not have been given out. What should he have done?

Unit 3 Assessment

Keeping customers happy: Scenario

When customers spend money they expect good customer service.

In this assessment you will have to investigate how one leisure and tourism organisation provides customer service. The second part of the assessment includes keeping a record of your involvement with customers in a variety of situations.

What you have to do
Obtaining a pass grade

Task 1

The first part of the assessment can be done as a presentation. You will need notes, OHTs and handouts. Your tutor will assess you on the basis of the content of your presentation, the back-up material to support it and the way you performed. In your presentation you should:

- give five examples of situations in the organisation that require staff to have contact with customers; for example, face-to-face, over the phone, giving information, selling products, handling complaints, serving drinks

- describe, with examples, how the organisation meets the needs of internal and external customers

- describe the organisation's complaints procedure

- describe what type of customer records the organisation keeps. Wherever possible, include examples of the actual forms, e.g. membership records, letters of thanks/complaints/enquiry. Bear in mind

that the organisation won't let you have personal details of members but you may include some blank forms.

- describe how do you regard the organisation's customer service policy. Evaluate it in the light of repeat business, customer comments, your own opinion.

Task 2

- Provide evidence of your own personal dealings with a variety of customers. For this you have to provide a record of involvement which could include witness statements from a supervisor, photographs, or even a video of you in action.

- Provide evidence in a similar form to the previous task, showing how you handle complaints.

These situations may not always arise so you may have to carry out some role-play situations.

Obtaining a merit or distinction grade

To obtain a merit or distinction grade your work must show:

- a sound review of customer service, with relevant examples of the ways in which the organisation provides for different customer needs

- a resumé comparing and contrasting the way the organisation serves its internal and external customers

- a clear description of the employee's responsibility to provide good customer service

- the ability to communicate clearly with customers in a manner that is helpful and friendly

- the ability to provide customers with valid information and handle their complaints appropriately.

Obtaining a distinction grade

To achieve a distinction, your work must show:

- a thorough and knowledgeable review of customer service, including detailed information on the ways in which the organisation provides for different customer needs

- an analysis of the consequences of poor customer service for the organisation

- the ability to communicate effectively and confidently with customers, listening carefully and providing a full and effective response

- the ability to evaluate your own performance in the customer service situations undertaken.

Helpful hints

For part one of the assessment it might be worth choosing a leisure and tourism organisation you are familiar with, perhaps you know the manager, or you may have a relative who works there. The alternative is to choose a place where you would like to work, for example a hotel or leisure centre. Your first task is to contact the manager and fix up an appointment.

Here are a few tips when using the phone:

1 Try to make your voice friendly and not too formal. It might be an idea to prepare a script so that you don't forget what you have to say.

2 'Smile as you dial' – putting a smile in your voice is likely to get results.

3 State who you are, what you want and ask who is the best person to speak to.

4 Rehearse the call with a friend. 'Practice makes perfect'.

5 Keep calm, sound interesting, and enthusiastic. Remember, enthusiasm spreads.

Unit 3 Test

1 Instructions at a hotel are written in several languages.

This would meet the needs of which group of guests?

2 Which type of communication skill is most important for an instructor in an outdoor pursuit centre?

3 If customers never seem to complain, what does this suggest to you?

4 Why should staff in a leisure centre be familiar with the services and facilities it offers?

5 Who would give visitors on an all-inclusive package holiday information about daily itineraries?

6 How would you give directions to a non-English speaking visitor to a destination across a city?

7 Why does a hotel provide information about evacuation of the premises on every door and in every room?

8 What are the two most likely outcomes for the restaurant customers leaving a restaurant feeling they have received good value for money?

9 A restaurant is evaluating the customer service skills of its staff. Which factor best shows positive improvement?

10 How do you think customers feel about organisations which deal with complaints in a positive and constructive way?

11 Name three contributing factors to the poor reputation of a leisure and tourism organisation.

12 What is the main reason for an organisation keeping a lot of customers' names and addresses?

13 Explain why different age groups have different holiday needs.

14 A guest at a hotel reception is asking for details of prices but reception is very busy. What is the best way to help?

15 How would you deal with a customer who complains that he didn't get value for money from his two-week holiday in Majorca?

Running an event

This unit covers the knowledge you will need to meet the assessment requirements for Unit 3.

It is written in three sections. Section one shows how careful planning leads to events being a success. Section two looks at actually taking part in an event and the third section shows how to review the event.

What you need to produce

You have to produce a record of an event related to leisure and tourism identifying your involvement in the planning, running and evaluation of the event.

This unit is assessed through your portfolio work only. The grade awarded will be the grade for the unit.

Introduction

Events play a big part in the leisure and tourism industry. They range from small, local activities, like a village garden party to multi-million pound events like the World Cup or the Olympic Games. Whatever their size, different events have many similarities in the way they are planned and staged.

Think it over

What kind of events could you and your colleagues consider organising? Some ideas are given below.

Examples of events which you and your colleagues could organise might include:

- a day trip to the seaside for senior citizens

- a party for a group of special needs children

- a table-top sale with all proceeds going to the local hospital

- a sports day for the local junior school.

It is a great way to find out how well you can work with people. It also gives you the responsibility to help plan, organise, run and evaluate an event. What's more, your experience in planning, running and evaluating an event will stand you in good stead at a job interview. Employers look favourably at people who can show organisational skills and working with others, which is what this unit is all about.

How to plan an event

For any event to be successful, it must be planned properly. This is where teamwork comes into it because, after all, it is virtually impossible to plan, organise and run an event on your own.

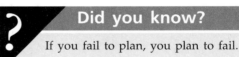

? Did you know?

If you fail to plan, you plan to fail.

Good communication between team members will ensure that everyone knows the details of the event. Without effective communication the old saying, 'The right hand will not know what the left hand is doing' certainly applies.

Think it over

What sort of communication skills do you think will be necessary for you as you and your team start to plan your event?

Try to list ten famous sports events, such as Wimbledon. Choose one and discuss what sort of planning must take place.

The event planning process

All leisure and tourism events aim to attract customers, increase sales, help promote an organisation and provide enjoyment. However, good events don't just happen by themselves; there's usually a lot of time, money and hard work attached to them. In order to have some chance of being successful, events go through a planning process like the one shown in Figure 4.1.

What will the event be?

When you have formed a team the next thing to do is to choose an event. A good way of doing this is to have a 'brainstorming session' and to come up with anything you can think of. Don't dismiss any ideas at this point. Remember that this is a 'live' unit: you will actually be doing the planning, running and evaluating of the event and using this as evidence for your portfolio.

Ideas could include:

- a sponsored walk
- a school/college 'open' day
- a raft race
- a trip on 'le shuttle'
- a swimathon
- a day trip to the seaside
- a 'toga' party
- a trip to a theme park
- 'stars in their eyes', etc.

It's great to come up with the ideas but in the end you have to be:

- realistic – is it feasible for the team to do it?
- aware of health and safety issues – is anything dangerous?

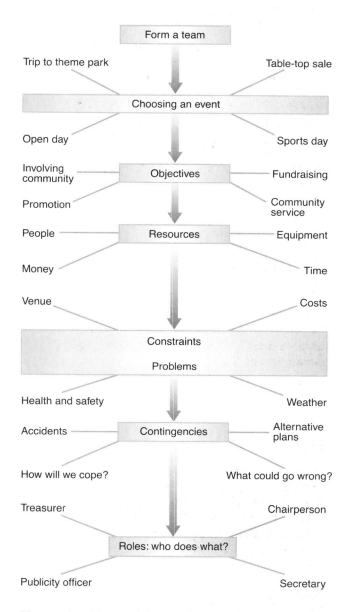

Figure 4.1 You will be working through this process as your event takes shape

- aware of the time – eight to twelve weeks from start to finish
- aware of any costs involved – can you afford it?
- able to manage the scale of the event – have you got the resources and the expertise?

Remember that your tutors have ultimate responsibility for the health and safety of the group and they will not want to see you or anyone else in a situation where you are put at risk. It is therefore important to be realistic and sensible when assessing your ideas. Look at the snapshots which follow.

SNAPSHOTS

Two less than successful events

*A **fashion show** A fairly successful fashion show had been organised by a group of leisure and tourism students in March. The sum of £200 was raised towards an overseas trip. About 100 people had turned up on the night.*

The students decided to hold another fashion show in October, again to raise funds for their trip. They hoped the same people who attended the last show would turn up and this time bring their friends. As a result, they didn't do too much publicity as they thought they would gain 'repeat business'. On the night the hall was set up for 150 people. As it happened, only 23 people turned up. It was a disaster from a financial point of view as the students had to pay a £100 deposit to the fashion show company if less than 100 people came. Add to that the cost of refreshments and hire of the hall and the event quickly became classed as a disaster.

*A **10-mile road race** Three leisure and tourism students in a group were keen athletes so a race seemed the obvious event to organise. They had all competed in road races themselves so had an idea of how to organise such an event. Or so they thought. They enlisted the help of the local athletics club secretary who advised them about the safety of competitors, the need to apply for a race permit and the requirement to liaise with the police regarding traffic control.*

The students sent out all the necessary publicity material and expected an entry of about 200 runners.

But on the day, only 30 people turned up. It just happened that the London Marathon was being held on the same day. To make things worse, the police refused to let the race start because they had been given insufficient notice of the event.

In the end, some athletes decided to go on a training run while others just went home, extremely disappointed.

SNAPSHOTS

Two successful events

*A **table-top sale** Six leisure and tourism students wanted to raise some money for the local hospital so they decided to hold a table-top sale.*

They produced leaflets and circulated them around their college and the local area: they actually did the direct mail themselves by posting the leaflets through letterboxes. They claimed the exercise did them good! A press release was submitted to the local newspaper.

The big task was to collect enough bric-a-brac, books, clothes, etc. to sell on the day. This turned out to be easy as there was a terrific response from staff and parents.

The event was held in the school hall and was due to start at 10 am. At 9.30 am, the students were wondering if anyone would turn up. At 9.45 am, there was a queue of customers. At 10 am the floodgates opened. Between 10 am and midday 300 people attended the sale.

The students were able to donate £357 to the local hospital. Their aim had been met. Teamwork, determination and some very hard work had paid off.

*A **trip to the seaside** The aim of this event was to take 40 senior citizens to Skegness for a good day out. The group of eight leisure and tourism students paid a visit to the local Community Centre on senior citizens' activities day and put the idea to them. The thought of a free day out to the seaside in June sounded very attractive and so the plan was put into action.*

The first task was to raise £210 for the 52-seater coach. This was accomplished through a sponsored car wash (an event in itself), sponsorship from local companies and a contribution from the college.

When the big day arrived, a great time was had by all. A quiz and a singsong were popular activities on the outward and return journeys. Even the weather was kind.

Afterwards the students received many letters of thanks from the senior citizens. There was an outstanding photograph of the coach party in the local newspaper. The students each received a letter from the college principal, congratulating them on their highly successful event.

Why did the first two events fail and the second two succeed? What would you have done differently?

The objectives of the event

An objective is a goal you want to achieve. The success of an event is measured by how well the objectives have been met.

Typical objectives for an event might include those outlined in Figure 4.2. Look back at the snapshots on page 170 and think about them again in the light of these objectives.

Figure 4.2   Some typical event objectives

Objectives must be SMART:

Specific   –   each objective must be exact in detail for each part of the event

Measurable   –   targets can be measured, e.g. numbers and sales

Achievable   –   objectives set must be capable of being achieved

Realistic   –   can the team achieve the objectives?

Timed   –   can objectives be achieved within a certain time scale.

> **S M A R T** objectives mean success

Examples of objectives:

⋄ Organise a day trip to Skegness for 40 senior citizens in June – promote a good image.

⋄ Raise £150 to be spent on sports equipment for the local junior school – fundraising.

⋄ Increase the number of people using the fitness suite by 25 per cent over the summer period – increase sales.

⋄ An open day at school/college to raise awareness to young people of the courses available – promoting an organisation.

Try it out

What do you think the objectives could be for the following events:

⋄ a table-top sale

⋄ a day trip to Alton Towers

⋄ a concert by junior school children

⋄ an exhibition of students' work?

The most important point to make about objectives is that everyone from the outset should be involved in setting them so that everyone knows what they are trying to achieve. It is also helpful to monitor the time scales and targets to see whether the objectives are likely to be met. The evaluation after the event will show if the objectives have been achieved.

When will it happen?

The timing of an event is always an important issue. For example, imagine your event is a Christmas concert for the local junior school. There are certain considerations to be taken into account regarding the timing of the concert. Remember that schools usually put on their own Christmas festivities any time from early December, so don't clash with existing activities and make sure you are not organising the same activity as the school. Also, because this event will have to take place in term time, it would be essential to liaise with the headteacher.

Likewise, a sports activity day for schools should really be programmed in the summer term, when, hopefully, the weather will be favourable. Again, there may be a clash with school exams so planning in advance is important.

CASE STUDY — Pop star party

Six GNVQ Leisure and Tourism students had to run an event as part of their course. Over a cup of coffee in the canteen they came up with a few ideas:

- a musical comedy concert – perhaps an established musical using their own words
- a day trip to a theme park for a group of students
- a Christmas disco
- a seaside trip for the elderly
- a Hawaiian party night
- a children's disco
- an open day for potential leisure and tourism students.

Each event idea was then discussed in more detail:

- The comedy musical – only a few members of the group showed any real interest and they need to do something that all of the team will enjoy doing. Also it would take ages to write the script and time was against them – after all they still had to clear their backlog of assignments!
- Christmas disco – there was not enough time to plan a disco properly as it was already November.
- Hawaiian night – their tutor liked this idea but they were not sure if anyone else would show any interest. There would have to be an awful lot of organisation to get costumes and decorations.
- The open day for students – the idea made them all yawn, they wanted more of a challenge.

The students then went back and discussed these ideas further with their course tutor. They narrowed their choice down to three:

- day trip to the seaside
- children's disco
- trip to a theme park.

Karen, one of the students, said,

'After discussing the three remaining options in great detail, we eventually decided that we were going to hold a children's party built around the theme of pop stars. We decided on this because:

- we think that it shows potential in helping us meet all of our team objectives which were to make sure that everyone involved had a lot of fun and enjoyment, to successfully complete the event management unit of our course, to break even or maybe even make a profit after all our fundraising and to have fun ourselves during the organisation and on the actual day of the event
- there is enough organisation involved in it to allow each team member an important role with a high level of responsibility
- it involves communicating with people outside our college which will help us to meet new people and will also improve our communication skills
- it has not been attempted by the previous leisure and tourism group, unlike the seaside trip
- we feel that we can learn something from the legal obligations that we have to consider
- we have not really got any competition from other people doing the same thing
- this was the event that all of our team members showed the most enthusiasm towards.'

Adam went on to explain the **objectives** of the pop star party. 'We want:

- to provide a party for 100 children aged between 7 and 10 years old
- to organise a car wash so that we can raise enough money to cover the cost of the event
- to work together as a team
- to promote the image of the college in the local newspaper by writing a press release and including photographs of the party.'

Question

What do you think of the students' ideas and objectives?

Try it out

Imagine you were organising a day trip to London for your event. What would be the best time of year for the trip? State your reasons.

We all need deadlines to ensure tasks are performed on time, for example deadlines for assessments. Each stage of your event should have a deadline otherwise the whole thing will not come together. For example, you will want to publicise your event. If you miss the submission deadline for the local newspaper, your advertisement or press release will not be printed. It is no use seeing an advertisement for an event the week after the event has taken place. It does not present a good image.

Your event, which you will plan, run and evaluate may take between ten to twelve weeks or perhaps one term. You will find when you are planning for your event that time seems to go quicker than usual and before you know it you've only got two weeks left when you thought you had four!

There is an answer to this problem. It comes in the form of careful scheduling, with a time scale for each stage of your event planning. Look at the example of a schedule in Figure 4.3.

Figure 4.3 Example of schedule for a students' disco

Week	Date	Task
Week 1	10–17 January	Aims/objectives/ date to be set
Week 2	18–25 January	Allocate team roles
Week 3	26 January– 1 February	Work out costs, decide on fund-raising ideas, book disco
Week 4	2–8 February	Publicity and promotion
Week 5	9–15 February	Publicity and promotion
Week 6	16–23 February	Confirm arrangements, publicity and promotion
Week 7	28 February	**EVENT**
Week 8	1–8 March	Evaluation

You will notice that the schedule runs a programme order leading up to the actual event itself. Getting things in the right order takes time and careful planning.

CASE STUDY – A sponsored carwash

Four Intermediate Leisure and Tourism students decided to do a sponsored carwash at the local supermarket. The first mistake they made was failing to ask the supermarket manager so when they got there, complete with buckets and sponges, they were questioned by the assistant manager as to what they were doing. They explained that they were raising money for charity by charging customers £3 to have their car washed. The assistant manager must have felt sorry for them and allowed them to go ahead. The next problem was with the water supply, or lack of it. The nearest tap was inside the supermarket warehouse, 30 yards away. With permission from the manager, they were able to use this. This was turning out to be a bit of a nightmare. On top of all this, they weren't getting any customers because the supermarket carwash cost only £2.

After five hours they had made the princely sum of £12 by washing cars belonging to their relatives!

Question

What do you think the students would discuss when evaluating their event?

Try it out

Divide the group into four so that each group works out one schedule for the following events:

◦   a fashion show

◦   a junior sports activities day

◦   a day trip to the seaside for senior citizens

◦   a garden fete.

It is worth remembering these points when planning your event:

◦   Make sure you give sufficient time to your planning.

◦   Planning stages can be missed if you are rushed.

◦   Put tasks in the right order.

◦   Missed deadlines spell disaster!

Where will it take place?

When selecting a venue for your event certain factors have to be taken into consideration:

◦   Location – as we saw from the marketing mix, this is an important factor. Are transport links available? Do people know where it is? Is there enough car parking?

◦   Suitability – you need to check whether the facilities are suitable for staging your event. For example, can you hold a social function in the sports hall, or will it damage the floor? Does the facility have to undergo major changes to put on the event, for example do you have to add coloured lights in the pool area for a Caribbean evening? What health and safety regulations have to be followed?

CASE STUDY — A junior sports evening

Mohammed's group decided to stage a junior sports evening followed by a meal and a disco. Mohammed and his colleagues were asked to describe their event to another group of Leisure and Tourism students. This is how it went:

'Our first task in organising our junior sports evening was to decide on a suitable venue. We wanted to follow the event with a meal and a disco. In fact we wanted everything to take place indoors because we didn't trust the great British weather!

We realised the school sports centre main hall was big enough to cater for all our needs. One end could be used for the sports activities for the 30 children and for their parents to spectate. The middle section was set up with tables and chairs for the meal and the third section acted as a dance floor. The three sections were separated by the purpose-made curtains which acted as partitions. As soon as the sports activities finished, we drew back the curtain to reveal the 'dining' area.

After the meal the disco/dance area was revealed, much to the joy and amazement of all the children.

The sports hall really showed the benefits of a multi-functional area which could be used for sports and leisure activities.'

The multi-purpose sports hall, as shown in the diagram below, was the perfect venue for these three separate activities.

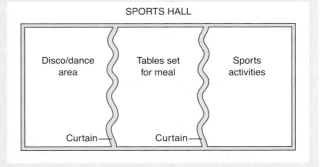

Question

What other facilities could be considered for this type of event?

CASE STUDY — Leadership qualities

Tariq

Tariq runs a very successful advertising and marketing company. He always involves his staff in decision-making but it is he who makes the final decisions.  Tariq plans things down to the very last detail to make sure all deadlines are met and that the work his company has produced is of the highest quality. Whenever the company secures a big contract he makes sure that his staff share the good news and thanks them for their efforts.

Jade

Jade is a senior air cabin crew member. She is responsible for six flight attendants on long-haul flights from Manchester to Orlando. She makes sure all her crew look absolutely perfect and if not they will be reported. She gives them all instructions before each flight and makes it clear that they must treat all passengers with the very best in customer service. Jade is strict but fair. Her crew know the standards she demands. They also know they can approach her with any problems.

Wesley

Wesley manages a dual use leisure centre. He has to liaise with the school PE staff during the day to try and strike a balance between the school and community activities. Wesley is also a member of the local community users group so he again has to try to fulfil the needs of specific community groups. He always tries to see other people's points of view and always lets them know if requests for bookings are turned down. He has to be a diplomat, leader and listener all rolled into one!

Question

What qualities do these leaders show?

- Spectators – is there sufficient seating and spectator accommodation?

- Is the facility open at the time you want it?

- Is the venue available on the date required?

- Is there a kitchen or other means of catering available?

Staffing for the event

The most important resource for any event is people and the skills they bring with them. You will have to identify how many people will be needed to help run the event on the day and allocate their specific areas of responsibility.

It is also important to make sure that team members have the necessary skills to make the event a success. For example, do you have someone who can design posters, word process letters, write press releases? Most important, does someone have the necessary leadership skills?

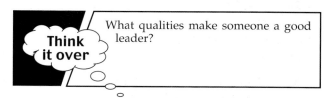

Think it over
What qualities make someone a good leader?

The idea that your team is a group of people united by a common purpose does not go far enough. Your group will show that it is a team when it displays certain characteristic behaviour that is, when:

- people keep an eye on each other's progress and will direct effort where it is needed most

- team spirit is high and people enjoy working together

- levels of communication are good – good teams solve problems well

- people accept responsibility for their actions

- any change to schedules is greeted with a positive attitude.

Each person should be given a role, or perhaps share one, in the team event. These could be:

- co-ordinator – has an overview of the event, makes sure all jobs are completed, keeps order at meetings, organises voting

- secretary – deals with correspondence, keeps accurate records, keeps minutes of meetings

- treasurer – overseas financial transactions, creates secure system for withdrawing cash, responsible for secure handling of income

- marketing officer – promotes the event, works with newspapers/radio, organises press coverage

- catering officer – orders all food and drinks, oversees preparation of food, ensures hygiene standards are met

- facility officer – finds venue, responsible for health and safety arrangements, arranges specialist equipment for the event, e.g. lighting.

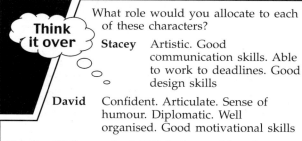

Think it over

What role would you allocate to each of these characters?

Stacey   Artistic. Good communication skills. Able to work to deadlines. Good design skills

David   Confident. Articulate. Sense of humour. Diplomatic. Well organised. Good motivational skills

Natalie   Well organised. Efficient record keeping. Good telephone manner. Good IT skills

Sophie   Reliable. Responsible. Likes maths. Trustworthy

Stewart   Well organised. Good team worker. First aid qualifications. Knowledge of hygiene

Robert   Well organised. Good communication skills. Good at solving problems.

Money and accounting

It is essential that detailed financial planning is undertaken from the beginning and that an income and expenditure balance must be achieved if the event is to be financially successful. Accounts of all payments made and all income received in relation to the event must be kept. This will ensure no one is wrongly accused of mishandling funds and that all financial transactions are monitored.

The financial objectives of your event could be a break-even situation or a profit which could go to an organisation you have previously agreed on, for example the local hospital.

Having set the financial objectives, it is then necessary to identify what the money will be spent on – the expenditure. This could include postage, telephone, transport, advertisements, food and drink and prizes.

It is important to produce a comprehensive and accurate set of costs. There is no such thing as a free event; everything costs money so realistic budget expenditure limits have to be set. The cost of any event varies with its size. The Olympic Games costs hundreds of millions of pounds to stage, whereas a junior sports day may need only a small amount of money to cover prizes and refreshments.

Try it out

As a group, write down the different ways you could raise money to cover the costs of your event.

Remember the six Leisure and Tourism students who planned to organise a children's pop star party do part of their course (see case study on page 172)?

The income and expenditure statement in Figure 4.4 shows the fundraising activities and sponsorship the students acquired to pay for the party. Any profit was put towards subsidising an overseas working trip. Can you work out how much profit was made?

The students opened a building society savings account to enable them to monitor the funds they were raising to finance their overseas trip. From this account they were also able to pay any costs incurred in their fundraising activities. A record of account transactions is shown in Figure 4.5.

Figure 4.4 GNVQ Intermediate leisure and tourism income and expenditure statement

Income	Amount	Expenditure	Amount
British Sugar	£50.00	Dress Material	£50.00
Travel Wright	£15.00	Lunn Poly Travel Agency	£735.00
Waitrose	£50.00	Fashion Show Deposit	£100.00
College Carwash Proceeds	£60.00	Carwash Shampoo	£4.00
Fashion Show Proceeds	£246.02	Fashion Show Refreshments	£10.00
Sponsored Walk Proceeds	£17.00	Pop Star Party Refreshments and Decorations	£58.02
Pop Star Party Proceeds	£247.00	Raffle Tickets	£1.98
Newgate Carwash Proceeds	£50.00		
Great Mills Carwash Proceeds	£127.37		
Holiday Payments	£285.00		
Table-top Sale	£140.03		
Charitable Donations	£4.00		
Gross Interest	£0.05		
Total	**£1291.47**	**Total**	**£959.00**

CASE STUDY — Caught in the act

Jack was in charge of finance for the disco which he and his colleagues had organised for the college students as part of their Leisure and Tourism course. It was his job to keep the ticket money and put it in the college safe. He also had to take care of any income that was generated from refreshment sales.

When it came to the evaluation of the event, Jack had to give his financial report to the rest of the group. He said that income from ticket sales was £100 and refreshment sales came to £76.35. As he was about to sit down, Sophie decided to ask Jack,

'If the ticket sales came to £100, with each person paying £2 per ticket, how come there were 75 people at the dance? Did 25 manage to get in free? And another thing, how come people were charged 60p for a can of soft drink when we decided that soft drinks should only be 40p?'

Jack went red. He said that some people must have got in free. But Sophie wouldn't let this drop. She went on,

'Then how was it that some of my friends paid on the door and weren't given tickets?'

Jack had been found out. He admitted that he had made £50 from people paying on the door and overcharging for drinks to make extra profit — which he had kept.

It was the group who decided how this situation should be dealt with. They felt let down. After a vote, it was decided they had to let their tutor know what Jack had done.

Jack's parents were invited in to see the principal who explained the situation to them. It was decided that Jack should pay the money back immediately. The principal said he did not want to call in the police, even though he could have done. He decided that Jack should be given 10 hours' community detention over the rest of the term. This included picking up litter around the college premises, clearing out the gymnastics storeroom and generally helping to keep the college tidy. Jack's parents were in agreement with this decision. They felt this was the right way to deal with the situation, taking into account the fact that Jack would have to face up to his fellow students.

Questions

- What would your group have done in these situations?

- How would you have dealt with Jack?

Figure 4.5 GNVQ Intermediate Leisure and Tourism Building Society account transactions

Date	Payee	Category	Amount (£)	Running Balance (£)
Opening Balance				50.00
Month Ending 31/12/98				
08/12/98	Dress Material Shop	Cash Withdrawal	-35.00	15.00
Total Month Ending 31/12/98			-35.00	
Month Ending 28/02/99				
01/02/99	Building Society	Cash Deposit (Gross Interest)	0.05	15.05
05/02/99	College Carwash Proceeds	Cash Deposit	55.00	70.05
26/02/99	Fashion Show Proceeds	Cash Deposit	22.02	92.07
Total Month Ending 28/02/99			77.07	
Month Ending 31/03/99				
02/03/99	Fashion Show Proceeds	Cheque	8.00	100.07
02/03/99	Charitable Donations	Cash Deposit	3.00	103.07
02/03/99	College Carwash Proceeds	Cash Deposit	5.00	108.07
02/03/99	Fashion Show Proceeds	Cash Deposit	46.00	154.07
05/03/99	Fashion Show Proceeds	Cash Deposit	160.00	314.07
05/03/99	Pop Star Party Proceeds	Cash Deposit	160.00	474.07
05/03/99	Charitable Donations	Cash Deposit	1.00	475.07
18/03/99	Pop Star Party Proceeds	Cash Deposit	70.00	545.07
26/03/99	Pop Star Party Proceeds	Cheque	7.00	552.07
26/03/99	Lunn Poly Travel Agency	Cash Withdrawal	-435.00	117.07
Total Month ending 31/03/99			25.00	
Month Ending 30/04/99				
20/04/99	Newgate Carwash Proceeds	Cash Deposit	50.00	167.07
23/04/99	Sponsored Walk Proceeds		17.00	184.07
Total Month Ending 30/04/99			67.00	
Month Ending 31/05/99				
26/05/99	Great Mills Carwash Proceeds		123.37	307.44
26/05/99	College Table-top Sale		125.00	432.44
Total Month Ending 31/05/99			248.37	
Month Ending 31/07/99				
07/07/99	College Table-top Sale		15.03	447.47
07/07/99	Holiday Payment		80.00	527.47
13/07/99	Fashion Show Deposit		-100.00	427.47
13/07/99	Lunn Poly Travel Agency	Cash Withdrawal	-300.00	127.47
26/07/99	Holiday Payment		105.00	232.47
Total Month Ending 31/07/99			-199.97	
Month Ending 31/10/99				
13/10/99	Holiday Payment		70.00	302.47
13/10/99	Holiday Payment		30.00	
Total Month Ending 31/10/99			100.00	
Grand Total			**282.47**	**332.47**

CASE STUDY — A tricky decision

The event planning was going well. A venue for the netball and football tournament had been found and a date had been set. Letters to local companies asking for sponsorship to pay for medals, trophies and refreshments had been sent out. It was decided that any profits should be given to the local special needs school to buy sports equipment.

One letter received from a local company had a cheque for £100 attached to it. It came from a company who transported live animals to the continent for slaughter.

This put the students in a dilemma. Some were strongly against this practice, others didn't mind. The debate which followed included arguments stating that the money was needed because no other sponsors had been found. Somebody suggested sending the money direct to the special school. Another student argued that it was 'dirty' money and should be sent back.

Question

Imagine you had a vote and it was decided to return the sponsorship cheque. Write a letter to the company explaining why you cannot accept their money.

Equipment and materials needed

The equipment and materials you will need obviously depends on your event.

Figure 4.6 shows just a few examples. The main thing to remember is that equipment and materials do not come free – you have to include them in your budget. The big question is how to know what you will need for your event. Some ideas might include the following:

- Find out if someone has organised a similar event and ask them what they used.

- Picture your event in your mind and, as a group, make a list of what you think you might need.

- Talk to someone who is used to organising events; it may be your tutor, relatives or friends. There's always someone in the community who has done this. It doesn't matter if what they have organised has nothing to do with your event – they will give you lots of ideas.

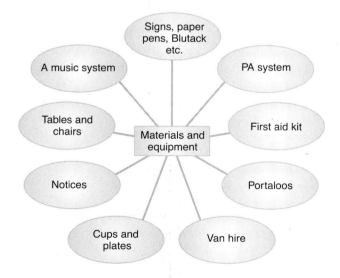

Figure 4.6 The equipment needed will vary according to your event

In your group, list the equipment and materials needed for a five-a-side football tournament for under-11s, with a slap-up tea afterwards.

How the event will be promoted
Definition

Promotion is all about publicising products and services in the right way to the right customer (see Figure 4.7).

CASE STUDY — Gala dinner

Richard has organised the Annual Gala/ Dinner for a major international company for the last five years. As secretary of all social activities his job is to organise the event for 580 staff at a major London hotel. He says,

'Everything must be perfect. Apart from booking the hotel and liaising with the hotel manager, I have to ensure that all the necessary equipment and materials are available both on the night and beforehand. Here's an example of my checklist:

- Raffle drum – for the grand draw
- Raffle tickets – sold on the night
- Place names – on tables
- Easels – for seating plans to stand on
- Microphones – speeches
- Prizes – employee of the year
- Invitations – make sure everyone is invited
- Wine lists – for guests
- Direction signs – show guests where to go
- Raffle prizes.

Over the years I've managed to plan things so that the night runs smoothly. The secret

is to look back on previous gala nights, write down what went right and what went wrong, and adjust the plans accordingly.'

Questions

- What type of reward would Richard receive for organising such a successful event?

- Imagine it was Richard's first time of organising the gala dinner, who could he turn to for help?

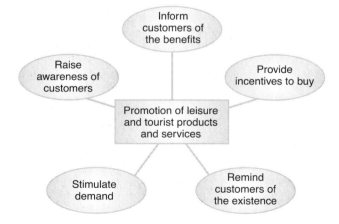

Figure 4.7   The main aims of promotion

Anyone who organises an event hopes that it will be well supported by everyone taking part and everyone watching it. An event could be promoted by:

- posters and leaflets
- press releases
- radio and TV advertising
- word of mouth.

These could be organised by the team publicity officer, but it is the task of everyone involved to spread the word. The different types of promotional activities are shown in Figure 4.8.

Figure 4.8 Different promotional activities

Try it out

Look at the Millennium Gala Day leaflet. How else do you think this event could be promoted?

This leaflet provides you with all the information needed to write a press release, so this is your chance to show off your journalistic skills to promote this event. Write the press release.

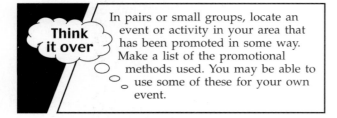

Think it over

In pairs or small groups, locate an event or activity in your area that has been promoted in some way. Make a list of the promotional methods used. You may be able to use some of these for your own event.

Health and safety

As a team member, you are responsible for the health and safety of the participants in your event and anyone who is watching it. Likewise, organisations that put on events, for example a Premiership football club staging a match, is also responsible for everyone in the stadium. You have only to look at the case study about the Hillsborough disaster on page 182 to realise that health and safety should be the number one priority at all events.

Laws such as the Safety of Sports Crowds and Stadium Act 1988 and the Health and Safety at

Source: The Lincolnshire and Nottinghamshire Air Ambulance Fund

This leaflet is promoting a local 'one-off' event

Work Act 1974 were introduced to try to prevent similar accidents happening. They cover the safety of spectators and employees at event venues.

When running an event you should consider:

◇ making health and safety a priority even in the planning stage

◇ ensuring that everyone involved in the event feels safe and secure

◇ the security of the facility

◇ the security of any information gathered for the event.

Ensuring health and safety and security

The Health and Safety at Work Act, 1974

This is the main piece of legislation governing the health and safety of employees, and others, in the workplace and at events like the one you are planning. The main aim of the Act is to make everyone aware of the importance of health and safety.

CASE STUDY – The Hillsborough disaster

Ninety-four fans killed in semi-final horror

NINETY-FOUR FOOTBALL FANS, including several children, were killed and about 150 seriously injured at Sheffield on 15 April in Europe's worst soccer tragedy. A senior police officer had ordered a gate to be opened, allowing fans to surge into the Hillsborough ground, and thousands of supporters were crushed on an overcrowded terrace at the FA cup semi-final between Liverpool and Nottingham Forest.

The dead and injured, who were crowded at the Liverpool end of the ground for the capacity all-ticket game, were buried under falling bodies when hundreds of fans poured into the ground as the game was kicking off. Several children died after being crushed against the security fence, where they had been sent to get a good view. Fans tore down advertising hoardings and perimeter boards and used them as make-shift stretchers until the arrival of the ambulance services.

Apparently, Liverpool fans, frustrated at the time it was taking to get into the ground, began to push towards the turnstiles about ten minutes before kick-off.

To ease the crush, the police opened a big metal gate and the fans surged in. They poured through the narrow, dark 30-yard tunnel in the centre of the stand, which offered them their first glimpse of the pitch. They careered into the central pens, crushing those at the front, although there was room to accommodate the latecomers in pens to either side. Those unaware of people dying at the front end of the terraces pushed forward for a better view of the action. As they did so, more were trampled underfoot and crushed into the perimeter fencing at the bottom of the terraces, which had been put there to prevent hooligans from invading the pitch. Because of the perimeter fencing, few of the spectators could get out, although some managed

to climb over the fencing or get through a narrow escape gate onto the pitch. Their plight was not immediately realised by the police inside the ground, but as soon as it was, a policeman ran onto the pitch to get the match stopped, some six minutes after it kicked off. Ten minutes later, the first ambulance arrived.

So for the third time in four years – after the Bradford fire and the Heysel Stadium disaster – the football authorities are left with the onerous task of restoring confidence in the flagging fortunes of Britain's national sport. One thing is clear. In the next few years, football must change its priorities and break away from what Graham Kelly, the Football Association chief executive, describes as 'the ritual of standing on the terraces'. In simple terms, that means a move towards all-seater stadiums – and quickly.

Source: *Daily Telegraph Football Chronicle*, 1993

Ninety-six people eventually lost their lives at the FA Cup semi-final at Hillsborough on 15 April 1989. What should have been a great match became one of the worst disasters in the history of British sport.

Question

How could this disaster have been prevented?

If we look at Richard's gala/dinner dance in the case study on page 180, we can highlight some of the health and safety considerations:

◇ Is the facility allowed to hold that many people?

◇ Are all fire exits clearly marked and illuminated?

◇ Are the staff trained to deal with evacuation procedures?

◇ Are all fire exits clear of obstacles?

◇ Is there a trained first aider on duty?

◇ Do the kitchen's hygiene standards meet the food hygiene regulations?

The Health and Safety at Work Act is enforced by inspectors who are appointed by the Health and Safety Executive. These inspectors have powers to enter premises and inspect them to see if employers and employees are following the instructions laid down by the Act.

If an inspector decides this is not happening, he or she can close down the facility until the problem is rectified and prosecute the organisation. For example, if a local authority swimming pool did not have a sufficient number of qualified lifeguards on duty in the eyes of the inspector, he or she could close it down until the pool's management made the appropriate changes. Why? Because if an accident occurred in the pool and there were not enough trained staff to deal with it then that accident could turn into a tragedy.

Finding information

The following agencies provide information about health, safety and security:

◇ the Health and Safety Executive

◇ the emergency services

◇ Trading Standards Officer

◇ Police Crime Prevention Officer

◇ professional organisations – the Institute of Sport and Recreation Management, the Institute of Leisure and Amenity Management.

Look it up

As a group, either phone or write to your local police station and ask if the Crime Prevention Officer can come and talk to you about organising security at events. Make sure you give him or her enough details about your course and the unit you are studying.

HEALTH AND SAFETY AT WORK ACT, 1974

Main Provisions
Employers' main duties

1 Have a written health and safety policy
2 Ensure that systems of working are safe
3 Provide protective equipment and clothing where necessary
4 Ensure that there are no risks to the health and safety of the public
5 Provide information about health and safety to all employees and ensure staff training programmes.

Employees' main duties

1 Take reasonable care not to endanger themselves or anyone else through their work activities
2 Co-operate with employers in meeting the requirements of the Act
3 Look after each other
4 Do not interfere with or misuse any equipment that has been provided in the interests of meeting the requirements of the Act, for example, 'fooling around' with fire extinguishers
5 Follow the rules regarding using safety equipment and wearing protective clothing

HEALTH AND SAFETY IS THE RESPONSIBILITY OF EVERYONE

Main laws and regulations applicable to the leisure and tourism industry

- Health and Safety at Work Act 1974
- Fire Precautions Act 1971
- The Reporting of Injuries, Disease and Dangerous Occurrences Regulations (RIDDOR) 1985
- Health and Safety (First Aid) Regulations 1981
- Food Hygiene Regulations/Food Safety Act 1990
- Offices, Shops and Railway Premises Act 1963

? Did you know?

The main security hazards at an event are theft of cash and theft of goods.

In the event of an incident occurring at your event it is important that detailed information is recorded accurately as soon as possible, while the details are still fresh in people's minds. In the event of an accident, the information will be recorded in an accident book and must include:

- details of the casualty – name, address, sex
- details of the incident – date, time, place, what happened, nature of injuries
- names and addresses of witnesses
- action taken – first aid, calling emergency services.

These details are recorded to help take any future remedial action and, if there is a claim for negligence, then the facts are available.

Security

There are two aspects of security relating to your event: security of the facility and security of information.

Security of the facility

Security of the facility is important for the reason shown in Figure 4.9.

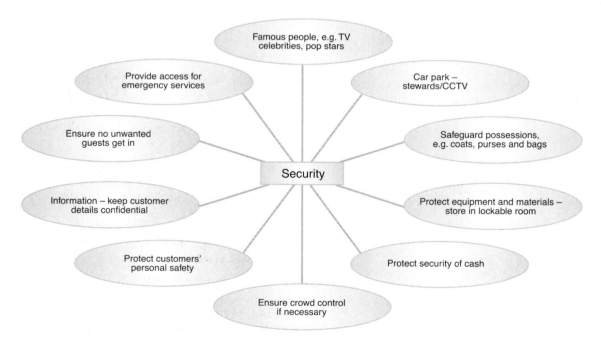

Figure 4.9   The security of the facility is important for a number of reasons

Try it out

Your group has organised a swimming gala. A very distressed lady rushes to you to say she has had her handbag stolen while she was in the café. What action are you going to take? Write down what you would put in the incident book.

Youth club disco

The venue for a youth club disco is in the church hall. Any equipment used must remain in the hall. It is highly likely that people without tickets will try to gatecrash so the organisers have to be aware of this.

Ticket money and money collected from refreshments must be collected by the organisers and kept secure until it can be banked.

Security of information

Details of customers and organisations must be kept confidential to ensure the privacy of the customer. Any information about an organisation's finances, its marketing plans or sales records belongs to that organisation. It could be very useful to a competitor so the information must be kept secure and confidential.

This may not apply to your particular event but it is worth making a note of it because you may well be organising big events as part of your future job.

Look it up

Find out the person responsible for safety and security in your school/college and write down the evacuation procedure.

Look it up

In groups of four, arrange a visit to a local leisure and tourism facility and look at the health, safety and security arrangements there. It may be an idea to contact the manager beforehand and explain what you want to do. When you have completed your study, report your findings to the rest of the group in the form of a presentation.

Talk about it

Sarah, Lisa, David and Greg are all Intermediate Leisure and Tourism students. They plan to organise a summer carnival on the local playing fields. This is an ambitious event because they want to include:

* a parade through the town
* fun events on the playing fields, such as obstacle races, 'wellie wanging' and challenges like lifting the bale of straw
* a grand finale with a fancy dress disco and barbecue.

What health, safety and security hazards would the students have to be aware of?

Insurance

Every event, no matter what size, should be covered by insurance. You may find that if you are using a facility such as a leisure centre or village hall to stage your event, it may already have the necessary insurance.

You may think that insurance is simply an extra cost which you could do without. What you have to consider is the cost implications of court action if you do not have insurance. Whoever is responsible for your event, and in this case it would be your tutor, must check that the relevant insurance cover has been met.

Insurance cover includes staff and the public, theft or damage against property and cars, and bad weather, for example money would be lost if an event is cancelled. Events such as Wimbledon and Test Cricket matches usually have this type of cover.

Alternative plans of action

If changes have to be made to your event because of the weather, problems with transport or a change in the numbers of people attending, then alternative plans of action have to be made. These are known as contingency plans – being able to deal with the situation if something goes wrong.

Things that may go wrong include bad weather. For example, heavy rain would ruin a garden fete or heavy snow may prevent people reaching the location because travelling conditions become almost impossible.

> ### ? Did you know?
>
> A few years ago, snow made it impossible for people to get to the NEC in Birmingham for the Clothes Show. The event was being televised and had to be screened. The models couldn't get to the venue so the staff at the Centre found themselves on television, modelling clothes usually worn by super models!

An event may be disrupted if it fails to attract the number of people expected. If the event is ticket only, than an accurate number of ticket sales can be determined. In some cases, events have to be cancelled if an insufficient amount of tickets are sold.

A final disruption to be considered, which hopefully won't occur but still has to be taken into account, is an emergency such as fire, accidents to staff or the public.

We will now look at different ways of dealing with disruptions.

Bad weather

The great British weather is very unpredictable. It has been known to snow in June! How many times have we seen cricket matches cancelled under the heading,

RAIN STOPPED PLAY

The Wimbledon Tennis Championship is always played during the last week of June and the first week of July in the hope of staging the event in glorious sunshine. Unfortunately we often see a headline saying,

ALL PLAY SUSPENDED FOR THE DAY

If your event is outdoors, you need to make plans in case of bad weather. For example, could the event be moved indoors? Should the event be cancelled? It is possible to transfer most of the activities which make up a garden fete into an adjoining village hall. Likewise, a five-a-side football tournament could be transferred into a sports hall.

The great British weather is unpredictable

Shortfall in numbers

How do you run an event when the number of participants is far lower than you expected? Armed with the motto, 'The show must go on', here are some examples of what you can do.

- A football tournament when 16 teams are expected and only four teams turn up – easy. Put them all into the semi-finals, have a third and fourth place play off and then stage the final so everyone gets two games.

- You have booked a disco in a massive room and you are expecting 300 people but only 50 turn up. Dim the lights and, put a partition across the room, thus making it smaller and more intimate for the guests.

- You have organised a trip to the seaside for 48 senior citizens but only 21 tickets have been sold. Simply hire a smaller bus (it's cheaper).

Accidents

Accidents happen in any situation. You have to try and ensure your event is as safe as possible for your colleagues and the participants. Look back at the section on health and safety (page 181) and remember that you should:

- have qualified first aiders on duty

- let the emergency services know in advance about your event

- ask an organisation like the St John Ambulance to be present at your event.

Talk about it

What sort of accident could occur at the following events:

- a pop concert

- a Premiership football match

- a raft race?

How could they be avoided?

Fire

To reduce the risk of a fire at your event, contact your local fire safety officer for advice about fire and safety regulations.

If your event is inside:

- ensure that all fire-exits are signposted and are not blocked

- know the evacuation procedure

- do not have more people in the building than you should – this is a very serious offence which could have tragic consequences.

Don't forget that health, safety and security should be your number one priority. Make sure you plan for disruptions which could be caused by accidents or fire. That way, you reduce the risk of injury.

Review and evaluation of the event

Plans must be made to review and evaluate your event. This is often a neglected stage in the planning process, probably because people are too busy concentrating on the event itself and not too bothered about what happens after it. By tying up the loose ends of the event, it shows you want to make a good impression and possibly do the same thing again another time.

Your evaluation of the event will tell you how successful it has been, whether it met its objectives, and how problems could be dealt with in future events. This is all valuable information and should therefore be included in the planning stage. The review of the event will be dealt with in the last section.

Taking part in the event

When you first start thinking about your event, all team members will need to meet on a regular basis to agree the details of your event plan. Meetings will be held and notes, known as minutes, should be kept so that everyone knows exactly what they have to do.

If the whole class or group is doing one event, it may be helpful to set up a committee to oversee the planning, and staging of the event. However, ideally, there should be around six people in a team for one event. That way, everyone knows what's going on and it's easier for a small group to meet together regularly rather than a big group. If the group is too big communication can break down and as said before, 'the left hand sometimes doesn't know what the right hand is doing'.

Completing the tasks you have been allocated

The success of your event will depend on team members completing the task they've been allocated fully and effectively. It will let the team down if someone has not done their job properly.

We have already looked at the different roles within your team event (co-ordinator, publicity officer etc). It is now time to look at how you can complete your tasks:

- **Co-ordinator**: make sure everyone knows exactly what he or she is doing and that it is done.

- **Publicity officer**: make sure deadlines are met for press releases and leaflets. The main purpose is to promote the event. The number of people being made aware of the event will show the success of the promotional campaign.
- **Catering officer**: has the food and drink been ordered? Are there enough plates and cups? Will there be enough food?
- **Facilities officer**: is the venue confirmed? Have health and safety arrangements been made? Has any specialist equipment been organised?
- **Treasurer**: has the money been banked? Is there a balance sheet? Have the bills been paid?
- **Secretary**: have all invitations been sent out? Have the appropriate dignitaries been invited? Are all the minutes in order?

It might be an idea to have a checklist of tasks which you can tick off when completed and submit to the co-ordinator.

Dealing politely with team members and others

In Unit 3, we studied customer care and, in particular, working with internal customers. This is just what working in a team is all about. Treat your colleagues in the team like external customers – respect their views, support them and be polite to them so that you work together to make your event a success (see Figure 4.10).

At the same time you have to work with people outside your team – the reporter from the newspaper, the supplier of food and drink, the leisure centre manager, the local fire officer. You need the co-operation of these people and the best way to get that is by being polite to them and dealing with them in a helpful and friendly way (see Figure 4.11).

Talk about it

Give other examples of people outside your team who you might have to deal with.

Figure 4.10   Good teamwork means working well with colleagues

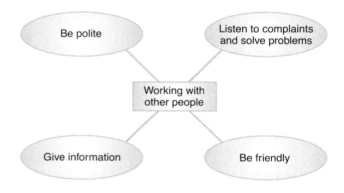

Figure 4.11   Working with people outside your team involves certain skills

Supporting other team members

Sometimes people don't have enough skills to cope with certain situations. For example, if a team member has to phone companies asking for sponsorship and keeps getting rejections, the individual may think he or she is doing something wrong. Another team member could encourage the person to keep trying and perhaps give some suggestions, very tactfully, to help to improve that person's telephone technique. If the team member does then manage to secure some sponsorship, i.e. is successful on the phone, he or she should be congratulated. In situations like this people need support and encouragement, even if they do not ask for it. Working together when things are not going well leads to team spirit being fostered and to a determination to keep going.

Other examples of support could be helping out with the distribution of leaflets, and, during the event, helping to serve food and drinks, or moving furniture. In other words, doing the jobs which you may not have been allocated but that you do in order to support other team members. You may also notice that some team members seem to do all the work!

SNAPSHOTS

Don't give up!

Whitney

Whitney is responsible for the publicity and promotion of her group's event. She volunteered for the job because she likes writing stories and eventually wants to become a public relations officer for a major international sports organisation. She says,

'When I approached my local newspaper with the press release I received a setback. The reporter pulled my article to pieces. But I didn't show how upset I was, just politely asked him how it could be improved. I was actually fuming inside, having been treated like a 7-year-old, but I didn't show it. He told me to go away and try again. I could have cried. But I did try again and made another appointment. Believe it or not, he liked it. I could not believe I was dealing with the same person. Maybe I had caught him on an "off" day on our first meeting. One thing I learned from this was never to give up.

In fact, I found I was becoming a bit of a "people" expert. I soon found out that whoever I approached, their first immediate reaction was either "No" or, "'I'm not the person to see about that". I began to develop a very positive attitude and did not take rejections personally. I must have contacted 40 potential sponsors by phone and met with at least 30 people face-to-face in my quest to publicise our event.

I've learnt to remain friendly, polite and positive in the face of rejection, rudeness and indifference. This is yet another part of my course that will stand me in good stead for my future career.'

> ### Talk about it

In your group identify where the following people would need support and suggest how you could give it.

- Stacey is the team's publicity officer. Her IT skills are quite basic although she is willing to learn. She wants to write to the local press informing them of the event but thinks her English might let her down.

- Kerry is 19 and is a single mother with a 3-year-old son. She was nominated as team treasurer. Each day she has to drop Matthew off at nursery before coming to college. Although she loves her course she has great difficulty finding the time to do her coursework on top of looking after Matthew.

- Nathan is shy and lacks confidence. He doesn't enjoy meeting people and becomes very tense and nervous in a group. As team secretary he will have to correspond with organisations to try and raise funds. By letter, this is no problem. Over the phone or in a face-to-face encounter he may have difficulties.

Reacting quickly and confidently to problems

Things don't always run smoothly at events and you will have to react quickly to any problems that may arise. You have already planned in advance for possible problems which should prepare you if the disruption actually happens. Let's look at some potential problems and how you can solve them.

Emergencies

Know what to do in the event of a fire – don't panic, direct people to emergency exits, evacuate the building in a controlled manner, take customers to the assembly point.

If there is an accident and you are a qualified first aider, you would obviously deal with it. If not, get help and, in the case of a bad accident, call the emergency services.

CASE STUDY — Dealing with emergencies

We have looked at the 4Ps of the marketing mix; we now have the 3Ps in first aid.

There are three principle aims of a first aider. These are:

- to preserve life
- to prevent the injured person's condition worsening
- to promote recovery.

In emergency situations such as near drowning, heart attack and severe trauma (e.g. broken neck), immediate action is required. These instances may require immediate resuscitation of the casualty. This may involve artificial respiration and external chest compression.

The qualified first aider should take charge. It is most unlikely that anyone else will be around. In taking charge the first aider should send someone else to call an ambulance. It is up to the first aider to deal with the casualty in the best way possible until the ambulance arrives.

Not every situation is an emergency. First aiders may have to deal with cuts and bruises but whatever the situation, the appropriate treatment should be given and the details of the accident must be documented in the accident report book.

Question

Have you or anyone in your family ever had to deal with a first aid situation? Share the experience with the rest of your group.

Changes of plan

These can be major or minor, as in the following example:

- A team member may be sick on the day of the event. You may have to cover his or her duties, but that's fine because at the team meetings everyone has communicated, he or she has told you his or her role and what he or she has been doing. Be flexible; be prepared.

- Timings during the event can alter. You may find that the final of the tug o' war will take place half an hour later than scheduled. Let the crowd know by announcing it on the public address system.

- The pop band hasn't turned up because of fog on the motorway. You have 150 people who have paid £3 per ticket. (This happened to me once.) What do you do? Apologise for the delay, tell them the truth and say that instead of a band there will be a disco (using the facility's equipment). People will be able to get a £1 refund on the way out.

You can rehearse 'what ifs' all-day and still not cover them all – although it does help to have some ideas for contingency plans. What is called for is **quick** thinking, and the **confidence** to go with it.

Keeping to any agreed time deadlines

The event co-ordinator should put pressure on people to ensure time deadlines are being met. All stages of your event planning process should be monitored so that deadlines can be met. A deadline for completion of each task should be timetabled. Remember:

- if you don't pay for something on time, you won't receive the goods

- if your newspaper advertisement is submitted too late, it will not appear when you want it to

- if the event starts late, it usually means it will finish late, which may have a knock-on effect for the facility and your customers

- if your deadlines *have* been met, your event will have a very good chance of being a success.

Knowing when to seek help and advice

None of us is an expert at everything and there are times when we need to seek help and advice.

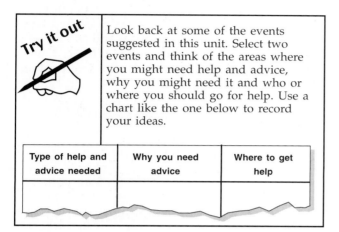

Try it out

Look back at some of the events suggested in this unit. Select two events and think of the areas where you might need help and advice, why you might need it and who or where you should go for help. Use a chart like the one below to record your ideas.

Type of help and advice needed	Why you need advice	Where to get help

Reviewing the event

Once your event is over it is important to reflect on how it went and if you achieved what you set out to do. One way of reviewing the event is for all team members to answer the questions set out in this section.

What went right and wrong for you individually?

This question is not to find out if you were perfect in carrying out your agreed role. It's to find out how you worked as a team member and to learn from your experience because it may have been your first time in helping to run an event. Questions you can ask yourself are as follows:

◦ **How well did I deal with disruptions?**
'I had to direct people to the emergency exits when the fire alarm went off after an electrician accidentally cut a wire. I was quite pleased really because I kept calm and was able to talk to people at the assembly point while we waited for the all clear.'

◦ **Did I stick to my agreed role and carry out my duties?**
'As publicity officer I wrote two press releases and designed the leaflets and posters. The journalist I met said I hadn't done too badly considering I was an amateur. Jamie had the flu on the day of the event so I had to help out in the kitchen, preparing sandwiches and serving drinks. I quite enjoyed this. It's a good job Jamie had given us a little bit of training in food hygiene and the do's and don'ts of working in catering.'

◦ **Did I use the resources well?**
'I like to think I did a good job. The only equipment I really used was the PC to write the promotional material and my brain to give me ideas. My computer never lets me down but I'm not sure about the other item.'

◦ **Did I carry out my health, safety and security duties?**
'As well as dealing with the evacuation procedure, I was also responsible for the participants' valuables, which were kept locked in the safe. I asked them all to sign for whatever they left with me and to sign it out when it was returned. This covered me against any accusations, and the system worked.'

◦ **How well did the team work? Did we meet our objectives?**
'Our objective was to raise enough money (£300) to cover the costs of staging the event and donate £100 to the local hospital's children's ward. We actually raised £450 so we decided to donate the extra £150 to the college nursery for new equipment.'

◦ **How did we all get on together?**
'We decided at the very beginning that we would do our best to listen to everyone's opinions and ideas. At first, we tended to criticise each other too much and there were one or two personality clashes. This was when Julie, our co-ordinator, showed her strength of character. She said that all discussions should be constructive and any criticism should not be taken personally. In fact, she repeated this at every meeting and it must have sunk in because although we still had some lively discussions, no one took offence. On the whole we solved our problems together, maintained a positive attitude and supported each other – even though Sarah was late for every meeting!'

◦ **Was health and safety maintained?**
'We made sure that the numbers we had in the sports hall did not exceed the legal capacity. All fire exits were illuminated and clear – this was put into practice during the evacuation.'

'There was one minor accident during the final of the five-a-side football match when one youngster was hit in the face and his nose began to bleed. Dan, our qualified first aider, dealt with the incident immediately and recorded the details in the accident book.'

'I'm glad we met the local fire officer last week to discuss evacuation procedures and call the emergency services. This planning stood us in good stead when the fire alarm went off.'

Were there any security problems?
'There were no incidents. The money was locked in the safe and three of us banked the cash the following day – it would have been too heavy for one person to carry as it was mainly coins, and we felt more secure with three of us taking it to the bank.

Did everyone carry out his or her role?
'There were one or two minor disagreements at first as to who should do what. Again, criticism can be destructive and people are sensitive so we tried to be as objective as possible. We found that team members volunteered their thoughts on their own roles and stated how they carried out their roles including both the good and not so good things they did.'

Did we handle disruption well?
'Our planning and training served us well. The evacuation and the minor injury were handled efficiently and, dare I say, professionally. We felt confident about handling disruption because we were prepared for any incidents.'

Would we change anything next time?
'The answer is quite simple: yes. Changes would include:

- make sure everyone turns up on time to meetings

- have qualified first aiders on duty – as there were 300 spectators

- keep reminding the press of the times of the event – they turned up with only five minutes to go so they missed a lot of the action

- seek more sponsorship, that way we could donate more to local charities

- warn the bank about depositing the money – it took ages counting the coins which meant the people in the queue were not pleased with the wait. Next time we could also collect some coin bags before the event. This would save the cashier time.'

How did working as a team help or hinder you?
'There were times when I wanted to go ahead and do things on my own, but that is because I am naturally impatient. Eventually, I learned how to co-operate with team members and to look at other people's points of view. This will no doubt stand me in good stead when I get a job. I valued the support we all gave to each other and I think we learned new skills from each other. It showed us all how to make food look presentable and attractive.'

What did the customers think?
One way of finding out if your event was successful is to ask the people who took part. Their opinion will play a big part in how you might plan future events. They may point out any strengths or weaknesses and you can find this out by asking them during the event – were they enjoying it? You could also carry out a survey after the event, inviting comments to find out what they thought of it.

Try it out

As a group, design and complete a team evaluation form which gives a full review of your event. It could look something like this:

| **Name**: (of student) | **Date of event:** |
| **Event**: (e.g. Family fun day) | **The team:** |

Criteria for evaluation	*Answers*
(Using the questions previously asked) Individual performance Did I carry out my duties? Team performance	
Improvements?	

Try it out

Design a simple questionnaire which will give you an indication of how people attending the event felt about it.

CASE STUDY – Team plan

Six GNVQ Intermediate Leisure and Tourism students had to run an event as part of their course. This is how they did it.

Team plan for 'Children's Pop Star Party', March 1999

Our team consisting of six members has been put together to plan a children's party. Our targets are:

- To come up with an effective and realistic plan for our event
- To organise an event that will have community benefit
- To make sure that the venue we use is suitable for the event and complies with health and safety regulations
- To make sure that the event runs according to plan
- To make sure that our party is the best that the children have ever been to and that everyone, including ourselves, has fun
- To contribute to evidence needed for Unit 4 of our course, 'Running an event'
- To raise enough money to cover the cost of the event and to go towards our holiday fund
- To work together as a team.

Key factors that could affect the party

The success of the party depends on a number of key factors:

- Making enough money – we want to make enough money to cover the costs of the party and then make some profit to go towards our holiday fund
- Promoting the event well – the event has to be promoted around local schools or else we will not sell any tickets
- Health and safety – if there is any threat to health and safety, the event will fail. We need to find out the maximum number of people allowed in the venue and the ratio of adults to children that we are going to need. We are also going to need an adequate number of first aiders and a first aid kit
- Security – we need to keep the children safe so we need someone on the door to keep out any undesirables
- Resources – we need to book the venue and organise any equipment that we are going to require or the event will not be able to take place at all.

Resources

- We need to start fundraising as soon as possible and we also need to write to local businesses regarding sponsorship. All money will be used to cover the cost of the party and any left over will go towards our holiday fund
- We need to arrange visits to local schools to promote the event and also for the writing, designing and printing of promotional materials
- The college is an ideal venue for the event, as it is very big and is easily accessible
- Most of the equipment that we need will be available from the college, for example tables, chairs, cups, plates, heating, lighting and the sound system
- We have plenty of staff with the skills needed to run the event. All of our team has agreed that we are going to work free of charge. The only extra help that we might need is with looking after the children on the actual day and with security of the premises.

Contingency plans

The college has already got detailed contingency plans in place for dealing with emergencies such as fire, bomb threats, medical emergencies and serious accidents. We will make sure that we are all aware of these procedures and review health and safety before the event. Other problems we might face include:

- Not enough people turning up – we can tackle this in advance because we will know how many tickets have been sold
- Extra staff not turning up to help with the children – we will try and get more helpers than we will actually need
- Team members being off sick – all of the key members will have a deputy to cover for them if necessary
- CD player breaking during our dance routine – we will have a backup tape with all of the required music and also a backup sound system.

Role allocations

The team is organised into the following roles:

Co-ordinator – Sally Sneddon

Vice co-ordinator – Nick White

Secretary – Kim Jones and Leigh Clarke

Treasurer – Andrea Hart and Illa Patel

Publicity officer – Adam Makowski and Illa Patel

Facilities officer/Health, safety and security officer – Sarah Dean and Peter Smith

Catering officer – Sarah Lam

Evaluating the party

The success of the party will be evaluated against our overall team targets, that is:

- Did our event have community benefit?
- Was the venue suitable for the event and did it comply with health and safety regulations?
- Did the event run according to plan?
- Did everyone have fun?
- Did we obtain evidence for Unit 4 of our course?
- Did we raise enough money to cover the costs of the event and go towards our holiday fund?
- Did we operate effectively as a team?

We will only be able to carry out this evaluation some time after the event, so we will hold a team meeting to evaluate in early April. In the time after the event and before the meeting we will collect feedback from people who took part or came to our event.

Questions

- What do you think of this plan?
- Does it cover all eventualities?

Unit 4 Assessment

The greatest show on Earth

Scenario

The local newspaper has just published an article implying that young people, and students in particular, have little sense of responsibility. It goes on to say that these people lack the organisational, planning and teamworking skills required in the outside world. Quite rightly, your group feels offended by this report and decides to prove the newspaper has got its facts all wrong. This is how you are going to do it:

Your group is going to organise an event. Each member will have a specific part to play and the end result will show you are capable of working together as a team.

What you have to do

Working in a group, come up with ideas for an event, related to Leisure and Tourism, which you could organise. Refer back to the section on 'Running an Event' (page 168), follow the guidelines and look at some ideas for the event.

In your assessment, you need to produce a record of your event identifying your involvement in the planning, running and evaluation of the event.

Your assessment work should include details of the objectives and the planning process. You should also give details of the venue, finance, staffing, equipment and materials needed. All events need to have an assessment of health, safety and security hazards and yours is no exception. Outline the promotional methods you use and show how you worked as part of a team. Finally, you have to show how you evaluated your event.

Obtaining a pass grade

You must demonstrate:

- that you can accurately plan, schedule and monitor all individual and team tasks for the event with some guidance from your tutor

- a clear description of the objectives, the stages of planning for the event and the resources needed, including accurate costings

- effective working as part of a team in planning and taking part in the event

- the importance of anticipating hazards, producing a simple risk assessment and effectively contributing towards the health, safety and security of the event

- an evaluation of the event, including both your own and other team members' contributions, making recommendations as appropriate.

Obtaining a merit or distinction grade

To obtain a merit or distinction grade your work must show:

- independent analysis of the main stages of individual preparation for the event through relevant plans and schedules, making changes to these when necessary

- an in-depth evaluation of the activity, clearly explaining how the event met the original objectives set

- a logical and well-structured format, clearly expressing your ideas and findings.

Obtaining a distinction grade

To obtain a distinction, your work must show:

* that you understand how planning, scheduling and monitoring has helped in meeting the event's deadlines and in creating better outcomes

* a thorough and effective risk assessment that enables the student to anticipate hazards and react quickly and confidently to any problems that arise during the event, knowing when to get help and advice from others.

Key skills available

Communication: C2.1a, C2.3

IT: IT2.3

Working with others: WO2.1, WO2.2, WO2.3

Application of Number: N2.2, N2.3

Resources

It may be possible to use examples of work produced by former students to get ideas about event management, or even get a former student to come in to talk about how he or she planned, ran and evaluated his or her event.

It might also be useful to choose an event that may have just finished, or is about to be staged in your area as an example. Perhaps the organiser could be brought in to explain what went on in the planning, running and evaluating of this event.

Unit 4 Test

1   What is the importance of health, safety and security regulations?

2   What do you think makes a good team?

3   What would be the individual roles and responsibilities in a team of six people?

4   What are some of the security hazards that could happen at an event?

5   Why do we set objectives in event planning?

6   Why is it important to deal with members of the team and others in a polite way?

7   What ways could you promote an event?

8   Who would you seek help and advice from during the planning stage of your event?

9   What factors would you take into account when you are choosing your event?

10   What do we mean by being flexible when working in a team?

11   Why is it important to evaluate the event?

12   How would you go about giving individual feedback about a team member's performance in the planning and running of the event?

13   How could you tell if your event was a success?

14   What makes a good team leader?

15   What do you think is meant by the expression 'thinking on your feet'?

This unit covers the knowledge you will need in order to pass the external assessment for Unit 7. You will learn that the leisure, sport and recreation industry not only consists of leisure centres but also other facilities such as snooker halls, theme parks, football clubs and nightclubs. You will gain an insight into the operation of leisure, sport and recreation facilities and how to organise them to be successful.

The unit is written in seven sections. Section one looks at the type of facilities in the industry and section two at their aims and objectives. Sections three and four consider staffing of facilities and programming, while section five describes health, safety and security requirements, including the Health and Safety at Work Act 1974 and the Control of Substances Hazardous to Health (COSHH) Regulations 1988. The final two sections look at how facilities are organised (i.e. administration and finance) and promoted.

This unit builds on Unit 1: Investigating leisure and tourism and Unit 2: Marketing in leisure and tourism.

What you need to produce

You need to produce evidence in the external assessment which shows your understanding of leisure, sport and recreation facilities and their working practices. This includes the aims and objectives of facilities and a knowledge of the programming, administrative and financial functions of organisations.

In addition, you will have to show the relationship between these functions and the organisations' aims and objectives. Finally you need to understand how organisations need to comply with health, safety and security legislation.

This unit will be assessed only through an external assessment. The grade you achieve in this assessment will be your grade for the unit.

Types of facilities

Introduction

The term 'facilities' refers to equipment, buildings and structures and also features of the natural environment. Facilities provide opportunities for people to take part in leisure and tourism activities. There are many different types of facilities in the leisure, sport and recreation industries.

Facilities may be features of the natural environment such as lakes or mountains, or can be structures and equipment which have been built; for example, a boating centre next to a lake, a concert hall or an out-of-town shopping complex.

Taking part in leisure, sport and recreation activities is only possible if access to the necessary facilities is available. In the case of a game of squash, this requires a specific purpose-built facility, whereas sailing, for example, would need part of the natural environment, i.e. a lake or the sea (or possibly a dam or reservoir – which, of course, will have been constructed). Walking or running are examples of activities that can take place anywhere.

Over the past 30 years there has been a change in the provision of leisure, sport and recreation facilities in the UK. We now have multi-screen cinema complexes, all-weather pitches, leisure pools with slides and flumes and floodlit playing areas. Facilities such as leisure centres are now expected to provide car parks, restaurants and function rooms.

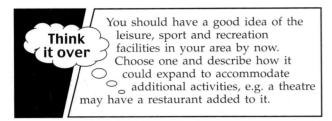

You should have a good idea of the leisure, sport and recreation facilities in your area by now. Choose one and describe how it could expand to accommodate additional activities, e.g. a theatre may have a restaurant added to it.

We will now look at the many different types of facilities which the leisure, sport and recreation industries offer.

Sports stadia

Sports stadia usually cater for spectators as well as participants. They mostly belong to the private sector and are used, for example, for professional football and rugby. Some stadia are used by local amateur athletic clubs and hockey clubs. Most running tracks in stadia are now synthetic, which leads to improved performances and less maintenance, although they do need replacing after about ten years. Sports stadia are also used for pop concerts, firework displays or political rallies.

Look it up

Try to find out some information about the Live Aid Concert in 1985 at Wembley Stadium. Why was it held? Who performed there? How many people attended?

Did you know?

More fans require medical treatment during rock concerts than sports events: over 3,000 people were treated for heat exhaustion during the Guns n' Roses 1992 stadium concert.

Try it out

In which cities are the following sports stadia situated:

- Nou Camp
- Millennium Stadium
- Elland Road
- Twickenham
- Stade de France
- Murrayfield
- Hampden Park
- Crystal Palace
- Don Valley?

(The answers are on page 235.)

CASE STUDY – The new Wembley National Stadium

The old Wembley Stadium, with its 80,000 all-seater capacity, was widely regarded as the world's premier venue for sport and entertainment. The new Wembley National Stadium will have a capacity of 90,000 people and a sliding roof. The famous twin towers will be replaced with a spectacular 133-metre high arch.

Key facts

- The National Stadium will attract some £229 million of total visitor expenditure each year, both at the Stadium and from spending by event visitors in shops, bars, hotels and leisure facilities elsewhere in

London. This would be an increase of £119 million over the expenditure attracted by the old stadium.

- The new National Stadium development, with its hotel and offices, will directly employ over 2,100 people permanently and some 2,200 more temporary staff on event days.

- The stadium will operate £229 million of spending in the UK economy each year.

Question

These are all positive effects of the new National Stadium. Can you think of any more?

You may have said the other positive effects of the new Wembley National Stadium could be:

- the local economy will prosper
- employment will increase
- major international events could be staged, such as the World Cup Final
- it would add prestige to UK sport.

Commercial indoor leisure facilities

These facilities include cinemas, bowling alleys and private health clubs. They have to make money in order to survive as the government does not fund them. They are run by either business organisations or individuals.

Commercial leisure facilities aim to make a profit – money generated by income after all overheads, such as wages and buying equipment, have been paid. Many of these facilities offer additional attractions intended to keep customers there for

Talk about it

What further attractions could the following facilities add to encourage customers to spend more money:

- an ice rink
- a cinema
- a health suite?

longer. For example, people coming in to play ten-pin bowling are encouraged to have a drink or a snack. This type of socialising after the game can generate more income for the facility.

Natural leisure and sporting facilities

The varied landscape and natural environment of the countryside offers opportunities for a wide range of sporting and recreational activities.

The National Parks (see Figure 7.1) provide opportunities for potholing (Peak District), hang-gliding (Yorkshire Dales), water-skiing (Lake District), skiing (Snowdonia), boating (Norfolk Broads) and hiking (Dartmoor, Exmoor). Of course some of these activities could take place in the other National Parks as well.

The Peak District National Park

Two distinct landscapes form the 1,404 sq. km. of the Peak District National Park. Around the north, east and west is the Dark Peak, an area of peat moorland and millstone grit which is ideal for walking and rock climbing.

The Lake District

Most of the Lake District's 2,280 sq. km. consist of moorland and fell. Windermere is the largest of the 16 lakes. The area is ideal for unrivalled walking and climbing, from gentle lakeside strolls to testing mountain ascents. It is also popular for sailing and water-skiing.

The Broads

Five rivers flow through the Broads making the area resemble the fingers of a giant hand. Popular activities include fishing, boardsailing, walking and birdwatching.

Try it out

Using a map or an atlas name the twelve National Parks of England and Wales labelled 1 to 12 Figure 7.1. (The answers are on page 235.)

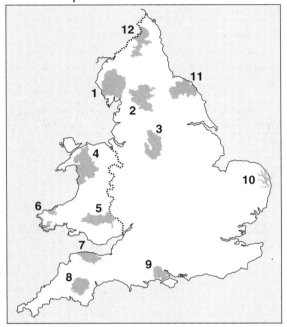

Source: Countryside Agency

Figure 7.1 The National Parks of England and Wales

SNAPSHOTS

Ray and Judy

Ray and Judy live in London. They both have good but stressful jobs. They escape to the countryside as often as possible to take in the fresh air and enjoy the peace and quiet.

They enjoy popping up to Norfolk and spending weekends on their houseboat. Judy says,

'The weekend breaks offer a complete contrast to the mad rush of the city. People seem to have more time for us and we seem to be far more relaxed. Ray enjoys his bird watching while I am quite happy going for long walks. It provides the perfect escape from our hectic lives in the city.'

Talk about it

What other groups of people would use the natural leisure and sporting facilities offered by areas like the National Parks?

Arts and entertainment venues

Arts and entertainment venues include facilities where pop concerts and exhibitions are held, as well as the more established art galleries, and theatres. The bigger venues are found in London and other cities in the UK. Arts venues in London include the Royal Opera House, the National Gallery and the Tate Gallery (including the new Tate Modern) which houses the largest collection of British paintings from the sixteenth century to the present day. The Royal National Theatre is based in the South Bank Centre and the London base of the Royal Shakespeare Company is at the City's Barbican Centre. The principal concert halls in central London include the Royal Festival Hall, the Barbican Hall and the Royal Albert Hall.

The biggest entertainment and exhibitions venue in the UK is the National Exhibition Centre (NEC) in Birmingham. Its 1.7 million sq. ft. houses 16 halls. It hosts more than 150 shows every year, 70 per cent of which are trade fairs. It seats 12,000 spectators. Other major events staged at the NEC include Crufts Dog Show, the Motor Show and sporting events such as the World Figure Skating Championships. Smaller events include seminars, product launches, presentations and conferences. Shops, banking facilities, catering and even a garden, all form part of the complex.

An important arts and entertainment venue in London

Try to find out some information about one arts and one entertainment venue from the following list:

Arts venues: The Royal Opera House, the Tate Gallery, the Royal Festival Hall, the Globe Theatre and the Newcastle Arts Centre.

Entertainment venues: the G MEX Centre, Manchester; the National Indoor Arena, Birmingham; the Sheffield Arena; the Royal Albert Hall, London; the Theatre Royal, Bristol.

Useful websites:

www.geoprojects.co.uk
www.english.sports.gov.uk
www.visitbritain.co.uk

Retail parks

The 1990s saw an increase in major out-of-town shopping complexes or retail parks, where you can buy more or less anything under one roof.

These retail parks are usually situated only a few miles outside town and city centres and have good road and rail links serving them. The big advantage of these places is that you can buy products and services from a very large range of shops under one roof. Once inside you do not have to worry about the weather or speeding traffic or finding a parking spot.

There is an argument to suggest that retail parks have killed off trade in some city centres. The other argument is that some retail parks have been built on what used to be derelict land which is now being put to good use. Developers will also argue that many jobs have been created by retail parks.

Well-known retail parks include Lakeside in Essex, the Trafford Centre in Manchester, Meadowhall in Sheffield and Fosse Park in Leicester. Bluewater in Kent is a new retail park built on derelict land (in this case an old quarry.)

? ## Did you know?

The Trafford Centre has its own Sky Wall – the largest TV screen in a shopping area in the world.

Retail parks usually have their own websites. Details about Meadowhall can be found on www.meadowhall.co.uk and the Trafford Centre on www.traffordcentre.co.uk. These websites also contain some very useful information on customer care.

? ## Did you know?

Meadowhall has 12,600 free parking spaces?

CASE STUDY – The Trafford Centre

Opened in September 1998, The Trafford Centre cost £600 million, took two and a half years to build and is designed to last more than 150 years.

The advertising brochures describe it as,

'more than a shopping centre – we have set out to create a world class experience: a breathtaking building, superbly constructed and beautifully decorated, and, within it, quality goods, high fashion, great food, top-class entertainment of all kinds **plus** a standard of service second to none'.

There's more to do than just shop there as it contains:

* a 1,600-seat food court
* a 20-screen UCI cinema
* a children's entertainment area with a crèche
* an 18 lane ten-pin bowling alley.

Question

What are your thoughts on centres like the Trafford Centre?

SNAPSHOTS

Sarah and Jo

Sarah and Jo are 17. They've been good friends for ages. They both study 'A' levels at their local college and on Saturdays work part-time as waitresses in a busy restaurant. About once a month they go to Meadowhall along with their other friends. Sarah describes a typical day out there:

'We catch a train to the Centre and arrive at about 10 am. We head straight for the Oasis catering area where one café sells a big breakfast with a pot of tea for only 99p, so naturally we "pig out". We then shop till we drop – fashion stores, music and video centres, shoe shops – you name it we go there.

The next stop is McDonald's which is based in the Oasis although we usually vary our choice between KFC, Wimpy and Pizza Hut.

To complete our day, we head for the cinema to see a favourite film star in their latest blockbuster: the Multiplex cinema is just upstairs from the Oasis!'

Talk about it

What makes retail parks so popular? In your group discuss the impact retail parks have had on the surrounding areas.

Look it up

Check out www.mcarthurglen.com for details about the Cheshire Oaks retail park.

Local authority facilities

Local authorities or local councils provide leisure, sport and recreation facilities such as local leisure centres, community centres, libraries and swimming pools.

These facilities exist to provide a service to the community. They have become an increasingly important element in local authority service provision, both in terms of the finance allocated to them and the political importance placed on them. In other words, if councillors are seen to be providing services to the community, then in return they hope to get votes. Today, it is generally viewed as a good thing for local authorities to support and promote leisure, sport and recreation facilities.

Local authorities receive funding from central government and from the local community in the form of council tax. Facilities are subsidised to a great extent so that a wide range of people can use the facilities, not just those who can afford them. In this sense, they are a true community service.

Local authorities provide staff and maintain a wide range of facilities, as can be seen in Figure 7.2.

Figure 7.2 All these facilities are run by local authorities

Did you know?

If the council did not subsidise a swimming pool, the true cost of a swim would be £6.

Think it over

What sort of leisure, sport and recreation facilities should local authorities provide? Do you think enough facilities are provided? If not, why do you believe this is?

The 1988 Local Government Act meant that local authorities had to invite tenders from commercial organisations for the management of a number of their services, the operation of leisure sport and recreation facilities being one. The idea behind this was that compulsory competitive tendering (CCT) could lead to improved services, more efficient management and value for money. Those opposed to CCT believe that some facilities may close because they are not profitable yet still provide a service to the community.

SNAPSHOTS

Shona

Remember Shona? The last time we met her she was a leisure centre supervisor in Birmingham. Well, she's got a new job and is called a 'Contract Manager'. Shona still works for the Council. However, her Centre is now run by a private operator under the terms of CCT. Shona's job is to ensure that the operator is still providing a range of activities to as many members of the community as possible with quality service. She says,

'I'm really now in charge of quality control, making sure the contractors are doing what they should. It is certainly not a 'them' and 'us' situation with the council and the private operator. This type of job is providing me with valuable experience.'

Aims and objectives of leisure, sport and recreation providers

All the facilities we have looked at have a similar approach to certain areas such as health and safety but will differ in other areas according to their aims and objectives. This section examines a range of organisations in detail.

It is also important to note that the aims and objectives of an organisation will vary according to whether they are in the private, public or voluntary sector. A cinema complex (private sector) will aim to attract a full house every evening by showing the latest films in attractive surroundings. A

community centre (public sector) aims to attract all sections of the local community by offering a varied activities programme, which might include bingo and tea dances for senior citizens, sports for young people and evening classes for everyone. An amateur dramatic society (voluntary sector) aims to provide entertainment to the local community by performing plays, musicals and pantomimes.

The private sector

Private sector leisure, sport and recreation facilities include cinemas, ice rinks, ten-pin bowling alleys, retail parks. The main aim of private sector organisations is to make a financial profit from the sales of products and services.

An aim is a target an organisation hopes to achieve and an objective shows how it is going to achieve it. Table 7.1 helps explain this.

Table 7.1 Private sector organisations

Aims	Objectives
• To make a profit for its shareholders and owners	Ensure income exceeds expenditure
• To increase its share of the market	Publicise and promote products and services to raise awareness
• To provide excellent customer service	Ensure all staff are trained and qualified in customer care
• To give value for money	Provide quality products and services to gain customer satisfaction

List four leisure activities which are usually provided by commercial organisations.

Name three commercial organisations involved in leisure, sport and recreation provision nationally and for each organisation identify their main area of interest, for example, Odeon – cinemas, McDonald's – fast food.

What are the aims and objectives of two of these organisations?

The public sector

At a local level, public sector facilities include leisure centres and libraries. At a national level, facilities provided by central government are National Sports Centres, for example Holme Pierrepoint, Nottingham. The aims and objectives of these facilities might be:

- to provide a service to the community by offering a wide range of affordable activities

- to keep within a budget by ensuring that targets for attendances and income are met

- to provide a wide range of facilities and activities to many different members of the community, including groups such as the unemployed, people with disabilities, single parent families.

Public sector organisations also provide leisure, sport and recreation facilities for their own staff. This provision can include:

- bar and catering facilities in the club room

- recreation room with snooker/pool table, dartboard, fruit machines, television

- social functions, such as dinner dances and quiz nights

- sports facilities, like football pitches, multi-gym, bowling green.

In all sectors, the aim of providing facilities for staff will be to promote good working relations and maintain a well-motivated work force.

These aims and objectives may be influenced by political factors. One political party may provide more resources for facilities than another. Their decisions to spend may relate to:

- the state of the economy – can the government afford to spend money on facilities?

- or whether the government of the day views these as necessary to the social structure.

Talk about it

Certain groups of people within the community have particular leisure needs; for example, the elderly, teenagers, the unemployed, single parents. As a group, discuss the leisure needs of these people and try to think of ways that these needs could be met.

The voluntary sector

This is made up of clubs, societies and associations such as amateur dramatic/operatic groups, sports clubs, or interest groups keen on conservation and heritage. Other voluntary groups include youth organisations and community action groups. They run on a non-profit making basis and raise funds through membership schemes and fundraising activities. The aims and objectives of voluntary sector groups might be to:

- provide facilities which neither the public nor private sector provide, for example a sports club

- ensure all subscriptions and fees cover administration and running costs and that any surplus is either re-invested back into the organisation or given to charity

- to raise funds to pay for the hire of premises, equipment or sports kit/costumes by organising sponsored walks and table-top sales

- to put pressure on organisations, for example a local authority, to provide a new activity for young people, such as short tennis.

Not all voluntary groups are small. Organisations such as the National Trust, the Youth Hostels Association and the YMCA/YWCA are all voluntary with funds coming from donations, membership subscriptions and entry fees.

Think it over

Do you think the government should provide leisure, sport and recreation facilities?

What benefits are there to society as a whole in having access to these facilities?

Talk about it

Discuss and note down two examples of voluntary organisations in each of the following areas:

a sports

b arts

c entertainment.

CASE STUDY — Nigel

Nigel has been secretary of the local running club for the past five years. His main tasks are to organise teams for races, deal with correspondence and organise fund-raising activities. Nigel says,

'I seem to spend more time as Club Secretary than I do at work. At the moment we are organising a 1960s/70s fancy dress disco for the public. All funds will go to the local hospital.

'Many of our social events are for club members. In the past I've organised picnics, dinner dances, barbecues, walking in the Lake District and treasure hunts. It's hard work but great fun. I have a big circle of friends and, what's more, I even get to go out for a run now and then!'

Question

What do you think are the benefits of belonging to a club?

Staffing of facilities

The success of all leisure, sport and recreation facilities is mainly dependent on the skills and qualities of the staff who work in them. The staff will know how to use the facilities to provide the very best in customer service.

Users of facilities expect their time spent in them to be enjoyable and problem free. The attitude and appearance of the staff will therefore directly affect their enjoyment. As the leisure industry is people based, staff should be enthusiastic and have the necessary communication skills to deal with people.

We will have a closer look at the skills and qualities needed to work in leisure, sport and recreation facilities.

Skills

Staff should possess:

* knowledge of the product or service – know your organisation, the staffing structure, the aims and objectives, the activities. This knowledge leads to self-confidence and could help progress your career

* information technology skills – almost all leisure and tourism organisations use IT in one form or another so word-processing and database skills are important. These IT skills could help improve your chances of promotion

* communication skills – whether it be face-to-face, on the phone or in writing, customers judge an organisation by the way staff communicate with them. It is the responsibility of all staff to give a good first impression and to be friendly and professional at all times.

Personal qualities

Leisure, sport and recreation staff should show the following qualities:

* Enthusiasm – be willing to help, show an interest in customers, give them your full attention. Enthusiasm spreads.

* Professionalism – giving good service in a clear, professional way means the customer has confidence and trust in both you and your organisation.

* Initiative – coming up with new ideas, solving problems, thinking ahead, making things happen, rather than waiting to let them happen.

* Sense of humour – a quality often lost in the rush of everyday life. A sense of humour is

SNAPSHOTS

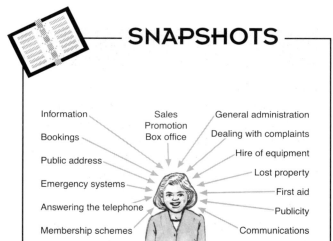

Figure 7.3   Role of a leisure centre receptionist

Mary

Mary has worked at the local leisure centre since it opened 15 years ago. She knows all the regular users and has become the familiar, friendly face in reception to her customers.

She says,

'People would rather be greeted by a smile than a scowl. My main task is to make people welcome, give them any information they need and try to make their visit here as enjoyable as possible.'

Mary's role as the receptionist is very varied one, as shown in Figure 7.3.

Anil

Anil works at a national sports stadium where he gives guided tours to visitors. Anil says,

'I get asked all sorts of questions ranging from "How many people can the stadium hold?" to "What world records have been set here?"! I really had to do my homework on the history of the stadium, the type of activities that go on and the different jobs people do here. You never know what to expect when giving guided tours. Fortunately, the knowledge I've gained since I started here a year ago has given me the self-confidence and ability to deal with the public in a professional and friendly way.'

Sarina

Sarina is the manager of a cinema complex. As well as being responsible for the staff and the health and safety of everyone in the building, she also has to meet certain financial targets. The computer skills she learned at college have come in very useful.

Sarina says,

'I need to keep a daily track on income and expenditure. The most accurate way of doing this is to look up the relevant information on my computer. My word-processing, database and spreadsheet skills mean I can keep track of income, stock control and outgoings. I can even make forecasts about future income based on the information I obtain from my computer. My IT skills have certainly helped me climb the career ladder.'

refreshing and entertaining – a smile can work wonders.

○ A clean, tidy appearance – look good, feel good. As we've said before, first impressions count and you don't get a second chance to make a good first impression.

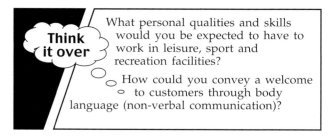

Think it over

What personal qualities and skills would you be expected to have to work in leisure, sport and recreation facilities?

How could you convey a welcome to customers through body language (non-verbal communication)?

The organisational structure of leisure, sport and recreation facilities

It is important that staff work as a team, each team member with his or her own particular tasks to complete and each having his or her own skills. It is equally important that staff know what is expected of them and so they receive instructions from supervisors or managers. This way, an organisation should run smoothly and efficiently.

An organisational structure shows the relationships and communication channels between different levels of staff; for example, lifeguards report to pool supervisors who in turn report to the deputy manager. The person at the top of the organisational structure is responsible for everyone below. Large organisations, such as theme parks or fast-food chains, have several management layers and departments. Smaller organisations, such as a travel agent, have a smaller simpler structure; for example, they usually only have a manager and three or four travel consultants.

CASE STUDY – The Blue Lagoon

Every morning the pool supervisor gets the team of six lifeguards together and briefs them on the day's tasks. There's a swimming gala today so the lane ropes have to be put out and the spectator seating has to be cleaned.

The pool supervisor then confirms with his immediate boss, the deputy manager that the pool hall is being set up for the gala. They then sit down and work out the rotas for the lifeguards for the following week. They also discuss training opportunities in lifesaving and first aid.

At 11 am every day, the assistant manager meets the centre manager and briefs him on the day's event. The manager wants to make sure everything is going to run smoothly because the mayor and several councillors will be attending the gala.

Question

What would happen if the manager gave instructions to the lifeguards without consulting the deputy manager and the supervisor?

Figures 7.4 and 7.5 show two different organisational structures.

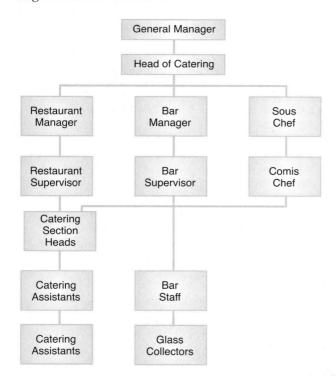

Figure 7.4 Organisational structure of a hotel's bar and catering facilities

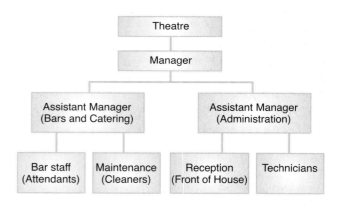

Figure 7.5 Organisational structure of a theatre

Each person forms part of the team and will have his or her own responsibilities. The ultimate responsibility lies with the manager who has to ensure that the organisation runs smoothly and effectively by employing willing and enthusiastic staff. Staff training can help to increase motivation and skills so that staff have the chance to improve their position and to work more effectively.

Look it up

Visit a local swimming pool or leisure facility with a pool and find out about its staffing structure. Then copy out the boxes below and try to fill in the staffing structure of the swimming pool.

(The answers are on page 235.)

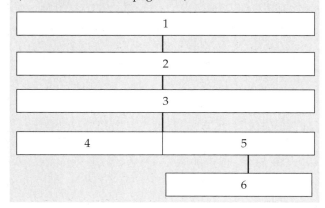

Types of jobs

Talk about it

What sort of jobs are available in your area of the leisure and tourism industry?

The leisure and tourism industry is a service industry and is concerned most of all with people. The opportunities for finding work are wide and varied and most of them involve direct contact with customers.

Because the industry offers many different types of work, there is no simple route into the area. Some jobs, such as an outdoor activities instructor, require specialist qualifications, while others, such as those working in leisure management, require general business or leisure qualifications.

Work experience counts for almost as much as qualifications. Council work that involves customer service while at school or college gives valuable experience because the leisure and tourism industry is all about helping and serving the public. Starting at the bottom of an organisation structure may not be ideal but it gives you the opportunity to build up experience,

'get your face known' and hopefully work your way up.

When asked about the worst parts of their jobs, many people in the leisure and tourism industry mention long and unsociable working hours and you will probably find you have to work in the evening and at weekends. This is the nature of the business. Leisure, sport and recreation facilities have to open when the rest of the population is not working.

However, people who work in the industry time and again stress the variety of the work, the enjoyment they get from meeting and helping people and the satisfaction they derive from providing a first-class service.

We will look at the types of job available in a little more detail.

Full-time work

In the leisure and tourism industry this usually includes weekend and evening work spread over 37 hours per week or more.

SNAPSHOTS

Stuart, recreation assistant

Stuart is a recreation assistant at a council-run leisure centre in Devon.

Stuart's typical day goes like this:

'*All the recreation assistants work a shift system, which varies from week to week. Last week, for example, I worked 6.30 am to 3 pm, then 2 pm to 10.30 pm, then 9 am to 5 pm and 12 pm to 9 pm!*

On the first shift, as soon as I come in I set the pool up, washing down the poolside and putting in lane ropes. I then act as lifeguard for the 'early bird' swimmers, making sure that they're safe while they swim. It's particularly important to keep an eye on the older swimmers because they're not so flexible. We have special swimming sessions for the over-50s and disabled people, who may need help getting in and out of the pool. We have a ramp that we take up to the water so that people in wheelchairs can just swim straight in.

continued from page 208

Safety is paramount. There are four recreation assistants on duty at any one time. When you're lifeguarding, you have to ensure that weak swimmers stay down at the shallow end and that no one runs along the poolside.

Sometimes you need eyes in the back of your head, especially during the school holidays! There are kids everywhere then and we have fun sessions with floats in the pool, water jets and rapids. You have to be very aware of what's going on and react quickly if anything's amiss. On one occasion I had to go into the rapids to rescue a toddler and return him to his mother. My knees went to jelly afterwards – but it's what we're trained to do.

We rotate our position every 20 minutes, from poolside to high chair, then off poolside to do some cleaning – wiping mirrors and windows, cleaning and general tidying. We're given daily cleaning sheets that show our responsibilities. In addition, we check the toilets every hour and get the equipment ready when there are changeovers in the sports hall. That might mean changing it from two football goals to four badminton courts, or from trampolining to an aerobics session or circuit training. The badminton nets are on wheels and the football goals in place already, so it's quite quick to do.

We have staff training once a week to make sure that we're kept sharp and up to standard (or above). One hour is theory work, resuscitation and first aid; the other hour is spent keeping your swimming up to scratch. It gets everyone working together as a team. I also have one day a week for my NVQ paperwork, which is working really well. I intend to get more qualifications as I go along.'

I would say, to work as a recreation assistant you need the following qualities:

- an outgoing personality
- be able to deal with the odd awkward customer
- a sense of humour
- a willingness to provide a high standard of service
- the confidence to act quickly if something happens.'

Finding a job as a recreation assistant

Stuart took an NVQ Level 3 in Sport and Recreation alongside an Intermediate GNVQ in Leisure and Tourism. He passed his National Pool Lifeguard Qualification (NPLQ) and was given his current position of recreation assistant. He takes his St John's First Aid Certificate next month followed by a Welcome Host – Customer Care

SNAPSHOTS

Stacey, conference and banqueting junior

Stacey has worked full time at a conference and banqueting centre for a year. She takes bookings and shows customers around the facilities. Stacey also welcomes guests to functions. The centre where Stacey works can accommodate up to 250 people in its banqueting suite for dinners, weddings and conferences. It also has facilities for smaller business meetings.

Stacey says,

'I had gained some experience of customer service from working in shops while at school and this was important in helping me get the job.'

A day in the life of Stacey might be like this:

'I start my work around 8.30 in the morning. My job is split between meeting people and showing them around the facilities, and office work. If we are holding a conference that day I have to check all the details are correct and preparations made. During the day I send information out to people enquiring about the facilities, take bookings and put together quotes for hiring the centre.

My working day is meant to end at around 5 pm, but I have to be flexible and most days are longer. For some of the larger events I have to work some Saturdays, for example when we are hosting weddings. For weddings I am on duty from the moment the guests arrive until they sit down for dinner. Luckily I get paid extra for weekend work.

I need to be very organised in my work and show patience and understanding to customers and guests. Customers often change their mind about what they want, which can be frustrating. The secret is to keep smiling – even if you don't feel like it. Remember: the customer is always right!'

The qualifications, experience and personal qualities required for Stacey's job are shown in Figure 7.6.

Try it out

Think about the job you want to do when you leave school or college, then describe what you would imagine to be a typical day, as Stacey and Stuart did. What skills and qualities do you think you will need?

Figure 7.6 What Stacey needs to do her job effectively

Part-time and casual work

Before you manage to obtain a full-time job in leisure, sport and recreation facilities you might have to start off working on a casual, seasonal or part-time basis. For example, before you find full-time work in a theme park you may have to work from April to October on a seasonal basis. Similarly with hotel work, you may be called in to work in the kitchen, washing the dishes or serving food and drinks during busy periods. One day you might work five hours, the next day it would be only two hours. This is known as casual work.

You may find that there are no vacancies for full-time work in, say, a theatre but there is a vacancy for a part-time receptionist for 25 hours a week. This is another way of starting out in your career. Table 7.2 looks at a variety of jobs, suggests where you could start off and the qualifications you will need.

Table 7.2 Different jobs and their requirements

Job title	Starting out	What you need
Information receptionist in tourist information centre	Not easy, as there aren't that many jobs around. Start as trainee with a local authority in either the Leisure or Tourism department. Gain as much experience as possible in working with the public	4 GCSEs, leisure, business or marketing qualifications. A friendly and pleasant manner with good communication skills and a knowledge of the local area. Language skills are increasingly useful
Sports development officer	Work in a leisure centre coaching and teaching various sports, progressing to supervisor or assistant manager. Start off as assistant sports development officer	GNVQ in Leisure and Tourism. 'A' levels or Advanced VCE in Leisure and Recreation. Certificate in Management Studies
Sales and marketing assistant	Part-time work in tourist attraction or any leisure facility or retail centre. Dealing with customers is the main task	A business and leisure qualification. Numeracy and computer skills are helpful. You need confidence to take people on guided tours and stamina for the long hours you work
Gallery attendant	Most museums and art galleries run by local councils require attendants to move and arrange displays, assist with routine maintenance and occasionally catalogue exhibits	17+ years, an interest in the arts, fit and able to work without supervision
Trainee chef	Work part time in a hotel/restaurant in the kitchen. Be prepared to take training and show an interest in food preparation	Three-year course leading to NVQ Level 4 in Food Preparation; Level 3 in Food Service and a Diploma in Cookery

Figures 7.7, 7.8 and 7.9 consider a variety of job opportunities in the leisure and tourism industry.

Figure 7.7 Job opportunities in a hotel or restaurant

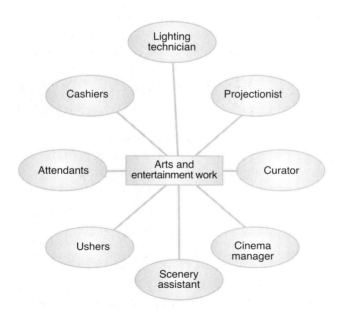

Figure 7.8 Employment in arts and entertainment facilities

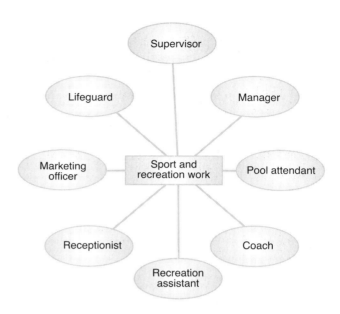

Figure 7.9 Jobs in sport and recreation facilities

Methods of employment

As well as full-time work, people can be employed in other ways.

Part-time work can be carried out by receptionists or cleaners who may work 15 hours a week spread over five days.

Seasonal work takes place in facilities which usually close for three or four months during the winter. Examples include theme parks (often open March to November) or seaside holiday centres where deck-chair attendants on the promenade or ride attendants on the Pleasure Beach work during the summer.

Casual work in the leisure and tourism industry takes place at special events – setting up a stage for a pop concert or riverside music festivals, or working as extra catering assistants. Opening an outdoor swimming pool at weekends in summer means additional lifeguards would be required.

Temporary work includes work for a specific short-term period; for example, required for one year, a trainee pool manager to learn the plant operation of a pool or a temporary six-month contract for a receptionist to cover maternity leave.

When people are employed, they are given a contract of employment. In principle, employers are free to include whatever terms they wish into a contract, but for the vast majority of people, contracts take a standard form.

In some cases there are a number of specific terms which can be written into contracts. They include the following:

- **Fixed-term clause** Employing people on a fixed-term basis is becoming increasingly popular, especially in the public sector where funding is limited or where the job is clearly of fixed duration. For example, Sport England has funded the post of sports development officer for the local council for three years. Therefore the successful applicant will be employed on a fixed-term contract for that period.

- **Waiver clause** Employees on a fixed-term contract for more than a year can be asked to sign a waiver clause giving up their right to a redundancy payment. For example, a consultant may be employed to oversee the development of a new ice-skating arena for 18 months. His fixed-term contract runs until the project is completed.

- **Probationary clause** Many employers initially employ people for a probationary period of six months or a year, at which point their performance is reviewed and a decision is taken on whether or not to confirm the appointment. Where this is the case, it is important to gain the employee's

agreement and to ensure that he or she understands the probationary arrangements together with the consequences of failure. For example, a receptionist who previously worked at a beauty salon has moved to work at the local theatre and may be given a six-month probationary period.

- **Restraint of trade clause** This clause can be put into contracts to prevent employees from working for rival employers in their spare time or using information gained in their employment to help business competitors. For example, a marketing officer in a private sector organisation who may possess information which could be very useful to competitors.

- **Restrictive covenant** This is like the restraint of trade clause but refers to the period after the employment has ended. It usually seeks to prevent employees from taking up employment with competitors for a certain period of time after they leave. For example, a company director who may possess sensitive financial information about the organisation she has just left will be prevented from going to work for a rival company straight away.

Working conditions, staff rotas and pay

Working conditions are usually laid down by law and apply to the physical environment where people work and employment.

CASE STUDY – Unfair treatment

Carmen is 17 and started work as a receptionist/cashier at her local cinema seven months ago. During that time she was never off sick and had done her very best in the job. She felt that the manager was pleased with her work. One day he even said to her, 'Well done, Carmen, you're doing a good job and fitting in well'.

Last week she was called into the office to see the manager. He told her that she had not passed her probationary period and so he would have to terminate her

employment. No reasons were given. There was no explanation. She was only in the office for three minutes. When Carmen walked out she was jobless, distressed and confused.

Questions

- What do you think Carmen could do?

- Was her employer within his rights?

- Do you know of anyone who has been treated unfairly at work?

The European Working Time Directive

These regulations, introduced in 1998, provide new rights for employees such as:

- a limit on the average weekly working time of 48 hours (although individuals can choose to work longer)
- minimum daily and weekly rest periods
- rest breaks at work
- a limit on night workers' average normal daily working time to 8 hours.

Talk about it

What are the implications of these regulations for jobs in the leisure and tourism industry?

The Health and Safety at Work Act 1974 and the Offices, Shops and Railway Premises Act 1963 ensure that employers provide safe working conditions for their staff. In particular, the Offices, Shops and Railway Premises Act is concerned with ensuring that:

- the general standard of cleanliness, hygiene and working conditions are acceptable
- heating, lighting, ventilation and toilets are satisfactory.

The leisure and tourism industry is not usually associated with 9 am to 5 pm hours of working. Long hours are part of the job for holiday representatives and recreation assistants. It is not unusual to work a 12-hour shift. It is up to managers to ensure that when rotas are planned, sufficient time off is given for staff to rest and recover. This is important because tired employees are ineffective employees as they cannot possibly give their best if they are worn out. What's more it could also prove dangerous – imagine a lifeguard falling asleep on poolside duty!

Shift work is necessary in the leisure, sport and recreation industry because facilities like leisure clubs are open from 7 am to 11 pm, seven days a week. It is unreasonable to expect staff to work 16-hour shifts every day so a shift system may be introduced.

A shift rota in a leisure centre could look like the one below for a recreation assistant. Staff would rotate these shifts over a three-week period.

Shift	Mon.	Tue.	Wed.	Thu.	Fri.	Sat.	Sun.
A	Early	Early	Rest	Rest	Late	Late	Late
B	Rest	Rest	Late	Late	Early	Early	Early
C	Late	Late	Early	Early	Rest	Rest	Rest

An example of a shift rota

Talk about it

As a group, what do you think are the advantages and disadvantages of working shifts? You may even be able to draw on your own experience.

You may have mentioned:

- *Advantages*
  - time off in the week: you can shop when it's quiet
  - extra pay
  - varied working week
- *Disadvantages*
  - interferes with social life
  - can affect family life and relationships
  - can affect health; late finish, early start, lack of sleep, poor diet (missed mealtimes)
  - you are working when others are 'playing'.

SNAPSHOTS

Enrique

Enrique works in a nightclub. 'It took me quite a while to get used to working late night shifts. At first, I kept feeling unwell because my body couldn't get used to the irregular sleep and eating patterns. I never knew which meal I was supposed to be eating. I have got more used to it now but still feel quite tired. Working shifts means I can't always go out with my friends but I have to accept it as part of the job.'

Pay

Some organisations, especially in the public sector, pay enhanced rates for shift and weekend work. For example, an annual lump sum, such as 12 per cent shift allowance with time and a half on Saturday and double time on a Sunday. Bank holiday rates could be double time and a day off in lieu. Many organisations in the private sector pay an all-inclusive rate to cover unsociable hours working.

Talk about it

Many students have part-time jobs. In your group, discuss what rates of pay you get. Do you get paid extra for bank holiday work or overtime? Try to find out what the minimum wage is for different age groups.

Programming of facilities

The use of facilities should be carefully planned and scheduled if they are to be used to the maximum. If an airline has empty seats or a sports centre has three empty badminton courts, and they are not filled or used, then the opportunity has gone and they can never be sold.

The size of a facility and the activities it is capable of putting on will determine what can be programmed. For example, if a leisure centre provides aerobics for women during weekdays, can it also offer a crèche?

Another point when planning a programme is to decide the type of use to which the facility will be put. For example, an exclusive private gym and health suite will aim to make a profit so it is unlikely that it will offer free use to the unemployed nor will it offer programmes for children. This is known as the 'philosophy of use' – in other words, the providers determine who uses the facility.

Programming in public, private and voluntary facilities needs to:

◦   ensure maximum usage

◦   make use of staff strengths

CASE STUDY – Open all hours

Sam works in his father's convenience shop and studies full-time at college. His day goes something like this:

6.00 am	I help my father stock the shelves and sort out the daily newspapers for the paper boys and girls.
7.00 am	The shop opens and I work on the till serving customers for an hour.
8.00 am	A quick breakfast then it's off to college.
9.00–3.30 pm	College. Given two assessments to start on and a project to be done by next week.

4.00–6.00 pm	Work in the shop.
6.00–7.30 pm	College work.
7.30–10.00 pm	Work in the shop, serving customers.
10.00–11.00 pm	Help with re-stocking shelves.

'It's a busy day and I do this every day. I don't mind hard work. My father and mother have always worked hard and have passed the work ethic on to me. One day I hope to take over my father's business and buy more shops. I was brought up to believe that hard work always brings rewards.'

Question

Could you work this hard every day?

◦ keep up to date with modern trends

◦ take into account different users.

Programmes can be devised by the manager of an organisation, particularly in the private sector, or by the community expressing their needs, for example, in a public sector leisure centre, where a particular group may want swimming lessons for adults or there is pressure for more club badminton. Whatever type of programming takes place, there must be:

◦ market research – to determine current and future programmes

◦ target marketing – to make sure the right activities are provided for the right people at the right times.

The facilities and activities can then be promoted to these groups.

How could a community group put pressure on a leisure centre manager to include short tennis on the centre programme?

Programming of activities

When planning a programme for a leisure centre, particularly if it is a public sector facility, it is important to take into account the different sport and recreation needs of the community – because after all the service is provided for everyone in the community (see Figure 7.10).

In addition, the programme should take into account:

◦ groups currently under-provided, e.g. the unemployed

◦ activities which are popular now

◦ an analysis of current activities – which are well attended, which are not so popular

◦ requirements of external groups, such as businesses wanting to put on conferences and exhibitions.

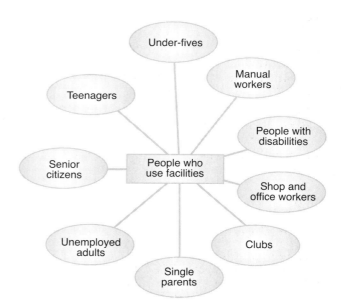

Figure 7.10 Different user groups to be considered

Look at the booking sheets of Victoria Leisure Centre 'wet' and 'dry' side on pages 216–217. Using the information about Star Leisure Centre design on page 218 complete two similar booking sheets of your own.

Programming mix

This is concerned with the balance of activities and the range of people using the centre. For example, the programming mix of a leisure centre can be made up of:

◦ individuals   – non members
    – open sessions, such as keep fit classes

◦ spectators   – special events, such as concerts
    – casual spectating

◦ special groups   – clubs, training, matches
    – disabled, special activities

◦ learners   – coaching classes.

In groups of four, try to work out a week's programme for a theatre – remembering that a variety of performances is required.

Victoria Leisure Centre: Wet Side

PUBLIC SWIMMING DURING SCHOOL TERM
Bank Holidays: Opening Hours 9.00 am to 4.40 pm – Public Swimming

DAY	EARLY MORNING	MORNING	LUNCHTIME	EARLY AFTERNOON	AFTERNOON	EARLY EVENING	EVENING
MONDAY	7.00 - 8.50 EARLY MORNING SWIMMING £1.00	9.00 - 10.20 RIVERSIDE CLUB 60+ and DISABLED 10.30 - 12.00 SCHOOL SW	12.00 - 1.50 LUNCHTIME SWIM	2.00 - 3.30 SCHOOL SWIMMING	3.45 - 6.25 EARLY EVENING SWIM * See below	7.00 - 8.30 ADULTS ONLY 16+	8.45 - 10.15 ADULT GROUP SWIMMING LESSONS
TUESDAY	7.00 - 8.50 EARLY MORNING SWIMMING £1.00	9.00 - 11.00 SCHOOL SWIMMING	11.00 - 1.50 LUNCHTIME SWIM 10.00 - 12.00 LADIES RECREATION PACKAGE (swim starts 11) (CRECHE) 10.00 - 12.00	2.00 - 3.30 SCHOOL SWIMMING	3.30 - 5.20 EARLY EVENING SWIM * See below	6.00 - 7.45 ADULTS ONLY 20+ 6.45 - 7.45 SECTION OF POOL LANE ROPED	7.45 - 8.30 AQUAFIT 8.15 - 9.45 LADIES ONLY 16+
WEDNESDAY	7.00 - 8.50 EARLY MORNING SWIMMING £1.00	9.00 - 11.00 SCHOOL SWIMMING	11.00 - 1.50 LUNCHTIME SWIM 10.00 - 12.00 MIDWEEK PACKAGE (swim starts 11)	2.00 - 3.00 SCHOOL SWIMMING	3.00 - 4.10 AFTERNOON SWIM PARENTS & BABIES SHALLOW END	4.15 - 6.15 SWIMMING LESSONS	6.30 - 10.00 PRIVATE CLUB HIRE
THURSDAY	7.00 - 8.50 EARLY MORNING SWIMMING £1.00	9.00 - 11.00 SCHOOL SWIMMING	11.30 - 1.50 LUNCHTIME SWIM 10.00 - 12.00 LADIES RECREATION PACKAGE (swim starts 11.30) 11.00 - 11.30 AQUAFIT	2.00 - 3.30 SCHOOL SWIMMING	3.30 - 5.20 EARLY EVENING SWIM * See below	6.00 - 8.20 EVENING SWIM	8.30 - 9.30 PRIVATE CLUB HIRE
FRIDAY	7.00 - 8.50 EARLY MORNING SWIMMING £1.00	9.00 - 10.50 RIVERSIDE CLUB 60+ and DISABLED	11.00 - 1.50 LUNCHTIME SWIM 10.00 - 12.00 PARENTS & BABIES SHALLOW END	2.00 - 3.30 SCHOOL SWIMMING	3.45 - 6.25 EARLY EVENING SWIM * See below	7.00 FAMILY NIGHT	AVAILABLE FOR PRIVATE HIRE
SATURDAY	7.30 - 8.50 EARLY MORNING SWIMMING £1.00	9.00 - 12.00 SWIMMING LESSONS AND COURSES	12.00 - 1.00 1.00 - 2.00 AVAILABLE FOR PRIVATE HIRE	2.00 - 4.40 FAMILY FUN SESSIONS (Floats 2.00 Slide 3.30)	AVAILABLE FOR PRIVATE HIRE	AVAILABLE FOR PRIVATE HIRE	AVAILABLE FOR PRIVATE HIRE
SUNDAY	PRIVATE CLUB HIRE	9.00 - 12.50 SUNDAY MORNING SWIM	1.00 - 2.00 AVAILABLE FOR PRIVATE HIRE	2.00 - 4.40 FAMILY SWIMMING	PRIVATE CLUB HIRE	PRIVATE CLUB HIRE	AVAILABLE FOR PRIVATE HIRE

PUBLIC SWIMMING DURING SCHOOL HOLIDAYS
Bank Holidays: Opening Hours 9.00 am to 4.40 pm – Public Swimming

DAY	EARLY MORNING	MORNING	LUNCHTIME	AFTERNOON	EARLY EVENING	LATE EVENING
MONDAY	7.00 - 8.50 EARLY MORNING SWIMMING £1.00	9.00 - 10.50 RIVERSIDE CLUB 60+ and DISABLED	11.00 - 1.50 LUNCHTIME SWIM 11.00 - 12.00 PARENTS & BABIES SHALLOW END	2.00 - 5.20 HOLIDAY FUN SESSION ** See below	6.00 - 8.00 HOLIDAY EVENING SWIM	8.15 - 9.45 ADULTS LATE SWIM 16+
TUESDAY	7.00 - 8.50 EARLY MORNING SWIMMING £1.00	9.00 - 11.50 MORNING *SWIM	12.00 - 1.50 ADULT LUNCHTIME SWIM	2.00 - 5.20 HOLIDAY FUN SESSION ** See below	6.00 - 7.45 ADULTS ONLY 20+ 6.45 - 7.45 SECTION OF POOL LANE ROPED	7.45 - 8.30 AQUAFIT 8.15 - 9.45 LADIES ONLY 16+
WEDNESDAY	7.00 - 8.50 EARLY MORNING SWIMMING £1.00	9.00 - 11.50 MORNING SWIM	12.00 - 1.50 ADULT LUNCHTIME SWIM	2.00 - 6.20 HOLIDAY FUN SESSION ** See below	PRIVATE CLUB HIRE	PRIVATE CLUB HIRE
THURSDAY	7.00 - 8.50 EARLY MORNING SWIMMING £1.00	9.00 - 11.50 MORNING SWIM	12.00 - 1.50 ADULT LUNCHTIME SWIM HALF POOL LANE ROPED	2.00 - 5.20 HOLIDAY FUN SESSION ** See below	6.00 - 8.20 HOLIDAY EVENING SWIM	8.30 - 9.30 PRIVATE CLUB HIRE
FRIDAY	7.00 - 8.50 EARLY MORNING SWIMMING £1.00	9.00 - 10.50 RIVERSIDE CLUB 60+ and DISABLED	11.00 - 1.50 LUNCHTIME SWIM 11.00 - 12.00 PARENTS & BABIES SHALLOW END	2.00 - 5.20 HOLIDAY FUN SESSION ** See below	6.00 - 8.20 HOLIDAY EVENING SWIM	PRIVATE CLUB HIRE
SATURDAY	7.30 - 8.50 EARLY MORNING SWIMMING £1.00	9.00 - 11.50 PUBLIC SWIMMING (except half-term holiday)	12.00 - 1.00 1.00 - 2.00 AVAILABLE FOR PRIVATE HIRE	2.00 - 4.40 FAMILY FUN SESSIONS (Floats 2.00 Slide 3.30)	AVAILABLE FOR PRIVATE HIRE	AVAILABLE FOR PRIVATE HIRE
SUNDAY	PRIVATE CLUB HIRE	9.00 - 12.50 SUNDAY MORNING SWIM	1.00 - 2.00 AVAILABLE FOR PRIVATE HIRE	2.00 - 4.40 AFTERNOON FAMILY SWIM	PRIVATE CLUB HIRE	PRIVATE CLUB HIRE

* During this session, the shallow end **may** be roped off for lessons.

** Floats 2.00 - 2.45   Slide 3.30 - 4.15
(These times are subject to alteration without notice at the discretion of the management)

Booking Sheet – Victoria Leisure Centre: Dry Side

Day Friday 1.9.00

Times	MAIN SPORTS HALL Badminton 1	Badminton 2	Badminton 3	Badminton 4	SIDE HALL	SQUASH 1	SQUASH 2	SQUASH 3	WEIGHTS ROOM
9–10									
10–11									
11–12	CONWAY SCHOOL								CONWAY SCHOOL
12–1	KENNINGTON		ACTION		ACTION	HAWKEY	JONES	DAVIES	ACTION
1–2	SCHOOL		SPORT		SPORT	SMITH	MORGAN	SHUTE	SPORT
2–3	FENWICK	JAMES	CARLOS		LADIES KEEP				
3–4		JAMES			FIT				
4–5	UNEMPLOYED FIVE-A-SIDE FOOTBALL						THOMAS		
5–6	JUNIOR SHORT					COLE	STEVENS	TURNER	
6–7	TENNIS				BRADBURY	DIXON	HOWE	JEROME	
7–8	CAVALIERS				TABLE TENNIS CLUB	MITCHELL	TAYLOR	COX	
8–9	BADMINTON				KITSU	OWEN		BRYANT	BEEFEATERS WEIGHT-LIFTING ASSOCIATION
9–10	CLUB				KARATE CLUB	ROBSON			

Star Leisure Centre

FACILITIES

Large Swimming Pool	– 1965	Squash Courts	– 1975
		Sports Hall	– 1983
		Social Hall	– 1983
Teaching Pool	– 1992	Floodlit All Weather Pitch	– 1988

Sauna, Sunbed, Fitness Room, Bar & Kitchen, Football Pitch, Caravan Rally and Touring Facilities also available.

Opening times
The Centre is open 7 days a week with occasional closure for Christmas and New Year.

Reception is open from 9.00 am – 9.30 pm every day.

MAIN POOL

25 m X 10 m
DIVING BASIN
(has limited sessions)
Disabled Persons Session
Swimming Courses
Swimming Club
Water Polo
Canoeing

TEACHING POOL

11 m X 8 m
overall 0.9 m depth
Kiddies Slide
Aquababes
Pre-School Lessons

SOCIAL HALL

12 m X 10 m
Aerobics
Crèche
Baby Gym
Judo
Table Tennis

SPORTS HALL

29 m X 16 m
4 Badminton Courts
Basketball
Cricket Nets
Five-A-Side
Gymnastics
Hockey
Short Tennis
Tennis
Volleyball

Other Activities include Roller Disco, Sports Activity Morning, Rackets Morning, Keep Fit and Swing Into Shape.

This venue is suitable for Wedding Receptions, Dances, Commercial Events, Meetings, Exhibitions, you name it – we can accommodate it.

Sports Activity Nights – whole or part facilities available – negotiable rates.

Star Leisure Centre
Day by day fitness

MONDAY

10.05–11.00 am	STEP AEROBICS	(SONIA)*
12.45–1.30 pm	AQUAFIT (term time only)	(FRAN)
6.15–7.15 pm	STEP AND TONE	(SONIA)
7.30–8.30 pm	STEP AND TONE	(SONIA)
7.15–8.45 pm	FITNESS WITH SWING	(JAMIE)

TUESDAY

10.05–11.30 am	FITNESS WITH SWING (term time only)	(JAMIE)*
10.30–11.30 am	STEP AEROBICS	(PRERNA)*
**10.15–11.15 am	SHAPE AND CIRCUIT	(JAMIE)*
**12.15–1.15 pm	C.V. CIRCUIT	(JAMIE)
7.30–8.30 pm	AEROBICS	(SONIA)
**8.30–9.30 pm	C.V. CIRCUIT	(JAMIE)

WEDNESDAY

9.30–10.30 am	50+ TRAINING	(SONIA)
6.10–7.10 pm	BODYTONE	(PRERNA)
8.30–9.30 pm	MIXED FITNESS TRAINING	

THURSDAY

10.05–11.00 am	TONE ZONE	(PRERNA)
11.30–12.15 pm	AQUAROBICS	(PETER)
6.15–7.15 pm	STEP AND TONE	(SONIA)
7.15–8.45 pm	FITNESS WITH SWING	(JAMIE)
7.30–8.30 pm	AEROBICS	(SONIA)
**7.30–8.30 pm	C.V. CIRCUIT	(JAMIE)
**8.30–9.30 pm	C.V. CIRCUIT	(JAMIE)

FRIDAY

10.35–11.35 am	KEEP FIT (term time only)	(FRAN)
**11.00–12.00 noon	SHAPE AND CIRCUIT	(JAMIE)
6.00–7.00 pm	BOXERCISE	(JAMIE)
6.05–6.50 pm	CRAZY COMBO FITNESS CLASS	(KAYLEIGH)
8.30–9.30 pm	AQUAROBICS	(PETER)

SATURDAY

| **11.00–12.00 am | C.V. CIRCUIT | (JAMIE) |
| 12.00–1.00 pm | BOXERCISE | (JAMIE) |

SUNDAY

| 11.30–12.30 pm | AEROBICS | (SONIA) |

*CRECHE AVAILABLE
ACTUAL START AND FINISH TIME HAVE BEEN ADJUSTED TO SUIT CRECHE OPENING TIMES.

**MUST BE FITNESS ROOM CARD HOLDERS

Programming for special needs

Groups who may have special needs include:

- people with disabilities
- mothers with young children
- people who are unemployed
- ethnic minority groups.

People with disabilities need to gain access to facilities, therefore:

- car parking bays should be close to the entrance
- corridors and doors should be wide enough to give access to social areas, toilets and activity areas
- ramps and, if possible, lifts should be provided.

The unemployed

Problems can arise through lack of money and lack of transport. Some of these problems could be overcome by:

- no charge for activities
- no equipment hire charge
- provision of transport where possible, e.g. putting on buses, especially in the countryside.

Ethnic minority groups

A minority group may have political, cultural or racial differences from the larger population. Within the UK ethnic minority groups might include Vietnamese, Ugandan, Asian, Afro-Caribbean and Polish people. Some of these groups may have problems with taking part in leisure and recreation activities because of language differences and cultural traditions.

CASE STUDY — Where is everyone?

Carfield Leisure Centre is a local authority run facility aimed at providing sports and leisure activities for all the community.

The manager had targeted certain groups such as teenagers, senior citizens and sports clubs, and had provided the necessary activities for them. His next target group was mothers with young children. He decided to promote a recreation class on Wednesday mornings between 10 am and midday, specifically for mothers, at a cost of £2.50 per person.

The course was publicised throughout the local housing estate and around the town. But only one person turned up to the first session and no one turned up on the second week.

The manager discussed this with his staff and they first asked themselves why no one was attending. They came up with the following answers:

- lack of transport
- lack of confidence
- lack of money
- who looks after the children?

This is what they did to try to increase usage:

- provided a crèche
- introduced concessionary family rates
- provided free tea and coffee after the session to emphasise the social aspects of the class
- provided free use of sports equipment.

The following week five mothers turned up, each with a toddler. Additional publicity and word of mouth advertising soon boosted numbers every Wednesday.

Question

How could you encourage the unemployed to use the leisure centre?

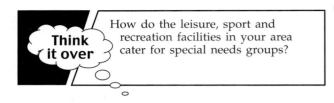

How do the leisure, sport and recreation facilities in your area cater for special needs groups?

Talk about it

The following times have been identified as off-peak in a leisure centre. What group activities could fill these times:

- 0700–0830 hrs
- 0930–1130 hrs
- 1300–1400 hrs
- 1630–1800 hrs?

Concessionary rates

Leisure facilities try to attract as many people as possible to use their facilities. Cheaper rates for different times and different groups help to attract more people. For example:

- senior citizens and unemployed – activities may be charged at a lower rate or there may even be free family tickets, e.g. at a theme park to target family groups

- off-peak rates are lower than peak rates

- a guaranteed block booking could mean cheaper rates.

Peak and off-peak usage

Peak times refer to times when facilities have no problem in getting people to use the place, for example evenings in a gym. Off-peak times refer to 'quiet' times when a facility is not used to its maximum, for example daytime in a leisure centre.

Good programming can ensure that off-peak usage in recreation and leisure facilities can be improved (see Figure 7.11).

Figure 7.11 Ways of improving off-peak usage

Private use

This is when an individual or group of people want to hire the facilities to hold a private function. One example of private use is when people hire a function room for a party, such as a silver wedding anniversary. They have the exclusive use of the room and disco. Sometimes they are able to have exclusive use of the bar as well.

Obviously people have to abide by the rules and regulations of the centre which would have been made clear to them at the time of booking. Such rules and regulations could be:

- the hirer shall leave the room in a clean and tidy condition

- the function must end at the time agreed

- people are not allowed to bring their own drinks

- any damage must be paid for

- the limit on numbers in the room must not be exceeded.

Club use

Managers of leisure facilities, especially leisure centres, have to provide a balanced programme which is fair to everyone. If a wide section of the community is to use the centre, then clubs must be allocated some time. It can be a difficult balancing act. Too much club use would cause an outcry from casual users. Little or no club usage would have the same effect on club members and officials.

Clubs will often utilise off-peak time, for example 7.00 to 8.30 am swimming or 9.00 to 10.00 pm football training. It is sometimes better to allocate club bookings after the programme has been set for the rest of the community.

Organising a league and fixtures

This job is usually carried out by the fixtures secretary, although organising a league may be done through a committee. Look at the information produced by the community sports leaders awards – this will give examples of league and fixtures organisation.

Health, safety and security

Leisure, sport and recreation facilities are potentially dangerous places, for example people can get into difficulties in a swimming pool, trampolining could be dangerous unless properly supervised by qualified staff, chemicals can damage buildings. It is with these risks in mind that the **Health and Safety at Work Act** was passed in 1974.

The main purpose of the Act is to maintain and improve health and safety standards for the public and employees. In other words, facilities must be made as safe as possible for everyone in them. It covers hazards such as:

- keeping fire exits clear
- making sure equipment is safe (e.g. see box on health and safety guidelines for inflatables)
- making sure staff wear protective clothing when necessary
- dealing with chemicals.

COSHH – the Control of Substances Hazardous to Health Regulations 1994 – refers to chemicals which must be treated with great care. In order to comply with this Act, facilities must provide:

- appropriate protective clothing/equipment
- suitable storage for chemicals, which must be labelled

Health and safety Guidelines for inflatables

Setting up procedure

1 A minimum of two people are required when handling, moving or positioning the inflatable. Ensure correct lifting techniques are used at all times.
2 Check the condition and operation of the fan before connecting to the inflatable.
3 Position the inflatable
4 Check the fabric for damage or for objects that may cause damage.
5 Attach the inflatable to the fan, ensuring that the collar is fitted securely to the correct surface of the fan tube.
6 Switch on the fan and inflate.
7 Position safety mats around the inflatable, leave no gaps.
9 Test the set up and sign the check list.

Operating procedure

1 Check that the set up procedure has been completed and signed by a member of staff.
2 A minimum of four staff members are positioned around the inflatable to act as spotters at all times that the inflatable is in use.
3 Users to remove footwear.
4 Any other equipment to be kept clear of the inflatable.
5 Operators to refrain from using the inflatable.
6 No adults to use the inflatable.
7 Number of users not to exceed 5.
8 Spotters to ensure stability of the inflatable and mat positions.
9 Any problems that may occur during the sessions: remove users from the inflatable, switch off the fan and report to the Duty Officer.
10 *Never switch the fan off* while users are on the inflatable.

- procedures in event of an accident
- details on toxicity of chemicals.

Other important codes of practice which you should know about include:

- Fire Precautions Act 1971
- Fire Safety and Safety of Places of Sport Act 1987
- Food Hygiene (General) Regulations 1970
- Health and Safety First Aid Regulations 1981
- Manual Handling Operations Regulations 1993.

Evacuation procedures

Evacuations are necessary in the event of:

- fire (see 'Fire action' box)
- bomb threats
- structural failures
- escape of toxic gases.

Emergency evacuations are also held to ensure that staff are familiar with the procedure. Observations can be made of the evacuation ('fire drill') in order that improvements can be made if required.

If you should discover a fire:

1   operate the fire alarm
2   call the fire brigade on 999
3   do not attempt to fight the fire unless you are sure that it is safe to do so.

All public buildings must have a fire certificate. This was specified under the Fire Precautions Act 1971 which was later amended by the Fire Safety and Safety of Places of Sport Act 1987.

This Act ensures:

- fire escapes are kept clear
- records on fire and safety matters must be kept
- warning notices must be prominently displayed
- staff training in fire drills must take place
- limits on the number of people in the building

Look out for fire action notices like this one in public buildings

- hose reels and fire extinguishers are regularly inspected.

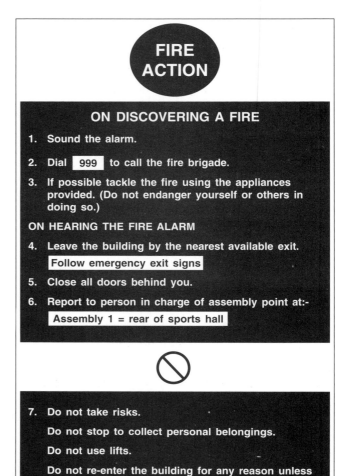

FIRE ACTION

ON DISCOVERING A FIRE

1. Sound the alarm.
2. Dial **999** to call the fire brigade.
3. If possible tackle the fire using the appliances provided. (Do not endanger yourself or others in doing so.)

ON HEARING THE FIRE ALARM

4. Leave the building by the nearest available exit. Follow emergency exit signs
5. Close all doors behind you.
6. Report to person in charge of assembly point at:- Assembly 1 = rear of sports hall

7. Do not take risks.
   Do not stop to collect personal belongings.
   Do not use lifts.
   Do not re-enter the building for any reason unless authorised to do so.

Source: HSE Crown copyright material is reproduced with the permission of the Controller of Her Majesty's Stationery Office

Risk assessment

Employers are required to ensure suitable and sufficient assessments of all risks in the workplace. The aim of this is to protect the public and staff. The risk assessment process follows a set procedure:

1   Identify the hazards – health/safety and security.
2   Who might be harmed?
3   What are the risks and do existing measures cover these risks?

4 Recommend and record how you could eliminate these risks.

5 Review and revise the assessment.

Over the next three pages are examples of risk assessment sheets, one of which was completed by a recreation student (see page 29).

Risk assessment

DEFINITIONS:

Hazard – anything that can cause harm (e.g. chemicals, electricity etc.)

Risk – is the chance high or low that somebody will be harmed by the hazard?

5 STEPS TO RISK ASSESSMENT:

Step 1: Look for the hazards.

Step 2: Decide who might be harmed and how.

Step 3: Evaluate the risks and decide whether the existing precautions are adequate or whether more should be done.

Step 4: Record your findings.

Step 5: Review your assessment and revise it if necessary.

Probability and severity of risk

	Probability	Severity
• Children tripping over cables	Medium	High
• A child falling	High	High
• A child falling due to spilt drinks	Medium	High
• A child cutting or grazing themselves	High	Medium
• Someone tripping over benches	Low	Medium

	Probability
Children tripping	50%
Children falling	100%
Children falling due to liquid spillage	50%
A child cutting or grazing themselves	100%
A child tripping over a bench	25%
Electrical faults	25%

A risk assessment for a children's party

RISK	CHECK	CHECKED BY
• Tables and chairs	Make sure that all tables are properly set up.	
• Cables or loose hanging wires	Make sure that all cables and wires are firmly stuck down.	
• Benches	Make sure that all benches are pushed as far to the walls as possible.	
• Fire exits	Make sure that all fire exits are clear, and there is nothing obstructing them.	
• Food and drink	Make sure that all food is covered and is not getting warm, for example egg or ham sandwiches. Uncover all food just before serving.	

Examples of risk assessment

RISK ASSESSMENT FORM

DATE: VENUE/FACILITY: ACTIVITY: GROUP: LEADER:

HAZARD	EFFECTS OF HAZARD	LIKELIHOOD OF OCCURRENCE	WHO MIGHT BE HARMED?	IS THE RISK ADEQUATELY CONTROLLED?	FURTHER ACTION	REVIEW
The potential to cause harm	*See key below*	*See key below*	*List groups of people who are specifically at risk from the hazards*	*List existing control measures in place or note where the information may be found*	*List the risks which are not adequately controlled and the action which could be taken where it is practical to do so*	*Review likelihood of occurrence following further action taken*
Facility						
Equipment						
Activity						
Participants						

RISK ASSESSMENT SCALES

Effect of hazard scale:

A: MAJOR: e.g. Death or major injury
B: SERIOUS: e.g. Injuries where people may be off work for 3 days.
C: SLIGHT: e.g. All other injuries including those where people are off work for a period of up to 3 days.

Likelihood of occurrence:

1: HIGH: e.g. Where it is certain or near certain that harm will occur.
2: MEDIUM: e.g. Where harm will occur frequently.
3: LOW: e.g. Where harm will seldom occur.

COLLEGE RISK ASSESSMENT

Area: *College Sports Hall Storeroom* Carried out by: *G. Knox*   Date: *1.11.00*

HAZARD	WHO/WHAT IS AT RISK	CURRENT CONTROL MEASURES	RISK FACTOR	HAZARD RATING	RISK RATING
Sports Hall Storeroom There is a big hole on the inside wall just as you walk into the storeroom	☑ EMPLOYEES ☑ STUDENTS ☐ VISITORS ☐ GENERAL PUBLIC ☐ MAINTENANCE ☐ STAFF ☐ GENERAL ☐ CONTRACTORS ☐ CLEANERS ☐ OTHERS ☑ EQUIPMENT ☐ PROPERTY	Activity leaders control the area ARE THESE ADEQUATE ☐ YES ☑ NO	Equipment could get caught or stuck whilst it is being removed, this could cause injury to the people who are removing it and the equipment	Serious. Injuries could result in the hazard.	

ACTION PRIORITY

A1: IMMEDIATE ATTENTION TO REMOVE OR REDUCE RISK ☐
A2/B1: URGENT ATTENTION ASAP TO REDUCE RISK ☑
A3/C1: ACTION NECESSARY TO REDUCE RISK ☐
B2: ATTENTION NECESSARY TO MINIMISE RISK ☐
B3/C2: ACTION PLAN FOR FUTURE IMPROVEMENT ☐
C3: LOW PRIORITY

RELATED RISK ASSESSMENTS

☐ WORK EQUIPMENT   ☐ NOISE
☐ COSHH   ☐ AIR MONITORING
☐ PPE   ☐ VDU/DSE
☑ MANUAL HANDLING ☐ WORK METHOD

RISK ASSESSMENT FORWARDED TO: *A Holden*
                    DATE: *18.11.00*
ACTION PLAN RECEIVED ON:
ACTION PLAN FOLLOW UP: DUE   COMPLETED
Nov   *Wed 14 Nov*   *Mon 19 Nov*

SIGNATURE OF ASSESSOR: *A Holden*
RISK ASSESSMENT IDENTIFICATION NO: *1073.*

Supervision of activities

Supervision is essential in leisure, sport and recreation because:

- it helps to ensure health and safety regulations are being followed

- it can reduce vandalism

- it can maintain the facility's standard of cleanliness, e.g. litter and chewing gum can be removed.

Regular patrolling by staff in smart, easily recognisable uniforms can help to improve the image of the organisation.

Pool supervision

Swimming pool attendants must be alert, vigilant and ready to move. They must never turn their back on the pool and must not stand chatting to other staff. All the water areas must be watched and pool supervision positions must be established to cover any particular zones that may require greater attention, for example diving areas, the wave machine or the deep end.

Toddler in pool tragedy

A little girl suffered serious internal injuries when she was trapped in a paddling pool water pump last Thursday.

Danielle Jeffrey, three, was playing in the toddlers' pool with her mother when the pump's grill broke and she was sucked into the filter.

Panic broke out as stricken parents searched for a way to turn the pump off.

Apparently there was no pool attendant present, and there was no one on site with a key to the engine room that powered the high-pressure pump.

The pool will remain drained and closed while a full-scale inquiry into what happened is carried out.

Source: *The Staines Informer*

Talk about it

What are the potential problems when the depth and gradient of the pool bottom changes?

Think of one rule which must be adopted by a pool attendant when watching the pool.

Pool attendant's duties

1   When on duty, constantly be on the lookout for potential accidents occurring in the water.

2   Prevent accidents by ensuring that users of the pool are following the rules and regulations governing the conduct of persons using the swimming pool.

3   Rescue persons who are in trouble in the water and administer any relevant first aid, making sure that colleagues are aware of the situation. Make sure an ambulance is called in case of any serious accident.

4   Maintain the swimming pool hall in a clean and tidy condition.

5   Call the pool supervisor or manager if assistance is needed in maintaining discipline of swimmers.

6   Report any potential health and safety hazards to the pool supervisor.

7   Be friendly and helpful to centre users and colleagues.

8   Assist as needed in any area of the pool when asked to do so by the pool supervisor or manager.

9   Be punctual when reporting for duty.

10 Maintain a very high level of appearance of both uniform and personal hygiene at all times.

Staffing of activities

The pool hall must be staffed by a sufficient number of pool attendants who are all trained and qualified in lifesaving and first aid. Accidents in pools occur either because of people getting into difficulty in the water or because of bathers running on the poolside. Qualified staff should be able to handle all situations from emergencies to minor accidents. This helps to ensure a safe environment and can give the public peace of mind.

It is worth remembering that additional qualifications can lead to extra pay which acts as an incentive to staff to increase their qualifications. What's more, trained and qualified staff will have the self-confidence to cope with most situations. Any member of staff who works on poolside, whether on full-time or part-time or even on a casual basis, should be qualified. It is up to the manager of the facility to ensure this because it is the manager who is responsible for the health and safety of the public and all the employees.

Security of valuables

Theft and vandalism are problems that never go away. Theft takes place in towns, cities and the countryside. It also takes place in car parks attached to leisure facilities. One such target might be a cinema car park where theft or damage could happen while the owners of the car are inside the facility. The same can happen in leisure centre car parks.

How can theft and vandalism be reduced? Possible solutions can include:

- closed-circuit television (CCTV) which is linked to reception
- regular patrols of the areas by staff or security guards
- signs reminding the public to lock their cars and not leave valuables in them.

Lockers in changing rooms

Most leisure centres have coin return or coin retain lockers; the main advantage of these being that they offer a secure place for clothes and valuables. Valuables go missing when the customer opens the locker to get a towel and shampoo and goes for a shower. This is a time when the door might be left open, which is an open invitation to a thief.

Talk about it

In your group, discuss the reasons behind theft and vandalism. Has anyone you know been on the receiving end of theft or vandalism?

What do you think can be done about it?

Look it up

What security systems operate in your local leisure centre changing rooms and car park?

CASE STUDY – The best policy

Honesty is not just the best policy, it is the only policy. This is something that the students of Greenbury College set out to prove after it was discovered that there had been a series of thefts from the college sports hall.

They organised a 'Stop the Thief Campaign' in the college. This included holding meetings to raise awareness of theft, producing a leaflet advising people on how to prevent theft and making signs to raise awareness, such as 'Careful. Thief on the loose'.

The campaign was such a success that the students were asked to go into local schools with their campaign message.

This campaign showed how citizenship, honesty and vigilance could reduce theft and vandalism. Such a high profile campaign must have deterred thieves as the outbreaks of theft at the college stopped soon after.

Question

Find out all you can about Neighbourhood Watch schemes. What are their main aims?

Providing safe facilities
Swimming pools

Have you ever thought why swimming pool water needs to be checked on a regular basis? Swimming pool water can be contaminated by many sources of pollution, including:

- sweat
- urine
- skin
- faeces
- saliva
- cosmetics.

Although much testing and analysis of pool water is now done automatically, some manual testing is still necessary. For all manual pool water tests:

- samples should be taken from as far below the surface as possible
- the container should be rinsed several times with the water to be tested
- the water sample should be tested promptly after collection.
- tests are usually carried out every four hours.

These tests show if the chemical balance of the pool is right and whether the water is clean enough to swim in.

Talk about it

What sort of checks should be made on the following:

- rides at a theme park
- food which is being stored
- equipment in use at a gym?

Maintenance of facilities

Correct maintenance of a facility and the equipment in it can make the place safe for staff and users. Regular maintenance checks could reveal any repairs that need to be carried out and any dangerous faults which need immediate remedial action.

As well as maintenance carried out on a day-to-day basis it is also essential that there is a properly planned, long-term maintenance schedule. This is important because:

- it ensures the facilities and equipment have been checked
- it means all areas are cleaned regularly to a daily, weekly or monthly timetable
- it makes the facility more attractive to customers
- it makes the facility more attractive to work in.

It is helpful when carrying out scheduled maintenance that records of all maintenance work are kept. Any work that is completed and any materials used should be written down by the person who has done the work.

Maintenance sheets (see below) help to ensure:

- that routine tasks are not overlooked
- there is communication between shifts
- that work has been carried out.

The term 'good housekeeping ' is usually connected with maintenance. This consists of:

- reporting problems, such as leaking showers, flickering lights
- investigating what is wrong
- instructing maintenance staff to carry out repairs.

Try it out

Give five examples of 'good housekeeping' in recreation and leisure facilities, for example turning off lights when the area is not in use.

Health and safety reminder

Health and safety relates to all leisure, sport and recreation facilities. Rules and regulations are put in place to protect employees and the public. Wherever you decide to work, make sure you are familiar with the health and safety procedures and do exactly what is expected of you when it comes to putting these procedures into operation.

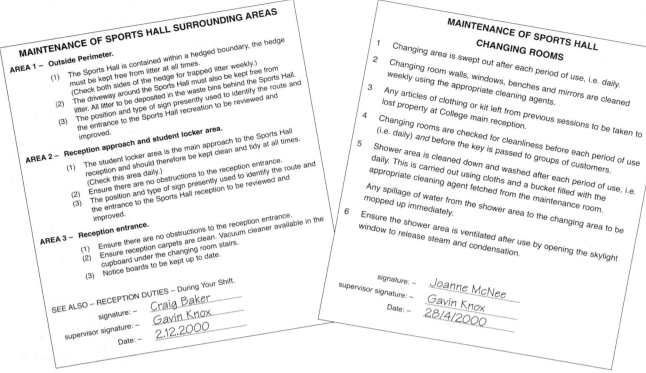

MAINTENANCE OF SPORTS HALL SURROUNDING AREAS

AREA 1 – Outside Perimeter.

(1) The Sports Hall is contained within a hedged boundary, the hedge must be kept free from litter at all times. (Check both sides of the hedge for trapped litter weekly.)

(2) The driveway around the Sports Hall must also be kept free from litter. All litter to be deposited in the waste bins behind the Sports Hall.

(3) The position and type of sign presently used to identify the route and the entrance to the Sports Hall recreation to be reviewed and improved.

AREA 2 – Reception approach and student locker area.

(1) The student locker area is the main approach to the Sports Hall reception and should therefore be kept clean and tidy at all times. (Check this area daily.)

(2) Ensure there are no obstructions to the reception entrance.

(3) The position and type of sign presently used to identify the route and the entrance to the Sports Hall reception to be reviewed and improved.

AREA 3 – Reception entrance.

(1) Ensure there are no obstructions to the reception entrance.

(2) Ensure reception carpets are clean. Vacuum cleaner available in the cupboard under the changing room stairs.

(3) Notice boards to be kept up to date.

SEE ALSO – RECEPTION DUTIES – During Your Shift.

signature: – *Craig Baker*
supervisor signature: – *Gavin Knox*
Date: – *2.12.2000*

MAINTENANCE OF SPORTS HALL CHANGING ROOMS

1 Changing area is swept out after each period of use, i.e. daily.

2 Changing room walls, windows, benches and mirrors are cleaned weekly using the appropriate cleaning agents.

3 Any articles of clothing or kit left from previous sessions to be taken to lost property at College main reception.

4 Changing rooms are checked for cleanliness before each period of use (i.e. daily) *and* before the key is passed to groups of customers.

5 Shower area is cleaned down and washed after each period of use, i.e. daily. This is carried out using cloths and a bucket filled with the appropriate cleaning agent fetched from the maintenance room. Any spillage of water from the shower area to the changing area to be mopped up immediately.

6 Ensure the shower area is ventilated after use by opening the skylight window to release steam and condensation.

signature: – *Joanne McNee*
supervisor signature: – *Gavin Knox*
Date: – *28/4/2000*

Maintenance sheets

Administration and finance

Handling money

The success of any business is ultimately dependent on the money it brings in and the profits it makes. This helps to keep people in jobs and organisations in business. When customers make a payment, for example for holidays, badminton courts or theatre tickets, they should always be issued with a receipt.

Try it out

List as many methods as you can which customers may use to make payments. As a guide, think of how you or your family pay for your purchases.

Each method of payment has its own procedures to follow along with any security measures that must be in place.

Cash is used mainly for smaller purchases like coach tickets, entry to a swimming pool or a ticket to the cinema. This method is the quickest and probably most advantageous for a business as it is immediate and can go straight into the account – no waiting for cheques to clear. However cash transactions can bring security problems because they involve a large amount of money being kept on the premises and mean that money must be taken to the bank.

Talk about it

Imagine a reception area in a theatre or cinema or a leisure centre. What items would be attractive to a would-be thief?

Security

The type of security which can be put in place might include:

* a safe with a combination lock, bolted to the floor, visible from outside

- the door to reception being locked at all times
- a burglar alarm fitted
- cash banked daily at different times, using different routes
- use of security companies to transport cash
- staff awareness of expired credit cards, forged bank notes.

When it comes to handling cash, you cannot be too careful. Make sure receipts are issued and that the money taken reconciles with receipts at the end of the day. This is called balancing the books. It is also a good idea to have two people to check the day's takings.

Petty cash

This type of payment is made when paying for such things as:

- travel expenses
- window cleaning
- entertaining important clients
- stationery and stamps
- tea and coffee.

A separate cash book for these items should be kept. Petty cash vouchers should be completed for every purchase and a receipt obtained. There are usually limits as to the amount that can be claimed and who can claim them.

Answering the telephone

It is important that all staff in an organisation should have a good telephone manner. When using the telephone remember to:

- answer it quickly – people get angry when they have to wait for their call to be answered
- give a 'verbal handshake' and smile
- answer in a friendly and professional manner
- ask the right questions
- take the caller's name
- take down messages quickly and accurately

- answer fully any questions about the organisation's products and services
- thank the caller
- say goodbye.

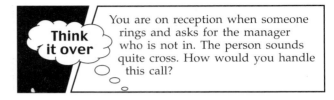

Think it over

You are on reception when someone rings and asks for the manager who is not in. The person sounds quite cross. How would you handle this call?

Fax

One of the most popular means of sending documents, in particular diagrams, maps and graphics, is by using a fax machine. This copies documents electronically and sends them down the telephone line to another fax machine which prints out the copy.

People like fax because it is easy to use and immediate. It has been proved through research that the informality of the fax is a bonus; it is now accepted working practice just to scribble down a message and send it by fax. A fax can be particularly important for airlines, travel agents and tour operators, when confirmation of bookings and other information is passed on.

Making a booking

The best way to explain this is by example:

Hire of hall by local amateur dramatic society to stage a play

Procedure

1 Hirer meets estates manager to explain what he wants.

2 Hirer completes booking form and returns it to the college.

3 Finance section works out costs and informs hirer.

4 Hirer pays for booking. Estates manager and head caretaker sign booking form and agree to the hire.

5 Head caretaker enters booking in computer diary and day-to-day log book.

6 Copy of form returned to hirer along with conditions of hire.

Caretaker briefs staff so that, 'Everything's all right on the night'.

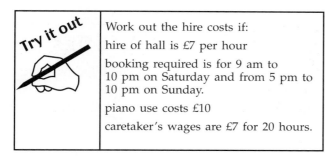

Work out the hire costs if:

hire of hall is £7 per hour

booking required is for 9 am to 10 pm on Saturday and from 5 pm to 10 pm on Sunday.

piano use costs £10

caretaker's wages are £7 for 20 hours.

Stock control

A restaurant keeps stock of food and drink. A sports centre may keep a stock of:

⋄ food and drink (for café or vending machines)

⋄ sports equipment

⋄ chemicals

⋄ stationery.

Stock control serves two purposes:

1 It shows the amount of stock left in the facility.

2 It shows how much has been used.

This control shows that any stock that has gone missing, through wastage, theft or loss, can be immediately identified.

A stock check shows what items are selling and what items may need replacing.

The stock check sheet above right gives a detailed breakdown of confectionery for April showing stock held, stock used, buying price, income and profit.

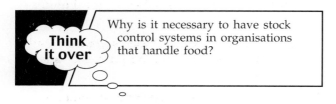

Think it over

Why is it necessary to have stock control systems in organisations that handle food?

Anytown Sports Centre Cafeteria

Stock items	Amount of stock	Stock sold	Stock remaining
Mars bars	6 boxes	4 boxes	2 boxes
Kit-Kat	5 noxes	3 boxes	2 boxes
Galaxy	5 boxes	4 boxes	1 box
Bounty	2 boxes	–	–
Chews	4 boxes	3 boxes	1 box
Lollipops	2 boxes	1 box	1 box
Fruit salad chews	3 boxes	2 boxes	1 box
Coke	8 trays (24 on a tray)	3 trays	5 trays
Sprite	6 trays (24 on a tray)	4 trays	1 tray
Lemonade	4 trays (24 on a tray)	3 trays	1 tray
Tizer	2 trays (24 on a tray)	1 tray	1 tray
Orange cartons	9 packs (12 in a pack)	5 packs	4 packs
Ribena cartons	5 packs (12 in a pack)	3 packs	2 packs

Date of stock take ___10.10.2000___

Signed by ___M Wa___

Stock check sheet

Staff records

Staff records contain a variety of information – see Figure 7.12.

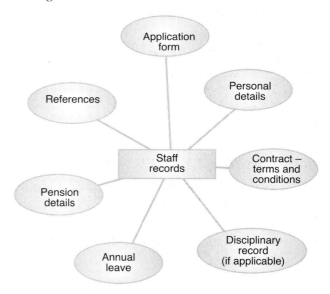

Figure 7.12 Staff records contain confidential information

These records, whether paper-based or on computer must be protected under the Data Protection Act 1984 (Access to Personal Files Act 1987) and therefore access to them must be restricted. Staff records give a brief history of an employee's past and present work and contains confidential information regarding salary, personal details (date of birth, address, etc.) and any other information.

Equal opportunities

Equal opportunities should spell out an organisation's determination to give equal opportunities to all irrespective of sex, race, creed, colour or marital status. This extends to equal rights in the workplace and employment issues generally. One college states, among other things: 'The college will take steps to ensure that no staff or student or potential staff or student receives less favourable treatment than anyone else.' Legislation such as the Race Relations Act 1976, Sex Discrimination Act 1975 and Equal Pay Act 1970 have sought to make discrimination illegal. The Disability Discrimination Act 1995 also has important implications for employers and providers of services.

Discrimination against anyone on the grounds of their sex, race, colour or national origins is illegal, whether it be in recruitment, conditions of work, promotion, training or dismissal. Job advertisements must clearly not discriminate. It is therefore necessary to make sure that interviews are conducted fairly, that pay is equal for similar work and that there is no sexual or racial harassment.

Talk about it

How can you relate equal opportunities to the leisure and tourism industry?

Promotion of facilities

It is important that customers know the location of leisure, sport and recreation facilities and what they offer. Let's look at some of the aspects of a facility which customers should be made aware of.

The existence of a facility

Promotion is concerned with telling existing and potential customers about a product or service, in this case a leisure and tourism facility. It must be promoted in such a way that customers know what the facility offers and where it can be found.

This can be done by including the relevant information in brochures, leaflets, posters and advertisements. Look at the Dudley Zoo and Castle brochure on page 233. This is a good example of promotional information.

Logos can be used to very good effect by organisations in order to identify themselves. A logo is the emblem of a facility which can be shown on all publicity material even on the outside of the building.

CASE STUDY — Equal opportunities

Ivan Petrescu has worked for the local authority as a theatre technician for five years. Ivan is a single parent and decided to put his child in the council's crèche. He felt this would be in order as the crèche was provided for employees who had worked for the local authority for more than three years. Unfortunately for Ivan, his request for a place for his child was turned down on the grounds that the crèche was only for the children of female employees.

Question

What sort of discrimination is this?

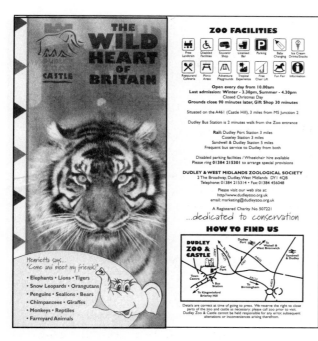

Source: Dudley Zoo and Castle

A good example of promotional literature

Logos can he helpful in identifying a facility

Try it out

Study the logos of the Cotswold Water Park, Snowdome and Chessington World of Adventures. Now design your own logo for a leisure, sport or recreation facility of your choice.

Where it is

The location of a facility is important in that it must be easily accessible to customers. More importantly, customers need to be able to find the facility easily. Sign posts showing the way, maps showing how to get there and media promotion can be used to help people find their way.

Any brochure should have a 'how to get there' section. Look at the material produced by Tamworth Castle and Thorpe Park. Each map is backed up by additional information about getting there.

Talk about it

How do leisure, sport and recreation facilities in your area provide information about their location?

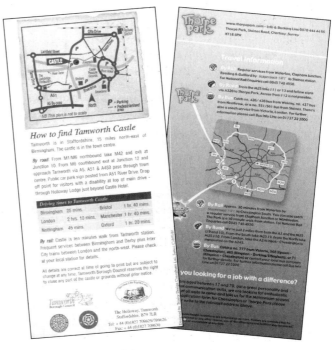

Sources: Tamworth Castle; Thorpe Park

It is essential to provide detailed information about how to find a facility

What facilities it provides and when

Customers like to know what facilities are provided in a leisure, sport and recreation facility so they can decide whether to use them. For example, a person who wants to concentrate on weight lifting would need to know if the facility has 'free' weights and bars, whereas someone who just wants to get fit may need a fitness suite with exercise bikes and treadmills. Another example is the serious swimmer who would prefer to swim up and down the pool as part of a training routine rather than a leisure pool which would be popular with families. Information about facilities and when they are available for use will therefore be important.

What activities it provides and when

A facility must offer a range of activities which appeal to customers. A cinema manager may alter the films shown in order to meet the current taste; for example, romantic comedies, disaster movies or 'blockbusters'. The manager must then make customers aware of the films being shown. This could be done by advertising in the local newspaper, posters in the cinema and press releases about 'What's On'. All these promotional activities can be used to raise a customer's awareness of the product or activity.

Look it up

Look in your local newspaper and find out what films are showing at your local cinema. Is all the information you need provided? Do all advertisements carry the same information? Could they be improved?

Prices

Price is probably the main factor that people take into consideration when deciding whether to use a facility or buy a product. People want value for money and need to have as much information about prices as possible.

THE PASSPORT TICKET

The Passport ticket offers excellent value for a day out and is substantially cheaper than buying individual tickets to separate sites. It includes a half price voucher for return to Blists Hill Victorian Town. There is also a chance to win a super British Waterways Canal Boat Holiday with every 2000\2001 Passport purchased. Tickets are sold at all the Museums, including the Tourist Information Centre or can be bought in advance on Freephone 0800 590258.
Adults £30.00 (2 adults, up to 5 children up to 18 years of age)
Adults £10.00
Child/Student £6.00 (5years of age upwards/in full-time education)
60 Plus £9.00
Prices valid until 31 March 2001

CAR PARKING & GETTING ROUND THE MUSEUMS
The Museum car parks are FREE. The Museum of the Gorge and the Iron Bridge & Tollhouse are adjacent to Local Authority Pay & Display car parks.

Pick up a Free Visitor Guide about Ironbridge & surrounding area, including accommodation from the TIC in Ironbridge or call FREEPHONE 0800 590285

Why do you think this might be a good piece of promotional material?

People can learn about the prices of products and services within a leisure, sport or recreation facility either by asking the staff who work there or looking on the board displaying the prices. This should be positioned in a prominent place where it is easy for all customers to see. Prices may also be displayed on leaflets and brochures.

Methods of payment

Nowadays there are several different methods of paying for products and services. Customers can use cash, cheque, debit or credit cards. It can be possible to pay in person, over the phone or even via the Internet. Organisations must cater for these needs by making payment for the customer quick, easy and convenient.

Box Office Information...

Box Office open. **Mon - Sat 10 am - 4 pm** (tel: 01636 655755)
Outside these hours a recorded message will give details of
current attractions.

To book either call in at theatre box office or phone during
opening hours. Alternatively we have agents (see listing).

Payment can be made by credit card, cash or cheque. An
additional change will be made on all credit cards.

Tickets may be reserved for cinema. Bookings open 7 days
before the first screening of each film.

Conditions of sale are printed on the tickets.

All listings are correct at the time of going to press. Some
cancellations or amendments do occur. Please check with the
Box Office.

Tickets cannot be exchanged nor monies refunded. However,
we will look at individual cases and attempt to re-sell your
tickets subject to a small exchange fee.

Doors open: Live shows 1 hour prior to showtime.
Cinema 30 minutes prior to screening

Data Protection Act: The Palace Theatre is committed to
upholding the Data Protection principles of good handling
practice. When processing your booking the Box Office will
ask your name, address and telephone number. This
information may be used to keep you informed of forthcoming
events and notify you of any changes to an event for which
you may have booked at the Palace. We will not forward any
personal details to any other organisation.

Does this provide enough information about payment?

Answers to 'Try it out'

page 198

Sports stadium	City
Nou Camp	Barcelona
Millennium Stadium	Cardiff
Elland Road	Leeds
Twickenham	London
Stade de France	Paris
Murrayfield	Edinburgh
Hampden Park	Glasgow
Crystal Palace	London
Don Valley	Sheffield

page 200

National Parks of England and Wales

1 Lake District
2 Yorkshire Dales
3 Peak District
4 Snowdonia
5 Brecon Beacons
6 Pembrokeshire Coast
7 Exmoor
8 Dartmoor
9 New Forest
10 The Broads
12 Northumberland

Answers to 'Look it up'

page 208

1 manager;
2 deputy manager;
3 supervisors;
4 trainee manager;
5 lifeguards; and
6 cleaners.

Unit 7 Assessment

This unit is externally assessed but the following assessment along with the test questions will provide you with the knowledge to pass your external assessment.

Theatre of dreams

Scenario

A group of leisure and recreation managers from Australia are on a fact-finding tour of facilities in the UK. As assistant recreation officer, you have been asked to produce a report about leisure, sport and recreation facilities and their working practices. This will assist your Australian guests in formulating a recreation policy back at home.

What you have to do
Obtaining a pass grade

Your report must give an introduction describing the public, private and voluntary sectors, aims and objectives, organisational charts, types of employment available, how customers' needs are met and different promotional activities.

Your report must also show:

- a clear and full explanation of the functions of organisations

- a clear description of the relationship between organisations' functions and the aims and objectives

- a brief description of relevant health, safety and security legislation

- you can enter transactions on a simple financial document.

Obtaining a merit or distinction grade

Your work must show:

- a logical and well-structured format and a well-designed organisational chart that clearly shows main job roles and lines of responsibility

- clearly expressed ideas and information to demonstrate a thorough understanding of the operation of two chosen functions

- your ability to complete calculations on a simple financial document.

Obtaining a distinction grade

For this your work must show:

- a thorough understanding of the relationship between the functions and organsitions' aims and objectives

- a high level of understanding of the importance to organisations of complying with health, safety and security legislation and an evaluation of the health, safety and security procedures of organisations

- your ability to complete more complex calculations on a simple financial document.

Key skills available

Communication: C2.1a, C2.2, C2.3

Resources

Some organisations now provide information packs for GNVQ students and are happy to host student groups. The Internet is another valuable source of information as are TV programmes. Specialist journals such as *Leisure Management* have the latest industry news and views.

Unit 7 test

1 Give examples of two famous stadia and say what activities take place there.

2 What sports can you do in the Snowdonia National Park?

3 What is meant by a public sector facility?

4 What is the main aim of a private sector health club?

5 How do voluntary sector organisations raise money?

6 What is the purpose of organisational structures?

7 What training and qualifications would you need to be a leisure centre manager?

8 What are the disadvantages of working shifts?

9 Name three special needs groups which should be included in leisure centre programming.

10 What is meant by peak and off-peak use?

11 What would you do as manager of a facility in the event of a fire?

12 Why do we have maintenance programmes in leisure, sport and recreation facilities?

13 What is petty cash used for?

14 What do we mean by 'equal opportunities' in relation to the leisure and tourism industry?

15 In what ways can you promote leisure, sport and recreation facilities?

Travel and tourism organisations

This unit covers the knowledge you will need to meet the external assessment requirements for Unit 8. It will give you a good idea about how travel and tourism organisations operate and will help you to decide whether these are the types of organisations that you would like to work for.

The unit is written in six sections. Section one looks at the different types of organisations in the travel and tourism industry. Section two examines the aims and objectives of different organisations and section three looks at staffing requirements. Administration and finance systems are described in section four; and section five describes the different products and services offered by travel and tourism organisations. Section six then investigates health, safety and security issues.

This unit builds on Unit 1: Investigating leisure and tourism. It is similar to Unit 7: Leisure, sport and recreation facilities.

What you need to produce

In the external assessment you need to produce evidence showing your understanding of two or more travel and tourism organisations and their working practices.

This unit will be assessed only through an external assessment. The grade you achieve in this assessment will be your grade for the unit.

Introduction

Travel and tourism is a growth industry with lots of job opportunities available to young people. It is now considered to be the largest business in the world, in terms of financial turnover and people employed. What's more, it is still growing.

The work opportunities range from jobs for people leaving school or college with leisure and tourism qualifications to careers for people with degrees who wish to enter management training.

Over 50 million holidays or short breaks are taken in the UK each year and we make over 20 million trips abroad annually. Therefore, it is not really surprising that about one and a half million jobs

in the UK depend on the travel and tourism industry.

The travel and tourism organisations that organise holidays, transport, accommodation and information vary in size and purpose. We will look at them in a little more detail.

Types of organisations in travel and tourism

Talk about it

Do you remember Unit 1: Investigating leisure and tourism? As a reminder of this unit, try to recall any organisations, big or small, in the travel and tourism industry and, in your group, make a list of them. Try to think of some before referring back to your notes!

Some organisations in the industry are very big and may employ hundreds or even thousands of staff. Others are very small and many only have one or two employees. The bigger organisations operate across the world while others may operate in only one location. In the 'Talk about it' activity you probably identified a range of sizes of organisations as well as different types.

Transport organisations

The different types of transport organisations are shown in Figure 8.1.

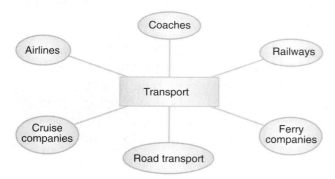

Figure 8.1 Different types of transport organisations

All transport organisations operate in the private sector, although some receive government subsidies to help develop new equipment and provide for future investment. They range from international airlines like British Airways to small car hire companies. They all aim to offer safe and reliable forms of transport so that passengers reach their chosen destination safely and on time.

The transportation of passengers is a highly competitive market so transport organisations must offer excellent value for money and top class customer service. Many transport organisations have a customer care charter to ensure that the demands of all passengers are met (see extract from Central Trains charter).

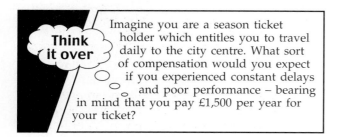

Think it over
Imagine you are a season ticket holder which entitles you to travel daily to the city centre. What sort of compensation would you expect if you experienced constant delays and poor performance – bearing in mind that you pay £1,500 per year for your ticket?

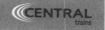

AS A BUSINESS OUR AIM IS TO OFFER YOU A VALUE FOR MONEY FORM OF TRAVEL THAT IS RELIABLE, CLEAN AND COMFORTABLE.

THIS PASSENGER'S CHARTER SETS OUT OUR COMMITMENT TO GIVE YOU THE SAFE, SECURE AND HIGH QUALITY SERVICE YOU HAVE THE RIGHT TO EXPECT.

To do this we will:

* Set standards for ourselves

* Tell you what our standards are and how we measure up to them

* Ask for your views and publish the results on questions such as:
  Are the stations clean?
  Are our staff performing well?

* Tell you what is happening, especially when things go wrong

* Give you discounts when you renew four weekly or longer season tickets if our performance falls below pre-set levels

* Give you compensation if you hold 7 day season tickets or non season tickets if your train has been seriously delayed or cancelled

Source: Central Trains

Extract from Central Trains Passenger's Charter

In the event of a complaint, this is what the rail company GNER will do:

5 per cent discounts
If on average over the previous 12 months, either punctuality has been more than two percentage points below target or reliability has been more than one percentage point below target, we will give a discount of 5%.

10 per cent discounts
If both punctuality and reliability were below those thresholds, we will give a discount of 10%.

Refund Later
If you decide for some other reason not to use a ticket you have bought, you can apply for a refund at any GNER ticket office within 28 days. We may charge an administration fee. No refund is given on most advanced purchase tickets in these circumstances

If you bought your ticket through a travel agent, GNER will make a refund to you and they will claim the money back from the travel agent.

We do not normally accept claims in cases where trains are delayed if the delay is notified before you buy your ticket and you still decide to travel. We cannot meet claims when the delay is caused by matters outside the control of the Railway Industry, such as acts of vandalism or terrorism.

Source: GNER

Transport organisations like National Express Coaches always try to be on time. They aim to provide clean coaches and have drivers and couriers trained in customer care to make the journey as pleasant and comfortable as possible.

Let's look at some transport organisations. This will give you an idea of what they do and what they hope to achieve.

Stena Line

Stena Line is an international transport and travel service organisation and one of the world's largest ferry operators. It has a modern fleet of 25 vessels — some for carrying passengers, others for carrying freight.

During 1999, 9.1 million passengers travelled with Stena Line while 1,750,000 cars and 712,000 freight units were transported over the same period.

CASE STUDY – Gina

Gina works as a courier for a national coach company. This is how she describes her typical day:

'I am given my travel schedule a week in advance so I know exactly where I am going each day. Today I'm on the London to Stratford-upon-Avon run which is one of my favourites as I am interested in Shakespeare.

Bob is my driver and we discuss the plans for the day including pick-up points, break stops and general timings throughout the day. It is essential to do this so I can give the passengers the right information and ensure that they get the best service possible.

We leave at 9 am with a full load of American tourists. They love England, especially all the history that goes with it. I do the introductions on the microphone and it's off to Stratford we go, stopping off for coffee.

My job is to ensure the passengers are entertained, looked after and comfortable. I get asked all sorts of questions like, "Are the fields always this green? How come we drive on the left-hand side of the road?". One day I was asked by a tourist from Texas, "Did Shakespeare write his plays for television?".

A tour guide takes over at Stratford which gives me the opportunity to stroll around and take in the sights. Although I have been many times, I still find it a fascinating part of the world. I also take a book with me to pass the time.

At 3.30 pm it's time to head back. My passengers have bought lots of souvenirs and presents and they feel they have been "in touch" with Shakespeare. The questions come thick and fast but I have done my research and can answer most of them.

It's back in London at 6 pm I finish off by saying,

"On behalf of my driver Bob and the ABC Coach Company, I would like to thank you for travelling with us and hope very much you enjoyed your day out with us. We hope to see you again soon."

Our passengers are often extremely generous with their tips which Bob and I share. Tomorrow it's York so I'd better brush up on the Vikings.'

Questions

- How could Gina keep showing her passengers that she was interested in them?

- What sort of personality do you need to have to be a courier like Gina?

CASE STUDY – British Airways (BA)

British Airways – BA – is one of the world's most successful airlines. In 1996–97, it announced pre-tax profits up 9.4 per cent on the previous year to £640 million. BA carried a record 38.2 million passengers during 1996–97. This was up by 6 per cent on the previous year. In 1996–97 the airline operated an average of over one thousand flights a day worldwide.

Its main base is London Heathrow Airport, the largest international airport in the world. It also operates an increasing number of services out of London Gatwick Airport. A total of 58,000 staff are employed by BA worldwide, 82 per cent of them based in the UK.

The airline's success has been built on quality service provided by a dedicated workforce, combined with marketing and continued cost reduction.

Employees

The motivation and commitment of all employees continues to play a major part in the success of BA. This is rewarded through the airline's Profit Share Scheme which, in 1999, gave every eligible employee a bonus equivalent to three weeks' basic pay. This bonus could be used by employees to acquire shares in the company or taken in cash.

BA's policy is to promote equal opportunity in employment regardless of gender, race, colour or disability. Wherever possible, employees who become disabled during employment are provided with an alternative job which makes full use of their capabilities.

Anyone wishing to enquire about working for BA should contact:

BA Recruitment and Selection
The Rivers
Cranebank
PO Box 59
Heathrow Airport
Hounslow
Middx. TW6 2SL

Some frequently asked questions for BA include the following:

Q Can I order a special meal for my flight?

A Special meals can be ordered at the time of booking, or by contacting your local BA office at least 24 hours before the scheduled time of departure.

Q What are the check-in times for all flights?

A In the UK, check-in time for domestic and European flights is one hour before departure and for international flights, two hours before departure.

Q Which BA flights are non-smoking and are there plans to introduce any more?

A All BA flights became non-smoking in March 1998 due to consumer demand and there are no plans to re-introduce smoking on board any flights.

Activity

Visit the BA website on www.british-airways.com and find out the following:

- What type of planes does it fly?
- What sort of long-haul destinations does BA fly to?
- On a map of the world, try to plot some of the different places to which BA flies.

National Express Coaches

This is Europe's leading network of express scheduled coach services. National Express coaches carry more than 15 million people every year to around 1,200 destinations throughout Britain and a further 400 in Europe and Ireland.

Look it up

Look up three other transport organisations that operate on either a national or international basis, one of which is a cruise company, one a rail company and one an airline. Write one paragraph about each and compare notes with your group. Also look up the name of a local transport organisation, e.g. a car hire company or coach operator and give brief details about what it does.

?   **Did you know?**

Some airlines, like Easyjet, sell one way fares which means you can go and come back whenever you like. How might this differ from other airlines?

Talk about it

There is an expression which says, 'the world has got smaller', meaning it is now very easy and quick to get to any part of the world. Imagine the England cricket team going to play Australia in Sydney. From the 1950s onwards the team were able to fly out there, but prior to that it was a six-week trip by ship. Nowadays, a non-stop flight from London to Sydney, with stopovers for change of crew and refuelling, takes only one day, to cover a distance of 12,000 miles.

How long do you think it would take to fly from London Heathrow to Charles de Gaulle airport, Paris?

In today's world of high speed transport, people can commute long distances to go to work; for example, there are people who live in York who travel to work in London every day, a journey time of 2 hours 15 minutes. This gives a total travelling time of four and a half hours each day. Add to this the time taken to travel from home to the railway station and you have a total of five hours per day of travel. This means five hours less spent at home with the family, not to mention the additional tiredness associated with this amount of travelling.

A second consequence of faster and more convenient travel is the fact that many people now live far away from the place where they were brought up (perhaps because of job moves) knowing that it is relatively easy and quick to return to see family and friends. At one time, most people used to live in the area where they were born and were thus able to keep in touch with their family, usually on a daily basis.

Travel today seems so quick and convenient. Many senior citizens go to Spain in winter for the warm weather yet they still manage to return for a few days to spend Christmas with their families back home!

Accommodation providers

Talk about it

What type of accommodation have you stayed in on holiday? Have you had any bad experiences with your accommodation while on holiday? Share your experience with the rest of the group.

There are many types of holiday accommodation (see Figure 8.2) and it is a big earner. Overseas visitors coming to the UK spend one-third of their money on accommodation. More than 50 per cent of the people employed in tourism work in this sector.

Hotels in the UK offer a great choice for guests. They provide accommodation, breakfast and at least one other meal if requested. City hotels offer familiar international names like the Hilton or the Ritz and they provide a particularly high standard (for which you pay a lot).

Figure 8.2 Types of holiday accommodation

Town house hotels are small, personally run town centre hotels. The emphasis is on luxury, privacy and very high standards of service. In addition, their central location makes them accessible to a wide range of restaurants.

Country house hotels are usually small and personally run, offering a combination of high standards of service and fine food in attractive, rural settings. Quality sports and leisure facilities are often a part of the package. Motels and motor lodges are usually situated next to motorways and offer functional bedrooms at reasonable prices. Not all provide meals but motor lodges tend to be next to roadside restaurants.

Bed and breakfast or 'B & B' as it is known aims to give the traveller two very important things: a warm welcome and comfortable facilities at a fairly cheap rate. B & Bs are usually private homes. The emphasis is on the quality of sleeping accommodation rather than facilities such as a bar and restaurant.

Bed and breakfast establishments have been a significant part of the tourism industry since its early development in the nineteenth century. The attraction of bed and breakfast establishments for tourists is mainly due to the value for money offered and the friendly close contact with the operator in their own home. It is therefore particularly attractive to those visitors interested in meeting local people and gaining local knowledge. As far as the provider is concerned, it is an inexpensive way of getting into the tourism

New rating schemes for accommodation aim to offer as much information as possible

and travel industry. Many of the facilities that need to be provided are already in place.

You can see that a variety of accommodation is available within a wide price range. The cost of

Facts and figures – the cost of accommodation (at 2000 prices)

Town prices (e.g. Newark on Trent)
Bed and breakfast £18–20 per person
Youth hostel £9–12 per person (breakfast £3)
Travel Inn family room £39.95 (breakfast not included)
Guest house double room £36.00
Holiday park caravan per night £11.00
Camping per tent £11.00

London
For youth travellers, shared rooms in hostel £18 per person including breakfast
Guest houses providing breakfast £50
Hotels £60
Business-class hotels £120
Luxury hotels £180

SNAPSHOTS

Vera and Jack

Vera and Jack run a B & B in Manchester. Their guests are usually businessmen staying for two or three nights during the week, although during the summer they welcome families from all over the world, who like the friendly homely atmosphere that Vera and Jack offer.

Vera says,

'It's me that does all the work really. Jack acts as if he is the Manager of the Hilton Hotel in London, meeting the guests and making polite conversation with them. I must admit, though, he does a good job because they all keep coming back. Personally, I think it's the full English breakfast I offer them – double eggs, bacon, two sausages, beans, tomatoes, mushrooms, fried bread and as much tea as they can drink. We welcome children, who love to be able to get out into the garden with its swings and slide. No wonder they keep coming back!'

the accommodation is dependent on the location and the type of service provided. Generally, accommodation in London is more expensive than in the rest of the country.

Think it over

Why do you think there is such a difference in prices in the different locations?

Visitors will be influenced as to where to stay by a number of factors:

- nearness to attractions or other facilities
- cost
- availability of certain services, e.g. bars, pets or facilities for children
- quality of service required.

Look it up

Try to find some information on the following types of accommodation: working farms; self catering holiday cottages; guest houses.

Did you know?

There are 11,700 B & B establishments in England with a total capacity of 105,000 bed spaces.

Look it up

Put together a summary of the range of accommodation facilities available in your area.

CASE STUDY – Alton Towers Hotel

"Alton Towers attracts more visitors per year than any other British paid attraction, with total annual attendances exceeding 3 million. Alton Towers cannot afford to sit back and enjoy its success however. There are other newer theme parks, others yet to be built which will be competing to attract customers.

Alton Towers has been considering the possibility of providing limited accommodation on site for more than four years – as they have seen the steady growth of visitors coming back for two or more days, staying at the various hotels and B & Bs in the beautiful Staffordshire and Peak districts. This now represents as many as 17 per cent of all visitors, so the opening of a hotel seemed a natural extension of the Park's activities. The short-break market (see below) is one of the most dynamic areas of the UK holiday scene, and the addition of the hotel puts Alton Towers firmly in that market – not because it can accommodate more than a tiny percentage of visitors, but because it will encourage many more visitors from further afield – London and the South East for example, and even more overseas, to look on a first visit to Alton Towers as much more than a day trip. We believe it will be an important catalyst for the whole area – and will bring additional business to the Park as well as local hotels and B & Bs. The hotel has 175 rooms including two themed family rooms."

Definition: short-break market

A short break is one to three nights or two to four days away from home, and the market for short breaks is couples and family groups.

Questions

- How will the local community benefit from the existence of the new hotel?

- The theme park closes in November but the hotel stays open throughout the year. Who is likely to use the hotel during this time?

Text reproduced with kind permission from Alton Towers

Tour operators

When you go into a travel agent to book a holiday you are usually given a selection of brochures to look through. These brochures are produced by the organisations known as tour operators that provide holidays for customers.

The role of the tour operator

Marketing research carried out by tour operators attempts to forecast changes in customer choice by asking customers how they view the product. By researching customer needs, wants and attitudes, the tour operator is able to predict more confidently the holiday resorts which most satisfy the market at any given time.

Customer preferences, regarding which countries tourists want to visit are constantly shifting between Spain, Italy and Greece. Preference between resorts tends to shift according to fashion, customer spending power and the facilities each resort can offer.

Over the past 20 years, the sun, sea and sand package tour to Mediterranean resorts has become a British tradition. Some people now want something different – they may have become bored with the traditional package holiday. Alternatives include cruises, long-haul destinations and activity holidays. If a tour operator wants to keep up with the times and ahead of the competition, new holiday opportunities must be explored such as safaris in

Kenya, cruises down the Nile, trekking in the Himalayas or wine-tasting in France.

Pricing is the most important factor in the tour operator's planning and preparation of any tour. Profit targets have to be met and the final price shown in the brochure must take into account the competition (i.e. other tour operators) and, as a result, brochure prices are a closely guarded secret right up until launch date. All profits and costs are built into the price of a holiday. The basic elements involved in pricing are the costs of: the aircraft seat, accommodation, transfers, overheads (reps' wages), profit mark up and travel agents' commission – usually 10 per cent leaving the tour operator with 90 per cent of the brochure price.

There is a wide range of tour operators within the UK. The largest ones provide a variety of holidays to suit most tastes, while smaller operators tend to specialise in a specific type of holiday.

There are five main types of tour operators in the UK, as shown in Figure 8.3.

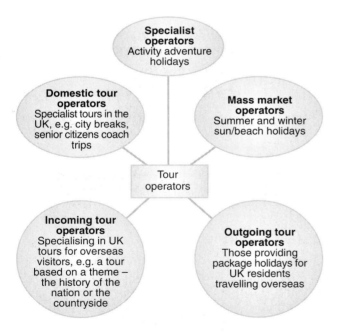

Figure 8.3 The five main categories of tour operators

Facts and figures – top five tour operators

1 Thomson Tour Operators
2 Airtours plc
3 First Choice Holiday and Flights Ltd
4 Kuoni Travel
5 Cosmoair

Look it up

Divide into five groups, with each group choosing one tour operator from the five listed. Find out as much information as you can about your selected tour operator.

Putting a package together

To provide the finished product the tour operator will have to organise accommodation, transport, visitor attractions and insurance – the components of the package holiday. The diagram below shows how it is done.

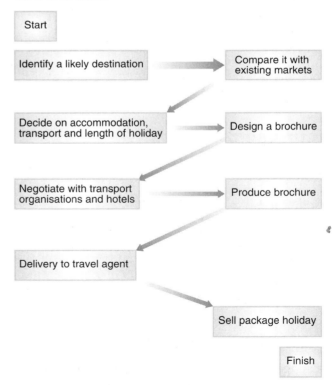

Figure 8.4 Putting together a package holiday

Specialist tour operators

In the past people used to organise their own holiday arrangements in pursuit of a special interest, for example climbing in the Himalayas or scuba diving in the Caribbean. Specialist tour operators now organise such packages for these groups which can be taken to the most appropriate location in the world. Specialist operators fall into six categories:

◇ those for specific groups, for example Club 18-30 for young people who want a fun and exciting holiday, SAGA holidays for senior citizens who may want a coach tour or a winter break in the sun

◇ tours to specific destinations, e.g. Australia, the Far East

◇ those taking people to exotic and exclusive places, e.g. safari in Kenya, sightseeing in China

◇ those who provide specific accommodation as part of the package, e.g. a villa in Spain, a caravan at the seaside, a camping holiday in the south of France

◇ those who have specific transport as part of the tour and as part of the attraction, e.g. a flight on Concorde, a journey on the Orient Express, a cruise down the Nile

◇ specialist interest operators, e.g. wine-tasting in Bordeaux, hang-gliding in Wales, train-spotting in India.

Mass market operators

A two-week holiday in Spain is usually organised by mass market tour operators. These 'cheap and cheerful' package holidays offer carefree relaxation, in a warm climate, often with basic food and accommodation. Most destinations are in south west Europe, which is within a short flight time.

The advantages of inclusive tours to the customer is shown in Figure 8.5.

Incoming tour operators

Although many tour operators organise tours for people from the UK to travel overseas, it is possible for an operation to bring in foreign tourists.

The target market for this type of tour operator would be those like American or Japanese tourists who want cultural and historical tours of the UK; in other words, they want to see and experience the 'atmosphere' of the country.

There are about 350 tour operators who derive part of their income from incoming tourists.

Look it up

Try to find an example of an incoming tour operator and give brief details of the organisation.

Domestic tour operators

Not everyone wants to go abroad for their holidays and many cannot afford to. Many people organise their own travel and accommodation arrangements for holidays in this country. However, there are others who are possibly used to inclusive tours abroad, and want the same type of service here.

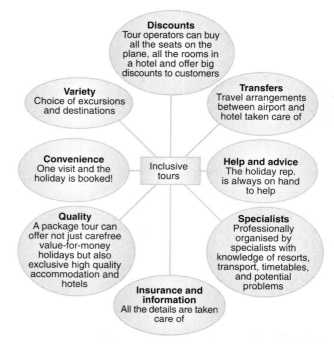

Figure 8.5 Advantages of the inclusive tour to the customer

The inclusive coach tour has become increasingly popular and this has led to a rise in the short break or mini holidays. One example of this would be a five-day tour of the Highlands of Scotland staying at three-star hotels and having the services of a courier on board.

SNAPSHOTS

Holly

Holly is deputy manager of brochure production for a large tour operator, having worked in airlines and hotels previously. She says,

'Brochures are extremely important to anyone booking a holiday and to the tour operator. If they are not attractive, customers won't buy the holidays: if they are not accurate in any way, there will be complaints and legal problems.

We first decide on the content of the brochure – how many pages to devote to each country, which hotels to feature, whether to have holiday prices and flight details on these pages or in a separate section and so on. We have to be absolutely certain that the brochure content is accurate; things can go wrong. A photographer may arrive at a hotel, for instance, to take pictures of the three-star rooms. If they are all occupied and the duty manager shows him the four-star instead, we have potential trouble.

We may have to slightly change the brochure before it can be sent out. Time marches on and during this time I organise photographic shoots overseas, get copy checked or rewritten and, of course, I work on several brochures at the same time. It's a brilliant way of earning a living.'

Try it out

Pick up a brochure from your local travel agent and explain why the content and the photos are set out the way they are.

Did you know?

The tour operating market is worth £8 billion. Most of the expenditure made through travel agents and tour operators is for overseas travel.

Travel agents

Walk down most high streets today and, alongside the clothes shops, banks, chemists and electrical stores, you are bound to find a travel agent. This is the first port of call for most people planning a holiday.

The travel agent's role is to sell ready planned (package) holidays, organise individual holidays, and make travel arrangements for their clients. They receive commission from the tour operators whose products they sell. The retail travel agent is therefore classed as a 'middle man' and fits into the structure of the industry between the supplier and the consumer.

Before the 1950s travel agents were a rarity, used only by those who earned high salaries and who could afford overseas holidays – and hardly ever by the average person in the street.

There are now around 7,000 travel agents. Many household names like Lunn Poly and Thomas Cook advertise their services widely on television and in the media. In many ways, travel agents operate just like other retailers. They display goods (holiday posters), give advice (the most suitable accommodation for a client) and arrange sales (sell the holiday or insurance).

In other ways, they act as an agent: no goods change hands and no stock is held. A travel agency is, in fact, considered to be an office and not a shop. Travel agents can make bookings with a variety of companies and these are referred to as principals. Some examples of principals are: airlines, rail companies, tour operators, car ferry companies, cruise lines, hotel groups and coach companies. Principals pay the travel agent to represent them and make bookings on their behalf.

The commission paid by a principal is a percentage value of the booking made by the travel agent. Commission earned by travel agents from principals on bookings varies between only 1 per cent on foreign traveller's cheques to 10 per cent or more on insurance. The average package holiday tour operator gives a travel agent 10 per cent commission; for selling scheduled international airline tickets the travel agent earns 9 per cent, with only 7.5 per cent on domestic tickets and about 9 per cent for car ferry bookings.

Examples of travel agents' commission

- A package holiday with a brochure price of £2,000 would earn the travel agent:
$$\frac{2000 \times 10}{100} = £200 \ (10\%)$$

- A scheduled airline ticket at £350: $\dfrac{350 \times 9}{100} = £31.50 \ (9\%)$

- A domestic airline ticket at £95: $\dfrac{95 \times 7.5}{100} = £7.12 \ (7.5\%)$

- A car ferry booking at £240 earns: $\dfrac{240 \times 9}{100} = £21.60 \ (9\%)$

- Insurance for two adult at £50 each: $\dfrac{100 \times 10}{100} = £10 \ (10\%)$

CASE STUDY – Zina

Zina has been a senior travel consultant for five years. Her time is divided between working on the travel counter and as a world travel consultant.

She says,

'On the counter I deal with everything. Customers vary from knowing exactly which package holiday they want, to simply saying that they want to go somewhere sunny and asking for advice. Others want to make independent arrangements. I love selling; when the company analyses sales figures, I am often in the top ten in the country.'

In the other part of her job, Zina provides a more specialised service on an appointment basis:

'Our larger branches have travel lounges, furnished like comfortable drawing rooms, where we can spend more time – and without constant phone interruptions – with customers who are planning long-haul trips. These are completely tailor made. Some people might be visiting relatives in New Zealand and are planning an interesting route to get there. Others want a special holiday. I have had some people wanting to go around the world; others to South America, or North and South America. In all cases I arrange the itinerary, book the flights, accommodation and any additional tours.

Once you have planned a good trip for someone, they start to trust you and expect you to know everything. It does involve knowing a lot, particularly as many customers have been reading up about the area they intend to visit before they come in! I am lucky in having been to many destinations around the world myself, either on holiday or on educational trips organised by the company.'

Questions

- What sort of skills would you expect a world travel consultant to possess?

- Zina is obviously very good at her job. How do you think her company would reward her for her excellent sales figures?

Think it over

Imagine you have worked as a travel consultant for six months. Your boss is sending you on an educational visit to Disneyland Paris for three days. What type of things would she expect you to learn from your trip? Discuss your ideas with the group.

The role and function of travel agents is shown in Figure 8.6.

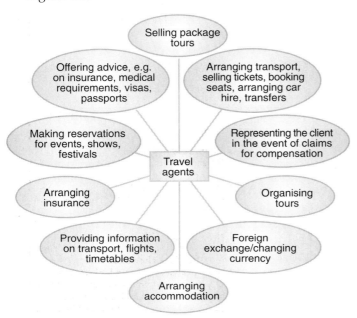

Figure 8.6 Role and function of travel agents

Location of travel agents

The main role of travel agents is to sell travel products from a convenient location. In the past many were located near to the travel terminals at pier heads, docks or railway stations. However, they are now usually located in major centres in towns and cities, where they can be easily found and used.

Ground floor premises in a busy street with convenient nearby parking make an ideal location. The window can be used to display posters, brochures and publicity about destinations. The street window can paint a picture of a world of glamour and excitement, waiting to be explored.

Types of travel agent

There are several different types of travel agent: independents, national and regional multiples, and business travel agents. We will look at each in turn.

Independents

These travel agents do not form part of a national chain. They usually consist of one retail unit, however they can still be classed as independents if they have up to six branches. You can usually find independent travel agents tucked away in an office above another retail outlet. They provide a local service in the suburbs or villages. One disadvantage for independents is that they may be targets of take-overs by national multiples.

National multiples

These travel agents dominate the retail travel industry in the UK. They have agencies or branches throughout the country. Examples include Lunn Poly, Thomas Cook and Going Places. They sometimes form part of larger travel organisations, for example, Lunn Poly is part of the Thomson group. Because of their size they can offer discounts on holidays, which makes them so successful. However, they sometimes cannot match the variety of products offered by the independent travel agent.

Regional multiples

These have a number of branches in one region of the country. They enjoy close connections with business and leisure travellers in their region.

Independent travel agents provide a local service and offer a wider variety of products than the national multiples

They sometimes start out as one unit family businesses and develop over time. Like independents, their success makes them vulnerable to take-overs by national multiples.

Business travel agents

People going away on business have their flights, accommodation and transfers arranged by specialist business travel agents. Business travellers attend exhibitions, conferences, meetings and trade fairs both at home and abroad. Some large organisations like the high street chemists Boots, whose business travel requirements are high, have a business travel agent actually on site – this arrangement is known as an 'inplant' travel agency.

Organisations providing tourist information

Tourism is big business. It is good for the economy and provides jobs for about 1.5 million people. It brings new jobs to areas hit by the decline of other industries: on average, for each £30,000 spent on tourism, one job is created.

The Department for Culture, Media and Sport funds tourism (about £10 million per year) and has set up a department to help the tourism industry continue to develop and grow.

The English Tourism Council

The English Tourism Council is funded by the Department for Culture, Media and Sport. It aims to:

- improve standards in accommodation and service quality to meet the increasing demands of tourists

- provide forecasts, research and guidance to foresee future trends

- make a positive contribution to the social, economic and environmental well-being of national life.

Regional tourist boards

Regional tourist boards receive funding from the English Tourism Council. They oversee local tourist information centres and co-ordinate the

Cumbria Tourist Board

East of England Tourist Board
Cambridgeshire, Essex, Norfolk, Hertfordshire, Bedfordshire, Suffolk and Lincolnshire

London Tourist Board
Greater London

Northumbria Tourist Board
Durham, Northumberland, Tees Valley and Tyne & Wear

Heart of England Tourist Board
Derbyshire, Gloucestershire, Herefordshire, Leicestershire, Northamptonshire, Nottinghamshire, Rutland, Shropshire, Staffordshire, Warwickshire, Worcestershire, the West Midlands and representing the districts of Cherwell and West Oxfordshire

South East England Tourist Board
Sussex, Kent and Surrey

West Country Tourist Board
Bath, Bristol, Cornwall & Isles of Scilly, Devon, West Dorset, Somerset and Wiltshire

Yorkshire Tourist Board
Yorkshire and North East Lincolnshire

Southern Tourist Board
Berkshire, East & North Dorset, Hampshire, Isle of Wight, Buckinghamshire and Oxfordshire

NorthWest Tourist Board
Cheshire, Greater Manchester, Lancashire, Merseyside and the High Peak District of Derbyshire

Source: English Tourism Council

Figure 8.7 The ten regional tourist boards in England

promotion and development of tourism in their own region. The ten regional tourist boards and their locations are shown in Figure 3.7.

Tourist information centres

Source: English Tourism Council

The tourist information logo is quickly recognisable everywhere

There are over 560 tourist information centres in England. If you are in a town or city which is new to you and want to know what to see, where to eat and perhaps where to stay, it is very likely that you will head straight for the tourist information centre. They can also give you information about other parts of England. They provide information to tourists on accommodation, car hire, entertainment and facilities in a particular locality.

Look it up

Find out where your nearest tourist information centre is, giving its exact address and telephone number.

Many local authorities have their own leisure departments which usually include a tourism section. They fund local Tourism Information Centres and promote tourism in their area.

British Tourist Authority

This was established in 1969 with the aim of promoting Britain to overseas visitors. It does this by having sales offices in many countries abroad including, for example, Germany, Australia, France, Saudi Arabia and the USA. These offices distribute promotional leaflets and brochures about the UK to overseas visitors. In addition, they liaise with overseas travel agents and tour operators by organising seminars, exhibitions and travel trade shows.

SNAPSHOTS

Manny

Manny is a manager of a very busy tourist information centre in Canterbury, Kent. The centre has three full-time and three part-time staff who assist over 250,000 visitors a year.

Today they have had the usual spread of enquirers from Britain, the USA, Japan, France and Germany, asking for anything from bus timetables to the way to visitor attractions.

Manny says,

'We keep information on theatres, buses, trains, day trips, local clubs and societies. You could book a theatre seat, join the Youth Hostel Association or one of the motoring organisations here. Oh, and we also sell stamps and phone cards.'

What about the job? Manny goes on to say,

'You really have to like meeting people and helping them. You must be able to work under pressure, because it gets very hectic when there are people waiting. Obviously you have to be courteous and patient – and have a good telephone manner, because a lot of enquiries are made by phone. You cannot worry about working at weekends. We are open on Saturdays which means that staff have to work one Saturday in three, and in summer we also open Sunday afternoons.'

The British Tourist Authority also promotes the UK by sponsoring stand space at the world's largest tourism exhibitions like the World Travel Market which attracts visitors and trade representatives from all over the world.

Visitor attractions

Visitor attractions include theme parks, like Blackpool Pleasure beach, and museums like the Victoria and Albert Museum in London.

When tourists travel to destinations they find suitable accommodation and look for something to do. Tourist attractions provide the activities, fun, excitement or interest that tourists look for. After travel and accommodation, visitor attractions are the third most important component in the tourism mix of products and services.

Attractions are often the very reason why tourists visit a destination and, as a result of this demand, the number of attractions in the UK has more than doubled in the last ten years.

Most of the attractions on offer are relatively new, with examples ranging from theme parks and educational museums to sea-life centres and butterfly farms. Other attractions have been around for quite some time and include, for example, cathedrals and churches, historic houses and monuments, parks and coastal and countryside areas.

Museums

During the past 15 years, museums have changed almost beyond recognition. Gone, at least in most of the major museums, is the dark and dingy atmosphere – to be replaced by new galleries, new displays, interactive computers and audio tours as well as improved catering facilities. One of the reasons for this change came in 1988 when the government made museums responsible for their own buildings, collections and staff, and allowed them to keep their own income. Previously their income had to be sent to the government.

For information on theme parks in the UK check out the following website: www.geoprojects.co.uk

Aims and objectives of organisations in travel and tourism

All organisations in travel and tourism have to ensure their businesses are managed properly if they are to be successful, so you will need to understand how organisations work. Their aims and objectives can vary and are often influenced by the sector to which they belong – private, public or voluntary.

The private sector

The travel and tourism industry in the UK is dominated by large and small private sector organisations owned by individuals or groups of people (see Figure 8.8). The main aims and objectives of these organisations are to make a profit from what they sell, for their owners, directors, employees and shareholders.

Many organisations which you are familiar with operate in the private sector; for example, Virgin, Alton Towers, BA, Lunn Poly, Travel Lodge hotels.

Figure 8.8 There are many different types of private sector organisation in travel and tourism

Select one private sector organisation from the travel and tourism industry in your area. How do you think it meets its aims and objectives?

Examples of private sector organisations

Eurostar

Source: Eurostar

The first commercial Eurostar service to Paris left Waterloo International in November 1994. In June 1996 it launched its daily service from Waterloo to the gates of Disneyland Paris. In October 1998, Eurostar's own package holiday service was launched called Eurostar Holidays Direct, for the growing market in short breaks. Eurostar now has up to 28 departures a day to Paris, Brussels, Little

Calais and Disneyland Paris.

◇ **Thomson Travel Group**

Thomson Group is one of Europe's leading holiday and leisure travel groups with around 14,000 employees, 7 million holidaymakers, over 800 retail shops and a charter airline with over 40 aircraft. The group operates in the UK, Ireland, Sweden, Norway, Denmark, Finland, Germany and Poland.

The Thomson Group's objectives are to:

◇ be an industry leader through the efficiency and profitability of its business

◇ provide its customers with holidays which offer excellent value for money

◇ maintain its reputation for product innovation and service quality

◇ deliver better quality products and services than its leading competitors.

The public sector

The main aims and objectives of the public sector are to provide a service to the community. Examples include the English Tourism Council, regional tourist boards, tourist information centres and local authority tourism departments.

Funding comes from either central or local government and, although the public sector does not run to make a profit, it is expected to offer value for money and meet set targets.

The public sector first became involved in tourism in the nineteenth century when local authorities invested money in tourist facilities in places like Blackpool, Skegness and Scarborough. Today the English Tourism Council heads up tourism in England and by working through the regional tourist boards, and local tourist information centres, helps to develop and improve tourism in England.

Regional tourist boards

The regional tourist boards are responsible for identifying the issues and needs of tourism in their own areas and presenting proposals to the English Tourism Council for funding to help tackle them.

Their aims are to:

◇ develop a leadership role. They will develop a high profile position regionally and be able to represent the tourism industry and become the 'accepted voice' of tourism at regional level

◇ develop regional partnerships with local authorities and regional development agencies

◇ provide key services to assist tourism businesses by delivering training programmes and supporting the tourist information network.

The voluntary sector

This includes organisations which are concerned with preservation and conservation, for example the National Trust. They operate on a 'not for profit' basis and funding is raised through membership schemes and fundraising activities. Another example of a voluntary sector organisation is the Youth Hostel Association.

The Youth Hostel Association

Hostel accommodation is unique in that nearly all facilities are shared with other guests. Rooms are dormitory style and are usually furnished with bunkbeds. Other areas such as bathrooms and lounges are shared as well. These shared facility arrangements keep the cost per guest low and create a warm and friendly atmosphere between guests. It needs to be experienced to be fully understood.

Tourists of all ages, including those with families, stay in hostels and the youth hostels in the UK encourage this. Although inexpensive compared to hotels and B & B's, staying at a hostel requires a different type of person. For example, the services available in hotels cannot be had in a hostel and in most cases the 'guests' have to cook for themselves and clear up in the morning. Most guests who use the facility do this as a matter of routine. In the UK, as in most other countries many foreigners stay at hostels, and it can be a good way to meet people while travelling.

The Youth Hostel Association is a registered charity founded in 1930 whose original aim was 'to help all, especially young people of limited means, to a greater knowledge, love and care of the countryside, particularly by providing Hostels or other simple accommodation for them on their travels, and thus to promote their health, rest and education'.

Hostels are located all over the country. There are still hostels in remote areas, including Tycornel in mid Wales which does not have electricity but does have a cosy fire. Costs vary but are within the budget of most travellers.

The National Trust

The National Trust's primary objective is and always has been the conservation of the buildings and landscapes in its care.

It came into existence in 1895 and now boasts 2 million members from whom it derives most of its income. The National Trust is a charity and not a government organisation. It is the largest private landowner in the country, protecting more than 600,000 acres of land and 200 houses and parks. Because for most of its history the Trust has opened its properties to visitors, the charity has become a major provider of tourist attractions in England, Wales and Ireland. National Trust properties include Fountains Abbey (North Yorkshire) – a World Heritage Site, Bodiam Castle (East Sussex) and Sissinghurst Garden (Kent).

Most of the National Trust's countryside properties are open to the public, free of charge, all year round. Many of its historic buildings are open from April to the end of October, with an admission fee. Membership of the National Trust gives free entry to all of the Trust's properties.

Staffing

The success of organisations within the travel and tourism industry is mainly dependent on the skills and qualities of the staff who work in them.

The type of people employers in the travel and tourism industry look for are the ones who are enthusiastic and good at communicating.

Think it over What qualities do you think employers look for in staff working in the travel and tourism industry.

Managers will often employ people who have the right personality and qualifications and then train them in the job. Your GNVQ in Leisure and Tourism will demonstrate your commitment to learn and your interest in the industry.

Staffing levels

If an organisation is to operate efficiently it needs to have the correct staffing levels. Imagine a busy travel agency with only two travel consultants. Customers would probably look at the queues and go elsewhere. Business would be lost.

Facilities like theme parks also need correct staffing levels from a health and safety point of view; for example, checking the safety of customers on rides. The staffing levels might include a mixture of seasonal, part-time and full-time staff. Seasonal staff are employed between Easter and the end of November at Blackpool Pleasure Beach. The facility closes for winter, so the seasonal staff have to find employment elsewhere. Hotels employ part-time staff at the week-ends and evenings to cover the long hours of operation. A waitress in the restaurant may work from Monday to Friday, 6.30 to 10.30 am serving breakfasts and clearing up. Another waiter may work from 7 to 11 pm serving dinner and drinks. In the same way, a travel agent's busiest day is usually a Saturday, so additional part-time staff may be brought in to deal with the extra customers.

Permanent, full-time employment is often being replaced by part-time and seasonal staff working in short fixed-term contracts as a way of reducing costs. Also, the introduction of new technology has meant that staff are able to cope with greater workloads and so in some cases, additional staff are not required.

Talk about it

It is actually cheaper to employ part-time and seasonal staff than full-time staff. Why do you think this is?

CASE STUDY – Katie

Katie left school at 16 and took a business and finance course at her local college. The following year she took a GNVQ in Business. She says:

'I first worked from Easter to October 1995 as a part-time ride assistant at a theme park. During the winters of 1996 and 1997 I worked as a catering assistant in a hotel and restaurant. In 1998, I became a seasonal ride operator back at the theme park and in 1999 I became a seasonal relief team leader. I started full-time work there in the same year as a secretary to the entertainment's manager and the following year I was back out in the theme park where I was promoted to team leader and then ride manager.

The work demands an ability to motivate and lead staff. Taking quick decisions while always remembering that the health and safety of the staff and visitors to the park comes first is an important part of the job, as is getting on with people – both staff and customers.'

Question

Katie is a good example of how you can progress from part-time to seasonal to full-time staff member. Can you think of other jobs which offer this type of progression?

Organisational structure with lines of responsibility

Organisational structures show the relations and communication channels between different levels of staff. For example, in a travel agency a travel consultant would report to the manager, who in turn would report to the regional manager. The regional manager would be responsible for a number of travel agencies in the area and all the staff who worked in them.

Each person in the structure has his or her own responsibilities and tasks. In our two examples, shown in Figures 8.9 and 8.10, the managing director and the curator have the ultimate responsibilities. They are responsible for the smooth running of their organisations and are ultimately responsible for all health and safety issues.

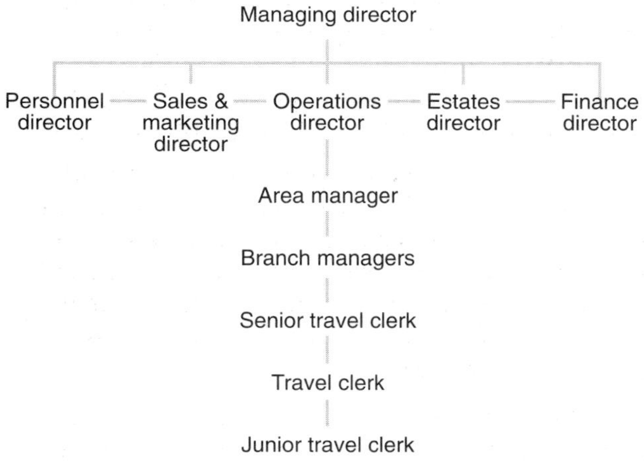

Well-trained staff

The opportunities for finding work in travel and tourism organisations are wide and varied. Promotion and career development can come about through training.

Managing director
Personnel director — Sales & marketing director — Operations director — Estates director — Finance director
Area manager
Branch managers
Senior travel clerk
Travel clerk
Junior travel clerk

Figure 8.9 Organisational structure of a national travel agency

Figure 8.10 Organisational structure for an art gallery or museum

Try it out

Copy and complete the boxes of the staffing structure for this theme park.

Complete the staffing structure of this imaginary theme park if the manager is in overall charge.

(The answers are on page 273.)

Manager
2
3
4
5

Staff can be trained at work (on-the-job training) or away from work, for example attending a day-release course at college (see Figure 8.11).

Well-trained staff can give a high level of customer service and improve the organisation's productivity because of their increased skills and knowledge of the job brought about by training. Another important aspect of staff training is that it can lead to increased staff morale which in turn leads to good teamworking.

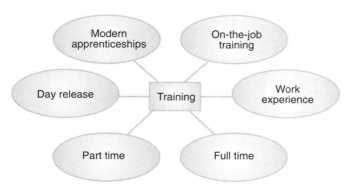

Figure 8.11 Types of study and training

Talk about it

What sort of study and training would you like to do after leaving school/college?

Training programmes

Employers in travel and tourism organisations often offer training programmes which enable staff to carry out their work more effectively. Some organisations have their own training departments which carry out this in-house training.

An example of a national training scheme is Modern Apprenticeships for 16 to 23-year-olds. This government-funded scheme enables young people on a work placement to study on a day-release programme. The employer pays them a basic wage and the government pays for their training which starts at NVQ Level 2 and progresses to NVQ Level 3.

We will now look at three jobs in the travel and tourism industry.

The holiday representative

Representatives, often referred to as 'reps', stay in one resort, and liaise with hotel managers, sorting out day-to-day problems and selling excursions to clients. They work long hours and are always on call. They look after departures and arrivals of holidaymakers, provide information about the area, deal with queries – and complaints! It is estimated that, in the peak holiday season, about 5,000 reps are employed abroad by UK package holiday companies.

In some countries, nationals of the country concerned are employed. Representatives recruited in Britain have to be at least 20 or 21 years, and for some companies, 23 or 25 is the minimum age. Some operators, specialising in holidays for the over 50s, look for 'mature' staff.

Reps need to be able to speak the language of the country in which they will live. Mostly they are employed on a seasonal basis and there is very stiff competition for jobs. After some experience as a rep., it is now sometimes possible to move into 'head office' positions, perhaps in marketing or customer services.

Qualifications and training Having the right personal qualities is often regarded as important as having formal qualifications, although some employers may ask for 3 or 4 GCSEs at grades A–C, or the Intermediate or Part 1 GNVQ in Leisure and Tourism. Many entrants offer GCSE qualifications or higher, such as A levels or

Advanced VCEs or degree. Useful subjects are Maths, and English, a foreign language and perhaps geography.

Once employed, there are many opportunities for further training. NVQs in Travel Services are available up to Level 4, which can be gained through assessment in the workplace. Most large travel and transport organisations – BA, for instance – run their own training schemes for employees. Some independent companies provide training courses, introducing you to the work of guiding and resort representative, for example. Regional tourist boards can advise on training of approved guides for site in their area.

Tour guide

The best route in is to take the Blue Badge qualification, which is the national qualification in guiding, through the local tourist board or the Guild of Registered Tourist Guides.

Prospective Blue Badge tourist guides are interviewed to gain places on the course, trained over a six-month period and then examined. At the selection process would-be tourist guides are given a general knowledge test and have to demonstrate their ability to get information across in an interesting way.

'Training includes how to guide on a coach, with a microphone, guiding on a walking tour in a town or in the country, and how to work at sites such as museums and churches. Each of these environments requires a different guiding technique. At the end of the course tourist guides have to pass a written examination on their local and national knowledge, as well as a coach, walking tour, museum and church examination.

Jobs in holiday centres and theme parks

Entry qualifications vary according to the job. For many jobs no particular academic qualifications are required. These basic level jobs, such as catering assistants, shop assistants and ride operatives provide good experience and a foothold in the organisation for anyone planning to work their way up. They are also a good source of employment for students looking for holiday work.

This industry has a high turnover of seasonal staff. After an initial induction, employees' training tends to be on-the-job, in-house training, very specifically related to the tasks of the particular job. For example, in a fast-food outlet, training will be given in specific tasks like making pizza bases or preparing burgers.

Theme parks and holiday centres offer lots of opportunities for keen and hard-working employees to work their way up the promotion ladder. However, in the early stages of their career they may have to accept seasonal work alternating with periods of unemployment.

Theme parks and holiday centres also offer many opportunities for students to work in their vacations. This experience can be very helpful in subsequently developing a career in the leisure industry.

Talk about it

What sort of training would be useful for the following jobs in travel and tourism:

* hotel manager
* holiday rep.
* marketing assistant for a tour operator?

(The answers are on page 273.)

Useful addresses for details on training

Association of British Travel Agents, 68–71 Newman Street, London W1P 4AH
www.abtanet.com

British Tourism Council, Thames Tower, Black's Road, London W6 9EL
www.visitbritain.com

Guild of Registered Tourist Guides, The Guild House, 52D Borough High Street, London SE1 1XN
www.blue-badge.org.uk

Hospitality Training Foundation, Third Floor, International House, High Street, London W5 5DB
www.htf.org.uk

Museum Training Institute, 1st Floor, Glyde House, Glydegate, Bradford, BD5
www.mti.org.uk

The Travel Training Company, The Cornerstone, The Broadway, Woking, Surrey, GU21 5AR
www.ttc.co.uk

Appropriate pay and conditions for staff

The idea of working in travel and tourism organisations is often very popular and attractive to young people. However, it is important to want to work in them for all the right reasons. While it gives the impression of being a glamorous 'fun' industry, the work in travel and tourism is a job like any other and not a paid-for holiday. In fact, some of the jobs do not have a lot to do with travel and tourism directly and are much more like any other job. You may have to work under pressure and difficult conditions and, in many cases, you cannot just sign off and leave at 5 pm.

We will have a look at some of the conditions and types of work environment you might experience when working in travel and tourism organisations (see Figure 8.12).

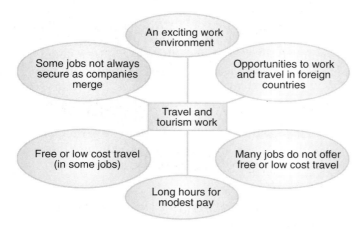

Figure 8.12 Some different conditions of work in travel and tourism

Jobs in travel and tourism organisations offer pay and conditions which are quite comparable to jobs in other industries. However, just because the industry makes profits does not mean that the pay is high. The strong competition for some jobs keeps pay down to very modest levels.

When you start out in your career in travel and tourism organisations you will find that, traditionally, the pay is low. As you progress up the career ladder, higher than average pay is possible if you are prepared to work hard. In some jobs, such as in a travel agency, you can receive performance-related pay. This means that you receive a commission or bonus on the amount you sell or the profits you make for your organisation.

Facts and figures – examples of pay
(at 2000 levels)

- Junior travel consultant: £5,000–8,000 per year plus bonus
- Air cabin crew
  - short haul: £8,000–10,000 plus £100 per month 'air time' (time spent in air).
  - long haul: £15,000–20,000 plus £150 per month air time.
  Also add commission for selling drinks and souvenirs on plane.
- Holiday rep: £8,000 including free accommodation, plus bonus and commission on excursions. For example 10 per cent of all tickets sold on an excursion to a waterpark in Crete: total ticket sales 350,000 drachmas (approx. £700), therefore commission of 10 per cent = £70.
- Hotel front office staff: £8,000–12,000, plus additional £2,000 per year for working shifts.

Some employers offer free or reduced price travel and holidays, but only if you have worked for them for at least six months. These benefits are a privilege, not a right, and can be withdrawn at any time.

Working conditions

We will look here at the working conditions of three people in the leisure and tourism industry: an events organiser, a flight attendant and a holiday rep.

SNAPSHOTS

Jill

Jill is a conference and event organiser. She says,

'Preparation for the event takes place in a busy office environment. Leading up to the event you could be working in a comfortable modern conference venue or out on a windy site for a rock concert. The days leading up to the event are very long and run over into weekends. On the actual day, you start at dawn and work till dusk. It's a very long but enjoyable day.'

Josie

Josie works as part of the air cabin crew for an international airline. She says,

'The job sounds glamorous but in reality it is really hard work. Flying long distances can cause jet lag and tiredness. Obviously I work shifts and sometimes finish at 3 am. I need my car to cope with the early and late starts and finishes. Despite all of this, I wouldn't change my job for the world.'

Sean

Sean is a holiday rep. This is what he says,

'I've been working in Corfu as a holiday rep. for two years. Most of my day is spent outdoors visiting clients in hotels and apartments, travelling to the airport to meet guests, and heading back to the office again.

'There's no 9 to 5 day. In fact change-over days can be very long, when I see off one group of guests and welcome another group. I tend to snatch short breaks during the day. Thursday is offically my day off although if there's a crisis I may be called into work.'

Talk about it

Do you think you still want to work in the leisure and tourism industry? The descriptions given have been honest and open. On page 255 you discussed qualities employers might require. What other qualities do you feel you might need to work in this industry?

Administration and finance

Good administrative and financial systems are required in all travel and tourism organisations, leading to efficiency and time-saving. Some of the systems may still be paper-based while others may use computers.

Reservation systems

Airlines, ferry companies, tour operators and hotels have reservation systems to keep records, invoices and track payments from customers.

Travel agents keep track of bookings. A travel booking for a package holiday, accommodation and transport will often be paid for in stages. Clients may have the option of paying a deposit then after a period of time, paying the balance. A system to keep track of accounts provides immediate information on all booking transactions.

Manual reservation systems are kept in ledgers recording enquiries, bookings, money paid and critical dates – such as when the balance is due or when tickets should be sent.

A personal computer in a travel agency can also be used to keep track of bookings and administrative tasks. Information can be entered into a database, as it might into a manual filing system, but there is a big difference. The data entered can be re-ordered in seconds. The same file of information could be used to select bookings which have been made in a particular month arranged alphabetically, or showing those clients who are flying from a particular airport.

Payment systems

Travel and tourism organisations use different systems to take payments from customers. This might be done by cash, cheque or credit card. Receipts are always issued and a record of payment is kept.

Each method of payment requires a number of procedures to be followed, some of which are specified by the bank or building society, others by the organisation itself.

Cash

Cash is normally used by clients for smaller purchases such as local coach or rail tickets. Occasionally a client may wish to pay for a flight ticket or holiday in cash and this can run into hundreds of pounds.

Large sums of money should always be counted out in front of the client and checked by a colleague. The cash should then be transferred to the safe. If you are in doubt about the validity of any note, compare it with a good note from the till.

Look at the statements below and insert the correct word from the words in the box.

(The answers are on page 273.)

> • customer's • receipt • desk or counter • cash • watermarks • money • till • check • forgery.

If a client is paying using large amounts of .... always get another member of staff to .... with you in the .... presence. A mistake could cost your company a lot of .... !

Always check the .... and metal strip of all large banknotes in case of ....

Never leave money on your ...., put it straight into the ....

Write out a .... straight away.

Cheques

With the increasing use of credit cards, you may not deal with many cheques. Nevertheless, it is still important to know what to do.

Unlike cash or credit cards, a cheque by itself does not guarantee payment. It is necessary for it to be accompanied by a valid cheque card, which will usually guarantee payment up to a certain limit – usually £50 or £100. For any payments in excess of the guarantee, the cheque must be cleared by the bank before the payment is

guaranteed. Cheques usually take a week to clear in the banking system.

When accepting payment by cheque, there are certain things you must check, such as seeing that the date on the cheque is correct, and the amount in words and figures agree.

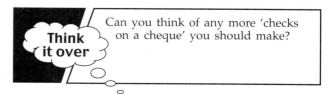

Can you think of any more 'checks on a cheque' you should make?

Other checks you might have suggested are:

- the amount does not exceed the cheque guarantee card limit
- the signature on the cheque matches the signature on the cheque card
- the cheque card has not expired
- the cheque is signed in front of you.

Credit cards

Customers increasingly use credit cards nowadays instead of cash and cheques, because of the added security and convenience. A credit card can be swiped on an automatic machine giving approval of the client's credit rating. People can arrange payment over the phone using their credit cards. Additional information is needed such as the expiry date of the card and the cardholder's name and address. Staff should check that:

- the company accepts this type of card
- the card has not expired
- the card is not listed as lost or stolen
- the card has the client's name on it
- the client's signature matches that on the card.

Receipts

Receipts should be issued for all cash, cheque and card transactions as a record that payment has been made. For security purposes, receipts should include the amount, the client's name and address

```
THE NEWWORLD GROUP                    № 03017

| LEAD NAME | FILE No. | PRINCIPAL | DEPARTURE DATE |
|           |          |           |                |

This document is a receipt issued for your financial protection. It is not
a "confirmation invoice". The invoice will be sent to you as soon as it
is received from the Principal or ATOL Holder with whom you have a
contract. Full details of your booking will be shown on your "confirmation
invoice" and your booking is subject to the terms and conditions of the
Principal or ATOL Holder. Monies are taken on behalf of the Principal
or ATOL Holder named. We act as agent for the Principal or ATOL Holder.

                                          RECEIVED WITH THANKS FROM
                                          ...............................................
                                          Date:
                                          £
                                          Cash/Chq/Card
                                          Signed: ..............................
ATOL NUMBER .....................          on behalf of The Newworld Group

The Newworld Group Limited  Registered Office:  1 Central Road, Manchester. M1 4PY
Registered in England and Wales No. 320 743   V.A.T GB 261 4912 59
```

An example of a travel organisation's receipt

and the date of the transaction. It is usual practice to have three copies of a receipt: one for the client, one for the file and one for the organisation's accounting system.

Look at the receipt of the NewWorld Group. Copy it out and complete it as if you were the travel agent.

Petty cash systems

Petty cash is used to pay for such items as stationery, travel expenses and staff refreshments.

Look at the statements below and decide whether they are true or false. Give reasons for your choice.

◊ The cheque card guarantee means that I can accept a cheque for any amount.

◊ The cheque can be completed and signed at any time before or during the transaction.

◊ Any mistakes can be simply crossed out and re-written.

A separate account or petty cash book should be kept for every purchase and a receipt obtained. Each item may be small in itself, but added together they can amount to significant costs.

Handling clients' complaints

Travel and tourism organisations usually have a complaints procedure. In the case of holidaymakers, this procedure is outlined in the booking conditions. A client on holiday should notify their holiday rep. of their complaint and also put it in writing. On return from their holidays, clients usually have about 28 days to write to the complaints department at the tour operator's office in the UK. Anyone who makes a complaint in writing should include their holiday reference number, a copy of the report made in the resort and their contact details.

Complaints are usually dealt with by the company's customer services department, whose role it is to try and solve the problem – either in the form of an apology or compensation. Sometimes an 'ex-gratia' payment is made to the client if their complaint is valid. This payment is made on the understanding that the organisation does not accept any responsibility for whatever has gone wrong with the holiday. The payment is simply a goodwill gesture.

Try it out

You have been asked to design a complaints form by the travel and tourism organisation you work for. You should include the following headings on your form:

- the nature of the complaint
- how and where to send the form
- what happens next
- what to do if the customer is still not satisfied.

Talk about it

Why do you think it is important for travel and tourism organisations to have good administrative and finance systems?

Effective administrative and finance systems are necessary to enable travel and tourist organisations to achieve their aims and objectives. For example:

- reservation systems ensure payments are made so income is maintained and profits can be achieved
- complaints procedures ensure that organisations put customer service high on their list of priorities
- effective administrative and finance systems help to ensure the smooth running of travel and tourism organisations, thus enabling them to meet customer needs and stay in business.

Products and services

Definition The activities of many travel and tourism organisations result in a product which may include goods and/or services to the customer. For example, a hotel may sell a weekend break as a product which also contains several services: meals, accommodation, entertainment.

Availability

Travel and tourism organisations succeed if they fulfil people's needs by providing the right products and services at a price they can afford. Different groups of clients have different needs, for example families, senior citizens, 18–30s. It makes sense therefore to be able to offer what the client wants – otherwise they may well go to another company.

People usually have more than one need when buying a product or service. A business person in a hotel may want:

- room service
- fax and photocopying facilities
- a restaurant to entertain clients
- a desk
- assistance with transport.

Trained staff would be able to identify the customer's needs through a combination of experience and skill.

SNAPSHOTS

'Meeter and greeter'

A group of students were taken to the Trafford Centre in Manchester. They were met in the coach park by a 'meeter and greeter' whose job it was to welcome them to the centre. He gave everyone a welcome pack and a brief history of the area on which the centre was built. They needed the information about the centre as none of them had been there before. What's more, it was nice to be warmly welcomed after a two-hour trip.

Open all hours?

Another way of satisfying customer needs is to ensure that facilities are open at a time when customers can use them. Many people work from 9 am to 5 pm. Monday to Friday. If a travel agent was only open the same hours, many working people would not have the opportunity to go in and book their holidays. So travel agencies usually stay open until at least 6 pm for six or maybe seven days a week.

Tourist information centres are usually open seven days a week so they are always on hand for

Look it up

Find out the opening times of two travel agents in your area. Either visit or phone your local tourist information centre and ask them their opening hours. Is the centre open all year round? If not, why not?

visitors to seek information about local accommodation, car hire etc. in the area.

A comfortable and safe environment

Customers need to feel comfortable and safe. They expect travel and tourism organisations to have:

- a safe environment
- trained staff
- clean premises
- security, e.g. against theft of belongings
- food that is prepared and served correctly
- evacuation procedures in case of emergency.

The requirement to feel safe and secure is one of our basic human needs: organisations should be aware of this.

Talk about it

How does a theme park provide a safe and comfortable environment for its customers? How does an airline?

CASE STUDY – GNER

'At Great North Eastern Railway, all our customers receive the best possible care and attention at all times. Our dedicated service includes assistance for customers with special needs. We offer:

- wheelchair space in First Class and Standard accommodation
- a toilet and washroom on all 225 trains for wheelchair users
- disabled toilet facilities at many stations.

Discounts for people with disabilities
The Disabled Railcard costs only £14 per year and dependent on the type of disability, entitles the holder and a companion to a discount of one third off First Class and Standard rail fares.

Parents with babies and children
All trains have baby changing facilities, as do many stations. To make your journey even more rewarding, children under 5 can travel for free.

Kids Go First
We have developed an 'unaccompanied minor' train travel service. This is available on direct journeys on GNER services to most stations on our route. Customers should phone the dedicated booking line. Your child must be aged 8 to 15 years and can travel on a service which departs between 1000 and 1500 hours, any day subject to availability. Your child will be escorted to and from the train by GNER staff and a regular check is made on the child during the journey, however this is not a babysitting service and therefore is not suitable for children who require close and constant supervision. The fare is the appropriate Standard Child fare plus an administration charge, for which your child is reserved a dedicated seat in First Class and provided with a soft drink.'

Source: Adapted from GNER leaflet, 'Information for customers with special needs'

Question

Why do you think GNER provides this type of assistance to customers with special needs?

Facilities for those with special needs

All customers have their own special needs, whether they are business people, senior citizens or young children. In addition some people will have specific needs and require extra understanding and sensitive treatment. They include:

- visitors with mobility problems
- visitors with sensory and learning difficulties
- elderly people
- visitors with small children or babies
- non-English speaking visitors
- visitors from a different cultural background.

How can we help?

- Visitors with restricted mobility – car parking bays need to be close to main entrance to the building; corridors and doors should be wide enough to give access to all areas, e.g. toilets, ramps, signposting.

- Visually impaired visitors – avoid intrusive background noise such as loud piped music as blind people rely far more on their hearing than sighted people.

Look it up

Find details from another travel and tourism organisation which show how it provides assistance for customers with special needs. Your research may include the following special provision:

- information in different languages
- translation services
- brochures in Braille
- the special prayer area at Heathrow airport
- 'signing' in theatres.

Think it over

What do you think an organisation could do to provide extra help for the following people:

- * disabled visitors
- * non-English speaking visitors
- * visitors with young children or babies
- * the elderly?

Entertainment or crèche facilities for children

Sometimes parents like to do things on their own, such as going shopping without their children. This can be done if organisations, for example shopping centres, provide crèche facilities where qualified staff look after youngsters. In fact, 'keeping kids happy' is a phrase adopted by some airports that have special areas for youngsters to play under supervision. This makes sense, especially if a plane is delayed. Some family restaurants, also provide a play area with a bouncy castle, slides and ball pools.

Many organisations provide crèche facilities where parents can leave their children whilst shopping

Health, safety and security

Travel and tourism organisations, by law, have to ensure that their premises are safe for both customers and staff. There is a range of government legislation requiring organisations to operate safely. One such piece of legislation is the Health and Safety at Work Act, 1974 (see page 182). This imposes a duty on employers to provide a safe working environment. It protects employers, employees, the self-employed and customers and outlines the employer's responsibilities regarding:

◇ safety in the workplace

◇ safety in working practices

◇ hygiene and welfare

◇ electrical and fire safety.

The employee's responsibilities are:

◇ to follow the rules on health and safety

◇ to observe safe working practices.

Look at Figure 8.13 – would you like to work in such an environment?

There are various ways organisations can ensure that they are complying with health and safety regulations. The remainder of this section shows how they do this.

Figure 8.13 How many hazards and dangerous practices can you spot here?

Staff training

It is important that all staff know what to do in the event of an accident or emergency. Having well-trained staff ensures such incidents are handled professionally and properly. For example, in the event of an evacuation, staff who have been well trained will know exactly what to do and where to assemble outside the building. Imagine the chaos and confusion that would come about if staff had no idea what to do if the fire alarm went off. At best, staff would be confused and not know where to assemble after leaving the building; at worst they could panic, get lost in the building and perish.

> **?** **Did you know?**
>
> In 1997, UK fire brigades attended over 36,000 fires in workplaces. These fires killed 30 people and injured more than 2,600.

Some organisations have an appointed health and safety adviser and an appointed first aider. As well as providing the necessary health and safety advice and first aid cover, this gives reassurance to employees and the public that the organisation is taking health and safety issues seriously. It is also a way of improving working relations if the organisation is seen to be doing the right thing in looking after the welfare of employees.

One advantage for the staff appointed as health and safety advisers or first aiders is that they may receive additional pay for their extra responsibilities.

> XYZ Organisation
>
> Your Duty First Aider is
> Georgina Coulham

The importance of induction

When new employees start work they should be given induction training. This is a period of time, which could last from one day to one week, when they will receive training in working practices and they can familiarise themselves with their new workplace. It is particularly important that staff induction should include health and safety issues (see Figure 8.14).

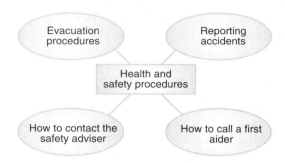

Figure 8.14 Induction training should provide information about health and safety in an organisation

Staff induction

1. The employee shall be shown all risk assessments. These will be systematically explained by the section manager.

2. For each of the tasks covered by the risk assessments the section manager will explain the training and instruction that must be received before the individual can carry out the task.

3. For each of the tasks the employee shall be shown any procedures for serious or imminent danger, and shall be introduced to any individual responsible for implementing evacuation procedures.

4. The employee shall be introduced to the first aiders and informed of the first aid procedure.

5. The employee shall be shown the location of the fire call points and emergency exits.

Induction training should include all full-time, part-time and seasonal staff. In fact, training in health and safety for all employees should not stop at the end of their induction period but should be ongoing. Employers are given this responsibility to ensure this actually happens.

Look it up

Does your school/college/place of work have staff training in health and safety? Try to find some evidence of this.

Risk assessments

Risk assessment involves identifying the hazards in the workplace and assessing the likelihood that these hazards will cause harm to employees and others. It is part of the systematic approach that employers are now required by law to adopt in order to manage health and safety effectively. It helps spot the prevention or control measures needed to protect workers and the public from harm.

Employers are obliged by law to undertake risk assessments. All aspects of all jobs should have been vetted for hazards and 'reasonably practicable' measures should have been taken to ensure workers are not put at risk.

Carrying out risk assessments

No one knows the problems of a job better than the worker who has to do it. Health and safety officers liaise with staff to work out risk assessments in order to try and spot anything that is potentially dangerous, for example electrical equipment, loose wires.

Risk assessments benefit employees and the public by trying to reduce the risk of accidents, injury or illness in the workplace. It also means employees are properly informed about their working conditions, the risks and how to avoid them – if risk assessments are done right. It is up to the safety adviser to make sure this happens.

Did you know?

More than two million people each year suffer ill health caused or made worse by their work, many suffering from stress, strains or sprains.

Talk about it

What sort of dangers are attached to working in a large office? What could you include in your risk assessment of an office environment?

Look at the risk assessment checklist below. Also look at the following problems associated with working with computers, as stated in the Health and Safety (Display Screen Equipment) Regulations 1992.

Badly organised VDU workstations and work can lead to discomfort including:

- aching hands, arms and necks
- temporary eyestrain, headaches
- tiredness.

Discomfort can lead to health problems like upper limb disorders or stress.

Risk Assessment Checklist

1 Are members entitled to regular breaks?
2 Do members take a lunch break?
3 Do any members work long hours? (more than 48 per week)
4 Are members allowed to consume food and drink in working areas?
5 Are suitable rest and meal facilities provided?
6 Are the facilities smoke-free?
7 Are adequate numbers of toilets provided for men and women?
8 Is there an adequate supply of soap and hand drying facilities?
9 Are toilets and washbasins kept in a clean, orderly condition?
10 Is there enough space provided in all work areas?
11 Does the amount of equipment and furniture in the area make it unsafe?
12 How can the work area layout be improved?
13 How often is the workplace cleaned?
14 What arrangements exist for the disposal of refuse?
15 How are hazardous substances disposed of?
16 Is special attention paid to areas where high hygiene standards are necessary? (e.g. kitchens, canteens)
17 Are there any trailing wires and cables?
18 Is the electrical equipment switched off at the end of the working day?
19 Are there any damaged electrical sockets or plugs?
20 Are building/refurbishment works carried out during normal working hours and in normal work areas?
21 Are building materials and substances safely stored whilst building work is on-going?
22 Are pregnant workers exposed to any health and safety risks?
23 What arrangements does the employer have for preventing/controlling such risks

Regular maintenance checks

Maintenance work is carried out to keep buildings, machinery and equipment at an acceptably safe standard. The lack of an effective regular maintenance programme could lead to problems, as shown in Figure 8.15.

Figure 8.15 Regular maintenance checks are essential to avoid problems like these

A planned regular programme includes the inspection, adjustment and servicing of facilities with the aim of preventing breakdowns.

Regular maintenance checks include:

- cleaning to prevent stoppages caused by dirty equipment

- testing and checking – to make sure everything is working properly

- visual inspections – to spot any problems

- replacement – as necessary.

Records of all maintenance work should be kept up to date and should state clearly what work has been carried out, who has done it and what materials were used.

The use of daily/weekly maintenance sheets can be effective in that they:

- help ensure routine tasks are not overlooked

- provide a record of the work done.

Look at the examples of maintenance record sheets.

Low priority tasks	Status	Due Date	% Complete
North block - gents toilet (Sports hall)	Completed	Fri 28/04/00	100%
Handrail on ramp - rear of main block	Completed	Fri 28/04/00	100%
North block - ladies toilet (Sports hall)	Completed	Mon 03/04/00	100%
Lab - room 103, décor	Completed	Fri 31/03/00	100%
Laboratory	Completed	Sun 26/03/00	100%
Door closers	Completed	Fri 24/03/00	100%
Pam Geary's office	Completed	Fri 03/03/00	100%
West block - ladies toilet, mirror	Completed	Fri 03/03/00	100%
Room 115	Completed	Fri 03/03/00	100%
World map - room 20	Completed	Fri 25/02/00	100%

Medium priority tasks	Status	Due Date	% Complete
Main gate - Clipstone centre	In Progress	Fri 16/06/00	0%
Parking spaces, Nursery - Grange	Completed	Fri 16/06/00	100%
Security bars - 'Old Magnus cookery'	In Progress	Fri 16/06/00	0%
Ramp handrail - rear of main block	Not Started	Fri 16/06/00	0%
West block - notice boards	Waiting on...	Fri 16/06/00	50%
Security bars - Engineering workshop	In Progress	Fri 16/06/00	25%
Security bars - Welding workshop	Not Started	Fri 16/06/00	0%
Yellow lines	Completed	Fri 16/06/00	100%
Windows - Edwinstowe centre	Completed	Fri 02/06/00	100%

High priority tasks	Status	Due Date	% Complete
Repair toilets at Edwinstowe	Not started	Thu 15/06/00	0%
'Northern light' leaking - Mount	Completed	Fri 26/05/00	100%
Water heater - Edwinstowe centre	In Progress	Fri 26/05/00	50%
Roof - Beauty salon, Grange	Completed	Fri 26/05/00	100%
Fire exit door - Edwinstowe centre	Completed	Fri 19/05/00	100%
Floor covering - Beauty salon, Grange	Completed	Thu 18/05/00	100%
Drains - Edwinstowe centre	Completed	Fri 12/05/00	100%
Signs - Grange	Completed	Fri 12/05/00	100%
Grange - porta cabin 133, leak	Completed	Fri 12/05/00	100%

Examples of maintenance record sheets

Emergency procedures in the event of a fire

Fire evacuation drills should be practised on a regular basis to ensure that people know automatically what to do in the event of an evacuation. For places of public entertainment, large shops and department stores the fire drill should be practised every six months. They should be done on an annual basis for industrial and commercial premises.

Fire drills should be conducted to simulate fire conditions; that is, one emergency route should be obstructed and no advance warning should be given, other than to specific staff for the purposes of safety. The fire alarm should only be operated for a fire drill on the instructions of the management. The fire brigade should not be called for the purposes of a drill but a joint exercise *can* be arranged with the local fire brigade. The fire alarm itself should be tested on a weekly basis to ensure that it is in full working order.

Fire And Emergency Evacuation Procedure

Practice emergency evacuations are held during the first few weeks of a new academic year to ensure that staff are familiar with the procedure and observations can be made of the evacuation in order that improvements can be made if required. It is essential that all staff and students are aware of and understand the following procedures that should be brought to attention as part of any induction programmes.

On discovering a fire:

1 **Operate alarm** at nearest point and ensure evacuation of anyone under your control.
2 **Call the fire brigade** by dialling 9-999 on any telephone.
3 **Notify**, by suitable means, **emergency staff** at the Assembly Point of location of fire, action taken and any people unaccounted for.
4 **Do not attempt to fight fires unless you are sure that it is safe to do so.**

On hearing the Alarm Bell:

The senior member of staff present will *immediately* evacuate the room and accompany the people present to the Assembly Point (as indicated on the notice in each room) and retain the people there.

Note for Evacuation - leave the building by the nearest exit, closing doors behind you, making use of the emergency exits. Do not necessarily follow the normal routes which can lead to congestion. Where necessary make way to the assembly areas around the perimeter of the campus buildings.

Be prepared to deal with any unforeseen problems, and take account of the circumstances of specialist rooms, e.g. 'switching off' equipment.

Having assembled, **everybody remains in their places and follows instructions given by the emergency staff.**

Talk about it

How do you feel when the fire alarm goes off? Have you ever had to evacuate a building when it wasn't a practice?

Protective clothing for staff

The Health and Safety at Work Act states that:

'Employers' duties include, so far as is reasonably practicable, that the handling, transport, use and storage of articles and substances is done in such a way as to prevent risks to health and safety arising and to make sure that protective equipment and clothing is provided and used when required'.

In places like theme parks and theatres this will include the lifting and storage of heavy equipment and the use and storage of chemicals used for cleaning.

FIRE ALARM SYSTEM – RECORD OF TESTS

Date	Fire Alarm		Automatic Door Releases	Automatic Detectors		Remedial action taken	Signature
	Call point Location or Number	Satisfactory Yes/No	Satisfactory Yes/No	Location or No.	Satis. Y/N		

FIRE INSTRUCTIONS AND DRILLS – RECORD OF WHEN GIVEN

Date	Instruction Duration	Fire Drill Evacuation Time	Personal/Department Receiving Instruction/Drill	Nature of Instructor etc.	Observations of Instructor etc.	Signature

It is important that careful records are kept regarding the fire alarm and fire drills

What sort of duties in travel and tourism organisations would require staff to wear protective clothing? What sort of protective clothing would they have to wear?

Rules about handling cash and cheques

Although this has been covered on page 261 it is worth reiterating that cash and cheque transactions present security hazards, such as fraud or theft. To ensure that this does not happen, it is important always to check the validity of any cheque card and make sure all cash is counted in front of the customer. If it is a large amount of cash, ask a colleague to check it with you.

Make sure tills and cash boxes are never left open and at the end of the day all the tills must be emptied and the cash locked away securely in the safe or deposited in the bank.

A manual for all staff members

A staff manual should include everything connected with the health and safety of employees, the public and any contractors working in the facility.

It should cover all the important points about health and safety in a simple, easy-to-read format which can be studied at staff training sessions. As procedures change, the manual should be updated.

For further information about health and safety, access the Health and Safety Executive website on www.hse.gov.uk or write to them at:

HSE Information Centre, Broad Lane, Sheffield S3 7HQ

European Union Directives on health and safety at work

These regulations cover a number of issues, as shown in Figure 8.16.

Figure 8.16 EU regulations cover a variety of health and safety issues

These regulations are especially relevant to tour operators and travel agents whose employees have to use visual display units (VDUs) in their work. Employers now have a duty to:

◦ plan display screen work so that there are breaks or changes of activity

◦ provide information and training for display screen users.

Employees using VDUs are entitled to free eye tests. Employers may also contribute towards the expense of special glasses when normal glasses cannot be used.

CASE STUDY – Apex International

Our Safety First Policy

As a company. Apex International places great emphasis on the safety and well being of its entire staff and customers. Our commitment to this extends beyond the working environment. This booklet is primarily to ensure the health and safety of the working environment, although a lot of the information can be used at home as well. The aims are to reduce risks and identify potential problems in your everyday working life. Vigilance, care and continued commitment to safe working practices can help to achieve a safe working environment.

Make every area in your working life an accident-free zone.

Accidents are no accident – they are caused.
You can minimise them by observing the following guidelines. The first section is a reminder of the possible causes of accidents that may occur at work – and how to avoid them. The second section offers practical guidance on how to steer clear of difficult situations whilst travelling in work vehicles.

We have produced this booklet to help you to recognise potential accidents and suggest how to prevent them happening to you and our customers.

REMEMBER - Safety is everyone's responsibility.

Health and Safety at Work

Introduction

Take the time and effort to read this handbook, it will help you to understand:
- Your new company's health, safety and security standards, policies and procedures.
- Why they are important.
- How you can help to maintain them.

If you have any questions or need further explanation your manager will be happy to assist you.

What you can expect from us.

Our policy is to ensure that:
- Your health, safety and welfare are protected at all times.
- Our customers' health, safety and welfare are protected.
- No employee's activities at work cause danger to colleagues or customers.
- All parts of the workplace, equipment and work systems are safe and properly maintained.
- All materials and substances used in the workplace are handled, stored and transported in accordance with approved safety procedures.

We will provide:
- All appropriate safeguards.
- Proper supervision, instruction and training.

What we expect from you:

Whilst at work we expect you to:
- Always act in a safe and responsible way.
- Take reasonable care of your own health and safety.
- Take reasonable care of the health and safety of others.
- Have respect for the working premises and equipment.
- Follow all the health, safety and security standards set out in this handbook.

In whatever career we choose to follow, everyone has the right to work in a safe and healthy environment, and it is our duty as your employer to provide this.

Maintaining Health, Safety and Security

We as a company aim to:

- **Provide a safe, enjoyable working environment for our staff**

This is made possible if we all make sure premises are clean and rubbish free at all times, also all stairs and floors must be cleaned at least once per day.

- **Keep yourself alive longer**

You make this possible as employees using common sense. Just by being aware of the dangers and removing risks to yourselves you can prevent serious injuries. For example, you wouldn't put your wet hands near an electrical socket.

- **To our staff**

As your employers we have a caring nature and uphold all legal obligations. By implementing legal obligations we prevent/reduce the risk of injury and improve performance because no one has to have any time off work through injury. For example, following guidelines to ensure no employee gets repetitive strain injury.

- **To our customers**

We provide a safe and enjoyable environment and therefore provide customer satisfaction. If the customers do not think the place is safe they will not come back. If the place of work is very dirty, and there is rubbish everywhere, customers will not return and may even tell their friends and family.

- **Ensuring customer care**

Health and safety must be a major part in customer care. It is very important to look after our customers' needs, for example, not exposing our customers to risk of injury. An example is making sure anything that had been spilt on a slippery floor is immediately cleaned up.

- **To public relations**

If we were to ignore health and safety regulations we would be prosecuted and this would be very bad for our excellent reputation, also accidents are very costly, it is easier to do things right in the first place.

- **To the protection of the environment**

These days everything that an organisation does can have an effect on the environment and for this reason it is important to make sure waste is disposed of properly and safely.

- **To the organisation**

Maintaining health, safety and security can:

- Prevent prosecution and or fines.
- Improve efficiency and effectiveness.
- Improve productivity and profitability.
- Provide a very positive organisational image.

Fines and being sued for criminal and civil negligence can be costly:

- Bad publicity.
- Loss of income.
- Time consuming.
- Annoying.
- Petty.
- Counter productive.

The thing to remember is always to take care and help us to maintain all our heath, safety and security procedures.

Slips and Trips

- Loose equipment
  - *Store equipment correctly*
- *Cracked tiles or worn carpet*
  - *Always keep good maintenance routines*

- *Wires and leads*
  - *Check for fraying and ensure they are not left across walkways*
- *Baskets and equipment*
  - *Always follow good housekeeping guidelines*

Questions
- What do you think of this as a staff manual?
- Should anything else be added?

Answers to 'Try it out'

Page 257
Your answers may have been:
1 Manager
2 Assistant manager
3 Park supervisor
4 Ride manager
5 Ride attendants.

Page 261
The correct order is:
1 cash
2 check
3 customer's
4 money
5 watermark
6 forgery
7 desk or counter
8 till
9 receipt.

Answers to 'Talk about it'

Page 258
Your answers may have included:

- hotel manager – customer care, management training, finance, IT

- holiday rep. – language, customer care, basic numeracy

- marketing assistant – numeracy, IT, customer care.

Unit 8 Assessment

Take a summer break

Scenario

As part of your ongoing training in the travel and tourism industry, your manager feels you should broaden your experience of the industry. He has asked you to produce a report showing your understanding of two or more travel and tourism organisations and their working practices.

What you have to do
Obtaining a pass grade

You must give a full and accurate introduction to the organisations describing the sectors they are in, their aims and objectives, organisational charts, the types of employment available and how customers' needs are met.

You then have to give a full and clear explanation of the administrative and financial functions of the organisations and describe the relationship between their functions and their aims and objectives.

Your work should also include a brief description of any relevant health, safety and security legislation. Finally, your report must show your ability to enter transactions on a simple financial document.

Obtaining a merit or distinction grade

Your work must show a logical and well-structured format and a well-designed organisational chart that clearly shows main job roles and lines of responsibilities.

You must clearly express ideas and information to demonstrate a thorough understanding of the operation of two of the organisations' functions. Finally, your report must show your ability to complete calculations on a simple financial document.

Obtaining a distinction grade

Your report must show a thorough understanding of the relationship between the functions and the organisations' aims and objectives. Secondly, you must demonstrate a high level of understanding of the importance to the organisations of complying with health, safety and security legislation and an evaluation of the health, safety and security procedures of the organisations.

Finally, to complete your distinction, your work must show your ability to complete more complex calculations on a simple financial document.

Resources

Useful websites:

www.museums.gov.uk Provides a gateway to UK museum information. Features an extensive range of facts and figures.

www.visitbritain.com Contains much information about tourism

www.englishtourism.org.uk Useful facts and figures on tourism

Specialist journals such as *The Travel Trade Gazette and Leisure Management* are helpful.

You may also find it useful to visit travel agents, hotels and transport organisations asking for information that could be useful to your assessment. It is a good idea to phone to make an appointment before your visits.

Key skills available

Communication: C2.1a, C2.1b
Improving own learning and performance: LP2.1, LP2.2
IT: IT2.2, IT2.3

Unit 8 Test

1 Why must travel and tourism organisations offer excellent customer service and value for money?

2 Who or what are principals?

3 What are independent travel agents?

4 Give five examples of accommodation providers.

5 Why do you think B & Bs are so popular?

6 What do tour operators organise?

7 What do domestic tour operators provide?

8 What skills and qualities does a travel agent need to possess?

9 Apart from selling holidays, what else can travel agents arrange?

10 How are museums financed?

11 What is the main aim of an organisation like Lunn Poly?

12 Why do travel and tourism organisations employ part-time and seasonal staff?

13 Why is it important to have well-trained staff?

14 Why do travel agents keep track of holiday bookings?

15 What security procedures should be followed when handling cash?

16 Name five responsibilities of employees according to the Health and Safety at Work Act.

17 What is the purpose of risk assessment?

18 Why is it important to have a regular maintenance programme in a leisure centre?

19 How often should a fire alarm be tested?

20 What is a staff induction programme?

Impacts of leisure and tourism

This unit examines the impacts the leisure and tourism industry has on people, the economy and the environment. It gives you the opportunity to investigate what can be done to make the most of the positive impacts, while at the same time reducing the negative effects.

The unit is written in four sections. Section one looks at the impact of leisure and tourism on people. Section two looks at the impact on economies and section three examines the impacts on the environment. The final section looks at ways of reducing the negative impacts of leisure and tourism.

This unit builds on the work you did in Unit 1: Investigating leisure and tourism.

What you need to produce

You will be expected to show your understanding of the impacts, both positive and negative, of leisure and tourism on people, the economy and the environment, and you will also be required to offer solutions to reduce the negative impacts. You will need to select a suitable locality which has sufficient leisure and tourism facilities and investigate its impacts on the local people, the economy and the environment.

This unit will be assessed only through your portfolio work. The grade you achieve in your portfolio assessment will be your grade for the unit.

Introduction

Leisure and tourism has three main impacts. The first is on the people who live in the area, sometimes known as the host community. It gives local people the opportunity to mix with a variety of people from different parts of the country and world. From a more negative viewpoint, the prices of food, houses and services may be forced up due to the popularity of the area with the result that local people may not be able to afford to live there.

The second impact is that it can bring in extra income to an area which means that new jobs and new businesses can be created. Many of the new jobs may be only seasonal or part time making it difficult to support a family.

The final impact is the environmental impact. Areas of countryside can be conserved and protected by management projects with the aim of allowing visitors to enjoy the countryside without harming it. This increase in visitors, however, may also cause an increase in traffic congestion and noise and litter pollution.

This unit examines in detail both the positive and negative impacts leisure and tourism has on people, the economy and the environment.

Impacts on people

Leisure and tourism can have a dramatic impact on people and the way they live their lives. For example, a tourist attraction may give local people more facilities to enjoy. At the same time, these facilities can create traffic congestion and extra noise.

But first of all let us look at the positive impacts which leisure and tourism has on people.

Better quality of life

Some of the beneficial effects of tourism on people can include those shown in Figure 13.1:

In some developing third world countries, tourism can offer greater opportunities for local people, especially those who transfer employment from agriculture to the service industry. This may give

Figure 13.1 Tourism can have some positive impacts for people

people higher wages, and better job prospects. It is possible that tourism can also give people – both tourists and locals – a broader outlook, which could result in less prejudice towards different cultures.

Tourists themselves can be altered by their holidays. They may change their views of other cultures and develop a respect for the culture and tradition of other people. They may feel a need to conserve and promote the culture of the area they visit. Tourists may return home and influence friends and relatives with their new views and opinions.

Talk about it

Have you ever experienced a different culture to yours while on holiday? What were the cultural differences? Tell the rest of the group about it.

More leisure and tourism facilities for local people

Tourism can create wealth in an area. This wealth can help provide facilities for local people, such as those shown in Figure 13.2.

These facilities, often provided initially for the enjoyment of tourists, give local people the chance to improve their quality of life and take part in community activities for the benefit of everyone.

Figure 13.2 Tourism can lead to improved leisure facilities for everyone

Additional facilities will enhance the scope for recreation for local people. There would not be the volume of trade nor the financial support for such facilities without the tourist trade.

Many local businesses would not survive without the tourist population and the money which is brought in from outside. Without tourists, some areas would certainly be poorer. The existence of shops and businesses supported by tourism helps to keep communities alive and active.

Try it out

Imagine a big new theme park was being created in your area. How would local people react to the addition of such a facility? Try to think about both positive and negative reactions and make a list of all of them.

Talk about it

What sort of businesses are created by tourism? Are some just for tourists and others for local people? What businesses would cater for the needs of everyone?

Public transport could be badly affected without the boost in population brought about by tourists. It could lead to a reduction in the frequency or the number of bus and train services. It could also reduce the viability of taxi businesses in rural communities if there is less demand for taxis. The loss of or reduction in transport services would cause some severe hardship, especially for rural communities.

Businesses whose survival is aided by such tourist population increases include:

- retail – shops
- accommodation – hotels, guest houses
- catering – cafés, restaurants, public houses
- transport – buses, taxis
- entertainment – cinemas, theatres.

Many rural areas of the UK have little industry and hence little opportunity for employment. Agriculture is becoming increasingly mechanised and, with reductions in subsidies, employment in the industry continues to fall. Tourism can provide much-needed employment and can help to keep young people in a rural community; otherwise they are likely to move away, resulting in rural depopulation. Employment created through tourism can help to maintain a social balance in rural populations.

Health and fitness opportunities

Tourism can offer local people a better quality of life. It can provide greater opportunities to improve their health and fitness if they are able to use the facilities developed for tourists.

SNAPSHOTS

Lorenzo

Lorenzo is 42 and has been a keen runner for the past ten years. A year ago he damaged his Achilles tendon and so he hasn't been able to do much running. During this time he piled on the weight due to his inactivity.

A new swimming pool opened in Lorenzo's locality recently, so he decided to pay it a visit. He became a member and now swims regularly. Swimming is ideal for him because it supports all of his body weight, minimising the strain to his muscles.

He says,

'This new facility has enabled me to get back to a good level of fitness and I've lost weight as well. Plus I'm enjoying a new form of exercise. I can't say enough for the centre. It's fantastic.'

Try it out

Think of a place you have visited either on holiday or a day trip. What sort of facilities were provided for tourists like yourself there? What sort of impact do you think that visitors – like you and your friends and family – might have on a holiday destination?

Nowadays many people are taking more interest in leading a healthy lifestyle; possibly because exercise and a sensible diet can help to relieve stress, reduce weight and increase fitness.

The development of public sector leisure centres and private health clubs, brought about by the demand for a healthier lifestyle, has meant there are now more health and fitness opportunities than ever before. People of all ages can enjoy such activities as aerobics, fitness training and jogging. The leisure and tourism industry has helped provide facilities for people to become fit and to lead a healthy lifestyle.

The chance to meet new people

For many people going away on holiday is an opportunity to make new friends. Likewise, if you join the local leisure centre and use it on a regular basis, you will meet up with people who will become friends.

The leisure and tourism industry is people-based. Working in leisure and tourism can lead to friendships with colleagues and the public. Imagine working in a tourist information centre. In one day, you could meet up to a hundred new people from different parts of the country and different parts of the world.

Better community spirit

Facilities like village halls and community centres provide a focal point where people can meet. They are usually run by volunteers for the benefit of the local community.

A community spirit can be built up if volunteers work together to organise activities for the local community such as playgroups, yoga, flower arranging or bridge. Not only do these facilities encourage socialising they can also provide a place where people have the chance to learn a

SNAPSHOTS

Dave

Dave is studying sports science at Manchester University. He comes from Scarborough and, during the summer break, he hires out deckchairs to holidaymakers.

He says,

'I must have one of the best student jobs going. I get to meet loads of people from different parts of the country. Their one aim is to enjoy themselves so there is always a great atmosphere in the town.

'Everyone from Scarborough in the tourist industry knows that without tourists there would be no businesses. As a result, they all help each other out by looking after tourists, promoting the town and generally working together. This builds up a community spirit in the town.

'After work, I go down to our brand new leisure centre and swimming pool for a work out and swim. The town wouldn't have been able to support such a massive leisure centre without tourist income and tourist use of the facility.'

Talk about it

What do you think we mean by the term 'community spirit'?

Read the following paragraph and discuss it in the light of your answer.

'A huge fire completely gutted the town's biggest hotel. Fortunately no one was seriously injured. However all 90 staff are now without work and 300 holidaymakers have nowhere to stay. The town relies a lot on tourism. It's a sad day for the resort. So, community leaders have all rallied round with friends and family and everyone has somewhere to go. Many of the staff have been able to find temporary employment and some will be able to go and work in the hotel company's sister hotel. In fact, it's all become quite good fun!'

How has community spirit helped in this situation?

new hobby, like photography, still life painting, or a sport like table tennis.

Talk about it

How does the leisure and tourism industry in your area help to promote a community spirit? What do you think could be done to make things better?

Negative impacts of tourism on people

Tourism does, however, bring with it some negative social and cultural impacts. For example, there are often major cultural differences between tourists and the residents of the places they are visiting. These differences could include food, language, dress and moral codes.

Around 80 per cent of all tourists come from twenty of the world's richest countries. This has often meant that people who have had little experience of the western way of life are suddenly brought into contact with another culture – with the possible result that their own culture may be absorbed and lost. In the same way, local languages and dialects can be lost.

Regional arts and crafts can die out because the people who followed them choose to take up new careers in service industries. Where they survive, their character is often changed in order to meet tourists' demands and the need to produce larger numbers of items for sale.

As local economics adapt to exploit the potential of tourism, traditional industries which have played a large part in forming both the landscape and the culture of native people, such as agriculture, often go in decline because of labour shortages.

Tourism can create other problems for host communities. An area which is reliant upon tourism economically, or is inflicted with heavy numbers of visitors, can suffer great damage to its society. Tourism can lead to:

- loss of privacy
- overcrowding
- a dilution in religious values

Clovelly in North Devon has a resident population of approximately 400; in the summer holiday period it can receive almost 400,000 visitors. This swamping of a tiny village, with its steep narrow cobbled streets, can give an unpleasant feeling of over-crowding and make residents feel that they are 'living in a goldfish bowl'.

⋄ a demeaning of traditional activities

⋄ noise and distraction

⋄ a dilution of local dialect or language

⋄ a distortion of local customs

⋄ a loss of traditional facilities

⋄ a disproportional increase in land and house prices.

Large numbers of visitors from other areas, having different social values, will have an influence on those of the host community. They may, for example, cause shops and facilities to remain open on a Sunday when they traditionally closed. They will also expose local people to different aspirations and expectations. This may well lead to changes in the community.

Traditional activities may be demeaned if scorned or taken as an amusement by visitors. Alternatively, they may be exaggerated or distorted to provide entertainment.

Land prices in poor rural communities can be inflated by tourism which demands land for speculative development. This can prevent its purchase for other developments, which may be more beneficial. Second or holiday home purchases can inflate house prices and prevent young people from being able to buy or rent houses in the area in which they have grown up.

Overcrowding on the roads and on transport

Leisure and tourism travel is mainly by car or coach. Cities like York, Bath, Canterbury, Lincoln and London suffer from traffic congestion because so many people want to visit these places.

A centre of historical interest like York now has pedestrianised areas but some of the streets are still open to traffic and unfortunately they are not suited to the size and volume of this traffic. People may want to avoid paying car park fees so they drive round looking for a place where they don't have to pay – so adding to the problem.

CASE STUDY – Thailand

Tourism, the world's biggest industry, reaches parts of the world other industries never reach, and often with tragic consequences. This is the case in Bangkok, in Thailand, for instance, where young girls – usually from poorer rural areas – are lured into prostitution. Thailand's once unspoilt and idyllic tropical islands now have airports and their seas are polluted by hotel sewage. The traditional 'Thai smile' is a thing of the past.

This is not to say that tourism does not bring much-needed employment and foreign currency to the area, but it is quite understandable that local people are becoming disillusioned with 'the industry without smoke stacks'. When locals are

forced out of their towns because of inflated prices for food and land, or when children can earn more in a day from begging and looking 'cute' for photographs than their fathers do from a week's fishing, whole societies are inevitably turned upside down.

Mr Kaewnou from Thailand explained,

'Prices have gone up, our lives have been commercialised and our traditions destroyed. It is no longer my home, just a tourist spot.'

Questions

• Do you think that this situation was inevitable?

• Could tourism in Thailand have been managed better? How?

Table 13.1 Impacts of tourism on people

Positive	Negative
• Improved quality of life for people	• Overcrowding – could lead to reduction in quality of life for those living in the area
• More facilities for local people	• Traditional jobs, e.g. in farming, might be lost to more attractive jobs in tourism
• Opportunity to learn about other people's beliefs and values	• Loss of traditional crafts in favour of mass-produced souvenirs
• Community spirit can be built up	• Increase in crime rates such as public disturbances, burglaries
• More income generated by tourism	• Local customs and traditions may disappear. Loss of local language and culture

The same problem arises in the countryside. Areas like the Lake District and the Yorkshire Dales are unable to cope with the vast number of cars and coaches on a hot summer's day. Narrow country lanes become clogged up, traffic comes to a standstill and traffic jams appear on even the motorways leading to and from tourist destinations.

Increased crime

Crime in holiday resorts can increase if local residents see tourists as wealthy targets. One example of this is in Miami, Florida, which often receives bad publicity. In places where the local population may be poor, the only benefit of tourism for them has nothing to do with job creation and wealth but is an opportunity to gain from tourists illegally.

On the other hand, it is sometimes tourists who are responsible for increased crime rates. This may be, for example, as a result of destructive behaviour – usually associated with too much alcohol.

Both the positive and negative impacts of tourism can be summed up in Table 13.1.

It is important to realise that the so-called experts still disagree over the positive and negative impacts of tourism on people. On the one hand, many people argue that traditional cultures have been ruined by the introduction of western values. Others will agree that tourism does more than simply bring prosperity to an area, it brings people who live there into contact with the western ideas of capitalism and democracy, thus broadening their outlook on life. Whatever the case, all leisure and tourism enterprises must

CASE STUDY – Ibiza

San Antonio in Ibiza is probably one of the liveliest and best known resorts for young people throughout Europe. Unfortunately, it presents a very negative image in terms of drugs, violence and abuse of alcohol. The image may be exaggerated by the press but unfortunately it has stuck. There is no doubt that tourism creates jobs and wealth for San Antonio. However, this must be balanced against the negative image which has been created.

Questions

• What do you think the local people might feel about the poor image of their town?

• What positive and negative impacts has tourism had on San Antonio?

Talk about it

Imagine the area where you live is to have a huge tourist attraction built there. What would be the negative impacts of that attraction on the people who live near it?

make sure that their activities have the minimum negative impact on local people.

Impacts on economies

Leisure and tourism has a major effect on the economies of countries and local areas. Looking on the positive side, the income generated by overseas visitor helps to pay for new attractions. At a more local level, the money coming in from leisure and tourism activities creates jobs and wages for local people.

Positive economic impacts

The leisure and tourism industry can have some positive effects on the local economy and we will look at these first.

Generating income for businesses, councils and individuals

Tourists who are drawn to an area by an attraction will spend money on accommodation, food and drink, entertainment, travel, gifts and souvenirs. This 'generated' spending on goods or services will benefit the businesses in which the money has been spent. The additional revenue will allow the employment of people who will in turn themselves have money to spend locally. Money generated elsewhere, which is brought into a region by tourists, will continue to circulate (until it has been used to buy goods or services from outside the area), so creating a more buoyant local economy.

Income is the money generated through wages and salaries, rent and profits, even taxation of leisure and tourism activities such as VAT on travel services, hotel accommodation or on a meal out. The sum total of all incomes in a country is called the national income and the importance of

the tourist industry to a country's economy can be assessed by looking at how much income it generates. It is estimated that tourism generates around £9 billion a year in foreign exchange alone, so you can see its economic importance.

The contribution of tourism to a local area is often greater than is at first apparent because of something called the **multiplier effect**. This suggests that money spent by tourists on goods and services provided by local people, helps to boost the local economy because a proportion of the money originally spent then circulates among other local businesses. The money generated by tourism 'multiplies' because of all the local people who themselves then have more money to spend on goods and services – a very positive economic impact.

Local councils can also benefit from tourism in that tourists spend their money in council-operated facilities such as leisure centres, museums and car parks.

A key sector of the economy

Given its size and the wide-ranging benefits it brings, tourism is one of the most important sectors of the economy:

- Tourism accounts for 7 per cent of the nation's jobs. It is as big as the British construction industry.

- The Joint Hospitality Industry Congress has forecast that up to a million new jobs could be created, directly and indirectly, by tourism and hospitality in Britain in the next decade.

- The industry's direct economic contribution is equivalent to over 5 per cent of Gross Domestic Product (GDP), the same as the energy and water-supply industries.

- The World Travel and Tourism Council has estimated that the total economic impact of tourism, when indirect contributions such as hotel construction and car rental are included, could be as high as almost 12 per cent of GDP.

- Tourism accounts for a quarter of our overseas earnings in services, more than any other service industry. It earns more from exports than North Sea oil, financial services or civil aviation.

- The UK is fifth in the World Tourism Organisation's league table of international earnings from tourism.

- Tourism provides a substantial proportion of the revenue that supports our heritage and culture. It is one of the main engines for economic regeneration in many areas and it makes a major contribution to the quality of life, supporting facilities and services from which local communities benefit.

Employment: creating jobs both directly and indirectly

The creation of income from tourism is closely bound up with employment. Almost one in every fourteen people in the world is employed either by the tourist industry or as a result of the tourist industry. In the UK, tourism provides employment directly or indirectly for around 2 million people.

The multiplier effect on employment is similar to that on income. If tourists visit an attraction, jobs are created directly at that attraction, for example ride operators at a theme park. These jobs support families, who in their turn require their own goods, which gives rise to indirect employment in the area for shops, pubs, leisure centres, clubs etc.

Travel and tourism acts as an economic catalyst:

- job creation – travel and tourism creates jobs more rapidly than most other industries

- multiplier effect – a wide range of other activities are stimulated by travel and tourism development, including infrastructure projects, agriculture, manufacturing, information technology and communications

- new business, formation – travel and tourism encourages small and medium-sized businesses which in turn help to generate service and entrepreneurial skills

- services stimulus – spin-offs like insurance, financial services and communications emerge alongside travel and tourism development, creating further job and training opportunities.

Talk about it

What will be the multiplier effect created by:

- a new airport development

- an out-of-town shopping development

- a new arts centre built by National Lottery funds?

Promoting a positive image of an area

Tourists travel to destinations in order to see the man-made or natural attractions of the area. When these attractions are kept in good condition it creates a positive image for the area and ensures that people will continue to go to the attractions. This is good for people in the area as it can promote a sense of pride and can increase the popularity of an area.

Regenerating derelict sites

Many tourist attractions and facilities have been built on derelict sites, thus putting waste land to good use. Two examples of this are Albert Dock, Liverpool and Meadowhall, Sheffield.

Negative economic impacts

Leisure and tourism does, however, have some negative economic impacts. It might be worth asking how an industry that creates so many jobs, generates so much wealth, and helps so many people to enjoy themselves, could be anything but a force for the good.

But things are not quite that simple. For example, tourism has totally transformed the Costa del Sol in Spain. Tiny fishing villages like Torremolinos have been turned into huge resorts, filled with high-rise blocks and holiday villas. Nightclubs, discotheques, restaurants and bars have appeared to service the entertainment needs of hundreds of thousands of European visitors to the area.

Tourism may have bought prosperity to the Costa del Sol, but it has also caused radical changes to the landscape and the culture. Such changes are

The differences between old and new can be startling

CASE STUDY — The Albert Dock, Merseyside

The multi-million pound restoration of Liverpool's historic dockland is spearheading the renaissance of Maritime Merseyside. Shopping pavilions, restaurants, office and conference facilities, a Maritime Museum, watersports and riverside promenades have already transformed a group of waterfront Victorian warehouses into one of Britain's most exciting tourist attractions - Albert Dock. Its warehouses and dock basins, restored by the Merseyside Development Corporation and the Arrowcraft Group, attract three million visitors a year.

Liverpool began as a muddy tidal creek and became the British Empire's second port. Its history is charted in one of the exhibitions of the Merseyside Maritime Museum. The Museum also has floating exhibits, working displays, demonstrations, a unique 'Emigrants to a New World' gallery and a Maritime Records Centre. In the Maritime Park, there is a reconstructed Piermaster's House and working cooperage, Pilotage House and Boat Hall, a schooner and pilot cutter.

The Tate Gallery opened at the Albert Dock in May 1998. Sister to the Tate in London, the Gallery houses the National Collection of Twentieth Century Art and will feature special international exhibitions.

The Mersey Ferries are one of Liverpool's oldest waterfront activities. Started in 1150 by the Birkenhead monks, ferries run frequently between the historic Pier Head and Wirral. The former P & O passenger terminal at Prince's Dock, close to the Pier Head, is now Liverpool Museum's Large Objects Collection and has working models of cars, coaches, engines and machines. The Museum has also developed one of only four Technology Testbeds in the country, to explain the principles of basic science with display models.

Watersport activities are fast becoming one of Maritime Merseyside's most exciting attractions. The Liverpool Watersports Centre, based at Albert Dock, is putting the restored dock basins to new use with activities such as sailing, rowing, canoeing and wind surfing.

Question

How does this development contribute to Liverpool's image?

not confined to Spain. Wherever tourism has made a significant contribution to a local economy, the environment and the lifestyle of the inhabitants have altered in response to the influx of visitors. This holds true for the UK as it does for Spain, the Greek Islands, Turkey and other well-known tourist areas.

Higher prices for goods, services and houses

The prices for goods and services in tourist areas are often increased during the peak season in order to gain maximum tourist income. This is a big disadvantage for local people, especially those trying to buy their own home. Second houses or holiday cottages in rural areas are used by tourists for only a small proportion of the year, for example 'weekenders'. This can make property much more expensive and put it out of reach for locals, especially first-time buyers.

More local taxes

Extra charges may be levied on the local community in order to finance facilities and services that are for tourists. Local people may have to pay for facilities like tourist information centres, brochures and leaflets which are mainly for tourists, through their council tax.

Loss of local services

Tourist areas usually have gift shops and cafés to meet the needs of tourists. In fact, tourist areas can often lose local shops in favour of retail outlets geared for tourists. This means that local people may have to travel further to buy goods, therefore increasing the costs of travel. It is also not very convenient when you can buy several different types of fudge from your local shop but not a loaf of sliced bread!

The balance of payments

The leisure and tourism industry contributes to the country's balance of payments. This is the term given to describe the difference in value between a country's imports and its exports. Imports are the products we buy from other countries. Exports are what we sell abroad.

CASE STUDY — Sunil and Indira

Sunil and Indira used to run a fruit and vegetable shop. They worked hard and built up a good business, which was used by many local people, six days a week, 12 hours a day. The quality of their food was good and fairly priced.

However, the business rates which they had to pay the council rose dramatically and they decided that they just weren't going to be able to make a future out of the shop for their family.

Sunil and Indira thought long and hard about the business opportunities available to them. Theirs was a thriving tourist area, but tourists did not usually buy their food because they had their meals in their hotels and guest houses. So they decided to diversify into tourist ware: T-shirts, mugs and mats, as well as some home-made sweets and cakes, for which they had to have a special licence. They had to work hard during the holiday season but soon found themselves doing well.

Indira says,

'We got to the stage where the fruit and veg business was only making ends meet. So far so good in the souvenir shop. Sunil is now talking about buying a corner shop to go back to the part of retailing he enjoys most, but I would keep the souvenir shop. We are determined that it will work.'

Questions

• What risks are Sunil and Indira taking?

• What types of shop do you think attract tourists? Are there any in your own area?

285

If the UK exports more than it imports it is said to have a surplus balance of payments, which is good for the economy. However, if we import more than we export there is a deficit in our balance of payments.

In a way, we 'export' tourists, people from the UK going abroad, who spend their money there. To balance this outflow of money, we try to attract visitors from overseas to come here. We can also try to encourage more domestic tourism.

The difference between UK residents spending money abroad and UK residents and foreign tourists spending money in the UK is called the **travel balance**. A healthy travel balance will help boost our balance of payments.

Income from tourism is known as 'invisible earnings' in that we do not import and export goods in exchange for money. Rather, tourism can be seen as a service which tourists either buy overseas or in the UK.

SNAPSHOTS

Phil and Inga

Phil and Inga go to France for their annual holiday. They use the Channel Tunnel to get across to France and then drive down to the South of France. They

stay in a hotel. They change their sterling into francs and spend money on souvenirs, meals and entertainment. All the money they spend is lost from the UK economy and goes into the French economy. This is bad for the UK's travel balance, but good for the French economy.

Fritz and Heidi

Fritz and Heidi are German tourists travelling round the UK for three weeks. They stay in bed and breakfast accommodation and in Youth Hostels, buy meals and souvenirs. The money they spend here goes into the UK economy and helps boost the balance of payments.

Talk about it

Nowadays, more and more people are going overseas for their holidays. Why do you think this is? What effect does this have on the economy?

Try it out

How do you think Britain can reduce the deficit in its travel balance?

You might have suggested:

- encouraging more overseas visitors to come to the UK
- encouraging more UK residents to take their holidays in the UK.

How could we achieve these suggestions?

Impacts on the environment

There are both positive and negative impacts on the environment from leisure and tourism.

Positive impacts

When tourism and the environment exist together without any harm being done, the environment benefits. Canals, parks and gardens which were once derelict areas have been developed to provide extra attractions for tourists.

When a building or area is given a new lease of life and is 'reborn' as something quite different from its original state it is said to have undergone a form of rehabilitation. Many buildings and areas have been saved through their rehabilitation as tourist attractions or as tourist accommodation. For example, derelict factories have found new lives as museums, industrial land has been used for garden festivals and a variety of castles and stately homes falling into disrepair have been given new lives as accommodation for tourists. Such examples demonstrate how tourism can benefit the environment by saving what otherwise might have been lost completely.

Negative impacts

Much of the damage to the environment as a result of tourism is caused simply by the volume of tourists arriving in these destinations. On a worldwide scale, tourism can have harmful effects on habitats such as coral reefs, and rainforest and mountain areas. In the UK, the countryside, the coast, towns and cities all suffer from the pressure of increasing numbers of tourists and their transportation.

The money and impetus which tourism brings to an area can help to restore and maintain the environment, but the pressure that it brings is often detrimental. Pressure from tourism can damage an environment by:

* causing physical erosion

* creating litter

* increasing pollution

* increasing congestion

* disturbing wildlife

* reducing habitats

* altering landscapes

* increasing demand for catering and other services

* encouraging inappropriate development.

Tourists inevitably congregate at both natural and man-made attractions. Most man-made attractions are designed and built to cope with the pressure. But often the infrastructure and approaches to such attractions cannot cope, and a popular attraction on a public holiday can cause a large traffic jam which leads to noise, pollution and frayed tempers.

Natural attractions can often suffer problems because of increasing tourism. In areas where visitors leave their cars and continue on foot, the damage to grass or heather can lead to erosion. Some areas like sand dunes and peat bogs are fragile and, particularly vulnerable. The pressure not only damages wildlife habitats but also disturbs and endangers wildlife itself.

Visitor numbers often boost local populations and so increase the pressure on sometimes over-stretched services. Water supply is often a problem in tourist regions during summer months, and the larger numbers also add to the sewage. The result is an increased pressure to

CASE STUDY – Local development protest

Protestors are still fighting to halt a planned £3 million hotel on an island in the River Trent at Newark. A petition against the development of Parnham's Island, off Millgate, was presented to Newark and District Sherwood Council.

It was presented by members of the Millgate Conservation Society, who are urging the council's planning committee to turn down the hotel plans. The issue is due to be discussed at the next planning meeting.

The society's main reason for objection is the impact on the environment, with traffic, leisure, heritage, wildlife and tourism being affected. This is despite the fact that the size of the hotel is smaller than first intended, being reduced from 125 to 69 bedrooms. The original plans, proposed more than a year ago by developers, also included provision for a helicopter pad and conference facilities, which are no longer proposed.

People who want to voice their views about the scheme can attend a public meeting in Newark Town Hall. Planning Committee members have been invited.

Source: *Newark Advertiser*

Questions

* If you were a member of the public attending this meeting, what objections would you have to this development?

* Imagine you were defending this development as a builder. What would your arguments be?

build more reservoirs, flooding more valleys and letting less water fill the rivers.

A major problem is the pressure to develop, possibly inappropriately, facilities to meet tourist needs. Tourists need shops, toilets, car parks and entertainments which often have to be developed without the means to meet such demands. Local building styles may be difficult and expensive to replicate, and there may be insufficient space to site buildings sympathetically or screen them with trees. Developments in a modern, efficient style can completely ruin the visual character of an old village or town; if visible from a distance the entire landscape can be spoilt.

The biggest problems are often caused by commercial developments which have been designed to attract trade rather than fit into the townscape or landscape. Neon signs and gaudy ill-considered building can destroy what the tourist initially came to appreciate.

Reducing negative impacts

The negative impacts of leisure and tourism can be experienced in many different places all around the world. For example, if you live near a Premiership football ground then nearly every week you will know about traffic congestion and noise brought on by the crowds. Similarly, if you were a resident of a Caribbean island your way of life would be affected by foreign tourists. It is now time to see if these negative impacts of leisure and tourism can be minimised in any way. We will look at some of the possibilities.

Managing visitors

One way of restricting access to a tourist attraction and thus managing the visitor flow is to increase the price of admission during peak times. For example, the most popular time to visit a castle could be a Sunday afternoon in summer. Different scales of pricing may make some people think again and plan their visit during cheaper off-peak periods, for example weekdays or Saturday mornings.

However, this raises a moral issue, particularly with heritage sites. Is it right to prevent the less well-off from having access to their heritage?

One of the most straightforward ways of controlling visitors to an attraction and preventing congestion and overcrowding at certain points is to provide clearly defined routes around the site, by using signposting and waymarked walks. In an historic building, this may mean operating a one-way visitor flow, and roping off certain sensitive and fragile areas so that the public can still see them – but only from a distance, in order to prevent damage.

In the countryside, the provision of footpaths – which may or may not be fenced – can encourage tourists to keep away from easily damaged areas. Highway authorities are legally required to erect a signpost at every point where a footpath, bridleway or byeway leaves a road, unless the parish council agrees that is not necessary. The sign must state whether it is a footpath, bridleway or byeway, and may give a destination and distance. Although many new signposts have been put up in recent years, many paths are still not yet signposted.

In order to help people follow the route, signposts or waymarks can be installed along a right of way. The latter are small marks (often arrows) that are fixed or painted to stiles, gateposts and sometimes trees. The Countryside Agency has designed an arrow with standard colours – yellow for footpaths, blue for bridleways and red for routes that can legally be used by vehicles. But you may find other colours and designs used locally.

In addition to waymarking, there are many routes for walkers and riders that are marked with their own distinctive symbols to identify the route and help people to follow it. These may be used alongside, or incorporated into, the waymarking arrow. An acorn symbol is used to waymark the Agency's National Trails. If you are following a particular route from a guidebook or leaflet, you may encounter other waymarked paths that are not part of that route.

Waymarking schemes carried out by volunteers, landowners and parish councils can help the highway authority to protect and enhance the rights of way.

Managing traffic

Public transport operators and local authorities have done much in recent years to improve public transport, both in terms of better services, clearer information and promotional activity. However, many people still imagine that it is impossible to travel in Britain's countryside without a car. In fact, the opposite is often true. Britain has one of the most comprehensive rural public transport networks in the world.

Rather than facing the increasing stress of traffic congestion in both town and countryside, visitors' enjoyment could be much increased by taking the train and bus. More information is now available which can give ideas about the many places you can reach by public transport and where to get further details.

With so many tourists visiting beautiful countryside areas, heritage sites or theme parks, it has become necessary to try to control the impact of people and traffic on the environment. One initiative is to try to persuade people to use public transport instead of using their own cars. Places like Lincoln, Nottingham, York, Oxford and Cambridge, which attract thousands of visitors each year, have introduced 'park and ride' schemes, using buses which reduce the amount of traffic in the city. Bus lanes that are given priority have been introduced to try to ensure that people using public transport do not suffer needless delays. In the same way, there has been increased investment in local rail services, again in the hope of reducing traffic congestion in cities.

Cyclists can take in the beauty of the scenery without causing pollution

take in the beauty of the scenery. Away from the countryside, cycleways in the city are another means of encouraging people to get round the area in safety and without causing pollution.

One useful way of controlling visitor flow is the siting of car parks. Most people are reluctant to walk more than 500 metres or so from their car. At a countryside property, siting a car park close to where you wish to concentrate visitors, or further away from where you do not want them, can be a useful way of controlling visitor flow.

Environmental action

Some tourist organisations are now trying to reduce the negative environmental impacts created by tourism. Those who provide accommodation have realised that the environment in which they work and welcome tourists may suffer if nothing is done to reduce the negative, crowded impact of tourism. Some examples to show what large hotels from Thailand, South Africa and Venezuela are achieving in their communities are given in the case study on environmental initiatives.

Legislation

There is a variety of legislation which has a direct effect on leisure and tourism and we will look at different items in turn.

Look it up

What sort of traffic management schemes are in operation in your town? Find out in small groups and discuss in class whether you think they are effective or not.

If not, what would you do about the traffic?

Some of the busiest roads in the National Parks are closed to traffic at peak times. This is aimed at encouraging hikers and cyclists to enjoy the countryside in complete safety and explore areas away from noise and traffic pollution.

Another initiative which many councils have introduced is the provision of cycleways in countryside areas. Obviously, cyclists do not cause pollution and it gives them the opportunity to

CASE STUDY – Environmental issues

Phucket Yatcht Club Hotel and Beach resort, Thailand

A major environmental education initiative is underway in Thailand, centred on the Phucket Yacht Club Hotel and Beach Resort. The hotel's environmental committee is holding workshops for groups as diverse as the Thai Hotel Association, hotel staff, provincial police and primary school teachers and children, on environmental problems and solutions. Police have been invited in order to build their understanding of the importance of enforcing environmental regulations. The Thai Ministry of Education is using the project to drive its new environmental curriculum into schools so that children grow up to live and care for the environment.

Sun Game Lodges, South Africa

Sun Game Lodges, a division of South Africa's leading hotel company, Southern Sun, sees neighbouring communities as the key to sustainable tourist development.

Michel Girard, General Manager, points out that attracting tourists to sensitive habitats places a great deal of responsibility on the hotel operator: 'Wildlife cannot live on emotional handouts. We realise that it is our greatest asset.'

Game reserves stand to benefit financially from income from the lodges and the policy is to limit the size of developments and the number of tourists at any one location. But perhaps the jewel in the crown of the company's environmental policy is its approach to supporting the local community.

'The construction of the Zululand Tree Lodge near Hluhhluwe is a good example of community involvement,' says Michel.

'The local chief and community leaders were consulted and involved in the construction project with one person in each household assured of a job.

The central theme of our approach to ecotourism is that local people benefit directly from the tourist industry,' explains Michel. 'We want to avoid our lodges becoming an island of opulence in a sea of poverty.'

The Hotel Inter-Continental Valencia, Venezuela

Some unexpected guests have turned up at the Hotel Inter-Continental Valencia – a colony of 236 iguanas! Research undertaken by experts in the hotel's grounds discovered the iguana colony thriving in the hotel garden, which provided plenty of big trees and lots of sun.

The hotel was classified as an official refuge for endangered species and a special dietary regime for the iguanas was established to keep the colony in health. Hotel staff have attended special courses to play a part in the protection of the colony.

Street signs have been erected in the hotel grounds warning drivers to look out for some unusual pedestrians and the hotel has also created a series of marketing initiatives, such as T-shirts and postcards, to promote this refuge for one of the world's oldest creatures.

Questions

- How can tourist attractions benefit from encouraging guests to look after the environment?

- What are the consequences of leisure and tourism organisations neglecting the natural enviroment?

Source: *Green Hotelier*, International Hotels Environmental Initiative

Holidays with Pay Act 1938

Between the two World Wars, time and opportunity for leisure increased and transport improved. Holidays had become more widespread and, after the passing of the 1938 Holidays with Pay Act, the majority of workers received paid time off work.

The National Parks and Access to the Countryside Act 1949

This Act defined the National Parks, set out their objectives and set up machinery for their creation and management. The Act created a National Parks Commission – later to become the Countryside Commission – to designate certain areas as National Parks and Areas of Outstanding Natural Beauty. Under this Act the first ten National Parks were created between 1951 and 1959.

Countryside Act 1968

This led to the development of countryside recreation and conservation activities, including the provision of country parks and picnic sites. The Countryside Commission was set up under this Act. There was increasing interest in the countryside and a government spokesman at the time said,

'The movement away from the towns during people's leisure time is constantly growing and it is taking place in mid-week as well as at weekends, and in spring, autumn and winter as well as summer. No one wants to halt this process.'

Development of Tourism Act 1969

This Act established the British Tourist Authority and the English, Scottish, Welsh and Northern Ireland national tourist boards. It was the first Act ever to be specifically devoted to tourism.

Environmental Protection Act 1990

This Act was introduced to deal with the control of pollution from man-made sources, such as factories, and the protection of natural resources, such as natural landscapes and wildlife. Local authorities were given new responsibilities with regard to controlling litter and noise and were given the powers to impose stiffer penalties for pollution caused by litter and noise.

Powers were established to ban dumping waste at sea. A register was also set up to identify contaminated land.

By-laws

Local authorities have the authority to enact by-laws within their area of jurisdiction. Because they are local they will therefore vary from place to place. A failure to observe them is dealt with in the criminal courts, generally by fines.

By-laws are sometimes used to limit what you may do or how you behave in public places and on rights of way. For example, you may be restricted from flying noisy model aircraft. A by-law may require dogs to be kept on a lead or off the beach (perhaps at certain times of the year) or prohibit cycling on a right of way.

Codes of conduct

Codes of conduct are a set of guidelines that a governing body like the English Tourism Council or The Countryside Agency may devise, laying down standards for people to follow (see 20 Tips for Visitors below). Probably the best known code of conduct is the **Countryside Code** which asks people to:

- enjoy the countryside and respect its life and work
- guard against all risks of fire
- fasten all gates
- keep dogs under control
- keep to public paths across farmland
- use gates and stiles to cross fences, hedges and walls
- leave livestock, crops and machinery alone
- take litter home
- protect wildlife, plants and trees
- take special care on country roads
- make no unnecessary noise.

Source: English Tourism Council

ETC 20 tips for visitors

Customer charters

Customer charters set out the minimum levels of service customers can expect when using facilities or buying goods and services. A charter indicates clearly what organisations aim to achieve in terms of looking after customers.

Education

There are various ways in which education can be used to reduce the negative impacts of leisure and tourism. Initially, students at school can learn about social, economic and environmental issues during humanities, geography and leisure and tourism lessons.

Documentaries on television about the destruction of the environment can make people more aware of these negative impacts. Staff like countryside rangers can give advice, information and guided

Customer Charter: The Countryside Agency

In the Countryside Agency, we want the very best for rural England and the English countryside, its people and places. We will:

- lead with research and advice

- influence others, especially central and local government

- demonstrate ways forward through practical projects.

Our aims are:

- to be professional and informative, fair and efficient, and undertake our work promptly and courteously

- to make sure our work and services provide good value for money

- to be open in everything we do and to consult you on matters that affect you

- to improve standards of service wherever possible

- to put matters right when things go wrong.

Our standards of service

All our staff have guidance on how to conduct themselves when dealing with customers and the general public.

Identifying ourselves

We aim to provide an efficient, friendly and helpful service to you – our customers. Our staff will clearly identify themselves in correspondence and when answering the telephone, meeting members of the public and attending meetings where they are not well known to other participants. They will wear name badges on appropriate occasions.

Source: Countryside Agency

tours, illustrating the need to protect the environment.

Some nature reserves have educational facilities on site and some facilities have residential accommodation where students can stay for a few days and carry out project work. Information

Reducing negative impacts

leaflets and brochures can also raise people's awareness about the impacts of leisure and tourism.

All leisure and tourism organisations must try to ensure that their activities have the minimum negative effect on local people.

Talk about it

In small groups, identify a leisure and tourism venue in your area (or even outside your area if you have enough information) and consider:

- how it manages to function with minimal negative impact on the environment

- if the way it is organised, i.e. setting, access etc., could be improved. How could this be done?

SNAPSHOTS

Solomon

Solomon is a countryside ranger in a country park. Part of his job is to talk to students about the environment within the park and set them projects to complete.

He says,

'Many people who come to the park have little idea of the wildlife that exists here and the way we try to conserve the park's natural beauty. The guided tours and question-and-answer sessions help the public learn about what we are trying to achieve. Some of the questions I get asked are quite varied, for example:

"Have you ever been chased by a wild boar?"

"How often do trees shed their leaves?"

"Do the snakes bite?"

'At least these questions show they are interested in the countryside!'

CASE STUDY — Blackpool

Positive impacts

Today, Blackpool attracts millions of visitors per year, generating £435 million – more than all the Greek Islands and mainland Greece combined! There are 3,500 hotels, guest houses and holiday flats, containing 120,000 holiday beds – more than the whole of Portugal!

Blackpool has lots of attractions and activities for holidaymakers. However, it must be remembered that local people also use these facilities. The people who work in the tourism industry in Blackpool – hoteliers, traders, publicans, deckchair attendants, tram conductors – come face to face with holidaymakers every day. They have a chance to meet and get to know people. In fact, some holidaymakers return to the

same hotel every year because they have got to know the owners and know they will be well looked after.

Local people not involved in the industry also get the chance to meet tourists in their local pubs, leisure centres or restaurants. Local people are often friendly towards tourists because it is in their nature to be so and also because they know tourists are good for the town.

There are many positive social effects of tourism for people in Blackpool. The tourists benefit from the facilities and activities provided for them, but the locals have the same opportunity to use these facilities where they have the chance of meeting new people or learning new sports or hobbies. Senior citizens can benefit from the public transport system built up around tourism, students benefit from getting summer jobs – e.g. hiring out deck-chairs or working on the trams – and local businesses benefit from tourist money.

Negative impacts

Blackpool does get busy - very busy. It gets overcrowded and the tourists tend to stare into people's windows. This can make life difficult for local people who want to go about doing their everyday things. The roads get blocked with the increased volume of traffic, which can increase journey time to work, and the trams and buses and trains can be full of tourists. There are obviously no special seats for local people.

The increase in visitors can lead to more crime – whether from rowdy or drunken holiday-makers causing damage or locals committing theft. Unfortunately, this is inevitable wherever there is a massive influx of visitors determined to enjoy themselves.

Most jobs in Blackpool are geared towards the tourism industry and this has spread to the surrounding villages, which are now doing a roaring trade in B & B's and

afternoon teas. This 'modern' tourist industry has tended to take over traditional jobs.

Positive economic impacts

Thousands and thousands of holiday-makers bring in millions and millions of pounds. Money is spent on food and drink, accommodation, tourist attractions, souvenirs, taxis, entertainment and presents. As a result, local businesses are booming, money for tourism is invested in new facilities which everyone can use and improved services can be provided by the local council – all because of the money brought in from holiday-makers.

Job creation is another 'plus' – whether it is a summer job in a café, a permanent job on the Pleasure Beach or a waiter in a restaurant, there are many job opportunities available. These opportunities arise directly as a result of tourism. However, jobs are also created in the supplies of goods and products necessary to run the hotels, for example butchers, dry cleaning for hotel laundries and factories for souvenirs. People in local shops, newsagents, bookmakers or clothes shops all gain extra income from tourism and jobs created in these areas are as a result of the money brought in.

Promoting a positive image of Blackpool

Blackpool is booming. It has a reputation as Britain's number one fun spot. It attracts political party conferences, business conventions, international superstars and millions of tourists. It is famous and known throughout the country as one of the most popular seaside resorts.

The image it creates is one of vibrancy, life, energy and activity. These are all very *positive* images. Old, derelict sites like the airfield (now Stanley Park) have been developed, in the case of the airfield into a magnificent zoo, an exclusive hotel and an international standard golf course. The old open-air swimming pool is now the Sandcastle leisure pool, where a 'tropical temperature awaits the castaways who land on Blackpool's treasure island, the water is warm so you don't mind a soaking as you soar down swirling slides and frantic flumes'.

Tourism has transformed Blackpool. Its partytime image is aimed at entertaining everyone – families, 18–30s and senior citizen activities. It has managed to keep up with the times to stay as the number one seaside resort in Britain.

Negative economic impacts

However, there are also some negative impacts:

- Prices tend to rise in tourist areas such as Blackpool for goods, services and houses – including increased local taxes and higher business rates.

- Seasonal work – Blackpool isn't open as a resort all year round so tourist jobs tend to be available only from April to November.

- As long as the economy is stable, people will be able to visit Blackpool. However, external factors such as increases in taxation, interest rate rises or if there is an economic recession would mean that people have less disposable income to spend on places like Blackpool.

- Loss of local services – shops which may previously have served the local community are now geared towards tourism, selling gifts and souvenirs or afternoon teas, rather than vegetables or groceries.

- Jobs in tourist areas are notoriously low paid, which means those employed have to cope in a relatively expensive area.

Positive environmental impacts

- Derelict areas have been cleaned up and regenerated.

- Old buildings, especially disused barns in rural areas, have been converted into restaurants and accommodation.

- Blackpool town centre has been pedestrianised, some areas covered in, and decorated with flowers. Good signposting and one-way systems have made traffic flow easier.

Negative environmental impacts

- Traffic congestion occurs along the promenade and en route to Blackpool on the M55.

- Problem of litter along the promenade, beach and town centre.

- Increased air and noise pollution.

- Pollution in sea – increased demands for water particularly sewage systems in 'high' season.

Reducing the negative impacts

- Managing visitors and monitoring the number of tourists, good signposting; peak and off-peak prices throughout the year.

- Managing traffic – the M55; public transport – trams and park and ride.

- Legislation – codes of conduct and customer charters.

- Education – to reduce negative impacts of leisure and tourism.

Questions

- Why is Blackpool so popular?

- Would you like to live there? Give your reasons.

CASE STUDY — The Mediterranean

It is a long way from the UK, but everyone is familiar with the Mediterranean as a holiday destination.

Key facts about the Mediterranean

- One-third of all tourism takes place on the shores of the Mediterranean.

- In 1999 there were over 100 million visitors to this area, making it the favourite destination in the world for tourists.

- It is the dirtiest sea in the world. The air over many resorts is polluted.

- The Mediterranean is almost completely enclosed by land. Because of this, and because the tidal range is generally less than one metre, the beaches are particularly susceptible to pollution.

- Almost half the world's oil pollution is found in the Mediterranean.

- Wildlife habitats are under threat. A major cause of the near-extinction of the monk seal is because it breeds near tourist resorts.

- The number of tourists and the world population generally is set to rise in the next few decades, putting intolerable pressure on this beautiful region and the resources of land and sea.

Questions

- What are the negative environmental impacts of tourism on the Mediterranean

- Why do you think this area is so popular with tourists?

- What factors need to be taken into account when planning the future tourist use of this area?

A final word

It is important to remember that the impacts of leisure and tourism on people and the environment can be both positive and negative. A new holiday centre may create jobs in an area and provide new facilities but at the same time it could cause traffic congestion resulting in air pollution and noise, and possibly some damage to the environment.

The creation of a balance between the positive and negative effects is a challenge for the leisure and tourism industry. When you start your career in the leisure and tourism industry you can play a part in reducing the negative impact of tourism. First of all you at least will be aware that tourism can have a negative effect on the environment, even though it can be beneficial too. Many people are unaware of or at least ignore this fact. Think about how you can influence your friends, family or even your employer! You could encourage the use of public transport, cycling to work, being careful about the use of resources or even making sure you have recycling facilities in your place of work.

The knowledge you will gain from studying this interesting area can really benefit the world around you if you use it well and sensitively.

You are about to embark on a fascinating career. Good luck and happy travelling!

Unit 13 Assessment

Going green

Scenario

There is currently much debate about the positive and negative impacts that leisure and tourism provision can have. The arguments for positive impacts include job creation and income for local people, whereas the negative effects include traffic congestion and air pollution. You have to come up with a balanced look, which shows both positive and negative effects in a selected locality.

What you have to do
Obtaining a pass grade

1 Choose a locality that interests you – it could be your local area, somewhere else in the country or even overseas. Give a full description of the leisure and tourism facilities in that locality.

2 Describe the positive and negative impacts that leisure and tourism can have on the people, the economy and the environment of the chosen locality.

3 Choose one organisation in this locality and show how it is trying to reduce its negative impacts on the area.

4 Finally, choose a leisure and tourism activity in the area and describe the positive and negative impacts it has on the people, the economy and the environment.

Obtaining a merit or distinction grade

Your work must show:

- an independent approach to research

- a description of practical measures taken by users of the activity and the organisation to limit the negative impacts they have on the locality

- a logical and well constructed presentation of your findings, communicating your ideas clearly and concisely and using appropriate technical terms when necessary.

Obtaining a distinction grade

Your work must show:

- an in-depth and independent investigation of the locality explaining clearly the reasons why negative impacts occur and any measures being taken to limit the impacts

- an evaluation of the positive and negative impacts that leisure and tourism facilities and activities have on the chosen locality, with practical and realistic suggestions for improving the locality.

Resources

Local authorities usually have an Economic Development Section, or the equivalent, which can provide up-to-date information on where future leisure and tourism development is possible and areas where there should be no possible leisure and tourism development.

Local newspapers usually have information on local planning issues. On a national level, Sport England has information on facility provision and development.

Other resources on the Internet are English Heritage, the Countryside Agency and the National Tourist Offices.

Key skills available

Communication: C2.3
IT: IT2.3
Improving own learning and performance: LP2.1, LP2.2, LP2.3

Unit 13 Test

1   How can leisure and tourism offer people a better way of life?

2   Name three jobs in the leisure and tourism industry where you would meet new people.

3   List three ways that can help to overcome traffic congestion.

4   Some country areas suffer from erosion caused by the number of visitors. Is this a: a) positive social impact; b) negative economic impact; c) negative environmental impact; d) positive economic impact?

5   Why is there an increase in crime during peak season at holiday destinations?

6   What do we mean when we say jobs are created 'indirectly' by leisure and tourism?

7   What part can leisure and tourism play regarding the reclamation of derelict land?

8   The Glastonbury Festival is held every year in Somerset for three days and large crowds are expected. What will be the positive and negative effects of this?

9   What are the positive economic impacts on a local area by the development of a new tourist attraction?

10   Why does the price of goods rise in tourist areas?

11   Nowadays people are becoming more and more aware of the need to protect the environment. What steps can be taken to protect it?

12   Which type of impact is involved when B & B's and guest houses employ extra staff for the summer season?

13   How can education promote ways of reducing the negative impacts of leisure and tourism?

14   What is sustainable tourism?

15   How could we encourage car owners to use public transport?

ABTA Association of British Travel Agents. Founded in 1950. It represents both tour operators and travel agents. ABTA maintains contact with government and organisations concerned with the development of travel and tourism both in the UK and abroad.

Activity holidays These range from water-skiing and mountaineering to walking and golf. Their popularity has increased in recent years due to the concerns about health, fitness and exercise for the majority of the population.

Advertising A promotional technique aimed at raising awareness and boosting sales. Advertising is carried out in magazines and newspapers and on television, radio, billboards and posters. The most powerful, yet most expensive advertising is television as it attracts big audiences.

After-sales service After a sale is made, customer service continues in the form of dealing with complaints or contacting customers to find out if they were pleased with the product.

Agenda Items of business to be considered at meetings, e.g. Apologies for absence, minutes of last meeting etc.

Areas of Outstanding Natural Beauty (AONB) These areas were set up under the 1949 National Park and Access to the Countryside Act. Although they are popular destinations for leisure and tourism, these areas are designated as such for conservation rather than recreation.

Bed and Breakfast (B&B) An establishment providing sleeping accommodation with breakfast, usually operated by private households. Very common in Great Britain.

Body language This refers to non-verbal communication where our emotions and feelings are transmitted when we're not even aware of it.

Branding Using a name or trade mark to make individual products easy to distinguish from competitors' products and to establish them in the minds of existing and potential customers.

British Tourist Authority Set up in 1969 under the Development of Tourism Act to encourage overseas tourists to visit the UK.

Brochure Promotional material involved in selling holidays, short breaks, coaching courses. A good brochure should convert an enquiry into a sale.

Budget estimate of income and expenditure over a stated period of time, e.g. annual budget.

Business travel Trips and visits made by employees in the course of their work, including attending meetings, conferences and exhibitions.

Byelaw Regulation made by a local authority or corporation e.g. a town or railway company.

Cabin crew These are the flight attendants on aircraft, who serve meals, attend to passengers' needs and look after their health and safety.

Catchment area An area from which the majority of users of an attraction, facility or service are drawn. Local theatres and swimming pools draw most users from within a few miles. Many theme parks and out-of-town shopping complexes have regional catchment areas.

Chair Individual who chairs a meeting, sometimes referred to as the Chairman or Chairperson.

Charter flights Charter aircraft are commissioned for a specific period of time and usually fly with a full load of passengers, mostly holidaymakers, to a given destination.

Check out This is the procedure for guests vacating their rooms and settling their accounts in hotels.

Check-in This has two meanings. First of all it is the term most commonly used to denote the latest time by which passengers are required to report at the airport terminal before flight departure. The term is also used in hotels where the latest check-in time denotes how late a reserved room will be held before it is let to another guest, unless the hotel is notified of late arrival.

Checkout This term refers to the desk or counter where accounts are settled.

Closed Circuit Television (CCTV) Observation by camera.

Code of conduct A set of guidelines laying down standards, to which members of a profession or association are expected to follow. In the UK, the Association of British Travel Agents provides codes of conduct for retail travel agents and tour operators

Commission Payment made to travel agents by principals. The payment made is a percentage of the value of the booking. The percentage of commission paid varies from one principal to another.

Committee Group of people, usually elected officials e.g. Chair, Secretary, Treasurer etc. Formed to work together to achieve certain goals such as running an event.

Commuter Someone who travels regularly, usually daily, between home and work.

Compulsory Competitive Tendering (CCT) The Local Government Act 1988 requires local authorities to subject a number of services to competition, including management of sports and leisure facilities.

Computer Reservations System (CRS) Computer based interactive electronic data systems providing direct access to airlines, hotels and other operators' computers, to establish product availability, make reservations and print tickets.

Consolidation Combining separate holiday bookings into a single trip in order to increase numbers.

Country park Established under the 1968 Countryside Act. An area for recreation usually near a town.

Countryside Agency A government department set up to, amongst other things, promote understanding of the countryside.

Curriculum Vitae (CV) This is a written description of an employee's qualifications and personal details which can be submitted when applying for a job.

Data Protection Act, 1998 Sets out to offer protection to living individuals in respect of personal data about them which is held electronically.

Database A collection of files, information and records, stored on computer or manually on cards. Customer details are kept on a database for quick and easy retrieval of information.

'DINKY' (double income no kids yet) couples with high disposable incomes and no family responsibilities who lead an affluent lifestyle.

Direct mail Mailing of promotional materials to potential customers. They may be previous customers but increasing use is made by many organisations of available lists of specifically targeted prospects. The mail received is sometimes known as 'junk mail'.

Domestic tourism Travel and tourism by residents of a country to other areas within the same country.

Dual use A term used when the same facility is used by two different organisations, for example a leisure centre is used by a school during the day and by the public in the evenings and weekends.

Duty free The term applied to goods on which tax or customs duty is not levied. It also applies to the shops at international airports, ports and ships in which passengers travelling abroad can buy such goods.

English Tourism Council A public-sector organisation, aimed at promoting tourism in England.

Equal opportunities An expression emphasising the rights of different people in society to be equal, regardless of age, sex, race or religion.

European Union (EU) This was established by the Treaty on European Union (Maastricht Treaty) in 1993. The Union seeks to promote further European integration.

Event This refers to activities with significant requirements for planning, resources and evaluation specific to the event.

Excursion A short journey taken for pleasure, usually lasting less than a day.

External customers People from outside the organisation who pay to use facilities or buy products and services.

Facility This is used in a leisure and tourism context to refer to equipment, buildings and structures of the natural environment where opportunities for leisure and activities are provided.

Fast-food outlet A limited menu outlet offering quick counter and takeaway service. Many fast food outlets are operated by organisations with brand names, e.g. McDonalds, KFC, Burger King.

Fax machine This produces a high speed electronic transmission of an exact copy of a document from one location to another using the national and international telephone networks.

Fly/drive The term used to describe package holidays where the client flies out to a holiday destination and a hire car is waiting for them at the airport.

Front of house This is the point where customers first come into contact with staff, usually at reception. Front-of-house staff are responsible for welcoming customers, giving them information and promoting the organisation.

Full board This term normally includes a room and three meals per day.

Grand Tour From 1670 onwards, young gentlemen from the UK were sent on the 'Grand Tour' of the cultural centres of Europe to widen their education before seeking positions at Court on return. Places like Venice, Florence and Paris were visited. The people on the Grand Tour were introduced to different cultures and societies.

Hazards This refers to anything that has the potential to cause harm.

Health and Safety At Work Act, 1974 This Act lays down the duties of employers and employees in providing a safe working environment in the workplace.

Heritage This refers to a country's monuments, countryside, culture, traditions and historic buildings. Overseas visitors come to the UK as it has a particularly strong heritage.

Holiday 'rep.' Employed by tour operators to inform clients about the local area, deal with any enquiries and to 'meet and greet' clients.

Home-based leisure This refers to leisure activities that take place in the home environment such as watching television, DIY, gardening and reading.

Hospitality A term used to describe the hotel and catering sectors of the leisure and tourism industry.

Host community People who live in a place where other people go for their holidays.

Human resources A term which includes all aspects of staff training, recruitment and discipline.

Incentive schemes Schemes offering rewards to successful employees e.g. subsidised travel, gifts.

Incoming tourism People coming from overseas to this country for their holidays.

Induction training Training new employees receive at the beginning of their employment, introducing them to the company's policies.

In-flight catering Preparation and serving of meals by air cabin crew to passengers.

Institute of Sport and Recreation Management (ISRM) An organisation promoting and providing guidelines on management of sport and recreation facilities.

Internal customers These are the people working within the same organisation who work and support each other. An internal customer should be treated as well as an external customer.

Internet This is a means of communicating with people worldwide for business or pleasure. It is sometimes known as the 'Information Highway'.

Invoice A statement of goods received by a supplier showing the outstanding balance owed by the customer.

Job description This is a written description of the roles and responsibilities of a job. The aim is to detail areas of responsibility, so that people are appointed to a job on the basis of information rather than a 'gut feeling'.

Job satisfaction This is the degree to which employees enjoy their work and feel motivated to continue to do so.

Job specification This is a written document which lists the skills and characteristics of the type of person needed to do a job successfully.

Joint provision The joining of two or more groups to design and construct a facility for mutual benefit.

Kite mark A mark placed on goods, showing that they conform to standards of quality specified by The British Standards Institute.

Laptop A portable computer which can be used without mains power supply. It gives the user freedom to access information outside of the office environment.

Leisure time The time available to people after they have completed duties and necessities such as work, sleep and household chores.

Local authority Refers to the local town or city form of government. It can also be used for county governing bodies.

Locality For the purposes of this qualification, this normally refers to the area local to students, within which the college or school is situated. However, the term may be applied flexibly to indicate any defined geographical area appropriate to the tasks set in the assessments.

Long haul This describes destinations beyond Europe, e.g. the Far East, USA, Canada and Australia.

Maintenance schedules These are work programmes connected with checking equipment and machinery which help prevent breakdowns and reduce the need to replace expensive equipment.

Market segmentation This is a method of dividing potential customers into groups with distinctive characteristics using criteria like age, gender, income, area of residence and lifestyle.

Marketing The process of finding out what customers need and want and then developing, promoting and distributing these products to them at a profit.

Marketing mix These are the factors which an organisation can vary to reach its sales targets including the product, price, place and promotion, the 4 Ps of the marketing mix.

Marketing research This involves the collection of information by personal surveys, telephone questionnaires etc. to assist in decisions relating to the marketing process.

Multiples National multiples are those travel agencies which have offices spread across the length and breadth of the UK, for example Lunn Poly and Thomas Cook. Regional multiples are travel agencies which are concentrated in one region of the country. Many have grown from a one-shop family business and have spread across the locality to a natural boundary, e.g. a county line.

Multiplex A very large cinema complex in which a number of films can be shown at the same time in different auditoriums.

National Lottery Set up in 1994 by the government. The main aims are to provide extra funds for a range of good causes including sport, the arts, charities, heritage and millennium projects.

National Parks These have been created to preserve the natural beauty of the countryside and to promote its enjoyment by the public.

National Trust This charity helps preserve buildings, gardens, and other sites of historic and architectural importance. It protects over 600,000 acres of land and over 400 buildings and gardens in England, Wales and Northern Ireland.

Observation This marketing research method involves looking at how customers behave. Information gained from observation can help make decisions about packaging or influence the choice of point of sale of materials designed to attract the attention of customers.

Occupancy rates A means of measuring how successful a hotel is based on the number of rooms occupied.

Off-peak times Less busy times in leisure centres, e.g. weekdays, or times outside popular holiday periods, which can make the package cheaper.

Organisational charts A diagram showing the division of responsibilities within an organisation, the lines of authority and the channels of communication.

Outgoing tourism People leaving their own country to take a holiday or trip abroad, e.g. someone from Manchester spending two weeks in Ibiza.

Overheads These are the costs attributed to the running of an organisation, e.g. rent, insurance, salaries and energy costs.

Package holidays These are put together by tour operators who charge an all-inclusive price for the holiday, including transport, accommodation, transfers and the services of a courier.

Park and ride Schemes which encourage motorists to park on the outskirts of cities and continue their journeys into the centre by bus. The aim is to reduce traffic congestion.

Peak times These are the times in leisure centres when there is the greatest demand for activities, e.g. 6pm–10pm and weekends or popular holiday times, e.g. July and August for summer sun or January to March for skiing.

Point of sale Items displayed where the customer makes a sale e.g. at the counter.

Primary marketing research (field research) This type of research is undertaken by the organisation itself to obtain information about its customers, products and services. Research is carried out using questionnaires, interviews and observation.

Principals The general term used to describe organisations with whom a travel agent may do business. Examples include tour operators, airlines, ferry companies, car-hire firms.

Private sector organisations Profit-making organisations such as hotels, health clubs and restaurants.

Profit This is the price charged for a product less the cost of making it.

Public Relations (PR) This is concerned with creating a good image for an organisation. It is most often associated with building up good working relations with the media.

Public sector organisations Largely funded by central or local government, these organisations aim to provide a service to the community and include facilities such as tourist information centres, art centres and libraries.

Questionnaire A document used in marketing research to gain information from customers which may help with future product development.

Recreation Any pastime undertaken by an individual for enjoyment outside that part of the day known as 'working time'.

Repeat business Customers who are happy with the product or service usually return for more of the same.

Risk assessment An assessment of how likely an incident is to happen and how to prevent it happening.

Sales promotions Special offers designed to produce a fast response from the customer, e.g. 'two for the price of one this week only'.

Scheduled flights These operate to a timetable and are committed to fly whether or not the aircraft is full.

Secondary marketing research (desk research) This is when information is gained from existing sources such as reports, statistics and general market surveys.

Self-catering holidays These are holidays where accommodation is provided but clients choose to make their own eating arrangements.

Serviced accommodation Accommodation such as a hotel where food and service are provided.

Sponsorship This enables organisations to promote their products and services through an association with an event, function or facility. Through sponsorship, organisations gain opportunities to advertise to a wider audience.

Sustainable tourism A term applied to all forms of tourism which are in harmony with their physical, social and cultural environment in the long term.

Target marketing All organisations need to know who their existing and potential customers are (i.e. their target market) so that they can provide the right products and services.

Time share This is a furnished and serviced holiday home used by a number of people, each of whom is entitled to occupy the property for one or more predetermined periods each year.

Tour operators They package and sell holidays which are offered in a brochure with a fixed price for accommodation, transport and transfers.

Tourism This is the temporary, short-term movement of people to destinations outside the places where they normally live and work. It also includes the activities they do once they have reached their chosen destination.

Transfers A cheque issued to a person in one country which can be exchanged by the cheque holder for local currency in another.

Travel agents These book holidays and travel arrangements for clients. They also offer advice regarding destinations, passports and visas. They receive their income from this service in the form of commission from principals with whom the bookings are made.

Travellers' cheque A cheque issued to an individual in one country which can be exchanged by the cheque holder for local currency in another.

Virtual reality Leisure facilities can use audio and visual technology to create an impression of real, dramatic events.

Visa A stamp in a passport giving the holder permission to enter or leave a country.

Visiting Friends and Relatives (VFR) When visiting friends or relatives there is usually no accommodation charge. The visitor still however spends money on goods and services like restaurants and pubs.

Voluntary sector organisations These are managed and operated by volunteers. They are often non-profit making or charitable. Examples include local sports clubs and amateur dramatic societies.

Welcome Host-Customer Care A training programme and qualification administered by the English Tourism Council. The training is geared towards dealing with customers.

White knuckle rides Examples include Oblivion at Alton Towers or The Pepsi Max Big One on Blackpool Pleasure Beach. They are intended to provide thrills and excitement by their changes in speed, height and direction.

Youth hostel A facility for travellers, including students, young people and the general public, which provides inexpensive accommodation and sometimes food.

Answers to tests

Unit 1

1 Visitor attractions.

2 It offers participation in sport and physical recreation.

3 Leisure tourism.

4 The main aim of an organisation in the private sector is to make a profit for its owners and shareholders.

5 Tourist Information Centres are in the public sector.

6 A summer playscheme might provide day trips, nature walks, camping and sports activities.

7 Outdoor activities centres are usually located in the countryside for ease of access to natural features, so that participants can take part in activities such as mountaineering and canoeing.

8 The best place to locate a theme park is the countryside, where there is plenty of land.

9 Careers officer, trade magazines, local newspapers, people you know who already work in the industry.

10 Rock climbing, sailing, mountaineering and canoeing.

11 Development of a tourist attraction may cause traffic congestion and noise, and may spoil the surrounding area.

12 Only you can answer this.

13 A receptionist would probably require communication, IT and telephone skills. They should also have a good personality and be friendly, polite and professional.

14 Apart from holidays, you can purchase insurance, exchange currency and organise car hire at the travel agents.

15 Ramps, wider car parking spaces, lifts and special toilet facilities can all help the disabled visitor.

Unit 2

1 Brochures are produced to encourage people to attend.

2 Promotion.

3 This is an example of sales promotion.

4 Mailshots are an example of direct mail.

5 Business lunches are aimed at business people.

6 This is market segmentation by gender.

7 People between the ages of 18 and 30 are most likely to be targeted.

8 The café might advertise in the college and offer discounts on food and drink for students.

9 Reduced day-time prices might benefit the unemployed.

10 Evaluation.

11 Sales of refreshments will increase, courses could be advertised, parents may accompany children and so additional interest can be built up.

12 The promotion could be evaluated by counting the number of vouchers brought into the theatre.

13 Press releases, an advertisement in the local newspaper and posters around town.

14 By seeing if attendance figures have increased as a result of the advertisement and by asking customers if they saw the television adverts.

15 Planning.

Unit 3

1 Foreign tourists/non-English speaking tourists.

2 Giving clear instructions about safety face-to-face.

3 They are either happy with the service or they are passive complainers: they don't say anything – they don't come back.

4 Because they will be able to answer any questions customers may ask, for example about courses, opening times. This will create a good image of the organisation.

5 The tour operator's holiday representative.

6 Use a map and body language, e.g. pointing in a direction, nodding to see if they understand.

7 In the event of an evacuation, e.g. a fire, guests will be able to leave the hotel quickly and safely.

8 They will tell family and friends about it who themselves may want to visit it. It can also bring repeat business.

9 An increase in repeat bookings, fewer complaints.

10 They will feel the organisation has acted professionally, that they have listened to customers and therefore will be thought of in a good light.

11 Poor customer service, dirty environment, e.g. dirty toilets, high prices for low quality goods.

12 So they can be contacted about future events – good marketing technique. Also, customers may feel important if they have been remembered.

13 Young people (18–30) may want fun and lots of socialising; senior citizens may want a quiet, peaceful holiday. It all depends on what people want, what they are used to, and their tastes.

14 Either give the guest a price list or say, 'I'll be with you as soon as I can'.

15 Listen to his complaints and contact the tour operator. Ask the customer to put his complaints in writing and say that you will be in touch about the outcome of his complaint.

Unit 4

1 They make sure that everything possible is done to avoid accidents or injuries to employees and the public.

2 Co-operation, being able to discuss problems without taking criticisms personally, working together in a supportive manner and listening to other people's points of view.

3 ◦ Co-ordinator – chairs meetings, ensures all jobs are completed, ensures everyone has the opportunity to speak at meetings, organises voting if necessary.
  ◦ Secretary – deals with correspondence, keeps accurate records, produces minutes for meetings.
  ◦ Catering officer – orders all food, drink and catering equipment, oversees preparation of the food, organises catering team members, oversees cleaning up of dishes etc. during and after the event.
  ◦ Marketing/publicity officer – promotes the event, organises press coverage, submits press releases, organises promotional materials, e.g. posters, leaflets.
  ◦ Treasurer – oversees all financial transactions, holds the team cheque book, ensures the team operates within the budget.

◦ Facility officer – finds and organises venue, makes security arrangements, arranges access into and around the building, makes health and safety arrangements.

4 Personal belongings, e.g. mobile phones, wallets and handbags, could get stolen. Cash generated by ticket and refreshment sales could also be stolen.

5 Objectives enable us to show exactly how the event is going to be run. They are a way of meeting the aims – what you want to achieve; objectives show how you are going to achieve them.

6 To create a good image and to get a positive response.

7 Press release, word of mouth, leaflets, posters, advertisements, direct mail.

8 Tutor, emergency services, e.g. for fire regulations, estates manager, caretaker.

9 Safety, time, finance, skills of team members, whether the event is realistic and feasible, i.e. practicalities.

10 Being prepared to do anything to help out colleagues.

11 To find out how things could be improved next time and to make sure everyone who should be thanked, is thanked.

12 Face-to-face on an individual basis.

13 If it met the aims and objectives.

14 The ability to motivate people and to give clear instructions; to be friendly, positive; approachable and a good decision-maker.

15 Making quick and effective decisions.

Unit 7

1 For example: Crystal Palace – athletics
Old Trafford – football

2 Rock climbing, mountaineering, hiking, sailing, canoeing.

3 A facility operated by a local authority where the main concern is to provide a service to the local community and the wider public.

4 To make a profit.

5 Subscriptions, membership fees, grants, sponsorship, donations.

6 Organisational structures define the relationship between workers. Organisation charts show lines of communication and the responsibility of different levels of employees and the person to whom each reports.

7 Training – in customer care, first aid, sports coaching, personnel, health and safety, management training. Qualification – Diploma in Management Studies; Degree in Leisure Management.

8 Affects health, family life, social life.

9 People with disabilities, senior citizens, the unemployed.

10 Peak use – busy periods, such as after 5 pm and at weekends.
Off-peak – less busy times, e.g. during the day. Usually cheaper.

11 Call the fire brigade, evacuate the building, co-ordinate activities at the assembly point – keep everyone calm.

12 To prevent equipment breakdown (and therefore ensuring health and safety), to ensure the facility has a good image, to ensure that income is not lost through closure of the facility.

13 Buying stamps, tea and coffee, for travel expenses, window cleaning bills etc.

14 Providing equal opportunities in leisure and tourism involves providing the same opportunities to all employees and prospective employees, regardless of their sex, age, ethnic origin, sexual orientation and ability.

15 Promotional activities include: using brochures, leaflets advertising, press releases, direct mail, posters, recommendations and 'word of mouth' by staff and, hopefully, customers.

Unit 8

1 To encourage repeat business and stop customers from going to the competition.

2 Principals are the companies that a travel agent does business with and whose products and services they sell.

3 An independent travel agent is one that is not part of a national chain. Often they are a single shop agency, usually run by one person or partners who are local and perhaps well known in the area.

4 Youth hostels, hotels, B & Bs, guesthouses, motels.

5 They are cheap, offer good personal service and are in plentiful supply.

6 Tour operators organise inclusive tours to a variety of domestic and international destinations. They organise the transport, accommodation and transfers for clients. They sell their products and services through travel agents.

7 Package holidays and trips within the UK.

8 IT and good communication skills, both face-to-face and on the phone. Personal qualities include politeness, enthusiasm and friendliness.

9 Holiday insurance, airport car parking and foreign exchange.

10 Central government, local government, sponsorship, the National Lottery, income from services provided to other museums and the public.

11 Make a profit.

12 In order to cover busy periods such as week-ends and summer. They are also cheaper to employ than full-time staff.

13 Well-trained staff have the product knowledge needed to answer customer enquiries. They are also familiar with health and safety procedures.

14 To ensure that payments are being made and show what balances are owed.

15 Count it in front of the customer and in the presence of a colleague. Never leave cash unattended; put it in the safe as soon as possible.

16 Observe safe working practices; abide by the safety rules; wear the appropriate protective clothing when necessary; co-operate with employers in meeting the requirements of the Act; use equipment properly, e.g. not 'fooling about' with fire extinguishers.

17 To reduce the risk of accidents and injury in the workplace.

18 To keep all equipment and machinery in good working order.

19 Weekly.

20 Training undertaken by staff when they start new employment.

Unit 13

1 People can use the leisure facilities; increased opportunity for a more social life; new jobs are created; more wealth introduced into area.

2 Air cabin crew; tourist information centre assistants; hotel receptionists.

3 Encourage people to use public transport; introduce park and ride schemes; close narrow roads in countryside to cars but keep them open to cyclists and hikers.

4 c) negative environmental impact

5 Tourists become a 'legitimate' target for some of the local population because of their greater wealth. Some tourists can add to the crime rate by drunkenness and rowdy behaviour.

6 A hotel employs staff to deal with guests. This is direct employment. That same hotel will need food for the restaurant, drinks for the bar, a laundry facility for cleaning the bedding. These are provided by people who don't work in the hotel but who do supply the hotel with goods and services. These people are employed indirectly by the leisure and tourism industry.

7 New facilities can be built on wasteland, putting to good use what previously may have been an eyesore.

8 Positive: money brought into the area; possibility of short-term casual work for local people. Negative: increased traffic congestion and noise.

9 Job creation, greater income brought into the area.

10 Greater demand for products and services, so traders increase prices.

11 Make people more aware of the damaging effects of leisure and tourism by publicity campaigns and education.

12 Positive economic impact.

13 Subjects on the school curriculum, documentaries on television, publicity material.

14 Tourism managed in such a way that the environment will not be damaged and so its future development can be sustained for the future enjoyment of people.

15 Introduce park and ride schemes, restrict access to cars, make public transport affordable and more convenient.

Suggestions for further reading and useful websites

Books

Dictionary of Travel, Tourism and Hospitality, S. Medlik (Butterworth Heinemann, 1997).

The Leisure Environment, R. Doggett and R. O'Mahoney (Stanley Thornes, 1994).

Manual of Travel Agency Practice, G. Syratt (Butterworth Heinemann, 1995).

The Leisure Environment, M. Colquhoun (Pitman, 1993).

Travel and Tourism, P. Lavery (Elm Publications, 1996).

Marketing in Travel and Tourism, V. Middleton, (Butterworth Heinemann, 2000).

Leisure Environment, A. Cheers and A. Sampson, (Thomson Learning, 1991).

Website addresses

www.culture.gov.uk Department for Culture, Media and Sport. Information about the department and its work, including a 'what's new' page.

www.detr.gov.uk Department of the Environment, Transport and the Regions. Details of the Department's work including local government, the environment, transport and the regions.

www.lottery.culture.gov.uk The National Lottery site. Gives information on distributing bodies and awards. Can search for statistical information on awards by region, good cause, name of recipient.

www.artscouncil.org.uk Arts Council of England. Information on grants, education and training, information sources, publications and funding.

www.24hourmuseum.org.uk 24-hour museum site. Provides an Internet gateway to enhance access to museums.

www.museums.gov.uk Museums and Galleries Commission. Outlines the work of the MGC and provides a global gateway to UK museum information. Features an extensive range of facts and figures, the latest news and details of publications, and links to related sites.

www.countryside.gov.uk Countryside Agency. Provides information about the organisation's work and initiatives.

www.english.sports.gov.uk Sport England. Very useful information on the organisation's work including information on the Lottery Sports Fund and the UK Sports Institute.

www.visitbritain.com British Tourist Authority. A site mainly containing tourist information. Also has information about the home countries tourist authorities and facts and figures on tourism in the UK.

www.englishtourism.org.uk English Tourism Council. Contains travel infomation, news, careers advice and useful infomation about English tourism.

www.geoprojects.co.uk Excellent websites for statistics and links on tourism.

www.staruk.org.uk Another useful website for statistics and links on tourism.

www.ilam.co.uk The Institute of Leisure and Amenity Management. Contains information on membership, education and training, an information centre with a searchable database and job advertisements, plus many other ILAM services.

www.isrm.co.uk The Institute of Sport and Recreation Management. Contains a large amount of information on sports development, jobs in the industry, publications and lots of other very useful information about sport and recreation.

The following company websites may be useful reference sources:

www.lunn-poly.co.uk
www.thomson-holidays.com
www.easyjet.co.uk
www.altontowers.com
www.nationalexpress.co.uk
www.eurostar.co.uk
www.english-nature.org.uk

Ready to move on?

This is exactly what you need for the Advanced VCE in Travel and Tourism or Leisure and Recreation

....

- Full coverage of the six compulsory units.

- Useful assignments will give you lots of opportunities to collect portfolio evidence.

- Lots of interesting case studies are drawn from real-life businesses, so you'll get a good insight into the working world.

There's an easy way to find out all the latest information about GNVQs. Just visit

www.heinemann.co.uk/gnvq

S 999 ADV 08

E823